Jeff Duntemann **Series Editor**

HIGH PERFORMANCE

Borland C++Builder

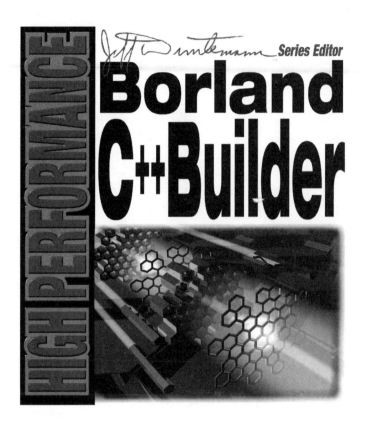

Series Editor

HIGH PERFORMANCE
Borland
C++Builder

Matt Telles

CORIOLIS GROUP BOOKS

an International Thomson Publishing company I(T)P®

Albany, NY • Belmont, CA • Bonn • Boston • Cincinnati • Detroit • Johannesburg • London
Madrid • Melbourne • Mexico City • New York • Paris • Singapore • Tokyo • Toronto • Washington

PUBLISHER	KEITH WEISKAMP
PROJECT EDITOR	DENISE CONSTANTINE
PRODUCTION COORDINATOR	APRIL NIELSEN
COVER ARTIST	GARY SMITH
COVER DESIGN	ANTHONY STOCK
LAYOUT DESIGN	NICOLE COLÓN
COMPOSITOR	ROB MAUHAR
COPYEDITOR	MARJORY SPRAYCAR
PROOFREADER	MERIDETH BRITTAIN
INDEXER	LAURA LAWRIE
CD-ROM DEVELOPMENT	ROBERT CLARFIELD

High Performance Borland C++ Builder

Limits of Liability and Disclaimer of Warranty

The author and publisher of this book have used their best efforts in preparing the book and the programs contained in it. These efforts include the development, research, and testing of the theories and programs to determine their effectiveness. The author and publisher make no warranty of any kind, expressed or implied, with regard to these programs or the documentation contained in this book.

The author and publisher shall not be liable in the event of incidental or consequential damages in connection with, or arising out of, the furnishing, performance, or use of the programs, associated instructions, and/or claims of productivity gains.

Trademarks

Trademarked names appear throughout this book. Rather than list the names and entities that own the trademarks or insert a trademark symbol with each mention of the trademarked name, the publisher states that it is using the names for editorial purposes only and to the benefit of the trademark owner, with no intention of infringing upon that trademark.

Published by The Coriolis Group, Inc.
An International Thomson Publishing Company
14455 N. Hayden Road, Suite 220
Scottsdale, Arizona 85260

602/483-0192
FAX 602/483-0193
http://www.coriolis.com

Copyright © 1997 by The Coriolis Group, Inc.

Printed in the United States of America
ISBN 1-57610-197-5
10 9 8 7 6 5 4 3 2 1

To my wife, Dawnna, without whom my life would be much more quiet and a whole lot less interesting.

Also for my kids, to whom the above applies tripled.

Acknowledgments

To the wonderful people at Borland for providing this tool.

For the great CBuilder mailing list which provided answers when I was stumped.

The designers and developers whose Web sites I haunted in writing this book.

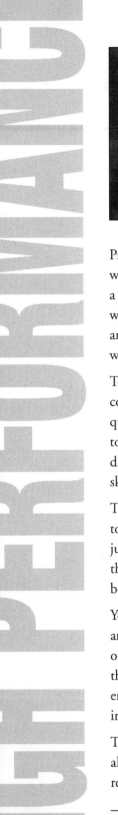

A Note From Jeff Duntemann

Programmers (especially those just coming up to speed) often challenge one another with questions like, "How good are your tools?" There was a time when this was a valid question. Compilers, debuggers, servers, database engines, and all the rest were just coming out of the Stone Age. There were tremendous variations in quality and power from one tool to another. If you bet on the wrong toolset, you could be working harder than you needed to—or worse.

Today, the more pertinent question might be "How good are you?" Relentless competition has given today's developer tools tremendous depth and amazing quality, such that a journeyman programmer is highly unlikely to push such tools to the limit. Long before your tools hit the wall, you will—unless you go the distance to learn everything you can about the tools that you use, and refine the skill with which you use them.

The Coriolis Group's High Performance series was designed to help you take your tools deep. These books explain the advanced tool features that the intro books just can't cover, and provide heavy-duty projects that force you to think through the development process at an expert's level—using those head muscles that lie behind everything we could call skill.

You could discover this knowledge by beating your head against the technology, and trying things randomly until they work. Or you can benefit from the experience of our authors, who've been up this learning curve before and took notes along the way. We've chosen the topics, the authors, and the approaches carefully to ensure that you don't get mired in introductory material you don't need and irrelevant technology that you can't use.

The goal is to take you and your chosen toolset as far as you choose to go. You've already got high-performance tools. Here's to your success at becoming and remaining a high-performance developer.

—Jeff Duntemann

Contents

Chapter 9   Working With The Windows API 275

Chapter 10   Working With Resources 303

Chapter 11   Working With Delphi   335

Chapter 12   Using CBuilder In MFC   351

Chapter 13   Working With Threads   377

Chapter 15   Frequently Asked Questions   453

Chapter 16 Other Sources Of Information 483

Chapter 17 Applications And Wizards 493

Overview

CHAPTER

1

- What Is C++Builder?

- Why Use C++Builder?

- Why This Book?

- What's In This Book?

- Who Is This Book For?

Overview

What Is C++Builder?

The industry is abuzz with C++Builder, a true Rapid Application Tool (RAD) for the C++ Windows programming world. You've no doubt heard the buzz, and the fact that you're reading this book must mean that you're interested enough to try it out. Given the title of this book, you're probably at least somewhat experienced with the tool and want to learn more about it. Before we tackle the details of the system, let's examine the big picture: What makes C++Builder such a powerful tool, and why is it so important to the programming industry? First of all, let's get rid of that tongue-twisting name and for the remainder of this book, refer to the integrated development environment known as C++Builder simply as CBuilder. We could even shorten that to Builder, of course, but that would get us into trouble with Borland's upcoming JBuilder Java development tool.

CBuilder is one of the very first true RAD tools available for C++, and it's the only RAD tool that provides true component-based drag and drop programming. It's really hard to overemphasize the impact this style of programming has had on the Windows world in the last few years. Originally, Windows programming was an error-prone nightmare of MS-DOS based editors, C compilers and linkers, and the Software Development Kit (SDK). Not surprisingly, therefore, the first Windows programs were bug-ridden and took years to develop. Today's programs are written in weeks instead of years (and are still filled with bugs, but that's another story). CBuilder, as you'll see throughout this book, will help you not only to develop applications faster, but also to develop them with fewer bugs.

The first evolution of the Windows programming model was the advent of the C++ programming language and C++ class libraries, which encapsulate the hundreds of lines of code needed to do even simple window display and processing into a few lines of C++ code. This code simply wraps up the few hundred previous lines of C code into C++ classes. Not only do we no longer have to write them, but also the number of errors in the code wrapped by the C++ classes drops precipitously. After

3

all, once code is written and debugged, it doesn't have to be written again. Code that isn't rewritten isn't likely to develop new bugs. Remember that point; it will become more important later.

This second generation of Windows development also brought with it the first Integrated Development Environments (IDEs for short). These tools allow programmers to edit, compile, and link all within a single application. Integrated debugging followed a bit later and was quickly embraced by the Windows programming community. It's hard to describe to you how wonderful these new tools are if you've never done original Windows programming using individual tools. If you've access to someone who was around in the good old days (say, before 1990), ask them, and I'm sure they'll be happy to tell you how bad it was. Try to ignore the part about having to walk uphill both ways in snowstorms to get the program to compile.

The next evolution of Windows development resulted from the development of *frameworks*. A framework is a skeleton application that holds all of the pieces of your application code together. Code frameworks are really quite similar to the girders, plumbing, and electrical paths of building frameworks. In retrospect, code frameworks may have actually been a step backward or at the very least sideways, although many people would disagree with this and remain staunch framework supporters. Then again, there are those who would passionately argue that MS-DOS is still a viable operating system. The reason that frameworks were a step backward is simple. Rather than making programs easier to write and more flexible, they forced us to write programs within a constricting set of rules.

The real problem with framework technology is that it's confining. Although frameworks speed the development of applications by providing many of the basic functions of normal Windows applications, they can quickly get in the way of applications that don't fit the norm. If you've ever tried to do something that the framework doesn't support (or worse, that the framework does differently), you know exactly what I mean. As soon as you try to do something non-trivial, frameworks quickly become like shoes that pinch.

> **Note:** If you don't believe in the problems associated with framework-based application development, consider this: Microsoft has virtually quit updating its flagship framework MFC in response to the newer technologies of ActiveX and COM (both component-based). I believe that most frameworks (MFC, OWL, and others) will disappear in the not too distant future.

Should we then abandon the frameworks and go back to old style linear programming with hundreds of lines of C code and billions of errors? Of course not. There is a better answer than frameworks: component-based programming. Components are like building blocks for applications. You start with specialized component objects that perform special tasks and then assemble the components in a way that you see fit for your own needs. It doesn't matter what sort of application you're developing because the components impose no structure of their own. Components, in fact, are the basis for ActiveX technology, the cornerstone of Internet programming.

CBuilder does components well. It does them simply and intuitively. Like most great applications, CBuilder works simply and consistently, thanks in large part to the component-based nature of the product. Each piece of the system has a specific job and does it as simply and easily as possible. Components are as close to pure C++ programming as you're ever likely to get and make the whole development effort easier. This, then, is the true legacy of CBuilder: It's the first true component-based RAD tool.

But Wait, There's More

There is another side to CBuilder that many programmers completely overlook in their zeal to embrace the drag and drop world of CBuilder forms. Hidden not so deep in the CBuilder system is an incredibly powerful, yet extremely flexible, database programming environment. CBuilder is, in fact, the first true database programming system for C++ programmers.

In many C++ development systems, database interfaces are often an afterthought intended to make some small segment of the database available to the programmer in a strictly enforced narrow set of objects. Database interfaces for most C++ systems consist of a series of objects that are thin wrappers around the underlying database's functionality. It's not at all uncommon for database objects to contain methods that require dozens of parameters to open and initialize a connection to an ODBC database. Contrast this with the complete suite of database drag and drop components built into the CBuilder system. CBuilder ships with a full complement of data-aware controls that require no programming at all. It's possible to write a complete database editing system that adds new records, edits existing records, and deletes unwanted records without writing a single line of C++ code. Try that in Visual Basic or Visual C++.

In the long run, CBuilder may be known as much for what you can accomplish with databases, tables, and SQL queries than for what you can do with the forms and other visual components of the system.

So what is CBuilder? A complete, flexible, RAD tool that offers superior database functionality, component-based technology, ease of use, and power of development. Oh yeah. It contains a pretty mean ANSI standard C++ compiler with complete support for such new technologies as templates, namespaces, exception handling, and the Standard Template Library (STL).

Why This Book?

Chances are that this is not the first CBuilder book that you own. As I write this, the current crop of CBuilder books fits neatly into one of two camps. One crop is aimed at experienced Delphi programmers moving to the CBuilder environment, a natural audience as CBuilder is really just Delphi using the C++ language instead of Object Pascal (although I suspect that most people who end up using CBuilder didn't start in Delphi at all). As I mentioned, CBuilder is just Delphi with a different language. Why switch? There is certainly a segment of the programming community that uses Delphi because of its superior components even though they hate Object Pascal. I suspect, however, that you're not one of those programmers. If you are, don't fret, there's plenty for you here as well.

The second crop of books is aimed at new programmers learning not only a new development environment but a new language as well. These people won't find themselves at home in this book until they've mastered the introductory books. This book is aimed at experienced programmers (or at least somewhat experienced programmers) who need to get the job done. Professional programmers will find the information they need to do all the little things that need to show up in their work. We'll also be looking at how to implement those final touches that make a program a success. Through short but thorough code examples, you'll learn what you to need to learn to do what you need to do. As a professional programmer, I know how frustrating it is to see other programs with neat features and not have the time or energy to figure out how to do them in my own applications.

So, this is really a component-based book. Read through the whole thing if you like, or just turn to the chapter that you need and steal the code you need to do the job. Hey, I've been there, too, and expect to be there again. I will certainly forgive you.

What Will We Be Covering?

Here is the short list of topics you'll find between these two thin covers:

- Using the VCL

- Using ActiveX controls

- Extending forms

- Writing components

- Developing database applications

- Writing complex C++ code

In addition to all of the code examples in the book (also found on the accompanying CD-ROM), we'll also be developing a full-blown CBuilder wizard that will allow you to develop complex components quickly and easily. Finally, at the end of the book, you'll find a complete copy of the C++Builder FAQ gathered from information posted by hundreds of people on the Internet. This easy question and answer list will certainly become a common place to turn as you begin to develop complex applications of your own.

What Should You Know Before Reading This Book?

First of all, you should know the C++ language. This book is not a primer on the C++ language; there are plenty of books that do this better than I ever could. This book will explain the differences between standard ANSI C++ and the version found in CBuilder. As you will see, these differences are primarily in extensions used by CBuilder. How well do you need to know C++? Not really all that deeply. If the following C++ class definition doesn't scare you, you should be fine with the remainder of the book. Anything more complex than this will be explained as it is introduced in the text.

```
class TMyObject : public TObject
{
private:
    int FnDigit;
    char *FpString;
    Foo  *FpFoo;
```

```
public:
    TMyObject(void);
    TMyObject( const TMyObject& aObject);
     virtual ~TMyObject(void);
     void DoSomething(void);
};
```

In addition to C++ programming skills, it would help if you have developed even simple applications in either C++Builder or Delphi before you start reading this book. This will get you used to the behavior of the environment and the workings of the compiler and linker. Simply reading this book and following along with the code will teach even beginners a lot about the CBuilder programming model, the VCL, and the inner workings of the system.

Finally, it would not hurt in the least if you have some sort of background in Windows programming. Although products such as CBuilder and Delphi make it easy enough for even a manager to develop serious applications (okay, maybe not simple enough for a manager but close), it's still necessary to understand the underlying Windows programming model in order to accomplish some tasks. We'll even devote one complete chapter to working with the Windows API to extend the CBuilder programming model. Even low-level systems programming grunts who sneer at the thought of a visual development system will be happy.

Who Is This Book For?

In general, this book is for experienced or professional programmers who want to learn more about the internals of the CBuilder system and how to make it work to the fullest. Beginning programmers will learn by doing the code in the book but will likely require multiple readings to get the full benefit of each example.

The book is organized into a series of discrete chapters, with few dependencies on previous work. This allows you, the programmer, to scan through the sections until you find the problem you're trying to solve (or find something else that catches your fancy) and then begin reading and digesting the code at that point in the book.

Although this book takes you through the process of creating several full-blown components, it's not intended to be a manual for CBuilder component development. If you're seriously into component writing, please pick up a book specifically aimed at that task in addition to this one.

What's Ahead?

There are three major sections to this book. In section one, we explore various pieces of the CBuilder environment and programming system through short example programs. In most cases, these example programs illustrate only one or two important points of CBuilder programming. In other examples, we'll explore more complex aspects of the system. Along the way we'll take side trips to explore some of the more interesting hows and whys of the CBuilder system. Some of the things we'll examine in section one include form painting, image processing, drag and drop component interaction, owner-draw controls, the standard template library, databases, and ActiveX controls. Not bad for one little section, hmm? As you might guess, section one is by far the single largest piece of the book.

Section two includes a complete application development, from initial design through complete implementation using the VCL and many of its components. This section will implement a complete Component Wizard that allows you to define not only the base class of the component (as the one that ships with CBuilder does), but also allows you to define new methods and properties (as well as publishing existing ones from the base component class). When you're finished with section two, you should understand just about everything there is to know about the pieces that make up the CBuilder system. You'll learn how to create extensions that have complete control over many of the pieces of the CBuilder IDE, including adding new files to a project, generating code, and loading files.

Section three contains the CBuilder FAQ (Frequently Asked Questions) list with dozens of questions and answers about CBuilder. The FAQ is organized by topic (General Programming, Components, Databases, the VCL) and broken down into simple single-topic questions. Also found in section three is a list of other places to go for information from Borland's Knowledgebase to specialized C++Builder Web sites on the Internet.

In short, this is a book for programmers by a programmer. I know from bitter and horrible experience what a drag it can be to buy a book that purports to help solve problems but turns out to be a rehash of the online help system. This book tackles problems that I've encountered in trying to write real C++Builder applications for real clients. I hope you'll find the answers to the questions that are driving you crazy here as well. What are you waiting for, turn that page and let's get started.

Forms And Event Handling

CHAPTER
2

HIGH PERFORMANCE

- **Creating A Form Without A Caption**

- **Drawing On Forms**

- **Inside The Form Definition**

- **Event Handling And Forms**

- **Dynamic Event Handling**

- **From Forms To MDI**

Forms And Event Handling

The form is the single most basic component in the CBuilder system. The form is the most visible part of the system and the part with which the user is most likely to interact. In most CBuilder examples, the form is used as a container for other components. In this chapter we'll explore the form as a component on its own.

What is a form? It's simply a window, of course. Like all windows, it can have child controls, such as toolbars, menus, and status bars. Forms, as windows, have certain unique properties of their own, such as captions, system menus, minimize and maximize buttons, close buttons, resizable (or not) borders, and other neat stuff. Let's take a moment to look at a form and the parts of it CBuilder will allow us to modify.

Figure 2.1 shows a typical blank CBuilder form that you would see when you initially start up the CBuilder application. Let's examine the pieces of this form in detail.

The first property of the form that jumps out at you is the title (**Form1**) of the form, shown prominently in the titlebar. This property is called the *Caption* property of the form. The **Caption** property can be directly modified in the CBuilder Object Inspector at design time or via code at runtime. Changing the **Caption** property will immediately update the form title at either design time or runtime with one exception: You can't simply set the **Caption** property to an empty string ("") and have the caption go away.

Here is your first expert tip in CBuilder: how to create a form with no caption and titlebar. It's not readily apparent how you can remove the caption and titlebar in a CBuilder form, but it can be done with a little bit of Windows magic and some knowledge of the Windows API. Because a form is really just a window, you can modify the starting properties of the form before it's actually created. If you change the window style bits to include the **WS_POPUP** flag and remove the **WS_CAPTION** flag, you'll create a window that has no caption bar. You'll also end

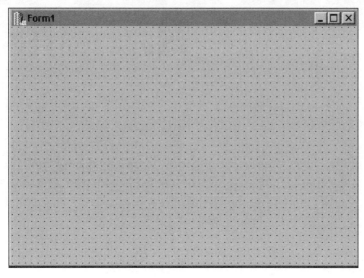

Figure 2.1
Standard empty CBuilder form.

up with a window that has no system menu, minimize or maximize buttons, or close button. For this reason you must provide some way to close such a form.

Let's experiment a little and create such a form. You'll find this complete application on the enclosed CD-ROM in the Chapter1\Captionless directory. Once you've finished playing with the **Caption** property, the next property to examine is the **Border** property, which allows you to control whether or not the form has a resizable border. There are several options available for the **Border** property, but the two you're most likely to use are the resizable border (bsSizeable) and the fixed dialog-style border (bsDialog). Take a minute to change the border style between these two styles and compile the resulting application. One thing to notice is that the two border styles are physically different on the screen. Figure 2.2 shows a typical form with a resizable border while Figure 2.3 shows a form with the dialog-style border. You'll see borders referred to as "frames." This name comes from the resemblance of the window border to a picture frame.

The third property is really a set of properties. The **BorderIcons** property consists of the set of icons or buttons that can appear on the caption titlebar of the form. This property is a true C++ set, containing options for the minimize button, the maximize

Figure 2.2
A form showing a resizable border.

Figure 2.3
A form showing a dialog-style or fixed border.

button, the system menu, and the close button. You can turn on or off any or all of the above buttons by simply setting the property to false in the Object Inspector or via your code.

Note: The changes you make to these properties will not be reflected at design time. The form displayed by the form editor is fixed at creation time. The changes you make will be made when the form is first displayed in your application. To demonstrate this, change the form to omit the minimize and maximize buttons, and you'll notice that the form does not change in the editor display. Compile and run the application and you'll see that the resulting form does not, in fact, have either the minimize button or the maximize button.

Color is another, less clear property of the form, which you can see in the following experiment. Starting with the basic form displayed in the Form editor of CBuilder, change the **Color** property to something else like clRed. This should display a form with a bright red background when the program is run. Compile and run the new application and look at the output. Surprise! The form is not red; it is instead the standard battleship gray. Why? Well, it appears to be (gasp!) a bug in the system. Fortunately, this particular bug is not hard to work around. Add a handler for the **OnFormCreate** event and add the following code to the handler:

```
void __fastcall TForm1::OnFormCreate()
{
    Color = clRed;
}
```

Amazingly enough, changing the **Color** property in the **FormCreate** method does the job and the form will then be displayed in the color red.

The Good Stuff: Scribble!

We've talked about many design time and runtime properties of the form, but we've conspicuously avoided talking about that big expanse of area in the middle of the form. The entire client area of the form is a single property called the *Canvas* property of the form. The **Canvas** property is responsible for the display of any text or graphics that belong to the form itself. It's also the part that responds to the **Color** property of the form, but this is done indirectly by the form object itself and is not of your concern.

Our first real example of the book concerns the **Canvas** property. Because Windows is generally thought of for its graphics capability, it's fitting that the first example be a graphical one. In the good old days of programming when Visual C++ was first shipped, Microsoft chose a program called Scribble as the tutorial for the Visual C++ programming system. This was basically a free-form drawing program that used the mouse to move around a window surface, drawing lines connecting all of the points that the mouse crossed on the window surface.

Scribble became something of an inside joke in the programming community because of the very simplistic nature of the example. Many programmers would go in for interviews claiming to have programmed in Visual C++ and the MFC (Microsoft Foundation Classes) when, in fact, all they had done was go through the Scribble tutorial. Scribble took quite a few pages to implement and required that the programmer be able to read a book and type in what the book said. This example showed nothing about the MFC and was even less useful to programmers wanting to leverage any MFC knowledge into writing useful programs. As a gentle tweak at the MFC community, we present the CBuilder version of Scribble. On a slightly more serious note, Scribble is good for a simple example because it provides some interaction with all of the elements of the form: properties, events, and methods. Let's implement a simple Scribble version in CBuilder.

Scribble: The Design

The purpose of Scribble is simple. When the user presses the mouse down, the program starts drawing. As the mouse is moved around the screen, the program should connect the dots that the mouse crosses, forming lines. This process allows the user to "draw" simple (and probably not so simple) figures on the screen. Figure 2.4 shows the result of a simple Scribble session, a smiley face.

> **Note:** You'll find the source code for the Scribble program in the Chapter1\Scribble1 directory on the accompanying CD-ROM for this book.

In the introduction to this book, I said that it would be useful to have a programming background in Windows to work with the examples presented here, and this is one of those times when it helps to understand something about the Windows messaging system. The process here is simple enough. When the user presses the mouse button down and moves it around, we draw connect the dots. What is less clear to the beginner is how you do that. If you're an experienced Windows programmer, you'll recognize that when the user presses the left mouse button down,

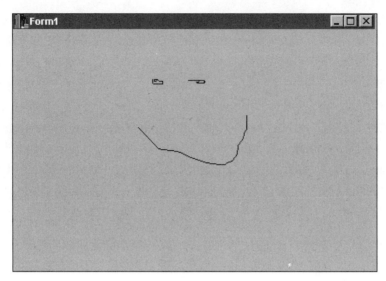

Figure 2.4
A Scribble session that results in a smiley face.

Windows will generate the WM_LBUTTONDOWN message to the window. When the user moves the mouse, Windows will generate the WM_MOUSEMOVE button. Finally, when the user releases the left mouse button, Windows generates the WM_LBUTTONUP message. The question is this: How does this information translate itself into the CBuilder environment?

CBuilder works by a system called event handling. Every Windows message that is sent to an object in the CBuilder environment is translated into an event that can be handled by that object. In the case of the above-listed messages, CBuilder Form objects call three event handlers, **OnMouseDown**, **OnMouseMove**, and **OnMouseUp**.

> **Note:** *If you're a Visual C++ or Borland C++ programmer, the notion of event handlers may seem a little strange. Both of these environments use the same concept, but approach it from a different direction. In both Visual C++ and Borland C++, message map entries define a message and the class method used to handle that message. In CBuilder (and Delphi, of course) the internals of the objects define which messages are handled and call user-defined event handlers. The difference is that CBuilder's event handlers are, as we'll see a little later, dynamic, while Visual C++ and Borland*

C++ message handlers are defined at compile time. Both use pointers to member functions to accomplish the job, but the CBuilder method is a little more clear and much more powerful.

With that out of the way, let's add a few handlers to our form to enable the Scribble application to do its thing. First, add a handler for the **OnMouseDown** event. Because this is the first example, I'll take you through the entire process in case you've forgotten. After this, I'm going to assume that you know what you're doing and will simply tell you which handler to add.

Bring up the Object Inspector window if it's not already visible by pressing the F11 key, or selecting View|Object Inspector. Select the form by clicking on it or selecting it from the drop-down combo box at the top of the Object Inspector. Move to the events form and find the **OnMouseDown** event on the left-hand side of the Inspector. The events are all listed in alphabetical order, so you should have little problem finding the event you want. Click on the right side of the Object Inspector grid next to the **OnMouseDown** entry and type in **OnMouseDown** as the name of the new event handler. Although it can be confusing to have an event handler of the same name as the event it's handling you'll see how we can change this a little later in this chapter. Press return in the grid cell to confirm your entry.

Once you've entered the method name and confirmed your choice, CBuilder will create the new handler in the edit window. Enter the following code into the **OnMouseDown** method in the editor window:

```
void __fastcall TForm1::OnMouseDown(TObject *Sender, TMouseButton Button,
                                    TShiftState Shift, int X, int Y)
{
    FbMouseDown = TRUE;
    Canvas->MoveTo(X,Y);
}
```

The **FbMouseDown** flag shown in the previous code needs to be added to your include file (Unit1.h) and initialized in the constructor. This flag is simply set to indicate whether the mouse is (TRUE) or is not (FALSE) currently down in the window. Here is the addition to make to your include file (shown in highlighted print):

```
//-----------------------------------------------------------------
#ifndef Unit1H
#define Unit1H
```

```
//--------------------------------------------------------------
#include <vcl\Classes.hpp>
#include <vcl\Controls.hpp>
#include <vcl\StdCtrls.hpp>
#include <vcl\Forms.hpp>
//--------------------------------------------------------------
class TForm1 : public TForm
{
__published:    // IDE-managed Components
                void __fastcall OnMouseDown(TObject *Sender, TMouseButton
                Button, TShiftState Shift, int X, int Y);
private:  // User declarations
    BOOL FbMouseDown;
public:         // User declarations
                __fastcall TForm1(TComponent* Owner);
};
//--------------------------------------------------------------
extern TForm1 *Form1;
//--------------------------------------------------------------
#endif
```

And finally, here is the change to make to your constructor for the class (in the Unit1.cpp source file):

```
__fastcall TForm1::TForm1(TComponent* Owner)
                : TForm(Owner)
{
    FbMouseDown = FALSE; // Initialize mouse down flag to be NOT down
}
```

Before we go on, let's take a look at what we've done. The class **TForm1** now has a private user-defined variable called **FbMouseDown**, which indicates whether or not the mouse is presently down. If the user presses the left-mouse button while within the bounds of the client area of the window, the **OnMouseDown** method will be called by the event-handling system. This method simply sets the flag to be TRUE and moves the current drawing position on the Canvas to the position of the mouse. CBuilder quite nicely gives us the information about where the mouse was when the user pressed the button in the event handler for that event.

You might be wondering how CBuilder knows to associate the **OnMouseDown** event with our own **OnMouseDown** method. It isn't the name, as the handler can be called anything you want. Looking through the above source and header code you won't find anything that does the association. Is this some form of Borland magic? The answer lies within the mysteries of the Unit1.dfm file, which contains information about the layout and processing of the form for Unit1. If you try to display the DFM file using a standard text editor or by typing it at the command prompt, you'll find that it's full of strange control characters that make little or no sense. How can we see what is going on?

Looking At The Form Definition File (DFM)

In order to look at the definition file for the form, you need to open it in CBuilder. There is nothing special about the process. You open a DFM file the same way that you would open a source file or a header file or any other text file. Click on the Open File button of the toolbar and select DFM files from the drop-down extension filter combo box. Select the Unit1.dfm file from the files displayed (there should be only one, but depending on whatever else you might have done, there could be more). Select the file and click the OK button. Two things should happen. First, the header and source files should disappear from the editor. Next the DFM file should be displayed in the editor as a simple text file. Here is the listing you would see if you followed this procedure:

```
object Form1: TForm1
  Left = 200
  Top = 108
  Width = 435
  Height = 300
  Caption = 'Form1'
  Font.Charset = DEFAULT_CHARSET
  Font.Color = clWindowText
  Font.Height = -11
  Font.Name = 'MS Sans Serif'
  Font.Style = []
  OnMouseDown = OnMouseDown
  PixelsPerInch = 96
  TextHeight = 13
end
```

As you can see from the above listing, there is all sorts of property information stored in the DFM file: position (**Left**, **Top**, **Width**, and **Height** entries), **Caption** (Form1), and all of the **Font** information is stored here. The event handlers are also stored here.

The line marked in highlighting is what associates the event (the left-hand side of the equation in the line shown) and the event handler in our form (the right-hand side of the equation). How does CBuilder differentiate between the event handler and the name of the method? Magic. Seriously, though, the internals of the mechanisms aren't within the scope of this book and aren't really of any importance to the programmer.

Doing The Drawing

Once you know how the process works, the next step is to finish the example by adding code to handle the drawing of the points as the mouse moves and to stop when the user releases the left mouse button. First, the code for the drawing. Add a handler for the **OnMouseMove** event as you did previously, and add the following code to that method:

```
void __fastcall TForm1::OnMouseMove(TObject *Sender, TShiftState Shift,
                                     int X, int Y)
{
    if ( FbMouseDown )
    {
        Canvas->LineTo(X,Y);
    }
}
```

This method is using the flag we set a little earlier to check if the mouse is currently down. If this flag is set, the **Canvas-LineTo** method is called. This method will draw a line from the current position to the position specified and will then set that specified position to be the current position for drawing. If you'll remember, the initial position was set when the mouse was originally pressed down in the window in our **OnMouseDown** method.

The final method that needs to be implemented is the handler for the mouse button being released. This method will simply clear the flag indicating that the mouse is down. Since the only other functionality that will normally occur is the mouse movement, this will also have the effect of stopping the drawing process.

Here is the code for the **OnMouseUp** method which you should add as a handler for the **OnMouseUp** event in the Object Inspector:

```
void __fastcall TForm1::OnMouseUp(TObject *Sender, TMouseButton Button,
                                  TShiftState Shift, int X, int Y)
```

```
{
    FbMouseDown = FALSE;
}
```

Believe it or not, the Scribble application is now complete. You can make the executable, run it within the CBuilder environment, and scribble away to your heart's content. A quick side note for those who prefer keyboard entries to using the mouse. You can use a quick key combination for making the project by pressing the Ctrl+F9 key combination. This will work from any editor window in the system.

Scribble Part Deux

Although the Scribble application we just finished writing is functionally complete, it's not quite perfect. We aren't going to make it perfect in this iteration, but we'll improve on it. To see the problem, bring up a Scribble window and draw a complex geometric shape in it free form using your mouse (I usually draw something vaguely approximating a square). Now, minimize the form using the minimize button (or by selecting minimize from the system menu). Bring the window back to full size by clicking on the icon in the Windows 95 or NT toolbar. Guess what—the form is now blank. What happened?

The Canvas property of the **TForm** object is not persistent. That is to say, anything drawn on the form surface goes away when the form is refreshed. Minimizing and restoring a window causes a refresh event to occur. If we want our masterpieces to stick around for awhile we'll need to deal with this little problem. The answer lies in the **OnPaint** event and its handler.

The **OnPaint** method is called for a form any time that the form window is invalidated. This can occur when you minimize and restore a form, as we've seen. It can also occur if you display another window over the form surface. For example, if you display a message box in the center of a form, the area under the message box will be invalidated. CBuilder detects the invalidation of the form by processing the WM_PAINT message from Windows. In response to this method, the form calls the attached **OnPaint** method for the form if one exists. Because no **OnPaint** handler currently exists in our form, nothing is called when the form needs to be repainted and thus nothing is displayed. It's time to rectify that situation.

Copying The Project

Normally, when you are creating a new project you would follow one of two paths. You would either create a new project from scratch and add the code you need to implement, or you would start with an existing project and clone it into a new project. The Object Repository can be used to store projects that you are likely to reuse and clone into new projects. For normal projects, however, you're more likely simply to open the project and use the File|Save Project As command to create a new project in a new directory.

Caution! Don't do this. Create a copy of the project in a new directory, even though the project save command appears to do what you want. It really doesn't. Instead, it creates a new project in a new directory, but *links all source files back to the original directory*. What this means is that you end up modifying source code in the original project without meaning to. Be very careful when saving a project as a new name. A better way to do this is to copy the entire project directory into a new directory and then open the project in that new directory. Once you've opened the new project, use the File|Project Save As command to rename the project in the new directory. Once you've done this you can delete the old project file.

Example: Let's copy the Scribble project to a new directory. Suppose that your existing Scribble project was found in the d:\work\Scribble directory. Copy the entire project tree from d:\work\Scribble to d:\work\Scribble2. Open the Scribble project in CBuilder in the d:\work\Scribble2 directory and use the File|Save Project As command to save the new project as Scribble2. Delete all existing Scribble.* files from the d:\work\Scribble2 directory and go about your merry way.

Once you've copied the project into a new directory (or, if you prefer, you can simply add the changes to your existing Scribble project, as you can always reload the project from the CD-ROM), bring it up in the CBuilder IDE. We now need to consider what changes need to be made to make the drawing of the form masterpiece persistent for the life of the form.

Obviously, in order for us to paint the form in response to a WM_PAINT message, we'll need to add a handler for the **OnPaint** event in CBuilder. The **VCL TForm** object will call our handler whenever it needs to update the form display. Fortunately, we don't need to worry about what pieces of the form need to be updated; CBuilder will deal with that for us quite well. All we need to worry about is how to duplicate the display of the figure that the user has input.

The first thing we need to do is to store the information as it is changed in the form display. To do this, we're going to create two arrays to hold the X and Y values for each of the points the mouse crosses during the figure creation. There are better ways to store the data than in static arrays, but we'll explore them a little later in the book when we talk about the Standard Template Library. At that time we'll also fix a few of the other problems associated with the program, so you'll have to wait for perfection until then.

First, add the following declarations to the header file for the Unit (Unit1.h). The changes are shown in highlighted print for ease of viewing.

```
//---------------------------------------------------------------------
#ifndef Unit1H
#define Unit1H
//---------------------------------------------------------------------
#include <vcl\Classes.hpp>
#include <vcl\Controls.hpp>
#include <vcl\StdCtrls.hpp>
#include <vcl\Forms.hpp>
//---------------------------------------------------------------------

const int MaxPoints = 100;

class TForm1 : public TForm
{
__published:    // IDE-managed Components
                void __fastcall OnMouseDown(TObject *Sender, TMouseButton
                Button,TShiftState Shift, int X, int Y);
                void __fastcall OnMouseMove(TObject *Sender, TShiftState
                Shift, int X, int Y);
                void __fastcall OnMouseUp(TObject *Sender, TMouseButton
                Button, TShiftState Shift, int X, int Y);
private:  // User declarations
    BOOL FbMouseDown;
    int  FnPoint;
    int  FPointX[MaxPoints+1];
    int  FPointY[MaxPoints+1];
public:         // User declarations
                __fastcall TForm1(TComponent* Owner);
};
//---------------------------------------------------------------------
extern TForm1 *Form1;
//---------------------------------------------------------------------
#endif
```

Once we have the storage area for the X and Y components of the points defined, the next step is to store something in that storage area. Let's tackle that one before we work on the painting process. Modify the **OnMouseDown** method as follows:

```
void __fastcall TForm1::OnMouseDown(TObject *Sender, TMouseButton Button,
                  TShiftState Shift, int X, int Y)
{
    FbMouseDown = TRUE;
    Canvas->MoveTo(X,Y);
    FnPoint = 0;
    FPointX[FnPoint] = X;
    FPointY[FnPoint] = Y;
}
```

The lines marked in highlighted print are those which you should enter, of course. All we're doing is storing the X and Y points of the mouse down position in the first position of the array. Naturally, you modify the **OnMouseMove** method accordingly:

```
void __fastcall TForm1::OnMouseMove(TObject *Sender, TShiftState Shift,
                  int X, int Y)
{
    if ( FbMouseDown )
    {
        Canvas->LineTo(X,Y);
        if ( FnPoint < MaxPoints )
        {
            FnPoint++;
            FPointX[FnPoint] = X;
            FPointY[FnPoint] = Y;
        }
    }
}
```

Again, no magic here. Just storing all of the points as we collect them into the arrays. Finally, add a new handler for the **OnPaint** method to do the display of the points in response to the paint message. Here is the code for the **OnPaint** method:

```
void __fastcall TForm1::OnPaint(TObject *Sender)
{
   if ( FnPoint > 0 )
   {
      Canvas->MoveTo(FPointX[0],FPointY[0]);
      for ( int i=1; i<FnPoint; ++i )
         Canvas->LineTo( FPointX[i], FPointY[i] );
   }
}
```

The final thing to do is to initialize the number of points to 0 in the constructor for the form. Here's the very last change you need to make:

```
__fastcall TForm1::TForm1(TComponent* Owner)
                 : TForm(Owner)
{
    FbMouseDown = FALSE;
    FnPoint = 0;
}
```

That's all there is to it. You've successfully duplicated the entire Microsoft Visual C++/MFC tutorial in just a handful of lines of code.

Now For The Good Stuff

Everything we have done up until this point was pretty trivial from the point of view of a CBuilder programmer or any other kind of programmer. It was a good way to get warmed up and stretch the old programming muscles before we get down to the real task at hand, showing off the real power of CBuilder.

One of the more powerful features of CBuilder is the ability to replace and remove event handlers dynamically. If you're accustomed to working with MFC or OWL, this is an incredible change from what you're used to.

In this example, we're going to add a menu to the Scribble form with two options on it. The first option will be to draw the lines as we are accustomed to. The second menu item will allow you to paste a bitmap on the screen at the position where you click the mouse. Along the way you'll learn a bit about how to change event handler names and how CBuilder helps you with the process. Finally, you'll learn how easy it is to load and display a bitmap in CBuilder. Given that most frameworks don't have any ability to display a bitmap, this is a pretty neat feature.

Scribble, Take 3

Scribble Part 3 will be a combination of drawing lines and drawing bitmaps. The result of this exercise can be seen in Figure 2.5, which shows a Scribble3 form after several bitmaps have been added and a complex figure drawn. The complete source code for the Scribble3 application will be found on the accompanying CD-ROM in the Chapter1\Scribble3 directory.

To implement this masterpiece, we need to make a few modifications to the interface. The first is to add a menu so that we can use menu commands to modify what happens when the user clicks the mouse in our form. Put a main menu component on the form and add the caption Draw to it. Add two menu items to the new main menu. For the first item, give it the name Lines. This menu item will result in the drawing of lines in the form. For the second menu item, give it the name Bitmaps. This will be the item for which we are going to add new functionality.

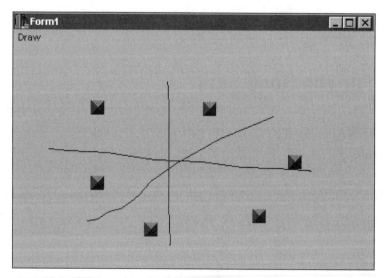

Figure 2.5
The Scribble form with both bitmaps and drawn lines.

The next thing you'll need to do in order to make the program readable is to change the name of the **OnMouseDown** handler to **OnMouseDownLines**. This is the same old handler we've been using all along, but giving it a new name will emphasize that this handler is to be used for drawing the lines on the form. In most environments, changing the name of the event handler would require either hand-editing the code and making sure all of the changes were made in the right places, or deleting the existing handler and then adding a new one with the new name. Isn't it nice, then, that you're working in CBuilder and not some other environment?

To change the name of an existing handler, simply go into the Object Inspector events tab and locate the name you want to change. Type in the new name for the event handler method and press Return or Enter. The code will automatically be updated in the source files to reflect the new change.

Next we'll add a new handler of our own without using any of the tools. For one thing this will show you how to accomplish the task, and it will prove that CBuilder really is a two-way tool. Changes you make by yourself to non-CBuilder generated code should not be affected by the tool itself. Let's prove that.

In the header file for the Unit1 form, add the following declaration in the section labeled **private: // User declarations**.

```
void __fastcall OnMouseDownBitmap(TObject *Sender, TMouseButton
  Button,TShiftState Shift, int X, int Y);
```

This is going to be our handler for the bitmap display. While you're in the include file, there is one other change that needs to be made. In order to display a bitmap on the form, we need to have a bitmap object that we can work with. Add the following line to the same private user declaration section of the include file:

```
Graphics::TBitmap *FpBitmap;
```

When you're finished, the completed include file private user section should look like this. All of the changed lines are shown in highlighted print:

```
private:  // User declarations
    BOOL FbMouseDown;
    int  FnPoint;
    int  FPointX[MaxPoints+1];
    int  FPointY[MaxPoints+1];
```

```
Graphics::TBitmap *FpBitmap;
void __fastcall OnMouseDownBitmap(TObject *Sender, TMouseButton
    Button, TShiftState Shift, int X, int Y);
```

The next step is to modify the constructor for the form to make it load the new bitmap. In this case we're going to use a standard Windows bitmap that should be found in your system Windows directory, by the name of Triangles. Here is the updated code:

```
__fastcall TForm1::TForm1(TComponent* Owner)
                : TForm(Owner)
{
    FbMouseDown = FALSE;
    FnPoint = 0;
    FpBitmap = new Graphics::TBitmap;
    FpBitmap->LoadFromFile("C:\\Windows\\Triangles.BMP");
}
```

As with most CBuilder objects, creating a bitmap to display is a two-step process. First, the bitmap object needs to be allocated and constructed using the C++ new operator. Note that since **TBitmap** is a non-visual element in and of itself, it doesn't require a parent argument. Most CBuilder objects are really windows and require that a window be used as their parent. This is not such a case. Once the object has been created and initialized using the new operator, the next step is to load the bitmap into memory. This is accomplished using the **LoadFromFile** method of the **TBitmap** class. This method will locate the bitmap file in the given directory and file name and will load the bitmap bits into the object so that they're ready to go.

Once the bitmap is loaded, it's time to implement the code that does the display of the bitmap when the user clicks the mouse in our form. Here is the implementation of **OnMouseDownBitmap** that you can enter in the source file (Unit1.cpp):

```
void __fastcall TForm1::OnMouseDownBitmap(TObject *Sender, TMouseButton
                Button, TShiftState Shift, int X, int Y)
{
    Canvas->Draw(X, Y, FpBitmap);
}
```

As you can see, there really isn't much to drawing a bitmap. The **Canvas** property of the form (and all other objects that have Canvas properties) already knows how to draw a bitmap. All you need to do is to provide a pointer to the bitmap object and the position at which you would like the bitmap drawn. It really is that simple.

So, we now have a complete form that knows how to draw lines and bitmaps. The only problem is that if you compile and link the application, you'll find that no matter what you do or where you click, the form will still only draw lines. Something is obviously missing.

Switching Handlers In Midstream

Missing in this little scenario is the ability to make the form call a different event handler, but we can add a handler for the menu item Bitmaps by bringing up the menu designer and double-clicking the Bitmaps item in the menu. A new method will be added to your form called **Bitmaps1Click**. Add the following line of code to the method as shown in the following listing in highlighted print:

```
void __fastcall TForm1::Bitmaps1Click(TObject *Sender)
{
    OnMouseDown = OnMouseDownBitmap;
}
```

Repeat the process for the Lines menu item and add the following code to that handler, also shown in highlighted print:

```
void __fastcall TForm1::Lines1Click(TObject *Sender)
{
    OnMouseDown = OnMouseDownLines;
}
```

Compile and run the application, and you'll find that selecting the Bitmaps menu item permits you to draw little triangles all over the form. Switching over to the Lines menu item will return the familiar behavior of drawing pretty lines all over the form as you move the mouse around with the left mouse button held down. What you just accomplished with a handful of lines of code—implementing a dynamic event handler that can be switched at runtime—is extremely difficult or impossible in Visual C++ or Borland C++.

Your program needs one last thing before it's really complete: a destructor for the class in the header file as shown in the following code listing:

```
public:          // User declarations
    __fastcall TForm1(TComponent* Owner);
    __fastcall ~TForm1(void);
```

And add the following code to the source module, Unit1.cpp:

```
__fastcall TForm1::~TForm1(void)
{
    delete FpBitmap;
}
```

It's important to delete anything you create using the new operator in C++. The only exception to this rule is an MDI child form created as a child of an MDI parent, objects that will be deleted by the system when the program cleans itself up at termination. In all other cases, you must delete anything that you create using the new operator by de-allocating it using the delete operator.

The Great Change: Moving To MDI Forms

Here's a sad but true story from my programming past. Once upon a time a few years back, I was working for a small company developing software. We got a request to convert an existing MS-DOS application to Windows 3.1 using Visual C++ and the MFC. After meeting with the development manager and the client, we were told to develop the software using a single document interface (SDI) framework. The other programmers on the team and I asked several times if this was really what they wanted, but they were adamant. It seems that the designer of the project had never worked with Windows before and was unfamiliar with the whole MDI concept. As a result, we spent six months developing a really nice product using the SDI model.

Six months came and went and the product was finally ready for systems test. Several senior management types were brought in for a demo because they had heard good things about it around the company. You can probably guess the rest of the story. One senior manager, who did have some experience with Windows (using Word and Excel), took one look at the interface for the application and said, "Looks great. Make it an MDI app."

We spent about a week trying to take the existing application and convert it into an MDI application. The problem was that all of the class names needed to be changed. All of the assumptions about a single document needed to be modified. All of the code eventually was scrapped and the relevant pieces copied into a completely new application built from scratch in the MDI model using Visual C++'s AppWizard.

What is the moral of this story? That you should know better than your client the right way to do something? Probably. But the problem is that the clients (your bosses) generally pay the bills and expect things to be done their way at any given moment. If they change their minds, it's your problem to make things right, not theirs.

Where is all of this leading? Well, let's suppose that your manager came up to you after a demonstration of the wonderful Scribble product and said, "Looks great. Make it an MDI app and let me draw in multiple windows. Oh yeah, make each one update all of the others." If you were using a previous product, such as Borland C++ or Visual C++, you would be faced with the same choice that my programming team was: rewrite the thing and pull out the relevant code to make it work. Fortunately, you aren't developing using Visual C++ and the MFC, and you don't use Borland C++ and OWL. Instead, you have the joy of using CBuilder.

In this example, we're going to convert Scribble to an MDI application, rather than the single form that it is today. You may be quite surprised how easy the whole process is, especially if you've worked with other systems.

What's The Difference?

The first important thing to know about the CBuilder approach to MDI is that there is really no difference between an MDI form and a normal form. MDI forms are simply one of two types: parents or children. In each MDI application, there is generally a single MDI parent form that acts as the frame for the application and contains all of the children. There can be, and usually are, multiple child MDI forms in an application that may be either the same type or different types. It's possible, for example, to have an MDI application consisting of five child windows all of different form types. I'm not sure why you would want to do this, but if your application needs such a thing, CBuilder will be there to support you in your effort.

Figure 2.6 shows the application we'll be developing. The frame window in this case is the main window that contains the main menu. The child windows are the Scribble windows. In terms of the internals of the design, there is almost no difference between the child Scribble windows and the single Scribble windows we used previously. In fact, were it not for the fact that we want all of the windows to share a single list of points, we could simply reuse the forms from the previous example.

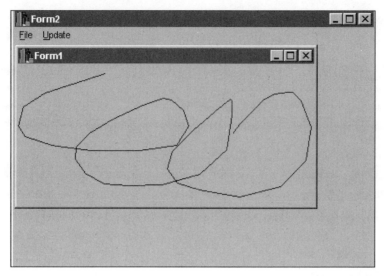

Figure 2.6
The Scribble program as an MDI application.

Doing The Conversion

The first step in changing from an SDI application is to understand what it is that makes a form an MDI form or an MDI child form rather than a normal form. The difference lies in a single property of the form, the **Form Style** property. For most forms in your applications, the **Form Style** property will be set to the value of **fsNormal**, indicating a simple form that can be thought of as a modeless dialog. For an MDI form, the **Form Style** property will be set to **fsMDIForm** for MDI parents and **fsMDIChild** for MDI child forms.

If a form is of type **fsMDIForm**, it will automatically be created with a single MDI child window, which will be the first MDI child form type found in the project. A form of **fsMDIChild** will be created within the boundaries of the parent form of the application.

The first step to making our Scribble application into an MDI application is to add a new form to the application that will act as the single parent of the whole application. Add a new form and set the Form Style to **fsMDIForm**. Add a menu to the new form and add two menu items to the menu with the captions File and View. Under the File menu, add the New and Exit menu items. Under the View menu, add a single menu item with the caption Update All.

The File|New menu item will be used to create new instances of the child forms in the application. The File|Exit menu item is provided to exit the application cleanly. Finally, the View|Update All menu item will force all child views to repaint, showing the same data in all view canvases.

Select the Scribble drawing form and change the Form Style to **fsMDIChild**. This is the basic view for our application. Although we have to make a few changes to make this form behave properly with all of the other forms, the basic code for the Scribble form remains the same. That single change of the **Form Style** property is the only change needed to turn it from a standalone form to an MDI child.

> **Note:** *When working with the forms, we'll be reverting to the Scribble2 example code because we don't want the sub-forms to have their own menus (which looks ugly on the screen). It's not difficult to add the second handler to these forms, but in the interests of space this example will only support drawing with the mouse rather than drawing bitmaps as well.*

The next step in the process is to make sure that the main form is created first in the pecking order by the auto-creation done by CBuilder. To change the order of the forms, select the Project Manager (View|Project Manager) and select the Options button. Click on the **Form2** object in the list and drag it to the top of the list box, before the **Form1** object. That's all there is to it. When you run the program, the **Form2** (main MDI form) will be created first, and the instances of the child forms (**Form1**, our Scribble drawing form) will be created next as a child of the parent window.

Each form in the system needs to know about the others, so we'll need to tell them about each other. To do this, select the main form (**Form2**) and select File|Include Unit Hdr. A list box will be displayed showing the **Form1** form. Select it and click okay. Repeat the process for **Form1** and include the **Form2** header.

> **Note:** *When you include the header for another form, you automatically enable the ability to use the object defined in that header file in your own form. If you look at the bottom of the **Form2** include file (Form2.h) you'll see a line that reads:*

```
extern TForm2 *Form2;
```

*This line enables you to use the **Form2** object in other forms or objects by simply including the header file. This is a nice touch by the CBuilder project team and shows the dedication in the product to making programmers' lives easier.*

Okay, so we now have an MDI parent form and an MDI child form. At this point, you can compile and link the application and you should see the MDI form displayed. The MDI child window within the parent frame is a Scribble drawing form and should permit you to press the left mouse button in the window and move the mouse, drawing merrily as you go. Give it a try.

Form Procreation

Exactly how do you make new little forms? This isn't a birds and the bees question, but the basic issue involved in the whole MDI window system. If you've worked with other systems, you're probably accustomed to letting the system create the MDI child windows and you know that generally it's a painful affair to create the child windows yourself. Because frameworks are designed for exactly this kind of work, it's painful to go around the framework to do things your way. Because it's component-based, CBuilder doesn't try to do things its way but instead gives you the power to do things your way.

To prove the point, let's take a look at the File|New handler. This handler is supposed to create a new MDI child form and display it on the screen. Typically, you would want to change the name of the form to something that shows its relationship to the parent. In our handler, we'll name the form "Scribble Child." Add a new handler for the File|New menu item and add the following code to the handler to do the job:

```
void __fastcall TForm2::New1Click(TObject *Sender)
{
    TForm1 *pForm1 = new TForm1(Application);
    pForm1->Caption = "Scribble Child";
}
```

The only strange thing about the above code is that it doesn't seem to have anything special in it for MDI. The form is created as a child form of the application. Because we set the Form Style property of the form to be **fsMDIChild**, it automatically knows at form creation time that it's an MDI child. As a result, all of the work of making it a child window of the main form window is done for you by the component itself.

The second line of code simply sets the **Caption** property of the window to be "Scribble Child," which will set the titlebar of the child window to be that text when the window is displayed. Once you've finished typing in all of the above code, compile and run the application. Select File|New from the main menu, and a new MDI child window appears, nicely offset from the first MDI child window.

> **Note:** You'll probably notice that the first MDI child window shown when the program initially is displayed does not have the Scribble Child titlebar text, because it was auto-created and did not go through the File|New process. There are two ways to fix this. Remove the auto-creation of the MDI child form in your application and start up the program with an empty MDI parent, fairly standard procedure in the Windows application world. The second approach is to set the title of the child in the form **Caption** property at design time and then simply append some unique identifier when the window is created at runtime. The Windows standard for this approach is to use some name (Scribble Child, for example) followed by the number of the MDI child window in the order in which it was created. For example, the first window would be Scribble Child 1, the second would be Scribble Child 2, and so forth.

The next step in our conversion process is to modify the drawing forms (Scribble Children) to use a single source for all points in the system. We want to centralize the points in a single place that all of the child forms can access. There are really two places that you can centralize data in the CBuilder system. The first is to put it at the same level as the **Application** object, which makes it a global object. This is generally frowned upon in the object-oriented community, but it certainly will work. The second possible approach is to make the data a member variable of an object in the system of which there is only a single occurrence. This is the approach we're going to take in this example. Your mileage may vary.

The best place to put the data in this example is in the one form that has only a single instance. Since the MDI child forms don't fit this criteria, the only place left to move the data is into the MDI parent form (the **Form2** class). This fits all the requirements neatly and allows us to have a certain level of control over the data in our application. So that is what we're going to do.

To move the data out of the Scribble MDI Child forms, we need to modify the code in the **Form1** (child) forms. Here is the updated code in the source file:

```
//-------------------------------------------------------------------
#include <vcl\vcl.h>
#pragma hdrstop

#include "Unit1.h"
#include "MainForm.h"
//-------------------------------------------------------------------
#pragma resource "*.dfm"
TForm1 *Form1;
//-------------------------------------------------------------------
__fastcall TForm1::TForm1(TComponent* Owner)
                : TForm(Owner)
{
    FbMouseDown = FALSE;
}
//-------------------------------------------------------------------
void __fastcall TForm1::OnMouseDown(TObject *Sender, TMouseButton Button,
                                    TShiftState Shift, int X, int Y)
{
    FbMouseDown = TRUE;

    // Move to this point initially
    Canvas->MoveTo(X,Y);

    // Now update the main form with the new
    // data. Indicate that we are clearing out
    // all existing points.
    Form2->ClearPoints();
    Form2->AddPoint( X, Y );
}
//-------------------------------------------------------------------
void __fastcall TForm1::OnMouseMove(TObject *Sender, TShiftState Shift,
                                    int X, int Y)
{
                if ( FbMouseDown )
    {
        Canvas->LineTo(X,Y);

        // Update the main form with new data.
        Form2->AddPoint( X, Y );
    }
}
```

```
//-----------------------------------------------------------------
void __fastcall TForm1::OnMouseUp(TObject *Sender, TMouseButton Button,
                                  TShiftState Shift, int X, int Y)
{
    FbMouseDown = FALSE;
}
//-----------------------------------------------------------------

void __fastcall TForm1::OnPaint(TObject *Sender)
{
    if ( Form2->NumberOfPoints() > 0 )
    {
        int X = 0, Y = 0;

        // Get the first point to anchor the thing
        Form2->GetPoint( 0, X, Y );
                    Canvas->MoveTo(X,Y);

        // Now, loop through each point, getting them
        // from the main form and drawing them.
        for ( int i=1; i<Form2->NumberOfPoints(); ++i )
        {
                    Form2->GetPoint( i, X, Y );
            Canvas->LineTo( X, Y );
        }
                }
}
//-----------------------------------------------------------------
```

Looking at the above code, you can, I hope, see that we really didn't change much apart from removing some of the code, such as the initialization of some of the objects and the point arrays (FPointX and FPointY). Looking at the header file, we see that they've also been removed here as well:

```
//-----------------------------------------------------------------
#ifndef Unit1H
#define Unit1H
//-----------------------------------------------------------------
#include <vcl\Classes.hpp>
#include <vcl\Controls.hpp>
#include <vcl\StdCtrls.hpp>
#include <vcl\Forms.hpp>
//-----------------------------------------------------------------
```

```
class TForm1 : public TForm
{
__published:    // IDE-managed Components
                void __fastcall OnMouseDown(TObject *Sender, TMouseButton
                Button, TShiftState Shift, int X, int Y);
                void __fastcall OnMouseMove(TObject *Sender, TShiftState
                                            Shift, int X, int Y);
                void __fastcall OnMouseUp(TObject *Sender, TMouseButton
                Button, TShiftState Shift, int X, int Y);
                void __fastcall OnPaint(TObject *Sender);
private:  // User declarations
    BOOL FbMouseDown;
public:         // User declarations
                __fastcall TForm1(TComponent* Owner);
};
//----------------------------------------------------------------------
extern TForm1 *Form1;
//----------------------------------------------------------------------
#endif
```

Okay, so we removed all of this wonderful code from the **Form1** class and replaced it with some strange-looking method calls to the **Form2** class. What, exactly, does this code do in the **Form2** class? Well, if you add the following lines to the **Form2.h** include file, you'll see just what is going on:

```
const int MaxPoints = 100;
class TForm2 : public TForm
{
__published:    // IDE-managed Components
                TMainMenu *MainMenu1;
                TMenuItem *File1;
                TMenuItem *New1;
                TMenuItem *Exit1;
                TMenuItem *Update1;
                TMenuItem *AllWindows1;
                void __fastcall New1Click(TObject *Sender);
private:  // User declarations
    int   FnPoint;
    int   FPointX[MaxPoints+1];
    int   FPointY[MaxPoints+1];

public:         // User declarations
                __fastcall TForm2(TComponent* Owner);
    void ClearPoints(void)
    {
```

```
        FnPoint = 0;
    }
    void AddPoint(int X, int Y)
    {
        if ( FnPoint < MaxPoints )
        {
            FPointX[FnPoint] = X;
            FPointY[FnPoint] = Y;
            FnPoint++;
        }
    }
    int NumberOfPoints(void)
    {
        return FnPoint;
    }
    void GetPoint( int Index, int& X, int& Y )
    {
        if ( Index >= 0 && Index < FnPoint )
        {
            X = FPointX[Index];
            Y = FPointY[Index];
        }
    }
};
//--------------------------------------------------------------------
extern TForm2 *Form2;
//--------------------------------------------------------------------
#endif
```

Does this code look familiar? It should. Most of it is simply copied from the old Scribble form and wrapped in methods for this object. This process is called *encapsulation* and is an important idea to understand in C++ programming. By encapsulating the access to retrieving and modifying the data in methods of an object, we protect that data from harm by objects. In addition, because we've moved the data out of the actual loop, so to speak, we have left it open to be able to change the way the data is stored. Suppose, for example, that the data was no longer stored in the simple array format as it is today. Suppose that we made the data into some sort of virtual array or even a hash table. Perhaps the points are actually to be stored on disk. Regardless of how the data is stored, this implementation will allow us to hide the actual format of the data from the other objects. No matter how the **Form2** object is restructured in terms of data, as long as the signatures (the function parameters and return type) of the methods **ClearPoints, AddPoint, NumberOfPoints,** and **GetPoint** don't change, the **Form1** object will not need to know anything about it. This is "data hiding" in C++. The actual data is hidden behind methods that are used to access the data. The purest form of data hiding is probably found in the idea of properties for VCL components, which we'll look at a bit later. I mention this only because many people have found the idea of properties disturbing and non-object oriented. As we'll see a bit later, this couldn't be further from the truth.

What does all of this buy us? The answer is simple. By moving all of the data into a single object and accessing it through that single object, we can now have all Scribble forms look the same when one of them is updated. Don't believe me? Try it out right now by compiling and running the application. Bring up several of the child windows by selecting File|New multiple times. Pick one of the windows and draw a masterpiece on the surface of the window. Now move to another window. You'll see that the window is automatically updated with the data from the other window.

There's ALWAYS A Problem

There is, of course, one slight problem with this approach. It only shows up if you have two of the child windows up side by side and modify one of them. In doing so, you'll see that the second child window doesn't update until you refresh it by either minimizing and restoring it or moving another window across it. The problem is that although the window will read its data from the central data repository (**Form2**) each time it's painted, it doesn't know that it needs to be painted. The solutions for this problem vary according to your application. We will examine one possible solution to the problem here via a menu item, but the same process could be used in any window.

Remember a while back when I asked you to add a menu item called Update All to the View menu? There was method to my madness. The Update All method was intended to solve the very problem we are talking about—forcing all of the child windows to update themselves.

First, let's take a look at the code that solves the problem, then we can get back to the discussion of the how the thing works and why it solves the problem. Add a handler for the Update All menu item and add the following code to that handler:

```
void __fastcall TForm2::AllWindows1Click(TObject *Sender)
{
    for ( int i=0; i<MDIChildCount; ++i )
```

```
   {
      TForm1 *pForm = static_cast<TForm1 *>(MDIChildren[i]);
      if ( pForm )
         pForm->Invalidate();
   }
}
```

What is going on here? The MDI Form has a property called **MDIChildCount**, which is the number of currently open MDI child windows. This property actually exists in all forms, but will be set to 0 if the form style for that form is not **fsMDIForm**. In addition to the number of children, the form also has a property called **MDIChildren**, which is a dynamic array of pointers to forms. We're looping through all of the forms that are children of our MDI parent and forcing them to update themselves by calling the **Invalidate** method.

If you're not accustomed to Windows programming, the painting model for a window is a little strange. Painting is accomplished by invalidating regions of a form. Invalidating means to tell the operating system that a portion of the window (or all of it) needs to be repainted. Anything can tell a window that it needs to be repainted by simply invoking the **Invalidate** method on that window (or form).

The last thing to mention about this little code snippet is the **static_cast** operation. The **static_cast** function is new to C++, only appearing in the latest ANSI release of the language specification. The **static_cast** function tries to cast an object to a given type. The general form of the **static_cast** operation is as follows

```
T *pT = static_cast<T *>(someobjpointer);
```

where **T** is a type (such as TForm1 above) that is defined in the system and **someobjpointer** is a given pointer. Note that this argument must be a pointer or you will get an error.

If the cast was successful, the returned value is a pointer in the correct format for type T. If the cast was not successful, the return is NULL. Therefore, check for the return of NULL before invoking the method Invalidate on the returned object. This is a basic sanity check that you would do well to invoke in your own applications. If you're working with pointers, verify that they are not NULL before proceeding.

The Very Last Step

This is the very last thing that we need to do to complete the Scribble MDI application. Even more impressive, this last step will only require a single line of code.

The File|Exit menu item has been sitting there, getting more and more lonely as we have ignored it to implement the remainder of the application. All it really wants to do is to have some code associated with it that will close down the program and return control to the operating system. What say we accommodate it by adding a handler for it?

Add a new handler for the File|Exit menu item and add the following line of code to the handler:

```
void __fastcall TForm2::ExitClick(TObject *Sender)
{
    Application->Terminate();
}
```

The **Application** object is a global interface to the operating system task that runs our application. The **Terminate** method of the application will clean up all dangling forms, pointers, and controls and then close all of the windows in the application. **Application->Terminate()** is the preferred method used to close down an application, and it can be used safely from pretty much anywhere in your application. Do not simply close all windows and assume that everything is okay; use the **Terminate** method.

What Did We Learn In This Chapter?

We've accomplished a lot in this first chapter of code in the book:

A form can be created with no caption. More importantly, the startup styles of a form can be modified by the program before the form is displayed on the screen. This is done in the **CreateParams** method of the form.

Forms have a variety of properties. The **Caption** property, for example, controls the text displayed in the titlebar of the form. The **Canvas** property is used to draw in a form client area.

Form event handlers can be defined for all sorts of user actions that occur in a form, such as mouse clicks, mouse moves, and pressing and releasing the mouse buttons.

Event handlers directly correspond to Windows messages. In CBuilder, rather than handling the messages directly, you allow the form to call event handlers indirectly by associating them with an event. This allows for dynamic modification of event handlers at runtime.

Form Definition Files (DFMs) can be viewed in the editor as plain-text files.

Copying a project should be done separately from saving the Project as a new name using the File|Save Project As command.

Bitmaps are simple and easy to use in CBuilder. They can be loaded via the **LoadFromFile** method and drawn via the **Draw** method of the **Canvas** object.

MDI Forms are nothing more or less than normal forms with a specific Form Style property set (**fsMDIForm**). MDI Child forms are exactly the same, except their Form Style is set to **fsMDIChild**.

The **Application->Terminate**() method is the recommended way to end an application.

That's all we have for Chapter 2. In the next chapter, we'll begin to explore the use of graphics in CBuilder by building a fun little game for you to play.

Image
Handling

CHAPTER 3

HIGH PERFORMANCE

- Displaying Images On A Form

- Creating Images At Runtime

- Changing Controls At Runtime

- Working With Pictures

- Creating Bitmaps In Code

Image Handling

Windows is a graphical operating system, CBuilder is a graphically oriented C++ development environment, the World Wide Web is filled with graphics. All of these things are related to images and image handling, and in this chapter, we explore image handling with CBuilder.

Graphics is far too exciting a subject to be handled as a dry series of examples, so we'll have some fun exploring the graphical aspects of CBuilder. We'll create two simple games using CBuilder, a matching game and a game of tic-tac-toe. Both offer the opportunity to have some fun while learning something about the system. Although neither game is likely to keep anyone below the level of manager happy for more than a few minutes, they might keep that three-year-old toddler at your house busy for awhile.

Example 1: Match Game Take One

For our first example in image handling, let's create a simple match game like one you probably played as a child where you try to match up like things. You may be familiar with versions of this game like Concentration or Match. Here's how we're going to implement the game. The board consists of 16 buttons arranged in a 4×4 grid, and each of the buttons has a name on it. If the two names match, the buttons disappear and a portion of a bitmap displayed behind the buttons will be displayed.

To implement the board we need two different kinds of VCL objects: buttons and an image control. This example shows how the image control is used and how you can display it. In this case, we aren't really doing any work—CBuilder is doing it all for us. You'll see the real power of CBuilder as we implement the entire match game, including displaying the bitmap image and processing all of the buttons, checking to see if they are the same, and making them vanish—all in 25 lines of code, including comments.

> **Note:** You'll find the complete code for the Match Game program on the accompanying CD-ROM with this book.

The first thing you need to do is to create the board for play. First, put an image control on the form, stretched across the entire size of the form. Set the **Image** property to whatever image you want to use for this game. We'll get into how to load a user-defined bitmap in just a few minutes. On top of the image control you need to arrange four rows of four columns of buttons. At this point you need to set the **Caption** property of each to blank. Figure 3.1 shows the board as it will appear when you're finished.

You might think that you need to select each of the 16 buttons and set the **Caption** *property of each one to blank, but you don't. Select all of the buttons at once by holding down the Shift key and clicking on each one. Then simply move to the Object Inspector. Only those properties that can be set for multiple objects (obviously not* **Name***) will be displayed. Select the* **Caption** *property and delete the contents of the property field. Press Return and all of the objects will be set to the blank Caption.*

Figure 3.1
CBuilder form for the Match Game.

Once you've set all of the buttons to blank, we need to start thinking about setting the captions of the buttons so that you can match them. We'll be doing this in the **FormCreate** method, which is called when the form is first created.

Setting The Button Captions

Before we assign the button captions a specific order, we need a list of captions to enter. Because I'm a big fan of classic Star Trek, we'll use names from that show. Modify the source file for Unit.cpp as follows to set the captions. Once you finish entering all of this we can talk about how the code for this particular function works.

Enter this at the top of the source file. These are the captions for the buttons. Because we have 16 buttons and want to be able to match each one, we'll need eight names, with two occurrences of each name on the buttons.

```
char *strNames[] = {
    "Kirk",
    "Spock",
    "McCoy",
    "Uhura",
    "Sulu",
    "Chekov",
    "Scotty",
    "Riley"
};

// Here is the modified FormCreate method.

void __fastcall TForm1::FormCreate(TObject *Sender)
{
    int nStringIndex = 0;
    for ( int i=0; i<ControlCount; ++i )
    {
        TButton *pButton = dynamic_cast<TButton *>(Controls[i]);
        if ( pButton )
        {
            pButton->Caption = strNames[ nStringIndex ];
            nStringIndex ++;
            if ( nStringIndex > 7 )
                nStringIndex = 0;
        }
    }
}
```

What exactly is going on in this method? This first piece of the puzzle is the **ControlCount** property that is used at the top of the for loop. The **ControlCount** property holds the number of child controls that are on the form. In this case, we have 16 buttons and one image on the form, so the **ControlCount** property for this form should be 17. We loop through all of the children by using the Controls property of the form object.

The **Controls** property of the **Form** class contains pointers to each of the controls found on the form. You can act on any of these forms in the same way because all of these controls are somehow related to each other in the hierarchy of the VCL. The **Controls** property actually stores objects of type **TControl**, which is the basic class for all controls in the CBuilder system.

Once we have a pointer to a control, we need to know whether this is one of the buttons on the control or if it's another kind of control altogether. If you've worked with other systems, you might try something like a form of IsKindOf or perhaps inspecting signal values in the object. CBuilder has a better way, the ANSI C++ standard function called **dynamic_cast**.

The **dynamic_cast** function in C++ has the following general syntax

```
T* pObject = dynamic_cast<T *>(somepointer);
```

where **T** is a type that you want to try to convert a pointer into and **somepointer** is a pointer to another object. If **somepointer** is not a pointer, you'll get an error from the compiler and the program will not compile.

You may remember the **static_cast** method talked about in the last chapter, which is closer to the normal way that C++ programmers work with casting of objects. A **static_cast** can only fail if the **somepointer** argument is NULL or invalid. A **dynamic_cast**, on the other hand, will only work if the object you're trying to convert is of the correct type to be cast. For the code we have in the above function to work, therefore, each Control entry will become a **TButton** pointer if, and only if, that control is really a **TButton** to begin with.

> **Note:** This last statement is true, but not complete. If the pointer is of a class derived from **TButton**, such as a user class like **TMyButton**, the cast will

*still work and you'll still end up with a valid pointer to a **TButton**. This is the magic of polymorphism, the concept that says derived classes behave exactly the same way that their base classes behave.*

Once we have a pointer to a button object, the rest of the process is easy. All we're doing is looping through the names in the **strNames** array. Each time that we reach the end of the loop we'll simply reset the index counter to the beginning of the loop.

Checking For Matches

Once we have all of the buttons initialized to some value, the next step is to check for matches. This is where the power of the VCL to have multiple objects share a common event handler is useful. Select all buttons on the form by holding down the Shift key while clicking on them. Move to the events page of the Object Inspector and add a handler for the **OnClick** event. In the entry on the right side of the grid, enter the name **HandleButtonClick**. This method will be created and associated with all of the buttons on the form. Here is the code for the **HandleButtonClick** method:

```
void __fastcall TForm1::HandleButtonClick(TObject *Sender)
{
    TButton *pButton = static_cast<TButton *>(Sender);
    if ( m_nClick == 1 ) // Second click
    {
        // Reset click
        m_nClick = 0;
        if ( m_pPrevButton == NULL )
            return;

        // Compare the two button captions
        if ( m_pPrevButton->Caption == pButton->Caption )
        {
            m_pPrevButton->Hide();
            pButton->Hide();
        }
        else
        {
            MessageBeep(MB_ICONEXCLAMATION);
        }
    }
    else
    {
```

```
        // First click
        m_nClick = 1;
        // Save the button
        m_pPrevButton = pButton;
    }
}
```

Notice the use of the **Sender** argument in the function for the first time in this book. When CBuilder calls an event handler for a form (or other object), the object that caused the event to occur will always be passed in the **Sender** argument of the event handler. Since we'll be clicking on a button, the argument to the method will be the button that we clicked on. We need to check whether or not the button that the user clicks is the same as the last button that they clicked. To accomplish this, we need to add a couple of member variables to the form class. Modify the header file for the form as follows, with changes shown in highlighted print:

```
< Code Omitted for Space>
                void __fastcall FormCreate(TObject *Sender);
private:    // User declarations
    TButton *m_pPrevButton;
    int       m_nClick;
public:         // User declarations
                __fastcall TForm1(TComponent* Owner);
};
```

The **m_pPrevButton** argument will be used to hold onto a pointer to the previous button click. The **m_nClick** argument is used to track which click this is in the form. Finally, modify the constructor for the form to initialize these member variables (something you should always do in your own applications, of course).

```
__fastcall TForm1::TForm1(TComponent* Owner)
                : TForm(Owner)
{
    m_nClick = 0;
    m_pPrevButton = NULL;
}
```

How Does It All Work?

When the user clicks a button for the first time, the **HandleButtonClick** method is called. At this point, the **m_nClick** variable is 0 and the previous pointer (**m_pPrevButton**) is NULL. The **HandleButtonClick** method drops through to the **else** section and sets the previous pointer to the button that was clicked. In addition, it sets the **m_nClick** variable to 1, indicating to the form that a button has been clicked and that a match is now going to be attempted.

The second time that a button is clicked, the method drops into the first part of the **if** statement that reads:

```
if ( m_nClick == 1 ) // Second click
```

This section makes sure that there is, in fact, a previous button (a sanity check to prevent a nasty program crash in case we forgot something). Next, the method simply asks the previous button for its **Caption** property and compares it to the **Caption** property of the button that was just selected. If the two are the same, it "hides" both buttons by calling the **Hide** method on each button object. This reveals the underlying image control and shows a part of the image peeking out from beneath the board. If the two buttons don't match, the speaker is beeped on the system by using the Windows API function **MessageBeep**.

> **Note:** Although we chose to use the **Hide** method in the code in this example, you could just as easily have accomplished the same task by setting the **Visible** property of each button to false in your application code. The code to do so would look like this:

```
m_pPrevButton->Visible = false;
        pButton->Visible = false;
```

Figure 3.2 shows a partially completed match game with several of the buttons gone and the image control showing from underneath the board of buttons.

Improving The Match Game Program

While the first cut at the Match Game program certainly works, it lacks certain aesthetics. First of all, the user is stuck with whatever image we chose to put in the image control when we designed the form. It would be nicer if the parent could set the image to whatever they want before the child starts playing the game. Also, it would be nice if the buttons could appear in new locations each time you ran the program. In this second cut at Match Game, we'll attempt to fix these two problems.

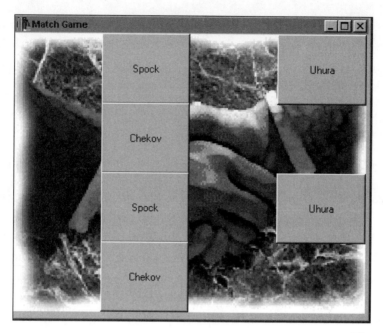

Figure 3.2
Partially completed Match Game.

Note: The source code for the second Match Game program will be found on the accompanying CD-ROM.

First things first, let's take care of allowing the user to dynamically load an image into the image control at runtime. Add a main menu to the form by dragging and dropping it onto the top of the form displayed in the form editor. Add a File menu to the main menu and add two menu items to the main menu. Give the first menu item the caption Select Image and the second menu item Exit. Finally, move to the Dialogs tab on the Component Palette and drop an Open Dialog onto the form. This is the dialog we're going to use to allow the user to select a bitmap file to display.

Add a handler for the Select Image menu item and add the following code into that handler:

```
void __fastcall TForm1::SelectImage1Click(TObject *Sender)
{
    OpenDialog1->Filter = "Bitmap Files (*.bmp)|*.bmp";
            if ( OpenDialog1->Execute() )
```

```
   {
      TPicture *pPicture = new TPicture;
      pPicture->LoadFromFile( OpenDialog1->FileName );
      Image1->Picture = pPicture;
   }

}
```

There are two interesting things going on in this simple method. First, you can see how to restrict files to a specific extension or type. By setting the **Filter** property of the **OpenDialog** object to the type you want to use, you restrict what shows up in the dialog file listing box. The format of the string has the following syntax

```
Name|Type
```

where **Name** is the text name that you want the user to be able to see in the filter combo box. The **Name** property is usually of the form Description (*.ext) where .ext is the extension you want to show them. In our example, the Description is Bitmap Files and the extension is bmp.

Type is the actual extension type that you want to enter. The pipe character (|) between the two pieces is important and must be entered as well.

The next thing that is interesting is the use of the **TPicture** object. We haven't dealt with **TPicture**s before, so it's worth taking a look at them. A **TPicture** is used to store bitmaps, icons, and other graphic images. A **TPicture** can be drawn, like the drawing of bitmaps in Chapter 2. In addition, you can load a **TPicture** object directly from disk using the **LoadFromFile** method and you can load a **TPicture** object from a resource file, which we haven't talked about to this point in the book.

Once you have the **TPicture** object loaded with the bitmap that the user selected in the OpenDialog box, simply assign that picture to the **Picture** property of the image control. That's really all there is to it. The Image control will do the job of displaying the picture in its Canvas.

That was step number one. Step number two is a little more complicated. In this step, we want to randomize the display of the captions to the button. Fortunately for us, the CBuilder runtime library contains a function called random, which will accept a number and return you a random number in the range 0 to the number specified. We'll make use of this property of the random function to accomplish our second task. Here is the code for the new **FormCreate** method:

```
void __fastcall TForm1::FormCreate(TObject *Sender)
{
    char strings_1[MaxStringCount*2][ 20 ];
    char strings_2[MaxStringCount*2][ 20 ];

    // First, copy all of the strings into the array
    for ( int i=0; i<MaxStringCount; ++i )
    {
        strcpy ( strings_1[i], strNames[i] );
        strcpy ( strings_1[i+MaxStringCount], strNames[i]) ;
    }


    // Now, randomize them

    for ( int i=MaxStringCount*2-1; i>=0; --i )
    {
        int nIdx = random(i);
        // Put that string into the second array
        strcpy ( strings_2[i], strings_1[nIdx] );
        // Copy the last string into that position
                        strcpy ( strings_1[nIdx], strings_1[i] );
    }

    int nStringIndex = 0;
    for ( int i=0; i<ControlCount; ++i )
    {
        TButton *pButton = dynamic_cast<TButton *>(Controls[i]);
        if ( pButton )
        {
            pButton->Caption = strings_2[ nStringIndex ];
            if ( nStringIndex < MaxStringCount*2-1 )
                nStringIndex ++;

        }
    }
}
```

Additionally, since I harped on the idea of not using magic numbers in your code, add the following declaration at the top of the file:

```
const MaxStringCount = 8;
```

This magic number is simply the number of strings we're going to use.

How Does It Work?

The randomizing process is a three-step deal. First, we copy all of the strings into a single array, which is twice the size of the number of strings we're dealing with. As a side note, this is another benefit of using the constant definition for the number of strings. If we ever change the number of buttons on the form and the number of strings we use to fill them, everything will adjust accordingly.

Once the strings are placed in the array, we step backward through them, selecting a single random string from the bunch each time using the random function we discussed previously. As we select each string in the first array, we move the last string in the array into the selected position, effectively deleting the old string from the array. The selected string is copied into a second array, which holds the random strings in the order they were selected. It's this second array of strings we'll use to display the captions on the buttons of our form.

The final piece is the now familiar section of assigning each of the buttons the new caption as we've done in the previous iteration of the program. If you now run the Match Game 2 program, you should see something akin to the screen shown in Figure 3.3.

At this point you have a fully functional game that your children can play for as long as they like. Unless you want your kids to grow up to be Star Trek fans, however, you might want to change the text to something more closely related to their age groups.

> **Note:** Although all along in this example we talked about using **TButtons**, if you examine the code on the accompanying CD-ROM, you'll notice that I actually use **TBitBtns**. The **TBitBtn** is a derived class from **TButton** that can display not only text but also an image on the button. If you have very young children who can't read yet, you might try your hand at modifying the code in the Match Game 2 program to use images rather than text. The process is pretty much exactly the same as we did here, but uses the **Glyph** property of the **TBitBtn** rather than the **Caption** property. In addition, you'll need to create **TPicture** objects (much as we did in the load procedure) for each image you want displayed. CBuilder comes with a nice assortment of images in the CBuilder\Images sub-directory of your application tree.

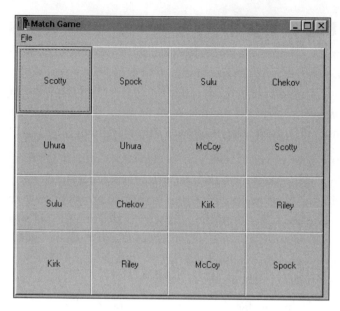

Figure 3.3
The updated Match Game program running.

Although this was a fun diversion and you learned a bit about **TPicture**s and **TImageControls**, you didn't learn a lot about the graphics built into CBuilder. In our next simple example, however, you'll learn quite a bit about some of the internals of the system.

The Tic-Tac-Toe Program

The X's and O's game of tic-tac-toe is one of the oldest games known to man. It's easy to play and most people already know all of the rules. In our version of tic-tac-toe, you'll learn quite a bit about the internals of CBuilder graphics, the processing of user-input, and the drawing capabilities of forms.

Figure 3.4 shows the complete form with all VCL components needed to build this application. Yes, it is indeed blank. All of the work for drawing this form will be done internally to the application itself.

> **Note:** The source code for the Tic-Tac-Toe program will be found on the accompanying CD-ROM.

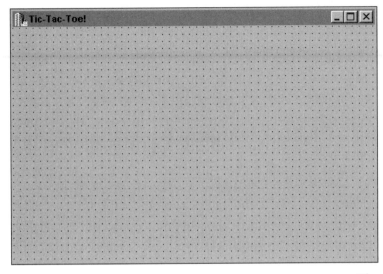

Figure 3.4
The form for the Tic-Tac-Toe program.

Step 1: Building The Bitmaps

In this example, we'll dynamically create bitmaps and the images associated with them. These bitmaps are fairly simple (an X and an O) but will illustrate how you can use the **TBitmap** object to create your own bitmaps within an application without relying on external files or resources. The first step is to declare some variables in the header file for the application. Modify the Unit1.h include file to add the following declarations:

```
class TForm1 : public TForm
{
__published:    // IDE-managed Components
                void __fastcall FormPaint(TObject *Sender);
                void __fastcall FormMouseDown(TObject *Sender,
                TMouseButton Button, TShiftState Shift, int X, int Y);
private:  // User declarations
    Graphics::TBitmap *FpXBitmap;
    Graphics::TBitmap *FpYBitmap;
    int       FnGameBoard[3][3];
    int       FnWhichPlayer;
```

```
public:          // User declarations
                 __fastcall TForm1(TComponent* Owner);
};
```

The two bitmap objects will be used to draw the bitmaps internally and to display them on the form to indicate user moves. The **FnGameBoard** array is used to store the currently selected squares on the board and to keep track of who owns what in the current game. Finally, the **FnWhichPlayer** member variables is used to keep track of who is moving.

Once you've added all of the variables, it's time to move on to the constructor for the form. Here we will initialize all of the member variables, like a good little C++ object, and do the work of initializing the bitmap objects in the system. Let's look at the code first and then learn how it all works.

```
__fastcall TForm1::TForm1(TComponent* Owner)
                : TForm(Owner)
{
   // Initialize to first player
   FnWhichPlayer = 1;

                 // Initialize the game board.
   ResetBoard();

   // Create the bitmaps
   FpXBitmap = new Graphics::TBitmap;
   FpXBitmap->Width = ClientWidth/3 - 2;
   FpXBitmap->Height= ClientHeight/3 - 2;

   // Fill in the bitmap with the form color
   FpXBitmap->Canvas->Brush->Color = Color;

   TRect r;
   r.Left = 0;
   r.Top = 0;
   r.Right = FpXBitmap->Width;
   r.Bottom = FpXBitmap->Height;

   FpXBitmap->Canvas->FillRect(r);

   FpYBitmap = new Graphics::TBitmap;
   FpYBitmap->Width = ClientWidth/3 - 2;
   FpYBitmap->Height= ClientHeight/3 - 2;
```

```
    // Fill in the bitmap with the form color
    FpYBitmap->Canvas->Brush->Color = Color;
    FpYBitmap->Canvas->FillRect(r);

    // Draw the X bitmap on the canvas
    FpXBitmap->Canvas->MoveTo(0,0);
    FpXBitmap->Canvas->LineTo(FpXBitmap->Width,FpXBitmap->Height);

    FpXBitmap->Canvas->MoveTo(FpXBitmap->Width,0);
    FpXBitmap->Canvas->LineTo(0,FpXBitmap->Height);

    // Draw the Y Bitmap on the canvas
    FpYBitmap->Canvas->Ellipse(0,0,FpYBitmap->Width,FpYBitmap->Height);

}
```

The first couple of pieces of the constructor are relatively obvious. We're initalizing the member variables to reasonable default states before proceeding. The hard part begins with the creation of the **TBitmap** object.

The Life And Times Of A TBitmap Object

Why do we need to set all of those properties of a **TBitmap** when we create it? In the past, all we've done is create the new object and then either load it from disk or assign a bitmap to it.

Like all good bitmaps in the Windows system, a **TBitmap** object starts out life as a 1×1 Windows bitmap, and in order to draw on it we need to "stretch" it out to the size we want to use. In our case, we want each of the two bitmaps to stretch to one-third of the size of the client area of the form. Why the client area? Well, the total **Width** property of the form includes the borders around the form, while the total **Height** property includes the caption bar. If you used these properties, your first two squares of the board would look larger than the third square. Since this isn't what we had in mind, we need to look elsewhere. CBuilder objects have two kinds of widths and heights. The **ClientWidth** and **ClientHeight** properties represent the width and height, respectively, of the client area of the form. The client area is the area left over after the menu bar, borders, caption, and status-bars are removed from the form surface.

Once we've defined the **Width** and **Height** properties, the bitmap objects are simply more graphical objects that are waiting for us to draw on them. A bitmap starts out life with a white background. Since this wouldn't look good on the battleship-gray background of our form, we need to reset the color of the background by using the **Brush** property of the bitmap, which contains a property of its own called **Color**. The **Color** property of the **Brush** will be used for the background of all drawing operations for that bitmap. In our case, we first need to fill in the white bitmap with our form background color. This is done via the **FillRect** method. To use **FillRect**, initialize a rectangle (**TRect** object) with the boundaries you want to fill. In our case, we use the boundaries of the bitmap itself because we want to fill in the whole bitmap.

```
r.Left = 0;
r.Top = 0;
r.Right = FpXBitmap->Width;
r.Bottom = FpXBitmap->Height;
```

Once we have the rectangle to fill defined and the color set in the brush of the **Canvas** property of the object we want to fill (in our case the bitmap), we invoke the **FillRect** method for that object (**Bitmap->Canvas**) and the rest is done automatically.

Once the bitmap is filled with color, the next step is to draw the image we want to appear on the bitmap. You can use any of the defined Canvas drawing methods to draw on the bitmap or you can pass the **Canvas->Handle** property to any Windows drawing routine you might have lying around. This is handy if you want to use a third-party drawing function in your CBuilder programs.

For the X bitmap, use the familiar MoveTo and LineTo commands of the Canvas to create two lines running diagonally across the bitmap forming the familiar X shape. For the Y bitmap, we use another method of the **Canvas** object, called **Ellipse**. **Ellipse** will draw an elliptical shape on a given Canvas. Because our bitmaps are very nearly square, the result of the **Ellipse** function is very close to a circle. The closer the **Height** and **Width** properties are to equal, the more circular the result.

At this point, we have a complete bitmap to use for drawing as if we had loaded it from disk or assigned it in the component editor. This is the nice thing about object-oriented technology. No matter how you reach a given position, you proceed from it in the same way no matter how you got there. This flexibility is the power of object-oriented programming.

> ***Note:*** *CBuilder also provides methods to save your bitmap to disk. You could create a complete drawing program using the CBuilder bitmap system. To*

*save a bitmap to disk, create a file steam object using the **TFileSteam** class and then use the **SaveToStream** method of the **TBitmap** object to write it out to disk.*

The utility function **ResetBoard** is called in the constructor as well. There are no great surprises here. All we do is initialize all of the game board segments to a known signal value, in this case 0.

```
void TForm1::ResetBoard(void)
{
   // Initialize game board
   for ( int i=0; i<3; ++i )
      for ( int j=0; j<3; ++j )
         FnGameBoard[i][j] = 0;
}
```

The worst part of the project is now out of the way. We have now dynamically created a bitmap object, made it the right size, and drawn on the Canvas of the bitmap to provide the image we want the user to see. The next step is to show the bitmap for the user. First let's tackle painting of the form and then move on to handling user input.

Add a handler to the form for the **OnPaint** method. The easiest way to do this is to move to the Object Inspector, locate the **OnPaint** event, and double-click on the right side of the grid next to it. CBuilder will automatically create a new handler with the correct name for the event. In general, the name assigned is Formxxx, where xxx is the name of the event minus the On. For the **OnPaint** event, therefore, the correct name is **FormPaint**. Here is the code to add to the **FormPaint** event handler:

```
void __fastcall TForm1::FormPaint(TObject *Sender)
{
    // The first thing we need to do is to draw
    // the vertical lines for the board
    Canvas->MoveTo( ClientWidth/3, 0 );
    Canvas->LineTo( ClientWidth/3, ClientHeight );
    Canvas->MoveTo( (2*ClientWidth)/3, 0 );
    Canvas->LineTo( (2*ClientWidth)/3, ClientHeight );

    // Next, we draw the horizontal lines for the
    // board
    Canvas->MoveTo( 0, ClientHeight/3 );
    Canvas->LineTo( ClientWidth, ClientHeight/3 );
```

```
Canvas->MoveTo( 0, (2*ClientHeight)/3 );
Canvas->LineTo( ClientWidth, (2*ClientHeight)/3 );

// Now we draw bitmaps based on who has what
// squares.

for ( int i=0; i<3; ++i )
    for ( int j=0; j<3; ++j )
    {
        int nXPos = (ClientWidth/3)* j + 1;
        int nYPos = (ClientHeight/3) * i  + 1;

        // See if X holds this square
        if ( FnGameBoard[i][j] == 1 )
        {
            Canvas->Draw(nXPos, nYPos, FpXBitmap );
        }
        else  // See if Y holds this square
            if ( FnGameBoard[i][j] == 2 )
            {
                Canvas->Draw(nXPos, nYPos, FpYBitmap );
            }
    }
}
```

There are no great surprises here. We draw the board by moving and drawing lines at one-third and two-thirds of the way across and down the client area of the form. Then we check each entry in the game board to see who owns that square. If the first player owns the square, we draw an X at that position using the X bitmap we created in the constructor. If the second player owns the square, we draw an O at that position using the Y bitmap we created in the constructor. Why call the bitmap for the O player a Y bitmap? The position of the bitmap is simply the position of the square with one pixel offset to avoid overwriting the lines of the board itself.

Handling The Mouse Clicks

At this point, we've done all that is necessary to handle the display portion of the game. It's time now to handle the actual processing. We would like to check for each time the user clicks the mouse in the game board, determine which square the user has clicked, and assign that square to the player whose turn it is at present. Of course, we also need to check to see whether the square is already occupied by another player.

The event for a mouse click in a form doesn't exist. There is, however, an event for the mouse button being pressed down and one for the mouse button being released (mouse up). We'll attach our handler to the **MouseDown** event. In general it doesn't matter which event you process unless you have specifically different behavior for the **MouseDown** and **MouseUp** events (such as we did in the Scribble exercises in the last chapter). Responding to the **MouseDown** event will give slightly faster reactions from the program than that of **MouseUp**, but neither one is likely to be noticeable to the average user.

Add a handler for the **MouseDown** event by double-clicking on that event in the Object Inspector. Add the following code to the **FormMouseDown** event handler that is created in your form source code:

```
void __fastcall TForm1::FormMouseDown(TObject *Sender, TMouseButton
                Button, TShiftState Shift, int X, int Y)
{
    int nRow;
    int nCol;

    // Determine which square it is
    if ( X < ClientWidth/3 )
       nCol = 0;
    else
       if ( X < (2*ClientWidth)/3 )
          nCol = 1;
       else
          nCol = 2;

    if ( Y < ClientHeight / 3 )
       nRow = 0;
    else
       if ( Y < (2*ClientHeight) / 3 )
          nRow = 1;
       else
          nRow = 2;

    // See if that square is already occupied
    if ( FnGameBoard[nRow][nCol] != 0 )
    {
       MessageBeep(0);
    }
    else
    {
```

```
    // No. Set the square to be that player's
    FnGameBoard[nRow][nCol] = FnWhichPlayer;

    // And toggle the turn
    if ( FnWhichPlayer == 1 )
        FnWhichPlayer = 2;
    else
        FnWhichPlayer = 1;
    Invalidate();

    // Check for winner! or tie game.
    if ( CheckForWinner() )
    {
        ResetBoard();
        FnWhichPlayer = 1;
        Invalidate();
    }
    }
}
```

The code in this handler checks to see which square the user clicked on. This is accomplished by using the X and Y parameters that were passed into the handler by CBuilder and comparing them to the grid squares. We're simply checking to see if the click was in the first third, second third, or last third of the horizontal and vertical pieces of the form. By converting each piece individually, we end up with two coordinates, a row in the grid and a column in the grid. This maps nicely to our data structure for the game board, which is a row and column oriented array.

Once the grid row and column are located, the game board is checked to see if that square is already occupied. If it is, the infamous **MessageBeep** method is called to tell the user that they can't do that. If not, the square is selected for that user. Once this process is complete, we call another method of the form to see whether anyone has won the game. Here is the code for that method:

```
BOOL TForm1::CheckForWinner(void)
{
    int nWinner;
    // Check the rows
    for ( int nPlayer = 1; nPlayer<3; ++nPlayer )
    {
        for ( int nRow = 0; nRow<3; ++nRow )
        {
```

```
      // Assume this player won.
      nWinner = nPlayer;

      // Check all of the columns. If one
      // doesn't have the player id, they
      // didn't win on this column.

      for ( int nCol = 0; nCol<3; ++nCol )
                  if ( FnGameBoard[nRow][nCol] != nPlayer )
          nWinner = 0;

      if ( nWinner != 0 )
      {
          String s = "Player " + String(nWinner) + " won!";
          MessageBox(NULL, s.c_str(), "Winner!", MB_OK );
          return true;
      }
  }

  // Next, check the columns
  for ( int nCol = 0; nCol<3; ++nCol )
  {
      // Assume this player won.
      nWinner = nPlayer;

      // Check all of the rows. If one
      // doesn't have the player id, they
      // didn't win on this row.

      for ( int nRow = 0; nRow<3; ++nRow )
                  if ( FnGameBoard[nRow][nCol] != nPlayer )
          nWinner = 0;

      if ( nWinner != 0 )
      {
          String s = "Player " + String(nWinner) + " won!";
          MessageBox(NULL, s.c_str(), "Winner!", MB_OK );
          return true;
      }
  }

  // Finally, check the diagonals
  if ( FnGameBoard[0][0] == nPlayer &&
       FnGameBoard[1][1] == nPlayer &&
       FnGameBoard[2][2] == nPlayer )
```

```
    {
            String s = "Player " + String(nPlayer) + " won!";
            MessageBox(NULL, s.c_str(), "Winner!", MB_OK );
            return true;
    }

    if ( FnGameBoard[0][2] == nPlayer &&
         FnGameBoard[1][1] == nPlayer &&
         FnGameBoard[2][0] == nPlayer )
    {
            String s = "Player " + String(nPlayer) + " won!";
            MessageBox(NULL, s.c_str(), "Winner!", MB_OK );
            return true;
    }

 }

 // If we get to here, check for a tie game
 for ( int nRow = 0; nRow<3; ++nRow )
 {
    for ( int nCol = 0; nCol<3; ++nCol )
       if ( FnGameBoard[nRow][nCol] == 0 )
          return false;
 }

 // Report the tie
 MessageBox(NULL, "No more moves possible!", "Tie Game", MB_OK );
 return true;
}
```

This method is interesting only for the use of the **String** object to form the output string to notify the winner. **String** is one of the more useful utility classes in CBuilder, and you should get accustomed to using it. **String**s are much more flexible than the char * or char array that you're probably used to using from C or C++ in other environments. **String** is also part of the Standard Template Library, which we'll be covering in much greater detail a little later in the book.

The nicest thing about the **String** is the ability to format things other than characters and strings. By passing an integer argument to a **String** constructor, you end up with the string representation of that integer. Two **String** objects can be pasted together using the + operator. By combining these two abilities, we build an output string of Player 1 wins from the strings "Player" and "wins" and the number 1, which seems pretty nice if you're accustomed to using sprintf and worrying about types of arguments and lengths of strings.

The last check in this method is for a tie game. If all of the squares are filled, the game is over and nobody wins. Unfortunately, this is rather common in tic-tac-toe games, as I'm sure you know.

We have the game more or less completed, but we need to free up the TBitmap resources that we allocated in the constructor for the object. The best place to do this is in the destructor for the object, and that is exactly what we need to do. Here is the code for the destructor:

```
__fastcall TForm1::~TForm1(void)
{
    delete FpXBitmap;
    delete FpYBitmap;
}
```

Note the __fastcall modifier for the destructor. ~TForm1 is an override of the base class TForm destructor. Because TForm is a VCL object and all VCL methods are declared with the __fastcall modifier, you must add this to your own override as well. If you don't, you'll receive an error message from the compiler stating that "Virtual function TForm1::~TForm1 conflicts with base class Forms::TForm." If you receive an error like that, check the modifiers.

The only thing left to do in our form is to update the header with the methods we added to the form in the source code. Here is the updated Unit1.h header file with all of the changes needed shown in highlighted print:

```
//-----------------------------------------------------------------
#ifndef Unit1H
#define Unit1H
//-----------------------------------------------------------------
#include <vcl\Classes.hpp>
#include <vcl\Controls.hpp>
#include <vcl\StdCtrls.hpp>
#include <vcl\Forms.hpp>
//-----------------------------------------------------------------
class TForm1 : public TForm
{
__published:    // IDE-managed Components
                void __fastcall FormPaint(TObject *Sender);
                void __fastcall FormMouseDown(TObject *Sender,
```

```
TMouseButton Button,
                TShiftState Shift, int X, int Y);
private:  // User declarations
   Graphics::TBitmap *FpXBitmap;
   Graphics::TBitmap *FpYBitmap;
   int      FnGameBoard[3][3];
   int      FnWhichPlayer;

             void ResetBoard(void);
             BOOL CheckForWinner(void);

public:        // User declarations
                __fastcall TForm1(TComponent* Owner);
   virtual __fastcall ~TForm1(void);
};
//----------------------------------------------------------------
extern TForm1 *Form1;
//----------------------------------------------------------------
#endif
```

Running The Game

The last step is always the most fun when programming games: testing the software. Run the program and select several of the squares. Try selecting the same square twice. Try selecting squares to complete a row, a column, and a diagonal. Verify that all of these combinations work. Finally, fill in the complete board without a winning position to verify that the tie game check works. When you're all done checking the positions, invite a friend or child over to help you play the game and enjoy.

Figure 3.5 shows a typical game in progress with several X and O bitmaps, while Figure 3.6 shows a completed game with one of the players with a winning position.

What Did We Learn In This Chapter?

CBuilder provides a rich assortment of graphic objects and components that can be used to easily define and show bitmaps, icons, and other graphics on the screen for applications.

Some of the things we learned about in this chapter include:

1. Loading bitmaps directly from files at runtime.

2. Drawing bitmaps on the screen using the **Canvas** object.

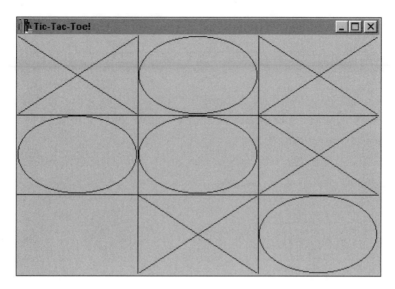

Figure 3.5
A typical game of tic-tac-toe in progress.

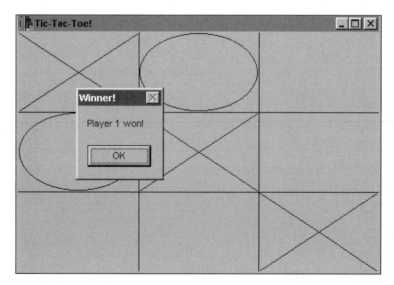

Figure 3.6
A winning position for Player 1.

3. Creating a bitmap at runtime and drawing on its surface.

4. Handling the display of graphics during runtime by drawing directly on the form surface.

I hope you learned a bit about the graphics sub-system in CBuilder. In our next chapter, we'll explore more of the VCL of CBuilder and learn more about these mysterious component things.

Components And Component Event Handlers

CHAPTER

4

- VCL Overview

- Dynamic Components

- Common Component Usage

- Drag 'Til You Drop!

- Secret Messages

- Owner Draw Everything

Components And Component Event Handlers

The heart of the CBuilder component system lies in the Visual Component Library, or VCL, a set of building blocks that includes components such as Forms, Edit Fields, List Boxes, ActiveX controls, File Open, and File Save dialogs. In the past few chapters of the book, we've touched upon some of the uses and several components of the VCL. This chapter is a whirlwind tour of the VCL and how it can solve your everyday programming problems in CBuilder.

This chapter doesn't have to be a reference on the VCL because Borland provides a pretty decent one of those in CBuilder documentation set. Instead, this chapter is a problem-by-problem analysis of what you can do with the VCL to solve common programming dilemmas. Just a few of the things we're going to talk about in this chapter include:

- Creating components at runtime

- Drag and drop between components

- Validating input in edit fields

- Working with progress controls

- Owner-draw components

Most books on CBuilder take you through fairly detailed examples of using the VCL, but few of them apply the VCL to problems of the real world of the programmer. In this chapter, we begin to explore the incredible power of the CBuilder programming model and what it means to you as a professional programmer. CBuilder really excels at the little touches that users expect from high-quality programs. Now that you have CBuilder to work with, there are really no excuses left for not putting that extra little bit into your programs to make them as easy as possible for the end user.

A Quick Overview From A Programmer's Perspective

From your perspective as a programmer, the VCL isn't really a hierarchy at all. It's a set of independent building blocks to drag and drop onto forms, set properties for, and use as programmers see fit. VCL components can be dealt with individually with little or no worry about how they fit into the grander scheme of things. Only component writers, those people who actually develop new components, really need to worry with the hows and whys of the VCL. The rest of us can simply sit back and bask in the glow of easily complete applications that happen to use VCL building blocks to assemble themselves.

There is, however, some rhyme and reason to the component system, and knowing the hierarchy of the system can help you to use some of the components. Let's take a quick look at the important levels of the component architecture before jumping into the thick of things with our first example.

The first, most important, class in the VCL hierarchy is the **TObject** class. **TObject** is the ancestor class of all other classes in the VCL and provides some of the most important methods to all classes. **TObject** has no properties of its own, however. If you look at the method listing for the **TObject** class, you'll find the **ClassName** method, which returns the actual class name of a given object. If you have a pointer to a base class that is really a derived class object, you can use the **TObject::ClassName** method to discover what class it really belongs to. Likewise, the **ClassParent** method will tell you the immediate parent of a given class. Using the **ClassParent** method, you could walk the tree of classes all the way back to the **TObject** level from any VCL object in the system. From the perspective of how things work, the most important method found at the **TObject** level is almost certainly **Dispatch**. The **Dispatch** method is responsible for passing messages to defined event handlers for an object. Using **Dispatch** you can send any message to an object and be certain that if that object supports a handler for the message, it will be routed to that handler.

After **TObject**, the next most important class is **TControl**, which forms the basis for all controls in the VCL system, i.e., forms, edit controls, and dialog boxes. **TControl** only refers to the visible components in the system. A visible component is one that the user can see and manipulate at runtime. This means that components such as **TTimer** or **TDatabase** are not derived from controls, but **TOpenDialog** (which is not visible at design time) is derived from it. Because **TControl** supports visual components, you'll find most of the visible properties of the control in the **TControl** class. Just a few of the properties you'll find here are **Height**, **Width**, **ClientHeight**, **ClientWidth**, **Hint**, **Cursor**, and others. Methods for the **TControl** class include **Hide**, **Show**, **Update**, and **Perform**. Looking at the how things work category, **TControl** provides the **WndProc** method, which handles specific messages. If you need to override the default handling of messages for a control, look at the **WndProc** method.

The final important class in our little tour is the **TComponent** class, which represents all components in the system. The **TComponent** class provides functionality to allow the component to appear on the Component Palette in the IDE, the ability to own and manage other components, and allows for streaming and other filing capabilities. **TComponent** includes all types of components, whether or not visible at runtime. Important properties of the **TComponent** class include **ComponentCount** (which represents the number of components owned by this component), **Components** (which contains pointers to all of the owned components for this object) and **ComponentState**, (which describes the current state of the component). **ComponentState** is most important for the **csDesigning** flag, which indicates that the component is currently in design mode.

That, in a nutshell, is the basis for the VCL system. Rather than go on in a long and dry manner about how to use VCL and what you can do with it, let's jump right in and start coding some examples to show off some of the power of the VCL. In our first example, we take on the problem of creating VCL components dynamically at runtime.

Dynamic Controls, Part One

If you were to browse the CBuilder newsgroups on the Internet, one of the most commonly asked questions you'd find is how to create controls dynamically at runtime. Although CBuilder provides a rich assortment of components and the ability to manipulate them easily through the form editor, many people do not want to be bothered by hidden components on a form. So-called dynamic controls are easy enough to implement in the form editor. Simply add the component to the form where you want it to appear later and then set its **Visible** property to false. When you want the component to appear on the form, set the **Visible** property to true and it will be visible for the user to use.

This, though, is not what all programmers want. Although it fixes the problems nine times out of ten, sometimes you really do need to create a component dynamically for the user at runtime. In this example, we provide the ability to create not one but three different component types are runtime. In addition, you'll see how to deal with responding to messages from dynamic components in your own code.

> **Note:** You'll find the source code for the Dynamic Component program in the Chapter4\DynControl1\directory on the accompanying CD-ROM for this book.

Figure 4.1 shows the form we'll be working with for this application. Create a simple form and drop three radio buttons and an **edit** component onto it. Move them around until they look something like the one shown in the figure.

The first thing we need to do is to modify the header file for the form so that it contains the definitions of the components that we're going to create. For this example, we will be creating three different component types at runtime. We need entries for a static text label, an edit field, and a button. Here are the modifications that you'll need for this example, shown in highlighted print:

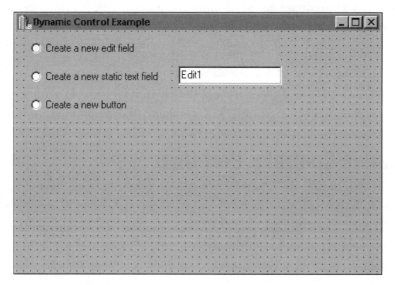

Figure 4.1
The dynamic component example form.

```
//----------------------------------------------------------------
#ifndef Unit1H
#define Unit1H
//----------------------------------------------------------------
#include <vcl\Classes.hpp>
#include <vcl\Controls.hpp>
#include <vcl\StdCtrls.hpp>
#include <vcl\Forms.hpp>
//----------------------------------------------------------------
class TForm1 : public TForm
{
__published:      // IDE-managed Components
                  TRadioButton *RadioButton1;
                  TRadioButton *RadioButton2;
                  TEdit *Edit1;
                  TRadioButton *RadioButton3;
                  void __fastcall RadioButton1Click(TObject *Sender);
                  void __fastcall RadioButton2Click(TObject *Sender);
                  void __fastcall RadioButton3Click(TObject *Sender);
private:     // User declarations
    TEdit *FpEdit;
    TLabel *FpLabel;
    TButton *FpButton;

                  void RemoveExistingFields(void);
                  void __fastcall OnButtonClick( TObject *Sender );

public:                 // User declarations
                  __fastcall TForm1(TComponent* Owner);
};
//----------------------------------------------------------------
extern TForm1 *Form1;
//----------------------------------------------------------------
#endif
```

The three component pointers will be used to create the new components on the fly. The **RemoveExistingFields** method will be used as a utility to get rid of the last component that was created and clear it off the screen. Finally, the **OnButtonClick** method will be used by our program to respond dynamically to the dynamic button being clicked by the user.

The first thing we need to do is to initialize all of the pointers to the components so that we know which one is active and which ones aren't. Add the following code to the constructor for the class:

```
__fastcall TForm1::TForm1(TComponent* Owner)
                : TForm(Owner)
{
    FpEdit= NULL;
    FpLabel = NULL;
    FpButton = NULL;
}
```

All that is happening here is that we're setting the pointers for the components to **NULL**. This invalid pointer value indicates that the components have not been created. This is important, because the plan is to create all of the components in the same spot on the form. If you didn't keep track of which one was active, the components could all be present at the same time and would overlap each other, making a mess out of the screen.

Creating The Edit Field

The first component we're going to create dynamically is the edit field. When the user clicks on the "Create a new edit field" radio button, the edit field will be created on the form. Add a new handler for the "Create a new edit field" radio button and add the following code to it. Once you've finished typing in the code (or looking at the code from the CD-ROM), we can talk about what it all means:

```
void __fastcall TForm1::RadioButton1Click(TObject *Sender)
{
    RemoveExistingFields();

    FpEdit = new TEdit(this);
    FpEdit->Parent = this;
    FpEdit->Left = RadioButton1->Left;
    FpEdit->Width = 200;
    FpEdit->Height = 20;
    FpEdit->Top = RadioButton3->Top + RadioButton3->Height + 20;
    FpEdit->Visible = true;
}
```

The previous code first removes any existing components by calling the **RemoveExistingFields** method. We'll take a look at this method in a few minutes. Next, the code allocates a new **TEdit** component using the new operator. This is needed because VCL components can only be created via the new operator. You can't simply define a new VCL component on the stack, such as by this statement:

```
TEdit mEdit(this);  // This won't work!
```

This is a limitation imposed by Borland on the VCL, necessary because the VCL was written in Pascal and certain behind-the-scenes manipulation must take place for everything to work correctly.

Once the component is created using the new operator (passing the owner of the component as the argument to the constructor), the next important thing is to set the **Parent** property of the component. The **Parent** property is essential to determining where the component is to exist. Failing to set the **Parent** property will result in the component never appearing on the screen because the component is created relative to its parent. If you dynamically create a component and it doesn't appear, check to be sure that you set the **Parent** property before looking at anything else.

Once the **Parent** is set, the next four lines of code simply position the edit field on the form. In our case we want the edit field to appear just below the last radio button, so we set the position properties of the edit field based on the **RadioButton3** position and all works well.

The last thing to do is to set the **Visible** property to true so that the component is visible to the user. This isn't strictly necessary, as the default for the **Visible** property is true for nearly all components. It's a good habit to get into, though, as you should not make assumptions about how things will work in the future.

To make the code compile and link, we need to add the **RemoveExistingFields** method. Here is that code:

```
void TForm1::RemoveExistingFields(void)
{
    if ( FpEdit )
    {
        delete FpEdit;
        FpEdit = NULL;
    }

    if ( FpLabel )
    {
        delete FpLabel;
        FpLabel = NULL;
    }
```

```
    if ( FpButton )
    {
        delete FpButton;
        FpButton = NULL;
    }
}
```

As you can see, all we're doing in this code is deleting any components that are not **NULL** and then setting them to be **NULL**. This is why the initialization of the components in the constructor was important. In this way we identify only a single component and clear it off the form.

At this point you've done enough to compile and link the form. You'll need to comment out the **OnButtonClick** method temporarily in the header file and then select **Project|Make** (or press Ctrl+F9) to compile and link the project. Run the resulting executable and click on the first radio button (create edit control). You should see the form as shown in Figure 4.2.

Adding The Static Text Field

Creating the static text field is quite similar to creating the edit field, but with a minor twist. The static text field, after all, requires that you enter some text for it. In

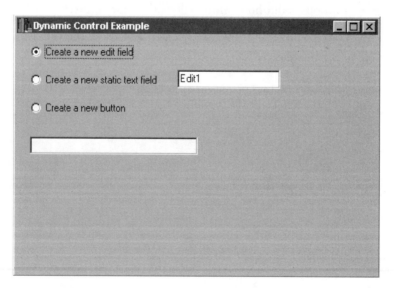

Figure 4.2
Dynamic form example showing new edit control.

this case, we'll use whatever text the user types into the edit field that lies next to the static text field radio button. This text will be used for the **Caption** property of the static text (or label) field.

Add a new handler for the "Create a new static text field" radio button and add the following code to it:

```
void __fastcall TForm1::RadioButton2Click(TObject *Sender)
{
    RemoveExistingFields();

    FpLabel = new TLabel(this);
    FpLabel->Parent = this;
    FpLabel->Left = RadioButton1->Left;
    FpLabel->Width = 200;
    FpLabel->Height = 20;
    FpLabel->Top = RadioButton3->Top + RadioButton3->Height + 20;
    FpLabel->Visible = true;
    FpLabel->Caption = Edit1->Text;
}
```

As you can see, the code for this handler is almost identical to the code for the edit component creation. All components are created pretty much the same way, differing only in the properties that you wish to set for the individual components. In this case, the **Caption** property of the label will be set to the contents of the edit field next to the radio button. To test this theory, compile and link the program and run it. Enter some text into the edit field, such as "This is a dynamic Label". Click on the static text field radio button and you should then see the result shown in Figure 4.3, with the new static text field occupying the position that the edit field was in a few moments earlier. In addition, the label should read "This is a dynamic Label" (or whatever it was that you typed in the edit field).

Adding The Button

The final step in this example is to add a new button to the form. Buttons are no different than edit fields or labels. In this case, however, we want to be able to know when the user clicks on our button. For that reason, we need to be able to create a handler for the button click and associate that handler with the **OnClick** event of the button.

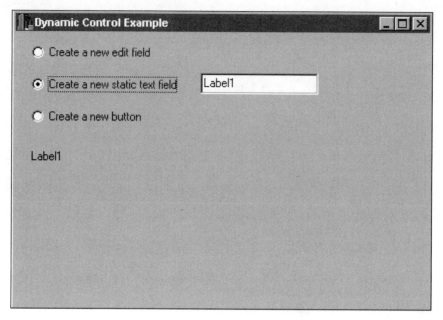

Figure 4.3
Dynamic form showing new label component.

The Object Inspector doesn't work for dynamically created components, of course. How then will we associate a handler with the button? Well, if you remember the Scribble3 example from Chapter 1, you can modify the handler for a component at runtime. If you can modify one, why wouldn't you be able to add a new handler? There is no reason why you can't.

Add a new handler for the "Create a new button" radio button and add the following code to the handler for the radio button:

```
void __fastcall TForm1::RadioButton3Click(TObject *Sender)
{
    RemoveExistingFields();

    FpButton = new TButton(this);
    FpButton->Parent = this;
    FpButton->Left = RadioButton1->Left;
    FpButton->Width = 200;
    FpButton->Height = 20;
    FpButton->Top = RadioButton3->Top + RadioButton3->Height + 20;
    FpButton->Visible = true;
```

```
    FpButton->Caption = "Button1";
    FpButton->OnClick = OnButtonClick;
}
```

Again, there is little difference between the button case and either of the preceding cases. We set up the properties (including the all-important **Parent** property) the same way we did for the static text field and the edit field. For buttons, we need a **Caption** property to appear on the face of the button. In this case we simply assign that property the string "Button1".

The line shown in highlighted print is the important one for the button. Here we are assigning our event handler for the button to the **OnClick** event of the button object. The only requirement for the handler is that it be of the right signature (function arguments and return value) for an event of this type. For the **OnClick** event, the method needs to accept a single argument (**Sender**, of type **TObject**) and cannot return any value (**void**). We therefore implement a simple handler by entering the following code into the source file for the form:

```
void __fastcall TForm1::OnButtonClick( TObject *Sender )
{
    MessageBox(NULL, "You clicked the button!", "Info", MB_OK );
}
```

Note that the signature for this event handler matches what is required for a button click handler. Notice also the **__fastcall** in the button handler modifiers. This modifier is required on all VCL method overrides. An event handler is, by definition, an override of the behavior of a component and therefore requires the **__fastcall** directive.

Remember to uncomment the line from the include file defining our **OnButtonClick** method and then compile and link the program. When you run the program and select the "Create a new button" radio button, a long skinny button should be shown on the form. Clicking on that button should produce the message box shown in Figure 4.4.

Congratulations. You now know everything that is needed to be able to create a simple dynamic control, assign properties to it, and respond to events from it. That wasn't so difficult, was it?

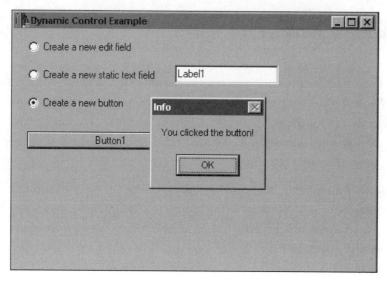

Figure 4.4
Dynamic form example showing button handler called.

Dynamic Controls, Part Two

One of the more useful reasons to create dynamic controls is to display a progress bar. This is not a control that you necessarily want around all of the time, but it would be nice to have the control around while a long operation is taking place.

In this example, we show how to create a progress bar dynamically. Not only will the bar be created at runtime, it will also be created as the child of another control on a form, the status bar of the form. This is a process that you see in many advanced programs, such as Microsoft Word and Internet Explorer. The progress bar is displayed on the bottom status bar during operations that require some time, such as loading and saving files or downloading HTML from a host. Now your applications can have this same functionality thanks to the power and flexibility of the VCL built into CBuilder.

> **Note:** You'll find the source code for the Dynamic Component program in the Chapter4\DynControl2\directory on the accompanying CD-ROM for this book.

Figure 4.5 shows the form we'll be working with for this application. Create a simple form and drop three buttons and a status bar onto the form. For the status bar,

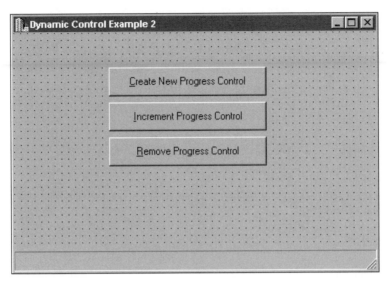

Figure 4.5
The dynamic control 2 example form.

make sure that the alignment is set to **alBottom**. This will not affect our example, but is the standard way to create a status bar along the bottom of the form.

The three buttons on the form are all stages in the life of the progress bar. Because we can neither set status bar properties until it is created nor can we delete it, disable the second and third buttons by setting the **Enabled** property to false. We'll automatically enable these buttons when the time is right.

The first step in the procedure is to add a progress bar component to the include file for the form. Add the following line to the Unit1.h include file for the project:

```
private:    // User declarations
   TProgressBar *FpProgress;
```

The next step, as always, is to initialize the pointer to **NULL** in the constructor. Modify the constructor in the Unit1.CPP source file to be as follows:

```
__fastcall TForm1::TForm1(TComponent* Owner)
            : TForm(Owner)
{
   FpProgress = NULL;
}
```

Creating The Progress Bar

When the user clicks on the first button (the one labeled Create New Progress Control) we would like to be able to create dynamically the progress control in the status bar. Add a new handler for the first button and add the following code to that handler:

```
void __fastcall TForm1::Button1Click(TObject *Sender)
{
    FpProgress = new TProgressBar(StatusBar1);
    FpProgress->Parent = StatusBar1;
    FpProgress->Top = 4;
    FpProgress->Height = StatusBar1->Height-6;
    FpProgress->Left = 2;
    FpProgress->Width = 200;
    FpProgress->Enabled = true;

    // Setup the range on the bar
    FpProgress->Min = 0;
    FpProgress->Max = 100;
    FpProgress->Step = 1;

// And enable the other two buttons
    Button1->Enabled = false;
    Button2->Enabled = true;
    Button3->Enabled = true;
}
```

As you can see, the code looks quite similar to previous dynamic control examples. First, the new component is created, then the parent of the component. In this case, we're going to use the status bar—rather than the form—to be the parent of the progress control. Remember that all of the position properties of the new component are relative to the parent of the control, not the component in which they are created. Even though the form is responsible for creating the progress control (because the creation occurs in a form handler), the status bar is now responsible for the control. Going back to our discussion about important classes, the **Components** array of the status bar would contain a pointer to the progress control, while the **Components** array of the form would not. It would contain a pointer to the status bar itself as well as the three buttons on the form.

We position the progress control to fit nicely within the status bar by using the bounds of the status bar to set the **Height** and **Top** properties of the control. This is something that you'll probably have to play with a bit to get it to look the way you want. Individual tastes vary, and there are no good hard and fast rules about this one.

Once the progress control is positioned, we set some of the important properties for it. In this case, there are three important properties that you should set. The **Min** value is the lowest possible setting for the progress display. The **Max** value is, not surprisingly, the maximum value for the progress display. The **Step** value is the amount that the progress control should increment its current value each time it's stepped. The progress control is a percentage indicator. It will show the values from 0 to 100 of the percentage the current value is of the range **Min-Max**.

Once the progress control is taken care of, the next step is to enable and disable the three buttons based on their current state. You can't create a second progress control in the same place as the first one, so disable the create button. It makes sense to allow it to be incremented or deleted, so we enable the second and third buttons.

Incrementing The Progress Display

The first thing that we'll add to the display is the ability to increment the progress display. This simulates what you would be doing in your own code to set the progress display to move along with whatever you're doing in the background (saving, downloading, loading). Add a new handler for the **Button2** object on the form (Increment Progress Control). Add the following code to the new handler:

```
void __fastcall TForm1::Button2Click(TObject *Sender)
{
   if ( FpProgress )
      FpProgress->StepIt();

}
```

All that this handler does is to verify (as a sanity check) that the progress control exists and, assuming it does, calls the **StepIt** method of the control. The **StepIt** method will increment the current value of the control by the amount set in the **Step** property of the control. To test what happens, add the previous code and then compile and link the application. Click on the Create button to create a new progress control in the status bar. You should see the control appear on the left side of the status bar. Click on the Increment button a few times. You should now see the display as shown in Figure 4.6.

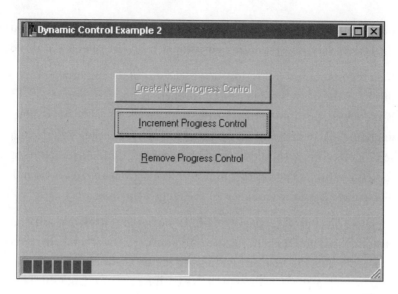

Figure 4.6
The dynamic control 2 form showing incremented progress control.

Removing The Progress Control

The last step in the process is to remove the progress control from the status bar. This simulates what you would do when the operation is complete. Note that once the progress control is removed, it's then possible to start the whole process all over again.

To add a new handler for the third button (Remove Progress Control), add the following code to the handler:

```
void __fastcall TForm1::Button3Click(TObject *Sender)
{
    // If it exists, delete it.

    if ( FpProgress )
        delete FpProgress;
    FpProgress = NULL;

    // Disable the relevant buttons
    Button2->Enabled = false;
    Button3->Enabled = false;

    // Allow them to create another one
    Button1->Enabled = true;
}
```

As you can see, removing a control from the form is as simple as deleting the VCL object pointer. Once we've deleted the pointer, we set it to **NULL** to make sure that everything else knows the pointer no longer exists. This is just a good practice that you should get used to doing in your C++ programs. Always **NULL** out a pointer when you're finished with it.

Once the pointer is deleted, we re-enable the first button to allow the user to create a new progress control and disable the second and third buttons because no control currently exists.

The Last Step

There is one final step. The form will work as shown and have no significant problems. If, however, the user closes the form without deleting a progress control there would be a memory leak in the system. To avoid this, we add a destructor to the class. Add the following declaration to the include file for the destructor:

```
private:        // User declarations
   TProgressBar *FpProgress;
public:                   // User declarations
               __fastcall TForm1(TComponent* Owner);
               __fastcall ~TForm1(void);
};
```

And then add the code for the destructor to the source file (Unit1.cpp):

```
__fastcall TForm1::~TForm1(void)
{
   if ( FpProgress )
      delete FpProgress;
}
```

Note that again we check to see if the component is **NULL** before trying to delete it. Deleting a **NULL** pointer can have disastrous effects in a program.

That's all there is to creating components dynamically in CBuilder. You now know how to create a dynamic control (remembering to set its parent), how to set properties of the control, and how to respond to events in the dynamic control. You also saw how to create the ever-popular progress bar in the status bar and how to make it display progress.

Next up, how to validate input in controls in CBuilder.

Data Validation Using Edit Fields

The most important facet in most corporate programs (at least to those silly user people) is the validation that the data being input into the application is correct. Once data is in an application and stored in some persistent data storage, such as a database, it's there for life, even if that data is incorrect or in an invalid format. I can't tell you how many times I've had a program crash because the allegedly safe data that it was reading from a production database was in an invalid format. Fields that were supposed to contain nothing but numbers ended up having alphabetical characters, and fields that were guaranteed to be integer values ended up having decimal points. The list goes on and on.

The surest way to avoid having a program receive invalid data is to make sure that the program that writes data into the database writes nothing but valid data. In this example, we explore ways that you can validate input from the user.

There are two general cases for validating input. The first is to make sure that only valid characters get into the input in the first place. For a numeric entry, for example, it makes no sense to allow the user to enter letters. If the input is supposed to be an integer, there is no reason to allow them to type a decimal point.

The second case of data validation is to verify that an input number falls within a given range. For example, if the data field is intended to enter a number between one and ten, you can validate that the user enters numbers and no decimal points. That won't help if they enter 12345678. This number is likely to cause problems on the data output side, which is expecting a two-digit number at worst.

CBuilder can help you validate input. It can help you screen out invalid input and verify that entries are valid once they are completely entered. In this example, we explore both of these cases and show how to use the CBuilder data validation model.

> **Note:** You'll find the source code for the Edit Validation program in the Chapter4\EditValidation\directory on the accompanying CD-ROM for this book.

Figure 4.7 shows the form we'll be building in this example. You construct this form by adding two edit fields, three radio buttons, and two static text fields in the design shown in the figure. From there we'll validate input in a variety of ways.

Once you've built the visual form, add a handler for the "Enter only numbers" radio button. If this radio button is selected, the edit field above the radio button will

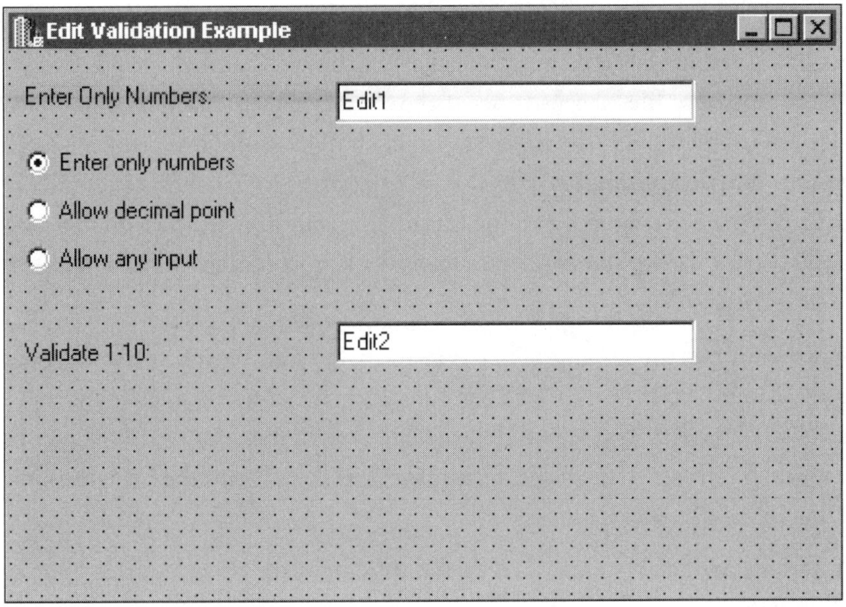

Figure 4.7
Data form for validation example.

only permit digits (0 to 9, no decimal point) to be entered into the field. Add the following code to the event handler for the form in CBuilder:

```
void __fastcall TForm1::RadioButton1Click(TObject *Sender)
{
    Label1->Caption = "Enter only numbers: ";
    Edit1->OnKeyPress = Edit1KeyPress;
}
```

In this example, we're setting the caption of the static text field label to read "Enter only numbers:". This gives the user a visual clue as to what is going on. After that we set the validation event handler for the edit field **KeyPress** event to be a routine called **Edit1KeyPress**. Here is the code to add for the **Edit1KeyPress** routine, which will be called whenever the user presses a key in the **Edit1** field while this first radio button is selected:

```
void __fastcall TForm1::Edit1KeyPress(TObject *Sender, char &Key)
{
  if ( !isdigit(Key) )
     Key = 0;
}
```

This routine simply screens each character that is entered by the user. The **isdigit** function, found in the ctype.h include file, which you'll need to include at the top of the form source file, checks to see if the character is in the range 0 to 9. If the character is in that range, the function returns TRUE. If the character is not in the range, the function returns FALSE. The **!isdigit** syntax is C++ shorthand, indicating that the following statement is to be executed if, and only if, the function returns FALSE. Setting the Key parameter to 0 tells the **Edit** component that this character is to be ignored.

Compile and run the program. Click on the first radio button for which we just added a handler and then click in the edit field. Try entering a letter, such as "a". Guess what happens? If you said that the character is not input into the edit field, you would be wrong. The edit field happily enters the "a" into the field, thus foiling the strategy of data validation.

Is this whole approach wrong? Can we not validate input on a character-by-character basis in CBuilder? If not, this would be a tragedy. Fortunately, it is not. The only problem is that we skipped one important step in the process.

Close down the application and bring the form back up into the form editor in CBuilder. Select the form by clicking anywhere in the client area of the form that does not contain a component. Or you can move to the **Object Inspector** and select the **Form1** object from the drop-down combo box at the top of the **Inspector** window. In either case, move to the **KeyPreview** property of the form and set it to true. Compile and run the application, and you'll notice that it has suddenly become impossible to enter non-numeric digits in the edit field.

The **KeyPreview** property of the form controls whether or not all keystrokes first come to the form and then go to the selected component. If the **KeyPreview** property is false, the keystrokes will all go directly to the component that has the input focus. If the **KeyPreview** property is true (as we just made it), the keystrokes will come first to the form level handler for keyboard input, such as our method, and will only then be sent on to the component with the input focus. This permits us to preview the keystrokes and modify them as we see fit. This is possible because the key-handling methods all pass the character by reference (**char &Key**), which allows the method to modify the value of the key.

With this in mind, add a new handler for the second radio button (Allow decimal point) and add the following code to the handler:

```
void __fastcall TForm1::RadioButton2Click(TObject *Sender)
{
    Label1->Caption = "Enter numbers or decimal point: ";
    Edit1->OnKeyPress = Edit1KeyPress2;
}
```

Again, we're notifying the user what sort of input is expected in this field and then setting the handler to verify it. Not suprisingly, the code for the **Edit1KeyPress2** function looks similar to the first input handler:

```
void __fastcall TForm1::Edit1KeyPress2(TObject *Sender, char &Key)
{
  if ( !isdigit(Key) && Key != '.')
     Key = 0;
}
```

Because we're now allowing the decimal point to be entered, we add a check for it. If you wanted to check for only a single decimal point, you could add a check to see if the decimal point had already been entered:

```
BOOL bFlag = strchr( Edit1->Text.c_str(), '.');
```

Then, if the **bFlag** boolean flag was true you could disallow the entry as well.

The final handler for the edit field allows any input. You would think that we would set the handler to something that allows any character, but there is any easier way. Add a handler for the third radio button and add the following code to the event handler:

```
void __fastcall TForm1::RadioButton3Click(TObject *Sender)
{
    Label1->Caption = "Enter anything: ";
    Edit1->OnKeyPress = NULL;
}
```

Again, we're setting the edit prompt to indicate what sort of input is allowed. However, rather than setting the event handler to a method, we set it to **NULL**. This clears the event handling for this function and permits the standard **Edit** component handler (which allows any character) to take precedence.

Along the way you'll have updated the include file to include prototypes for the event handlers we added. Here is the updated include file, in case you have any questions:

```
class TForm1 : public TForm
{
__published:    // IDE-managed Components
                TLabel *Label1;
                TEdit *Edit1;
                TLabel *Label2;
                TEdit *Edit2;
                TRadioButton *RadioButton1;
                TRadioButton *RadioButton2;
                TRadioButton *RadioButton3;
                void __fastcall Edit1KeyPress(TObject *Sender, char &Key);

                void __fastcall Edit2Exit(TObject *Sender);
                void __fastcall RadioButton1Click(TObject *Sender);
                void __fastcall RadioButton2Click(TObject *Sender);
                void __fastcall RadioButton3Click(TObject *Sender);
private:    // User declarations
                void __fastcall Edit1KeyPress2(TObject *Sender, char &Key);
public:             // User declarations
                __fastcall TForm1(TComponent* Owner);
};
```

Note that because I originally added the **Edit1KeyPress** function via CBuilder as a handler for the **KeyPress** function, it will already be in the area that CBuilder maintains.

Processing The Input After The User Is Finished

There are times when you don't want to or cannot input character by character into an edit field. In these cases, you would prefer to wait until the user is finished entering the data and then validate the input when they try to leave the field. Cases like this might result from data range input, date or time input, or another application-specific data entry.

CBuilder can help you in these post-processing validation cases as well. To deal with validating the data after the user has entered it, you must add a handler for the **OnExit** event of the edit field. To show you how this is done, add a new handler for the **OnExit** event for the second edit field, Edit2. To this new handler, add the following code:

```
void __fastcall TForm1::Edit2Exit(TObject *Sender)
{
    BOOL bFlag = TRUE;

    char *s = Edit2->Text.c_str();

    // First, check that all entries are digits
    for ( int i=0; i<(int)strlen(s); ++i )
    {
        char c = s[i];
        if ( !isdigit(c) )
            bFlag = false;
    }

    // See if it passed entry
    if ( bFlag == false )
    {
        MessageBox(NULL, "You should only enter digits in this field!",
          "Error", MB_OK );
        Edit2->SetFocus();
        return;
    }

    // Next, see if between 1 and 10
    long lVal = atol(Edit2->Text.c_str());
    if ( lVal < 1 || lVal > 10 )
    {
        MessageBox(NULL, "You can only enter values between 1 and 10!",
          "Error", MB_OK );
        Edit2->SetFocus();
        return;
    }
}
```

This handler first verifies that the entry contains nothing but digits. If it fails this test, an error message is displayed and input focus is returned to the edit field in question. If it passes this test, we then check to see if the field is within a valid range. If not, again an error message is displayed and the focus is returned to the input edit field.

> **Note:** If you've worked with the Windows SDK at all, you've probably tried to do something similar to this catching the **WM_KILLFOCUS** message. If so, you're probably aware that displaying a message box during the **WM_KILLFOCUS** message handler results in an infinite loop that eventually crashes the program. Don't concern yourself with these remembrances of

*things past; CBuilder suffers from no such problems. You can display mes-
sage boxes, set the input focus, and do anything else you would like during
the processing of an* **OnExit** *event. This is the modern era of programming,
not the dark ages.*

In this example, I hope you've learned the important lesson of how to validate input. Just as a quick recap, let's cover the important points of data validation in an
edit field in CBuilder:

- To catch individual keystrokes in an edit field you must first set the **KeyPreview**
  property of the form to true.

- When processing individual keystrokes for an edit field, set the character input
  to 0 to prevent the current entry from being added to the edit field.

- You can clear an input event handler by setting the event handler for the given
  object to **NULL**. Thus to clear a key processing method in an edit field, you
  would **set Edit1->OnKeyPress = NULL**.

- To validate input when the user tries to leave a field, handle the **OnExit** event. As a
  side note, to do processing when the user enters a field, handle the **OnEnter** event.

That's all there is to say about the general problem of data validation in an input field of
a CBuilder form. Although the issue of validation is wide open, CBuilder gives you
the tools you need to handle whatever problems might arise in your application.

Dragging Until You Drop

Another sad story from my programming past. A few years back I was called upon
to implement a fairly simple dialog box. This dialog contained two list boxes. The
first list box was supposed to contain all of the available entries for a given topic, and
the second was intended to contain the selected entries. Lying between the two list
boxes on the dialog were two buttons, labeled >> and <<. The >> button moved
things from the left-hand side list box (the available list) to the right-hand side list
box (the selected list). It was a pretty simple dialog, and I knocked it off in a couple
of hours. Then the nightmares began.

The first user review for the product immediately targeted my list box dialog for
changes. First, the user didn't like the >> and << buttons. "Not clear enough," they
said. Okay, said I, and changed the buttons to read "Select" and "UnSelect".

Right about then the popular topic of discussion in the Windows world (this was Windows 3.1) was drag and drop. One of the senior managers, who actually had some experience using Windows products, picked up on this right away. "What we need here," he said, "is a drag and drop system between the two list boxes." Sadly, this actually made a lot of sense. The user would simply select the items they wanted in the left-hand list box and drag them over to the right-hand list box. We mocked up a prototype of the list box using a third-party tool, and the users loved it. It was easy to select one or more items on the left and drag them to the right. The discussion was closed. The programming began and the problems started creeping out of the woodwork.

When this was all happening, the support for drag and drop in the system we were using (it happened to be MFC, but really could have been anything) was non-existent. Implementing the drag and drop for the two list boxes meant sub-classing my own list box, checking for the mouse button being pressed, and deciding what could be selected. Three days went by while I tried valiantly to implement the procedure for the two list boxes. Finally, I had something that worked most of the time without strange results. The program was unveiled for the end users who immediately liked what they saw. There were just a few changes desired, my manager told me after the demonstration (why aren't programmers ever invited to demo to upper management?). First of all, they wanted to be able to place the items where they wanted them in the second list. In other words, the dropping part of the list had to support positioning. Okay, I thought, this is a reasonable request. The second request, though, was the kicker: allow the user to move items around within a single list.

If you've ever implemented a drag and drop list, you've probably dealt with this problem. The issue is not only removing the existing item, but then figuring out where it should fall in the new list. It was ugly code, not helped at all by the fact that I was only guessing where the item should fall. This was outside the bounds of the normal list box functionality and required that I drop into the Windows API to get the job done.

Finally, three weeks after the initial demonstration, the dual list box dialog was completed and the user was satisfied. One week after that, the project was canceled and I was out of a job. The moral of this sad story? I'm not sure, but it's a whole lot easier to implement things like this in CBuilder than it was in the MFC.

Implementing Drag And Drop List Boxes

CBuilder was built around the kinds of things that programmers do all the time. It doesn't directly support drag and drop between two list boxes, but it does have drag and drop support built into it.

> **Note:** At this point it's worth noting that people mean really two things when they talk about drag and drop. The first is the system we are talking about, moving data between two components, two forms, or two objects in the system. The second is the drag and drop of files onto a program. This form of drag and drop, usually done from Windows Explorer to an application running in Windows 95 or NT, is a separate subject and will be tackled a bit later in the book when we talk about the Windows API.

So what exactly do we need to do to make drag and drop work in CBuilder? Not a lot, really. First of all, let's create a form to demonstrate the drag and drop of items between two list boxes. Figure 4.8 shows the form we'll use to illustrate the example. It has two list boxes and a label field that we'll use for a status display of what is going on.

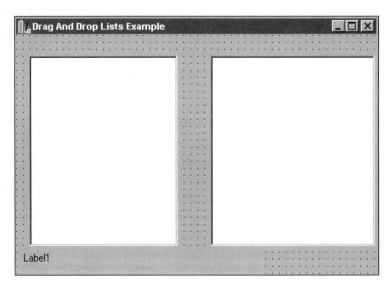

Figure 4.8
The drag and drop list example form.

In order to support drag and drop in your form, you must handle two methods for the objects you want to allow dragging and dropping. The first of these is the **DragDrop** method, which is called when the user drags something from your object and then again when something is dropped onto the object. The second method you must handle is the **DragOver** method. This method is called to check whether it's valid to drop data onto your object. If you don't handle the **DragOver** method the cursor will appear as a Not symbol (a circle with a line through it) while it's over the object.

> **Note:** You'll find the source code for the Drag Drop List program in the Chapter4\DragDropList1\directory on the accompanying CD-ROM for this book.

In this example, we'll handle both the **DragOver** and **DragDrop** methods for both list boxes in the form.

First, let's add an event handler for the **DragOver** method for both list boxes. Select both list box objects from the form and move to the Events tab of the Object Inspector. In the **DragOver** event, type the method name **OnDragOver** for the entry. This will assign the event handler to both of the objects at the same time and save you a little wear and tear on the mouse and keyboard. Enter the following code into the **OnDragOver** method for both list boxes:

```
void __fastcall TForm1::OnDragOver(TObject *Sender, TObject *Source,
                int X, int Y, TDragState State, bool &Accept)
{
   Accept = True;
}
```

This method is simply indicating that either of the list boxes can accept input. We'll accept that data, as it really doesn't matter where the drag and drop is coming from (we're assuming another list box). The output parameter **Accept**, which indicates whether the method will (true) or will not (false) allow data to be dropped onto it, is the only parameter of this method that matters to CBuilder.

The next method that we need to handle in the code is the **DragDrop** method. This method will be called when the user drags something onto our list box and releases the mouse. Add handlers for both list boxes for the **DragDrop** event using the Object Inspector. Call the new method **OnDragDrop** and add the following code to the handler for the list boxes:

```
void __fastcall TForm1::OnDragDrop(TObject *Sender, TObject *Source,
                                   int X, int Y)
{
   TListBox *pList1 = (TListBox *)Source;
   TListBox *pList2 = (TListBox *)Sender;

   // Whatever is selected, we need to copy
   for ( int i=0; i<pList1->Items->Count; ++i )
      if ( pList1->Selected[ i ] )
      {
          // Add it to the second list box
          pList2->Items->Add( pList1->Items->Strings[ i ] );
          // And remove it from the first
          pList1->Items->Delete( i );
      }

}
```

There are a couple of things to note about this code. First of all, it doesn't matter which list box you drag from and which one you drag to. This code will handle either one. The reason for this is that CBuilder sends you two parameters indicating where the drop is coming from and where it's going to. The **Sender** object is the object on which the drop is being performed. The **Source** object is the object from which the drag originated.

This might not seem clear at first glance. If you think about it, however, the **Sender** argument to all event handlers is always the object for which the event was generated. In this case, the event is the drop of the items. The **Source** argument seems more clear; it's the source of the information that is being dragged and dropped. Interpreting this data and deciding what to do with it is our responsibility.

The next thing that is of interest in the code is that it supports multiple drags and drops. If you drag three items from the left-hand side list box to the right-hand side, three items will disappear from the left-hand side, and three items will appear on the right-hand side. This is pretty much what you would expect. In order to make this work, by the way, you need to set the **MultipleSelect** property of the list boxes to true.

The third and final thing to notice in this code is something you probably won't see right away. This code will work if the source and destination for the drag-drop operation are the same. If you select an item in the first list box (left-hand side) and drag it to the first list box (left-hand side), the item will disappear from its current position in the list and will reappear at the end of the list. What it won't do is to appear where you happened to move the mouse. We will tackle that problem in a few moments.

The only way you can test this list box example is to have some data in the list boxes to work with in the first place. Add a handler for the form for the **OnCreate** event. Give the new event handler the name **FormCreate**. Add the following code to the **FormCreate** method:

```
void __fastcall TForm1::FormCreate(TObject *Sender)
{
    ListBox1->Items->Add( "Item 1" );
    ListBox1->Items->Add( "Item 2" );
    ListBox1->Items->Add( "Item 3" );
    ListBox1->Items->Add( "Item 4" );
    ListBox1->Items->Add( "Item 5" );
}
```

All we're doing here, of course, is putting some data into the list box that we can play with.

How Do I Know When I Start?

Drag and drop is rarely as simple as illustrated here. You'll often find that you need to know when the drag process starts so that you can set a flag somewhere or check to see that the data is valid to be copied. A list that contains mutually exclusive items is an example of this. You wouldn't want the user to select two items and add them to the selected list if those items couldn't work together. What you would like to be able to do is to find out when they start dragging the data and then clear out any items that aren't valid.

CBuilder, of course, provides a way to do this. Would we be talking about it if it didn't? Of course not. In this case, however, the **StartDrag** event handler is what you're looking for. When we originally created the form, I had you add a label to the bottom of the form. Let's make use of that label to tell us what's going on in the process.

Add an event handler for the **StartDrag** event for the first list box object in the form. Give the event handler the name **ListBox1StartDrag**. Add the following code to the **ListBox1StartDrag** method of the form:

```
void __fastcall TForm1::ListBox1StartDrag(TObject *Sender,
                                          TDragObject *&DragObject)
{
    Label1->Caption = "Starting the drag...";
}
```

There is nothing special about this event handler. All we do is set the caption (text) of the label to indicate when the list box drag has started. Likewise, we can add a handler for the **EndDrag** event, an event generated when the drag drop operation is completed. Add a handler for the first list box for the **EndDrag** method and give it the name **ListBox1EndDrag**. Add the following code to the **ListBox1EndDrag** method of the form:

```
void __fastcall TForm1::ListBox1EndDrag(TObject *Sender, TObject *Target,
                                        int X, int Y)
{
    Label1->Caption = "Finishing the drag...";

}
```

Compile and run the application. As you select items in the list box, watch the caption of the label at the bottom of the form. Notice that simply selecting an item in the list box and moving at all kicks off the drag process. The process ends when the mouse is released somewhere. If the mouse is still in the same list box, the end drag is still called.

At this point, you know enough about the drag and drop process in CBuilder to be dangerous. The Drag and Drop list box example shows you how to do some things, but not quite enough. There are a couple of enhancements that need to be made.

Drag And Drop List Box Part II

One thing about the drag and drop program really bugged me after I wrote it. It's the same problem that bugged me after the initial version of the drag and drop project I talked about at the start of the example. The problem is that the dropped items always end up at the end of the list they're dropped on. This is annoying to the user, who has carefully moved the mouse over the item they wanted to place the item after and had it go all the way to the bottom.

In the second cut at the drag-drop list example, we'll solve this problem.

Note: You'll find the source code for the Drag Drop List 2 Example program in the Chapter4\DragDropList2\directory on the accompanying CD-ROM for this book.

Starting with the code we wrote for the previous example, modify the **OnDragDrop** method to read as follows:

```
void __fastcall TForm1::OnDragDrop(TObject *Sender, TObject *Source,
                                   int X, int Y)
{
   TListBox *pList1 = (TListBox *)Source;
   TListBox *pList2 = (TListBox *)Sender;

   // See what item lies under what is selected
   POINT p;
   p.x = X;
   p.y = Y;
   int nItemIndex = pList2->ItemAtPos( p, false );
   String s = "Dropping at item: " + String(nItemIndex);
   Label1->Caption = s;

   // Whatever is selected, we need to copy
   for ( int i=0; i<pList1->Items->Count; ++i )
      if ( pList1->Selected[ i ] )
      {
         // Add it to the second list box
         pList2->Items->Insert( nItemIndex, pList1->Items->Strings[ i ] );
         // And remove it from the first
         pList1->Items->Delete( i );
      }

}
```

When you do this, you accomplish two things. First, you move the item to the correct position in the new list, and second, you implement a list box that allows the items to be rearranged by dragging and dropping them within a single list.

Note that we also added a little bit of code to indicate where the item is being dropped. The reason for this is simple. Try dropping the item past the last item in the list. You would expect that the **ItemAtPos** method would go berserk trying to figure out what item is at a position that has no item. That's certainly what I initially expected when I wrote the example, but it doesn't go berserk. In fact, it works exactly the way

I would have liked, returning a number one larger than the number of items in the list. This works well with the **Insert** method of the **TListBox** class **Items** property, which will happily append the item to the end of the list when given this value. Hmm. It's almost like someone actually thought about this problem.

CBuilder has examples like this throughout the VCL. You'll find that there is little need to consult the copious documentation because most of the time things work the way you expect them to. Every now and then something works a bit differently, but in those cases you'll generally find that your attitude is being colored by your prior experience. Instead of some complex methodology to implement something, CBuilder regularly takes the simplest approach. Simplest, that is, from the perspective of the programmer.

So, you now know a whole lot more about the drag and drop procedure than you used to, maybe more than you ever wanted to know.

Message Maps And CBuilder

Windows is a message processing system. Messages are sent from Windows to application programs to inform them of status changes, changes to the environment, things the user has done, and to inform the programs that something needs to be done by the application.

CBuilder, on the other hand, is an event-handling system. Events are generated by VCL components and the system and are passed on to the application forms and other objects via event handlers. These event handlers are called with the information that is needed to inform the application what is going on. Nearly every Windows message in the general system is wrapped by a specific CBuilder event. As an example, when the Windows system generates an LBN_SELCHANGE message to inform the application that the user has made a change in the selection of a list box, the CBuilder VCL object **TListBox** generates a **SelectionChange** event for the owner of the list box. Adding a handler for the **SelectionChange** event is all that is necessary to process the underlying Windows message LBN_SELCHANGE.

It isn't always this easy, of course. Windows contains literally thousands of different messages that can be sent on an extremely infrequent basis. Still other messages are not exposed by the underlying VCL because they're already handled by the underlying VCL object.

On occasion, there are times when you'll find that you need to process a message for which no corresponding event exists in the VCL object for which it would be handled. An excellent example of this problem is found in the **TForm** object with the WM_VSCROLL message. The WM_VSCROLL message is sent to a form when the form scrollbar (a part of the form itself) is clicked in one or another place. There are several times when this message might be generated. First, if the user clicks on either the top or bottom arrow portion of the scrollbar, a scroll message is generated with the code SB_LINEUP (for the top arrow) or SB_LINEDOWN (for the bottom arrow). Similarly, the SB_PAGEUP message is generated when the user clicks in the scrollbar itself above the "toe" of the bar. There are other good examples of these codes.

The point, however, is that you cannot trap the scroll messages in a form via event handlers. If you search through the list of defined events for the **TForm** VCL class, you'll not find events for **OnLineUp**, or **OnPageDown**. If you wanted to handle these events yourself, you would need to create a new component derived from **TForm** (a non-trivial exercise) and then specifically check for the message in the component or find some kludge to make the scrollbar messages available to you, the application programmer. Or you could use message maps.

Message maps are immediately familiar to Borland C++/OWL or Visual C++/MFC programmers, and are used by framework-based systems to deal with all messages. You write a function, attach it to a message map entry for a given message, and wait for the system to kick the function off in response to that message. Although they work, message maps aren't nearly as elegant as event handlers. It's much more difficult, almost impossible, in fact, to change message map handlers at runtime the way that event handlers do. Before adding a message map system to your application, you should consider seriously whether the message map route is the way you want to go.

Okay, all that said, you wouldn't be reading about them if there wasn't some reason to do so. Message maps do allow the CBuilder application programmer to solve problems that would otherwise not be able to be solved. Compare this to Visual Basic programmers, stuck with the messages that that system allows you to handle and no others. VB programmers often need to resort to third-party components, such as the Message Blaster VBX, to handle messages that aren't defined within VB. Until Version 5.0 of VB, in fact, you could not define **callback** functions for messages at all. CBuilder may not be perfect, but it's quite a step up from the competition in this area.

In this example, you'll see how to implement a message map in your application and how to handle the elusive WM_VSCROLL message from Windows. We'll use that message to change the display of the screen and we'll even see how to display information in a status bar pane.

Implementing Message Maps

Figure 4.9 is the form that shows off the power of the CBuilder message map system. To create this form, add a status bar at the top of the form by setting the **Alignment** property of the status bar to **alTop**. This will cause the status bar to take up part of the form area at the top and will cut down on the client area available to the form. This is necessary because we'll be vertically scrolling the form that would make the status bar appear all the way at the bottom of the virtual form, which is quite a ways down. It will be visible at the top of the form and can be used to display information about the current status of the form.

Once the status bar is taken care of, the next step is to set up the scrollbars for the form so that we can get input from them. To force a form to have a scrollbar, select the form in the Object Inspector. Find the **VertScrollBar** property and double-click on the left-hand side of the Object Inspector grid. This will open the property to

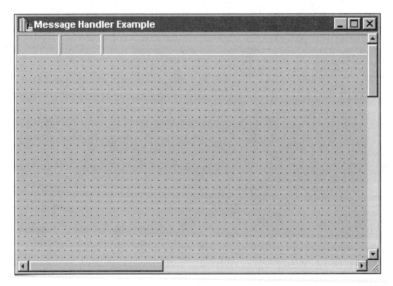

Figure 4.9
The message map example form.

show the sub-properties beneath it. Change the **Range** sub-property to be 1000; this should be big enough to allow the scrollbar to display.

Move to the **Horizontal** scrollbar property and repeat the process. When you're finished, the form should display with both a horizontal and a vertical scrollbar. Next, move to the status bar and click on the right side of the **Panels** property. We're going to add two small panels to hold the virtual row and column positions in the form. Add three panels to the status bar. Leave the text on all three blank.

At this point we're ready to being writing code for handling the message maps. Before we do so, let's take a look at what message maps are all about.

The general syntax for a message map is as follows

```
BEGIN_MESSAGE_MAP
MESSAGE_HANDLER(message, function)
END_MESSAGE_MAP(object)
```

where:

- **message** is the Windows message that you want to handle. In general, Windows messages look something like **WM_xxx**.

- **function** is the object level function that you want to use as the handler for the message. Message handling functions usually take a single parameter which is a reference to a **TMessage** object.

- **object** is the class for which you are defining this message map (**TForm**, **TListBox**, etc).

What we would like to do is to add two message handlers for the horizontal and vertical scrolling messages to our form. Modify your include file (Unit1.h) for the form to be as follows. First make the changes, shown in highlighted print, and then we'll discuss what the changes accomplish:

```
//------------------------------------------------------------
#ifndef Unit1H
#define Unit1H
//------------------------------------------------------------
#include <vcl\Classes.hpp>
#include <vcl\Controls.hpp>
#include <vcl\StdCtrls.hpp>
#include <vcl\Forms.hpp>
```

```
#include <vcl\ComCtrls.hpp>
//-------------------------------------------------------------------
class TForm1 : public TForm
{
__published:     // IDE-managed Components
                 TStatusBar *StatusBar1;
                 void __fastcall HandlePaint(TObject *Sender);
private:     // User declarations
                 void __fastcall HandleVScroll(TMessage& Msg);
                 void __fastcall HandleHScroll(TMessage& Msg);
   int FnStartLine;
   int FnStartCol;
public:                  // User declarations
                 __fastcall TForm1(TComponent* Owner);
BEGIN_MESSAGE_MAP
MESSAGE_HANDLER(WM_VSCROLL,TMessage,HandleVScroll)
MESSAGE_HANDLER(WM_HSCROLL,TMessage,HandleHScroll)
// Add any number of additional message handlers here.
END_MESSAGE_MAP(TForm)
};
//-------------------------------------------------------------------
extern TForm1 *Form1;
//-------------------------------------------------------------------
#endif
```

The first batch of changes define two methods (**HandleVScroll** and **HandleHScroll**), which we're going to use as message handlers in this form. The methods both accept a **TMessage** reference, which is the message input for the given message. Note that because these are message handlers and therefore override message handlers in the underlying VCL, you need to add the **__fastcall** modifier to the methods.

The **FnStartLine** and **FnStartCol** member variables will be used to track how far we've scrolled the form in the vertical and horizontal directions respectively. We'll also use these member variables to display the status in the status bar and to determine what will be painted on the form.

Painting The Form

In general, you handle scrolling in a form because you want to be in control of the painting of text, graphics, or other data on the form. For this reason, we'll next override the painting of the form by adding a handler for the **OnPaint** event. In the Object Inspector, add a new handler for the **OnPaint** event and give the new handler the name **HandlePaint**. Move to the source window and add the following code to the **HandlePaint** event handler:

```
void __fastcall TForm1::HandlePaint(TObject *Sender)
{
    int x = 0;
    int y = 0;
    for ( int i=FnStartLine; i<100; ++i )
    {
        String s = "This is line " + String(i);
        int nHeight = Canvas->TextHeight( s );
          Canvas->TextOut ( x, y, s );
        y += nHeight;
    }

}
```

As you can see, we're simply displaying lines of text in the form canvas surface. The lines of text show the line number beginning with the current starting line and progressing for 100 lines of display. Each line will be displayed on a separate line of the canvas, as we're incrementing the vertical (y) position by the height of the previous line.

Adding The Vertical Scrolling Handler

Handling vertical scrolling isn't a particularly tough job if you understand what the messages you're receiving look like. In general, if you would like to handle messages in the message map format, you'll need to know something about what the messages look like in the Windows API. For a scrolling message, for example, the **WParam** section of the **TMessage** object will contain a code which indicates what the user has done. This code can be either a single scroll move (up or down), a page scroll move (up or down), or a scrollbar drag. We aren't going to deal with the scrollbar drag in this example because it really doesn't mean a lot unless you have a percentage of the text to work with. We'll stick with scrolling up and down by single lines or pages because we're simply displaying random text lines on the form canvas. Here is the complete source code for the vertical scrollbar message handler:

```
void __fastcall TForm1::HandleVScroll(TMessage& Msg)
{
    int nStartPos = FnStartLine;
```

```
switch ( Msg.WParam )
{
   case SB_LINEUP:
      if ( FnStartLine )
         FnStartLine--;
      break;
   case SB_LINEDOWN:
      FnStartLine++;
      break;
   case SB_PAGEDOWN:
      FnStartLine+=10;
      break;
   case SB_PAGEUP:
      if ( FnStartLine < 10 )
         FnStartLine = 0;
      else
                    FnStartLine -= 10;
      break;
}

// If the position changed, redraw!
if ( FnStartLine != nStartPos )
               Invalidate();

StatusBar1->Panels->Items[0]->Text = "Row: " + String(FnStartLine);
StatusBar1->Panels->Items[1]->Text = "Col: " + String(FnStartCol);

}
```

This message handler is fairly complete in that it accepts a message and works with it without having to rely on the underlying VCL handler. Once we determine what the user has done in the scrollbar by checking the code, we simply increment or decrement the vertical position indicator, which we're storing in the **FnStartLine** variable. Once this is completed, we check to see if the ending position is the same as the starting position. If it's not, which will be the case most of the time, we repaint the form, which will redraw the lines of text, making it appear that the form text has scrolled. In addition, we update the status bar text panes with the current row and column positions.

Handling Horizontal Scrolling

Similar to the vertical scrollbar, the horizontal scrollbar reports exactly the same information using exactly the same codes. The only difference in our handler, therefore, is that we work with the column position rather than the vertical one. Note that in this example we don't do anything with horizontal scrolling, so there is no reason to redraw the form. Here is the complete source for the horizontal scroll handler:

```
void __fastcall TForm1::HandleHScroll(TMessage& Msg)
{
    int nStartPos = FnStartCol;

    switch ( Msg.WParam )
    {
        case SB_LINEUP:
            if ( FnStartCol )
                            FnStartCol--;
            break;
        case SB_LINEDOWN:
            FnStartCol++;
            break;
        case SB_PAGEDOWN:
            FnStartCol+=10;
            break;
        case SB_PAGEUP:
            if ( FnStartCol < 10 )
                FnStartCol = 0;
            else
                            FnStartCol -= 10;
            break;
    }

    StatusBar1->Panels->Items[0]->Text = "Row: " + String(FnStartLine);
    StatusBar1->Panels->Items[1]->Text = "Col: " + String(FnStartCol);

}
```

The last step that needs to be put into the form is the initialization of the member variables done in the constructor for the class. Add the following lines to the constructor to initialize the row and column positions before the form starts displaying:

```
__fastcall TForm1::TForm1(TComponent* Owner)
                : TForm(Owner)
{
    FnStartLine = 0;
    FnStartCol  = 0;
}
```

That's all there is to the message map example. As you can see, handling message maps is not particularly difficult. You just add message map entries, exactly as you would using Visual C++ or Borland C++. There is no built-in support for adding message map entries automatically in CBuilder, primarily because adding message map entries should be an effort of last resort rather than a first step as it is in framework-based products.

You'll probably find that you rarely, if ever, use a message map entry in your own applications. Component writers may find it a bit more common, but still rare. Look very carefully at the exposed events for a component before you decide to handle a message directly using the message map. There might be a very good reason for the message not to be exposed directly by the component.

Creating An Owner-Draw List Box

Although the VCL is quite powerful in its own right, there are a number of applications that need the ability to use things that are not directly implemented by the VCL. One of these extra things is the ability to use a Windows list box with a slight twist. Some applications want to change the color of each entry in the list box, others need to change the font that is used to display entries in the list box, and still others need to display some sort of image or bitmap along with text in the list box to show a thumbnail sketch of what data is stored in that list box entry. The VCL system makes it fairly easy to implement such a list box, provided that you know something about the Windows messages and API calls that are needed. In this example, we show you how to customize a list box to display things the way you want them to appear, including changing the font, color, and bitmap displayed with each entry in a list box.

There are really two ways that you can implement the kinds of changes we're talking about here. First of all, you can handle the drawing of the list box within the form in which it resides. This form of list box is generally specific to a form. The second kind of list box that implements this behavior is at the component level. By deriving a new component from the standard Windows list box component (implemented through **TCustomListBox**), you can then use this list box in multiple forms and multiple applications with ease. In this example, we're going to tackle the first case: drawing the list box from the form in which that list box lives.

Understanding Owner-Draw List Boxes

List boxes drawn by the application in which they're created are called owner-draw (this applies to list boxes in components as well). Owner-draw list boxes get the name from the fact that it is the owner of the list box, the form, which implements the drawing code for the list box. There are two kinds of owner-draw list boxes possible in Windows and therefore through the VCL. The first kind is called an owner-draw fixed list box. In this type of control, each entry in the list box is of fixed height. Nearly all list boxes you're likely to encounter in your application are owner-draw fixed.

The second kind of list box you can implement is an owner-draw variable type. This type of control allows each line of the list, in other words each list entry, to have a variable height. The example we're going to implement will be of the variable kind. As you'll see in the example, being variable sized does not mean that you can't have each entry the same height, just that it's okay to have each entry different. For our purposes, we're simply going to make it variable height so that we can demonstrate how you set the sizes of the lines in the list. Although we'll use a single height for all entries, based on the font of the list box, the example would be extremely easy to customize to allow multiple fonts for different entries, with each font having a different height.

In order to implement an owner-draw list box, you need to understand a little bit about the Windows messages that go on behind the scenes in the list box world. There are two Windows messages of paramount importance in creating an owner-draw list box. Fortunately, the VCL encapsulates both of these messages as events, and you can work through the standard event-handling system to implement them. There is no need for messy message map entries when working with owner-draw list boxes in CBuilder.

The first message that you'll need to process for your list is the WM_MEASUREITEM message. This message, handled by the **MeasureItem** event, is used by Windows to determine the height of each entry in the list. When Windows needs to draw an item in the list, it will call the **MeasureItem** event handler the first time that the item is drawn. The height is a returned parameter from the event handler, which the Windows list box uses to set aside enough vertical space for the item to be displayed.

The second message that you'll need to process for your list is the WM_DRAWITEM message. This message, handled by the **DrawItem** event, is used by Windows to do the actual rendering of each entry in the list. When Windows determines that an item needs to be drawn on the list box surface, it will call the **DrawItem** event handler for that item. This handler is going to be called multiple times for a list box, once for each time the entry needs to be drawn. Unlike some other systems, the VCL provides default handling for most of the pieces of the owner-draw system so that you only need to implement the parts that are unique to your application form.

These two messages are the only ones that you need to worry about for handling owner-draw list boxes. The trick is to handle them properly. Although it's not a terribly complex problem, it's usually easier for someone to show you how to do it the first time and then to simply cut and paste the solution into other applications. This steal-this-code mentality is important in CBuilder, and we'll stress it wherever possible. Don't reinvent the wheel if someone has already done the work for you. You'll find that while you can do whatever you want, things will go much faster and easier if you rely on pre-built, pre-tested components in the system rather than doing much of the work yourself.

Implementing The Owner-Draw List Example

In this example, we implement a fairly complex owner-draw list box. The form will permit you to select a new color for the list entries, as well as a new font for the list entries. We'll load bitmaps to display on the left-hand side of each list entry. In short, we'll probably do everything you could imagine for drawing list box entries on your own. When you've finished this example, you may award yourself the Masters of ListBox degree.

> **Note:** You'll find the source code for the Owner Draw List Box program in the Chapter4\OwnerDrawList\directory on the accompanying CD-ROM for this book.

Figure 4.10 shows the form we'll be working with for this application. Create a simple form and drop a list box onto it, more or less centered on the form. In addition to the list box, we'll also be working with **FontDialog** and **ColorDialog** objects as well as a main menu. Add all of these components to the form wherever you like. Don't forget to set the style of the list box object to be **Owner-Draw Variable** or none of the code we're going to write in this example will work properly.

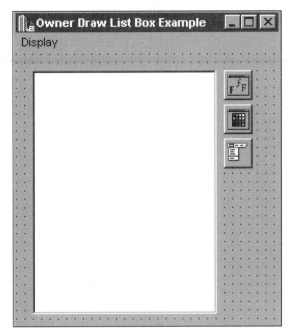

Figure 4.10
Owner-draw list box example form.

If you implement all of this code and nothing looks right in the list (you get only text), check this property setting for the list box.

Modifying The Include File

The include file (Unit1.h) for our application needs several modifications before we can continue with the development of the example. Modify the include file as shown in the following listing. All changes you'll need to make are shown in highlighted print:

```
//-------------------------------------------------------------------
#ifndef Unit1H
#define Unit1H
//-------------------------------------------------------------------
#include <vcl\Classes.hpp>
#include <vcl\Controls.hpp>
#include <vcl\StdCtrls.hpp>
#include <vcl\Forms.hpp>
#include <vcl\Dialogs.hpp>
```

```
#include <vcl\Menus.hpp>
//--------------------------------------------------------------------
class TForm1 : public TForm
{
__published:     // IDE-managed Components
                 TListBox *ListBox1;
                 TFontDialog *FontDialog1;
                 TColorDialog *ColorDialog1;
                 TMainMenu *MainMenu1;
                 TMenuItem *Display1;
                 TMenuItem *ChangeFont1;
                 TMenuItem *ChangeColor1;
private:     // User declarations
    TFont *FpFont;
    TColor FcColor;
    Graphics::TBitmap *Fbmp1;
    Graphics::TBitmap *Fbmp2;
public:                  // User declarations
                 virtual __fastcall TForm1(TComponent* Owner);
                 virtual __fastcall~TForm(void);
                 void SetListBoxItems(void);
};
//--------------------------------------------------------------------
extern TForm1 *Form1;
//--------------------------------------------------------------------
#endif
```

We're using a few things that we haven't used in the past in this example. First of all, the **TFont** pointer object will be used to store the font that we're going to display the list box entries in. This object is the encapsulation of a Windows HFONT and contains many methods for working with text displays. Fortunately, we need not work with many of the methods, because fonts are dealt with well in the CBuilder system. Mostly, the **font** object will be used to retrieve the current font from the font dialog and to set the current font in the display canvas for the owner-draw list box.

The **TFontDialog** class in CBuilder allows users to select all of the attributes of the font for display. They can select font families, sizes, and attributes (bold, italic, bold and italic, etc) for the text, and even see a display of sample text for the selections they've made. The best part of the font dialog is that you don't need to do anything for it. Just display the dialog, let users select the font attributes they want from the dialog, and then collect the new **TFont** object from the dialog when it's finished running. This is a vast improvement over earlier systems that required you not only to display the font dialog, but also to build a font from the pieces selected in the dialog.

The **TColor** object is a very simple object (it's really just a value) that contains Windows color definitions. Colors in Windows break down into two discrete categories: real colors and relative colors. Real colors, represented by RGB (Red, Green, Blue) values, are often used to select directly a color for display. In the CBuilder system, you don't need to deal directly with the RGB values because CBuilder provides constants such as **clRed** or **clBlue** for this purpose.

Relative colors are set in reference to objects in the system. For example, you might want to set your form background color to be the same as the button color currently in use in the system. CBuilder provides many constants for this purpose, such as **clBtnFace**. The advantage to using colors in this way is that your program will look like all other programs running on the system. If the user has some oddball color scheme because they are red-green color-blind, you'll be doing them a great disservice by using red and green extensively throughout your program. Although this kind of problem is rare, it's a serious concern when writing programs that are used outside of your company. Shrink-wrapped software should never make assumptions about the color scheme in use. At the very least, you should permit the user to customize any color selections you have made in your application at runtime.

The **TColorDialog** class in CBuilder provides the means to allow the user to customize colors. Built around the standard Windows 95/NT Color Dialog common dialog, this dialog will permit the user to select either a pre-existing color or a color of their own choosing. You don't need to worry about any of this. You simply display the dialog, allow the user to select some color value in whatever way they see fit, and then use the color value selected by the user. Any time that you decide to use a color in your application, consider whether this color should allow customization. This is essential for things like owner-draw list boxes that display the item text in a specified color.

Once we've added all of the pieces to the dialog, it's time to start implementing the code for the form. Let's begin with the constructor for the form. Here is the code to add to the constructor:

```
__fastcall TForm1::TForm1(TComponent* Owner)
            : TForm(Owner)
```

```
{
   FcColor = clBlack;
   FpFont  = NULL;

   // Create some bitmaps.
   Fbmp1 = new Graphics::TBitmap;
   Fbmp1->LoadFromFile(
     "d:\\CBuilder\\CBuilder\\images\\icons\\earth16.bmp" );
   Fbmp2 = new Graphics::TBitmap;
   Fbmp2->LoadFromFile(
     "d:\\CBuilder\\CBuilder\\images\\icons\\ship16.bmp" );

}
```

The first thing the code does is assign some defaults to the color and font properties for the owner-draw list box. We'll be using the **FcColor** object to store the color in which to display the text. The **FpFont** will be used to define the font for the dialog. For our defaults we'll simply define the text color to be black. The font will be initialized to NULL, which will indicate to our program that no font has been selected by the user. Like all good components, the list box canvas has a default setting for the font and will use it if we do not specify a font to use at runtime.

Implementing The Menu For The Form

Once we have all of the things added and initialized, it's time to get down to basics. Select the main menu on the form and add two menu items to the form. The first item should have the caption Change &Font. This item will be used to display the font dialog and gather the new font from the user. The second item should have the caption Change &Color. This item will be used to display the color dialog and gather the new selected color from the user.

Add a new handler for the Change &Font menu item. Add the following code to the handler for the menu item:

```
void __fastcall TForm1::ChangeFont1Click(TObject *Sender)
{
   if ( FontDialog1->Execute() )
   {
      FpFont = FontDialog1->Font;
      SetListBoxItems();
   }
}
```

As you can see, the handler is quite simple. The **Execute** method of the dialog will return true if the user makes a selection and clicks on the OK button in the dialog. If the user clicks on the Cancel button, the **Execute** method returns false. The C++ statement **if (FontDialog1->Execute())** is really shorthand for the more full statement:

```
if ( FontDialog1->Execute() == true )
{
```

As you can see, we'll run the code within the braces only if the user selects something in the font dialog and clicks on the OK button. Otherwise the return code from the **Execute** method will be false and the code will not be executed.

We'll get to the **SetListBoxItems** function in a moment. For now, though, let's take a look at the color change code. The implementation of the Change &Color menu item is remarkably similar to the code for the Change &Font menu item. Add a new handler for the Change &Color menu item and add the following code to the handler (call the handler the default, **ChangeColor1Click**):

```
void __fastcall TForm1::ChangeColor1Click(TObject *Sender)
{
    if ( ColorDialog1->Execute() )
    {
        FcColor = ColorDialog1->Color;
        SetListBoxItems();
    }
}
```

Once again, all we're doing is letting the dialog display itself and allowing the user to select a color in any fashion that they see fit. If you bring up the Color Dialog itself, you'll see the variety of options that the user has: selecting a pre-defined color, entering RGB values, or selecting from a color band. You get all of this for free in your own code.

Once the user has selected a new color, we store it away in the **FcColor** member variable for the form and reset the list box items.

Why Do We Need To Reset The List Box Items?

You would think that we would simply be able to invalidate the list box and have it redraw itself, and you would be right. The problem is that the Windows list box is just a bit too smart for us. Once the item is stored in the list box and the height of the item is set, that information is stored in the list box itself. It will not change that information even if you ask it really, really nicely. As a result, if the user selects a new font for the list box that has a different height from the old font, the list box doesn't know about it and will not reset the item height. This is a one-time change made when an item is added to the list. For this reason, we take advantage of the fact that the list will reset itself if items are added to the list. We will simply clear out the existing items in the list, reset the font, and measure the items again based on the new font. This does imply, however, that you know what items are in the list and what attributes are associated with those items.

If you were creating a general purpose color-font list box component, you would probably maintain four separate object arrays in your component. The first would hold the text for the item, and the second would hold the bitmap associated with each item. Remember that bitmaps can be **NULL** and need not be assigned for the item. The third array would hold the color to associate with the item, which would be used when the item is drawn on the list box. The fourth and final array would hold the font to use with the item, which can also be **NULL** and need not be applied. A better approach than four arrays, which would need to be kept in sync with each other as items are added and deleted, would be to create a new C++ object of your own to store these attributes. Just a thought for the future.

In our example we have only two list box items, so it's easy enough for us to keep track of what should be displayed with which bitmap, color, and font. Here is the complete implementation of the utility method **SetListBoxItems**, which does the adding of the list box entries:

```
void TForm1::SetListBoxItems(void)
{
   ListBox1->Clear();

   // Save them with the strings in the list box
   ListBox1->Items->AddObject( "Earth", Fbmp1 );
   ListBox1->Items->AddObject( "Ship", Fbmp2 );
}
```

There is nothing terribly complex about this routine. It first clears all existing items out of the list box by calling the **Clear** method of the list box object. Next, the two items are added to the list. If you've never worked with **TListBox** before and are accustomed to the normal way of associating items in the list with data from the user program, you're in for a treat. The **AddObject** method of the **TListBox** class will permit the programmer to add both the text and the associated data item at the same time. The second argument to the function, in this case our bitmap, is an untyped object. You can pass anything you want here as long as you're able to interpret it later on. As you'll see when we reach the drawing code for the list box, we need to store the same kind of pointer (or derived from a common base class at least) in the object to use it effectively.

Handling The Item Measurement

You might recall that we made the list box an owner-draw variable list. This will cause the Windows system list box to issue a WM_MEASUREITEM message to the list box window. CBuilder then routes that message through the **MeasureItem** handler for the list box, which in turn calls the **MeasureItem** handler for the parent window and the form, if one exists. Because we added a handler for the **MeasureItem** event, we should now implement this method. Add the following code for the **MeasureItem** event handler to the Unit1.cpp source file for the form:

```
void __fastcall TForm1::MeasureItem(TWinControl *Control, int Index,
                                                        int &Height)
{
    if ( FpFont )
        ListBox1->Canvas->Font = FpFont;

    // Get the canvas height
    Height = ListBox1->Canvas->TextHeight("M");
}
```

In this method we first check to see if the user has selected a font for use in the list box. If so, that font object is assigned to the **Canvas Font** property for the list box. Otherwise, the **Font** property for the list box canvas will contain the default font for the system. Once this is accomplished, we use the **TextHeight** method of the canvas to compute the height of the line. Because all characters on the line are in the same font and Windows only supports single-height fonts, we can simply check the text height of any character. The capital M is a good choice because it stands out well by itself on the line and because M and W are the two widest characters in any font.

You might ask what happens to any previous font that might have been associated with the font of the **Canvas** property of the list box. In other systems you would first need to get the font associated with the **Canvas**, delete it, and reset it with the new font. Then you would need to worry about whether the font had been in use somewhere else, which would cause a program crash the first time that it was accessed in the other place. Don't fret, CBuilder doesn't directly allow you to modify the **Font** property in the assignment statement. Instead, you're causing the system to invoke the **Set** method for the **Font** property in the **Canvas**. This **Set** method will automatically free up the **Font** property if it needs to be done, saving you the time and trouble. Just another nice thing about one of those so-called extensions to the language.

Drawing The Items

It's finally time to consider the work of actually drawing each item on the screen. As you might recall, we added a method called **DrawItem** to the event handler for the **DrawItem** event in the list box to handle this job. Each time this list box has to draw any item in the list, the **DrawItem** event handler will be called to do the job. The list box itself doesn't care what you draw or how you draw it. Instead, it concerns itself with managing the selection of items, the association of user-defined objects with the items, and the handling of keyboard selection from the end-user. Given the state of Windows programming, the list box is an amazing example of good object-oriented design in the system.

Here is the complete code for the **DrawItem** event handler for the form. Add it in the **DrawItem** stub that was generated by CBuilder in the Unit1.cpp source file:

```
void __fastcall TForm1::DrawItem(TWinControl *Control, int Index,
            TRect &Rect, TOwnerDrawState State)
{
    Graphics::TBitmap *pic = (Graphics::TBitmap *)
      ListBox1->Items->Objects[Index];
    if ( pic )
    {
                ListBox1->Canvas->Draw(Rect.Left, Rect.Top, pic);
                Rect.Left += pic->Width + 5;
    }

    // If the user selected a font use it
    if ( FpFont != NULL )
      ListBox1->Canvas->Font = FpFont;
```

```
   // Set the color based on user preference
   ListBox1->Canvas->Brush->Color = FcColor;

   ListBox1->Canvas->TextRect(Rect, Rect.Left, Rect.Top,
     ListBox1->Items->Strings[ Index ].c_str() );
}
```

The first step is to draw the bitmap image on the left side of the list box item area. The area itself is managed by the list box and given to us in the **Rect** parameter to the function. The **Control** parameter passed to the object is the control for which we are drawing. We already know what the object is (we only have a single list box on the form) so we can just use the canvas of our object. The **TControl** class does not contain the **Canvas** property, thus we would need to cast the **Control** object into the **TListBox** object that it represents before we could use it. We're simply bypassing the middle man.

As usual, drawing the bitmap is a matter of positioning it properly on the canvas. We already have the rectangle representing the position on the list box area of this item, as this is just a matter of using the top left corner of the passed rectangle. We then add the width of the bitmap to the position and add a five-pixel buffer so that the text doesn't run right into the bitmap.

If the user has selected a font for this form to use with the list box, it's set into the canvas. Likewise, the color of the item is set to the internal **FcColor** value. Finally, the **TextRect** method is called to draw the text onto the canvas. Note the use of the **Strings** property to get the text for this item before we draw it on the canvas. The **Canvas** object will automatically use the proper font and color that we have assigned in the **TextRect** method, so that is all that is necessary to draw the item.

Cleaning Up The Details

There are just a few details that need to be cleaned up before we can compile and run the application. First of all, we need to add the data to the list in the first place. To deal with this issue, add a new event handler for the **FormCreate** event and add the following code to the new event handler:

```
void __fastcall TForm1::FormCreate(TObject *Sender)
{
    SetListBoxItems();
}
```

Finally, add a new destructor for the class. This is where we do the final cleanup for the class before the form goes away forever. We'll need to free up the memory we allocated for the bitmap objects in the constructor for the class. Here is the complete implementation of the destructor for the class that you should add to the Unit1.cpp source file:

```
__fastcall TForm1::~TForm1(void)
{
            // Free the allocated bitmaps from the constructor
            delete Fbmp1;
            delete Fbmp2;
}
```

Compile and run the application. You should now see the display shown in Figure 4.11. Select a new font for the list by selecting Change &Font from the menu and make it larger than the existing one. Click on OK on the Font Dialog and watch the display change. Repeat the test using a new color from the Color Dialog by selecting

Figure 4.11
The new owner-draw list box example in action.

the Change &Color. When you're finished with the testing, sit back and marvel at the simplicity of owner-draw list boxes using CBuilder.

Exploring Tab Controls

The next area we are going to explore in the VCL excavation is that of tab controls. Tab controls, or notebooks as they are known today, are a method to display a large amount of related information in a small amount of space. Tab controls first made their appearance in Windows 3.1 but were not heavily used until Microsoft started using them in its applications (most notably Word). Basically, a tab control is a notebook metaphor that contains multiple dialog panes in a single space. As each tab is selected, the dialog corresponding to that tab is made visible and the previous dialog made invisible. Fortunately, with the new components it's no longer necessary to understand how the underlying functionality works, but rather what you can accomplish with the technology. In short, tab controls are an excellent example of component technology at work in the Windows programming world.

> **Note:** *You'll find the source code for the Tabs Example program in the Chapter4\Tabs\directory on the accompanying CD-ROM for this book.*

The easiest way to use tabs is in a tab dialog. This is also the most natural way to do it. While tabs can appear in main windows, it's not the way most applications work. Perhaps in the future this will change, but for now you'll normally consider a tab dialog the standard. CBuilder makes it really easy to create a new tab dialog that you can then modify to your heart's content. This is the initial approach we will use to create something that we can work with. To generate the tab dialog initially, you use the **Repository** to create a new one. Select File|New from the main menu in CBuilder. From the tabbed worksheet that is displayed, select the Dialogs tab. Find the Tab Dialog entry and double-click on it. CBuilder will generate a new tab dialog and add it to the project. Just how CBuilder is able to generate a new file and add it to the project will be tackled later on in the book.

The Tab Dialog form is called, by default, **TPagesDlg**. Let's take a quick look at the header file for this form and see what it is, exactly, that makes up a tab dialog:

```
//------------------------------------------------------------------
#ifndef Unit2H
#define Unit2H
```

```
//------------------------------------------------------------------
#include <vcl\ExtCtrls.hpp>
#include <vcl\ComCtrls.hpp>
#include <vcl\Buttons.hpp>
#include <vcl\StdCtrls.hpp>
#include <vcl\Controls.hpp>
#include <vcl\Forms.hpp>
#include <vcl\Graphics.hpp>
#include <vcl\Classes.hpp>
#include <vcl\SysUtils.hpp>
#include <vcl\Windows.hpp>
#include <vcl\System.hpp>
//------------------------------------------------------------------
class TPagesDlg : public TForm
{
__published:
                TPanel *Panel1;
                TPanel *Panel2;
                TPageControl *PageControl1;
                TTabSheet *TabSheet1;
                TTabSheet *TabSheet2;
                TTabSheet *TabSheet3;
                TButton *OKBtn;
                TButton *CancelBtn;
                TButton *HelpBtn;
private:
public:
                virtual __fastcall TPagesDlg(TComponent* AOwner);
};
//------------------------------------------------------------------
extern TPagesDlg *PagesDlg;
//------------------------------------------------------------------
#endif
```

The initial design of the tab dialog contains several important components. First of all, the **TPageControl** member variable (**PageControl1**) is the center of the whole thing. The page control object is the tab itself and controls which dialogs (called tab sheets) are displayed. The **TTabSheet** objects (**TabSheet1**, etc.) are the actual pages of the tab dialog, which are displayed when the tab is clicked. Finally, the OK, Cancel, and Help buttons are automatically generated at the bottom of the dialog for the user to work with the dialog. If you were making this form into a non-modal form (for example, an MDI child window), you would remove the buttons from the bottom and expand the panels on which the tabs reside to fill the form.

Displaying The Tab Dialog

First we'll display the new tab dialog. This gives us a chance to show off the difference between showing forms in a modal versus a modeless (normal forms) fashion. Add a new main menu to the main form and add a menu item with the caption Show Tab Dialog. Add the following code to the handler for the new menu item. Note that you'll need to do a File|Include Header to add the Unit2.h header file to the first form:

```
void __fastcall TForm1::ShowTabDialog1Click(TObject *Sender)
{
                PagesDlg->ShowModal();
}
```

This will allow us to show the new **Tab** dialog as a modal dialog. Displaying a dialog as modal means that you won't be able to return to the main form until such time as you close the dialog by selecting the OK or Cancel button or selecting the Close button on the form frame.

Dealing With Tab Events

Putting up a tab is easy. Working with tab events should be correspondingly easy, right? Well, yes and no. Actually defining event handlers for the tab events is easy, as any event handlers are in the CBuilder system. Figuring out which events you want to trap and how to deal with them—well, that is another story entirely.

The first tab event of any importance to us is the **OnTabChanging** event. This event is a member of the **PageControl** object on the form. This event is fired when a new tab is selected by the user. The **Page Control** object calls the event handler for the **PageControl** object of the current form to see whether it's okay to leave the form. For our first example, we'll do some checking to see whether it really is okay to move off the current tab page and how to stop it from happening.

Add three edit fields to the first page and a static text field, "Enter text in one of these text fields" above the edit fields. Set the **Text** property of all three edit fields to be blank. You can do this by selecting all three edit fields and deleting the text in the **Text** property field displayed in the Object Inspector. While you're at it, modify the tab captions by selecting the **TabSheet** objects and modifying the **Caption** property. Set the first page to Page One, the second to Page Two, and the third to Page Three. When you're finished, the first page should look like the one shown in Figure 4.12.

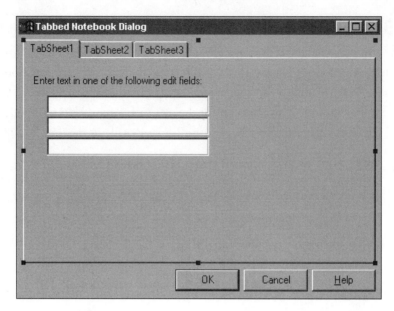

Figure 4.12
Tab dialog showing page one.

Add a new handler for the **OnTabChanging** event by selecting the PageControl (you do this by clicking on the tab portion of the dialog) and then moving to the Events tab of the Object Inspector. Give the new event handler the name **HandlePageChanging**. Add the following code to **HandlePageChanging** event of the new form:

```
void __fastcall TPagesDlg::HandlePageChanging(TObject *Sender,
                                          bool &AllowChange)
{
   // If this is the first page, only allow them
   // off if they have entered something in one of
   // the text fields
   if ( PageControl1->ActivePage == TabSheet1 )
   {
      if ( Edit1->Text == "" &&
           Edit2->Text == "" &&
           Edit3->Text == "" )
      {
         MessageBox(NULL, "We TOLD you to enter text!", "Error", MB_OK );
         Edit1->SetFocus();
         AllowChange = false;
```

```
                    return;
      }
                }

    // Otherwise save the active page
    FnCurTab = PageControl1->ActivePage->PageIndex;
}
```

You'll need to add a definition for the **FnCurTab** member variable to the include file. Add the following line to the private section of the form include file:

```
int  FnCurTab;
```

What's Going On?

In the code you just added to the handler, there are a couple of important things going on. The first is the concept of an *active page*. Each **PageControl** object has a single page that is active. In the case of the **OnTabChanging** event, the active page will be the one that is going to lose focus, not the one that the user clicked upon. The **OnTabChanging** event is, therefore, used to validate input on the current form. The **ActivePage** property of the control is simply a pointer to one of the tab sheets on the tab dialog. In our earlier check, we were looking to see if the current tab (the one that the user is trying to leave) is the first tab sheet. If it is, we want to make sure that at least one of the edit fields has been entered. That is, after all, what the message on the sheet says.

If the edit fields are all blank, which they would be if you didn't enter anything, the code then displays an error message, resets the focus to the first edit field, and modifies the output parameter **AllowChange** to be false. This stops the tab control from moving to whatever tab the user has selected.

If the user has entered something in the control, we want to allow them to move to another sheet. In this case, we don't modify the **AllowChange** output parameter, which is, by default, true. In this case, we'll simply remember the current page (the one that used to be displayed) for later use.

*How do you know that the **AllowChange** parameter to the method is an output parameter? In general, CBuilder passes objects that will not change by value or by pointer. Parameters that the method is intended to modify are passed by*

*reference normally using a reference object. A reference object is one with the &
(ampersand) symbol after the object (e.g., bool& AllowChanges, rather than
bool AllowChanges).*

If you now compile and run the application, you'll find that the first sheet will not
allow you to move off of it without entering something for at least one of the edit
fields. It won't stop you from entering more than one edit field, nor does it care
what you put in the edit fields. It simply verifies that some information is entered.
This same technique can be used to verify that an input field contains valid data or
that a single checkbox is selected on a tab sheet.

Handling The Move To Case

The opposite case of the moving off of a tab sheet is the case of not allowing a user
to select a given tab sheet by clicking on its tab in the **PageControl**. This case is a
little more complicated than the previous case. Microsoft, in its infinite wisdom,
did not give the Windows 95 tab control the ability to disable a given tab. Some
third-party tab controls do give this ability, but anything that is written using the
standard Windows 95 Tab Control will not be able to do so. CBuilder, of course,
uses the underlying operating system controls wherever possible to remain consistent with other applications. For this reason, you cannot simply disable a tab.

> **Note:** *It actually is possible to implement the behavior you want for dis-
> abling a tab control. It's not that easy, which is why we won't go into it here.
> Basically, what you want to do is to sub-class (derive a new component
> from) the **PageControl** object and check for a mouse down message
> (WM_LBUTTONDOWN) in the tab. If you find such a message, determine
> which tab the mouse click was made in. If that tab is disabled, don't allow
> the underlying tab control access to the mouse down message.*

To handle the case of moving to a tab rather than from it, we handle a different event for
the **PageControl**. In this case we want to add a handler for the **OnPageChange**
message. Let's look at an example of doing just this to check for a disabled tab.

Move to the second sheet of the tab control by either changing the **ActivePage**
property of the **PageControl** in the Object Inspector or by simply clicking on the
second tab in the form display. Add two buttons to the now blank displayed sheet.

The first should be labeled "Allow Page Three". The second button should be labeled "DisAllow Page Three". If the user clicks on the first button, we'll allow them to move to the third page of the sheet. If they click on the second button, we won't let them move to the third page. It's that easy. Figure 4.13 shows the updated page two of the **PageControl**.

Add a handler for the first button (Allow Page Three) and add the following code to the handler:

```
void __fastcall TPagesDlg::Button1Click(TObject *Sender)
{
    FbAllowPageThree = true;
}
```

Likewise, add a handler for the second button and add the following code to the handler:

```
void __fastcall TPagesDlg::Button2Click(TObject *Sender)
{
    FbAllowPageThree = false;
}
```

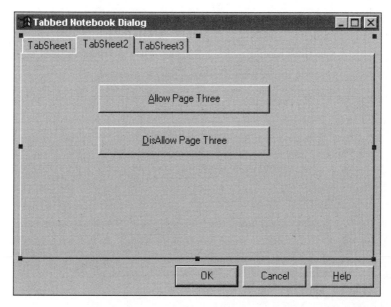

Figure 4.13
Tab dialog showing page two.

Modify the constructor for the form to initialize the boolean variable so that the page will start out being enabled:

```
__fastcall TPagesDlg::TPagesDlg(TComponent* AOwner)
              : TForm(AOwner)
{
    FnCurTab = 0;
    FbAllowPageThree = true;
}
```

Disabling The Tab Itself

Once we have all of the preparation out of the way, it's time to disable the tab. As mentioned earlier, it's not possible to disable the control directly using conventional means, so we need to be a little sneaky.

When a tab control sheet is selected, the tab first issues an **OnTabChanging** event to the form that owns the **PageControl** to see whether it's okay to leave the current tab. This doesn't help us because it isn't the current tab that we are concerned with. Instead, we're more worried about the tab the user is moving to. Unfortunately, the information for the tab to move to is not supplied in the **OnTabChanging** event. Once the tab has changed the current sheet, however, the **PageControl** sends another event to the form. This event is named the **OnTabChange** event. Add a new handler for the **OnTabChange** event and give it the name **HandlePageChange**. Add the following code to the **HandlePageChange** event:

```
void __fastcall TPagesDlg::HandlePageChange(TObject *Sender)
{
    // If the third page is becoming active, check if this
    // is allowed.
    if ( PageControl1->ActivePage->PageIndex == 2 )
    {
        if ( FbAllowPageThree == false )
        {
            switch ( FnCurTab )
            {
                case 0:  // First page
                    PageControl1->ActivePage = TabSheet1;
                    break;
                case 1:  // Second page
                    PageControl1->ActivePage = TabSheet2;
                    break;
```

```
            }
        }
    }

    // Change the caption of the form to reflect the
    // current page
    Caption = "Working on: " + PageControl1->ActivePage->Caption;
}
```

When the user selects the third page, the **HandlePageChange** event handler will be called. The **ActivePage** property of the **PageControl** will have been reset to be the third page. We check to see whether this is the case by checking the **PageIndex** property of the **ActivePage**. We could, of course, have simply checked to see if the **ActivePage** was the same as the **TabSheet3** object, but this allows you to see another way of validating what page something really is. That notwithstanding, if the page is, in fact, the third page, we check to see if it's okay to move there.

If the user has previously clicked on the DisAllow Page Three button on the second page, it will not be permissible to move to page three. The member variable **FbAllowPageThree** will be set to false. In this case, we check to see what the previous page was (remember that we set this previous page in the **OnTabChanging** method earlier) and reset that page to be current. Note that you can't use the **PageIndex** property to reset the **ActivePage** property. If you change the **PageIndex** property, you're really changing the position of the tab sheet in the array of pages within the **PageControl** object. You would be moving the third sheet into the second position (and therefore moving the second page to the third position). Instead, we simply set the **ActivePage** property to be the sheet object we want to be current (**TabSheet1** or **TabSheet2**).

Finally, we reset the caption of the form to be the string "Working on: " concatenated with the caption of the tab sheet that is current. This gives the user visual feedback of which tab they are working on even if the remainder of the form is not visible. If the user were to minimize the form, for example, the caption would still be set to Working on: Page Two (if Page Two were the current active page), and they would know where they were. It sounds strange, but several projects that I have worked on in the past have asked for functionality such as this. Live and learn.

That pretty much covers our tab examples. Tab controls are an extremely powerful way to collect related information into a notebook-like metaphor. Because tabs are becoming more and more a part of the Windows 95 system, it's important that you understand the functionality provided by this component so that you can use it in your own applications. As CBuilder makes it so easy to use the control in your application, there is really no excuse for not using the right tool for the job.

Drawing Your Own Menus

A little while back in this chapter we discussed the owner-draw list box. This form of the list allowed you to display whatever you wanted in a list box item (text, graphics, colors, fonts). You'll probably notice that a menu is quite a lot like a list box. They both allow you to display lists of items. In this respect they're quite similar. They're also similar in another way: Both allow you to display the items in the list in whatever format you like. In that regard, menus are even nicer than list boxes. Menus, as we'll see in this example, allow you to draw only the items you want to draw and even to modify whether or not the menu does its own display for an item at runtime. In this example, we explore some of the capabilities of drawing menu items using CBuilder and how you can modify this behavior to suit your own application's needs.

> **Note:** You'll find the source code for the Owner Draw Menu Example program in the Chapter4\OwnerDrawMenu\directory on the accompanying CD-ROM for this book.

If you'll recall from the discussion about the owner-draw list items, there are two Windows messages you need to process to handle owner-drawing. The first is the WM_MEASUREITEM message, which is sent for each item in the menu. This message expects you to tell the menu how tall each item will be in the display. The WM_MEASUREITEM Windows message is nicely wrapped by the **OnMeasureItem** event in CBuilder forms.

The second message that is dealt with in owner-draw menus is the WM_DRAWITEM message. This message is sent when each item in the menu needs to be drawn. Unlike the list box, the WM_DRAWITEM message will be sent every time that the menu is displayed because the state of the menu item might have changed since the last time that the menu item was displayed. You can do anything you like when drawing a menu item. Draw a bitmap next to the text, draw the text in a new font, or even display a bitmap or other graphic instead of text. In this example, we're going to display simple color bars for the menu items.

Dealing With The Windows API

If you look through the methods for the **TMainMenu** and **TMenuItem** components of the VCL, you'll not find any method that would naturally be associated with owner-draw menus. The reason for this is simple: There isn't one. Instead, you'll need to deal directly with the Windows API to get the job done. This isn't the nightmare that it might be in Visual Basic or even Delphi, which use different variable definitions than the API. Instead, you're working with C++, which maps nicely to the C language in which the API is written. We'll work extensively with the Windows API functions and CBuilder in a future chapter of the book.

The Windows API function we need to concern ourselves with in this example is the **ModifyMenu** function. The **ModifyMenu** function has the following syntax

```
ModifyMenuA(
    HMENU hMnu,
    UINT uPosition,
    UINT uFlags,
    UINT uIDNewItem,
    LPCSTR lpNewItem
    );
```

where:

- **hMnu** is the handle of the menu.

- **uPosition** is the position of the menu item you want to modify within the menu.

- **uFlags** is a set of possible flags to use when applying this menu item change.

- **uIDNewItem** is the identifier of the item to change.

- **lpNewItem** is either a string to display for the menu item or a handle to a menu, depending on the value of the **uFlags** parameter.

The **uFlags** parameter is where all of the confusion comes in with this API function. In general, you'll specify **MF_BYCOMMAND** or **MF_BYPOSITION** along another flag. The **MF_BYCOMMAND** flag means that the **uIDNewItem** parameter specifies the ID of the menu item (the value we specify in the **Command** property of the menu item). The **MF_BYPOSITION** flag indicates that the **uIDNewItem** parameter specifies a 0-based index into the list of menu items for the menu handle. Using this argument would mean that the first entry would be 0 regardless of the value of the **Command** property.

Along with the **command** versus **position** flag, the other flag you can set for the menu item is what kind of entry this menu item is. This can be **MF_STRING**, **MF_BITMAP**, or **MF_OWNERDRAW**. In the case of **MF_STRING**, the **lpNewItem** parameter is expected to point to a string to use for the text of the menu item. In the case of **MF_BITMAP**, the parameter should be the handle of a bitmap, and the **MF_OWNERDRAW** flag says the parameter is unimportant. We won't be using the **MF_BITMAP** argument in this example.

Rather than spending a lot of time discussing the way that the various flags can be combined and used, it's much easier to show you an example. First, add a main menu item with the name "Fred" to the menu. Add a second menu item with the name "Irving" and a third with the name "Modify." To the Fred menu, add two menu items with the names "George" and "Ralph." These are going to be our owner-draw menu items. Just to show that changes in one place don't affect menu items in another, add a menu item to the Irving menu with any name you like. To the Modify menu, add two menu items with the titles "Make Owner Draw" and "Make Normal." These two menu items will be used to toggle the owner-draw state of one of our items.

Add a new handler for the **OnCreate** event to the form. Give this new handler the name **FormCreate**. To this new handler, add the following code:

```
void __fastcall TForm1::FormCreate(TObject *Sender)
{
     ModifyMenu(MainMenu1->Handle,
       George1->Command,
       MF_BYCOMMAND | MF_OWNERDRAW,
       George1->Command,
       0);
     ModifyMenu(MainMenu1->Handle,
       Ralph1->Command,
       MF_BYCOMMAND | MF_OWNERDRAW,
       Ralph1->Command,
       0);
}
```

As you can see, we're using the **ModifyMenu** API function to change the two menu items (George and Ralph) to be owner-draw. The **ModifyMenu** command tries to change the command associated with the menu item, so we need to pass the current command twice to avoid changing it. The new item parameter (the last one) is not used, so we simply pass 0 to the command.

If you run the program now, the two menu items will not have anything displayed on them. Close down the application and add a handler for the George menu item. This will verify that the menu item is still working properly regardless of what we do to it. Add the following code to the handler:

```
void __fastcall TForm1::George1Click(TObject *Sender)
{
    MessageBox(NULL, "You clicked George!", "Info", MB_OK );
}
```

Run the program again and pull down the first menu. You should see nothing. Select the second menu item by moving the mouse down to the bottom of the menu and release the button. You should see the message box telling you that the menu item was clicked. We have at least verified that we didn't break anything—yet.

Drawing The Menu Items

The next step in the process is to add the handlers for measuring and drawing the items in the menu. The process itself is the same as for the owner-draw list box, so we won't go into excruciating detail about what is going on.

Add a handler for the **OnMeasureItem** for the form and give it the name **HandleMeasureItem**. Add the following code to the handler:

```
void __fastcall TForm1::HandleMeasureItem(TMessage& Msg)
{
            MEASUREITEMSTRUCT *lpmis = (LPMEASUREITEMSTRUCT) Msg.LParam;
            lpmis->itemHeight = 12;
    lpmis->itemWidth = 50;
}
```

This method simply modifies the **Measure Item** structure. Notice that because the message sent to us for this method is a simple **TMessage** object, we need to convert the **LParam** portion of the message into a pointer to the structure that we need to work with. Working with owner-draw menus is not quite as clean as working with list box items, but still it's pretty easy.

Next up, add a handler for the **OnDrawItem** method of the form. Give the new handler the name **HandleDrawItem** and add the following code to the handler:

```
void __fastcall TForm1::HandleDrawItem(TMessage& Msg)
{
                DRAWITEMSTRUCT *lpdis = (DRAWITEMSTRUCT *) Msg.LParam;
   TCanvas *canvas = new TCanvas;
   canvas->Handle = lpdis->hDC;
   if ((int)lpdis->itemID == George1->Command )
                canvas->Brush->Color = clRed;
   else
                canvas->Brush->Color = clGreen;

   // Assign the rectangle
   TRect r;
   r.Left = lpdis->rcItem.left;
   r.Top = lpdis->rcItem.top;
   r.Right = lpdis->rcItem.right;
   r.Bottom = lpdis->rcItem.bottom;

   canvas->FillRect(r);
   delete canvas;
}
```

Once again, because the owner-draw menu implementation is not quite as clean as the owner-draw list box, you need to cast a piece of the **TMessage** object structure into a pointer to the **DRAWITEMSTRUCT** object, which holds all of the pieces of the menu drawing code. Once we have the structure, we use the device context handle stored in this object to create our own **Canvas** object to use in the drawing code. Working with the **Canvas** object is a lot easier than working with the underlying device context handle, so this is done solely for our benefit. All we need to do then is determine which color to paint with based on the **itemID** identifier in the structure and then fill in the rectangle that was passed to us in the structure with that color. Easy as pie (or is that pi?).

Changing The Owner-Draw State At Runtime

The neatest part of the whole system is that we're able to modify the behavior of the menu items at runtime. We can toggle a given menu item to be either owner-draw or normal-draw any time we want to. Let's look at how to do that.

Add a handler to the menu item that reads "Make Owner Draw" under the Modify menu. Add the following code to the menu item handler (called **MakeOwnerDraw1Click**):

```
void __fastcall TForm1::MakeOwnerDraw1Click(TObject *Sender)
{
            ModifyMenu(MainMenu1->Handle,
        Ralph1->Command,
        MF_BYCOMMAND | MF_OWNERDRAW,
        Ralph1->Command,
        0);
}
```

If you're thinking that this command looks familiar, you're probably right. This is simply the command we used in the first place to make the item owner-draw. The second menu item, "Make Normal", is the more interesting of the two. Add a handler for it, called **MakeNormal1Click**, and add the following code to the new handler:

```
void __fastcall TForm1::MakeNormal1Click(TObject *Sender)
{
            ModifyMenu(MainMenu1->Handle,
        Ralph1->Command,
        MF_BYCOMMAND | MF_STRING,
        Ralph1->Command,
        "Ralph");

}
```

This is more the normal style of the **ModifyMenu** API function. This function call will reset the state of the Ralph menu item to be a normal string and will set the text to be Ralph. The command remains the same for the menu item because we pass the same command identifier in both the old and new positions. Notice that we pass the **MF_STRING** flag to indicate that we want to change the menu item text to a normal string. Once you compile and run the application, selecting this item will change the first menu to display one color bar and one text string (Ralph).

> **Note:** You may notice that the first time you select the Make Normal menu item and then bring up the first menu, the Ralph item is displayed in a larger than normal font. Moving the cursor down over the item (Ralph) will make it revert to normal font. This appears to be a bug in the Windows95/NT API.

That's all there is to work with and deal with owner-draw menu items in CBuilder. As you can see, they really aren't all that much different from any other kind of owner-draw item. Happy menuing.

Time In A Status Bar

The final example in our tour of the VCL is something that many programmers need in their applications but few seem to know how to implement. In many applications, there is a need to display the current time in one of the panes of the status bar. Although the Windows 95/NT desktop normally displays the current time in the lower right-hand corner, this is not always the case. Users who modify their desktop so that the time is not visible expect the current application to give them that information. CBuilder makes it pretty easy to make those users happy, so doing this for them isn't enough of an inconvenience to justify not putting it into your own application. In this example, we explore the process to display the data for the current time in the status bar. When you're finished, you'll know enough to display pretty much anything you like in the status bar panels at runtime.

> **Note:** You'll find the source code for the Time In Status Bar program in the Chapter4\TimeInAStatusBar\directory on the accompanying CD-ROM for this book.

Figure 4.14 shows the form we'll be using for this example. As you can see, the form has had a status bar, a timer, and three edit fields dropped onto it. The edit fields are there solely to show you that the code we're going to add to the form will have no impact on the performance and running of the application. Set the timer time span property to be 1000 milliseconds (timer units are milliseconds, so this simply indicates to enter 1000 in the property field). This is one full second. For this demonstration, the display will include seconds, although you might prefer to only display hours and minutes. As you'll see, this is up to you.

Add two panels to the status bar component. Make the first panel about three-quarters of the width of the status bar, and allow the second panel to fill the remaining space in the status bar display. The second panel is the one we'll be using to display the time, so make sure that it's wide enough to display the full hour, minutes, and seconds of the current time.

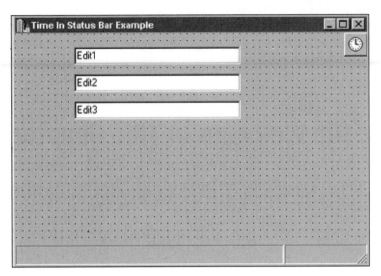

Figure 4.14
The timer in a status bar example.

Once you've set all of the properties for the form, add a single event to the form for the **Timer** event. This event will be kicked off each time the timer time span is met. Although there is no absolute guarantee that this event will occur once each second, it will be close enough for our purposes. The **Timer** event can be delayed if the system is quite busy or if something is eating up a majority of the processing power of the machine.

Add the following code to the handler for the **Timer1Timer** event handler (which is the default name if you simply double-click on the **Timer** event in the Object Inspector):

```
void __fastcall TForm1::Timer1Timer(TObject *Sender)
{
            StatusBar1->Panels->Items[1]->Text = Now().TimeString();
}
```

That's it, the whole example. The **Panels** property of the status bar contains objects that represent the individual panels of the status bar display. Within the **Panels** property, the **Items** property contains information about each panel including, as we see here, the text displayed in the panel. Compile and run the new application and you'll see the time displayed in the panel.

Isn't it amazing that such a tiny amount of code can produce such dramatic effects? This is the best example of component-based development that could be shown. With exactly one line of code written, we have a complete form that displays the current time in a status bar.

What Did We Learn In This Chapter?

Recapping everything that we did in this chapter would involve rewriting the entire chapter, so we'll simply hit the high points of what was covered in this whirlwind tour of the Visual Component Library (VCL) of CBuilder:

- We learned how to create controls dynamically and how to respond to dynamic controls.

- We learned how to trap edit keystrokes to validate edit fields.

- We learned how to handle drag and drop between controls in CBuilder.

- We learned how to handle messages that aren't handled directly by CBuilder events.

- We learned about owner-draw controls and menus and how to set them up in CBuilder.

- Finally, we learned how to use a timer object to update a dynamic display.

HIGH PERFORMANCE

The Standard Template Library

CHAPTER

5

- What's A Template?

- Vectors And Arrays

- Sets And Lists

- Maps To Go

The Standard
Template Library

Borland CBuilder includes, as we've mentioned earlier, a complete ANSI standard C++ compiler. One of the new requirements imposed by the ANSI C++ committee is that each C++ compiler must ship with a standard library implementation. This is intended to ease the problem of moving so-called portable code (such as utility functions and database functions) among compilers with a minimum of fuss. This change is one of the most important made in terms of making C++ a truly portable language among compilers, operating systems, and machines.

One of the parts of the Standard C++ Library is the Standard Template Library (STL), which contains generic classes needed by nearly all programs and systems written. CBuilder includes a complete implementation of the Rogue Wave Tools' STL, which contains classes for strings, containers, and other neat stuff. In this chapter, we begin to explore the STL, first outside of the graphical environment of CBuilder and then later as an addition to form-based application development.

What Is The Standard Template Library?

The STL is a template-based library of utility classes. There are no graphics, components, or anything else in the STL. It is intended to make it as easy as possible to work with a variety of data in a variety of ways. The STL provides the portable **string** class, which allows the user to quit worrying about string overruns in character arrays, how to extract pieces of a string, or anything else string-related. The **string** class is quite prevalent in the CBuilder environment, so you should seriously consider using it (or its related friend **AnsiString**, which is compatible with the VCL) instead of character arrays for strings in your own applications.

The STL's **string** class and its related functionality would be reason enough to use it in your applications and certainly enough reason to learn about it, but the **string** class is only a small fraction of the power of the STL. In addition to strings, the STL also offers complete implementation of arrays (called vectors in STL lingo), linked lists (both one and two directional), queues, maps (which are kind of like dictionaries), and other standard data structures.

All of the STL classes are *templated*. If you've worked with C++ for any length of time, you have probably run across templates, very smart macros that the compiler knows how to work with. To understand what templates are, consider the following scenario. You have an **array** class that stores integer values. It knows how to allocate an integer, store it in memory, retrieve it from memory based on its index into the array, and find a given integer in the array. This class works quite well for storing your integers, and you've been using it for some time, but now you need to store floating-point numbers as well as integers. You really have two choices. First, you could copy the entire integer array class and change all occurrences of the **int** keyword into the **double** keyword. Or you could work out some sort of fantastic system whereby you cast doubles into integers and lose all of their precision (making bank customers very happy, I'm sure).

Instead of going through the pain of cloning a complete class for a new data type, wouldn't it be nice if you could just have the compiler substitute the keyword **double** wherever it saw the keyword **integer** in your class? Well, perhaps not everywhere— and therein lies the rub. Let's take a look at a class definition for a portion of our mythical **integer array** class:

```
class IntegerArray
{
    int *pArrayOfInts;
    int  nNumberOfInts;
public:
    IntegerArray( int nNumberOfInts );
    ~IntegerArray(void);
    void Add( int nIntToAdd );
    void Remove( int nIntToRemove);
    int Find( int nIntToFind ); // Return the index of the found number
    int GetAt( int nIndex );
    void SetAt( int nIndex, int nIntegerToAdd);

};
```

Now, assume that you now need to store an array of floating-point numbers. You would probably do this by simply copying the previous code header to something that supported floating-point numbers (doubles). You would probably end up with another block of code that looks like this:

```
class DoubleArray
{
    double *pArrayOfDoubles;
    int  nNumberOfDoubles;
public:
    DoubleArray( int nNumberOfDoubles);
    ~DoubleArray(void);
    void Add( double dDoubleToAdd );
    void Remove( double dDoubleToRemove);
    int Find( double dDoubleToFind );  // Return the index of the
                                       // found number
    double GetAt( int nIndex );
    void SetAt( int nIndex, double dDoubleToAdd);

};
```

Of course, once you had implemented both the **integer** and **double** versions of the classes, you would immediately find a need for a class that stored strings. Then you would need one that worked with some object that you were storing in your application. The list could go on and on forever (or until you went insane implementing the classes).

Wouldn't it be nicer if you could write the class once and then have all of the other classes automatically generated from some sort of base copy? When you make copies of a car or other device, the base device is often called a template. This term, therefore, is appropriate for classes constructed from instructions stored in a base device. In the previous example, we would create a single class called **Array**, which worked from a single argument (the template argument), which represented the type that we want to work with. Then we could write the **template** class as:

```
template <class _Type>
class Array
{
    _Type *pArrayOfType;
    int  nNumberOfType;
public:
    Array( int nNumberOfType);
    ~Array(void);
    void Add( _Type tTypeObject );
    void Remove( _Type tTypeObject);
```

```
    int Find( _Type tTypeObject );  // Return the index of the
                                     // found number
    _Type GetAt( int nIndex );
    void SetAt( int nIndex, _Type tTypeObject);
};
```

When you wanted to create a new class of this templated class, you would use an argument, much as you do with a function. Therefore, to create an array of integers, you would write

```
Array<int> intArray;
```

while an array of doubles would look like this

```
Array<double> doubleArray;
```

and finally, an array of some arbitrary type such as the **string** class would look like:

```
Array<string> stringArray;
```

Something like that really would be nice, wouldn't it? You would probably never have to write another **Array** class. Well, that is exactly the functionality provided by the STL. This library contains templated versions of all of the common data structures needed by most applications. To use an array of integers, for example, you would use the **vector** class. To create a map of strings to integers, you would use the **map** class, and so forth.

Why Use The Standard Template Library?

While all of the generated code is certainly a powerful inducement to use the STL, there are other more persuasive arguments. When you're writing utility code, such as file handling functionality, database functionality, or simple business object classes, you'll often find that you need to support multiple platforms. The code might need to work on Windows 95 under CBuilder, along with the need to use the objects in ActiveX controls for the Internet and Unix applications. If you were to use proprietary data structures, such as those found in either OWL or MFC, you would be out of luck when you moved to other compilers or operating systems. Using the STL, which is available in source format for free from Hewlett Packard (the originators of the STL), you can be assured that the same code will run on any of the platforms you need it for. That routine you wrote for your beloved Amiga 2000 (yes, I really own one and yes, it still works) will work, unchanged, on the Pentium II you just bought yesterday.

If that is not a powerful enough inducement to use the STL, consider this. Borland was so impressed by the power and flexibility of the STL that it provides no other components in the VCL for handling arrays, lists, and so forth. You can use STL components directly in VCL components as well. In short, there is no good reason not to use the STL in your applications.

Getting Started: Exploring The Classes Of The STL

Before we actually start writing applications with the STL, let's take a few moments to explore the classes available to you in the STL and what those classes can be used for in your applications. We'll take each class one at a time and look at the methods available to the class as well as what the class is best used for—and not used for.

First let's consider the **string** class, which provides methods for processing characters. This class is essentially a smart, flexible character array. Rather than forcing you to limit yourself to a fixed number of characters for an array, the **string** class provides the ability to support any length of string (up to the maximum allowed allocation block for the operating system you're working with). The **string** class is quite similar to the Visual Basic string type and provides many of the same sorts of functions for manipulating the character data stored in the string.

Table 5.1 shows a list of the more commonly used functions of the **string** class, along with a description of what the function does for you.

The **string** class is the most useful generic class in the STL for most applications. It removes all of the messy code that we once wrote to access character strings, manipulate them, and the worry that we'll run over the end of a string and overwrite memory at the other end.

Let's look at a very simple example of a string in use:

```
#include <string>
#include <stdio.h>
#include <stdlib.h>
#include <string>
using namespace std;

int main(void)
{
   // Assign a character string to a string object
   string s = "Hello world";
```

```
// Get the first word of the string
int nWordEnd = s.find(' ');

string sub_string = s.substr(0,nWordEnd);

// Print out the results
printf("Original String: %s\n", s.c_str());
printf("SubString of First Word: %s\n", sub_string.c_str());

return 0;
}
```

Table 5.1   Commonly used **string** class methods.

operator[]	Allows access to individual characters in the string for either reading or writing access
c_str()	Converts the string into a char * for use with functions that cannot directly handle string objects
append	Appends characters to the end of a string
operator=	Provides a method for assigning other strings, character arrays, and even numeric values to a string
insert	Allows you to insert characters or other strings inside a string variable
erase	Allows you to remove one or more characters from a given string at a given position
replace	Allows you to replace one or more characters from a string at a given position
length (or size)	Returns the number of characters stored in a string
empty	Indicates if the string contains any characters
find	Allows you to find a given character or string within the specified string
rfind	Like find, but does its searching from the end of the string backwards
find_first_of	Allows you to find one of a collection of characters in a string. Useful for searching for word breaks, for example
substr	Returns a sub-string of a given string. Very similar to the Basic substr function
find_first_not_of	Allows you to find the first character in a string which is not in a given list of characters
compare	Allows you to compare two strings (also supported by operator !=, operator <, operator >)

This example shows off several of the important uses of **string** objects. First, you see that we can directly assign a character string (The "Hello world" string) to a **string** object. This makes it easy to use strings with data in our application.

The next thing we see is the use of the find method of the **string** object. The **find** method (and its related method, **rfind**) will find the first occurrence of a given character in a string. The return from the method is the position (0 based) of the character it found in the string or -1 if no matching character could be found in the string.

The **substr** method returns a copy of a piece of the string starting at the position specified in the first argument to the method and running for the number of characters specified in the second argument. If you leave off the second argument, the string returns the characters until the end of the string, making it equivalent to the BASIC function **Right$()**.

Finally, to print out the string, we use our old friend **printf** to print the string as a character array (the **%s** specifier in the **printf** format string) by using the **c_str** method to convert the string to a character string. I prefer to use **printf** in MS-DOS style applications. If you prefer to use the more modern streams such as **cout**, you could rewrite the previous lines as:

```
cout << "Original String: " << s << endl;
cout << "SubString of First Word: " << sub_string << endl;
```

Note that you do not need to use the **c_str** method in this case, as strings have overloaded operator methods for the << and >> streaming operators.

Working With Vectors

In the STL, variable arrays are represented by the **vector** class, which allows you to access items of any type (although only a single type per **vector** object) in either a sequential or random-access manner. Vectors are used in your application anywhere that you would normally use the array modifier for a type. For example, if you were storing an array of 100 integers, your program might contain a statement such as:

```
int nItems[ 100 ];
```

This is an error-prone statement, however. What happens a bit later when you suddenly discover that you really needed to store 200 items? You could use an allocated block of memory, such as:

```
int *pnItems = new int[100];
```

Then, if you wanted to make the array bigger, you could do something like:

```
delete pnItems;
pnItems = new int[ nSomeNewSize ];
```

The problem here is that when you delete all of those items you'll lose the values that they hold. Alternatively, you could revert to the old C style **malloc** and **free** functions:

```
int *pnItems = (int *)malloc( 100 * sizeof(int) );
```

And reallocating the items then is possible using the **realloc** method:

```
int *pnItems = realloc( pnItems, nSomeNewSize * sizeof(int) );
```

This method also has its problems. First of all, you need to remember to include the size of the integer in the allocation. Secondly, there is no way to tell if the items have been freed later on. Finally, there is the issue of working with **malloc** and **free** versus **new** and **delete**. All of these issues are serious enough that the STL contains a complete templatized version of the array class called **vector**. In the previous example, we would replace the declaration of the array of integers with the following statement instead:

```
vector<int> nItems;
```

This allocates a variably sized array of integers. To add items to the array, use the insert method:

```
nItems.insert( nItems.end(), 12 )
```

This statement appends the value 12 to the end of the array. If you've already set a value, you can access it either to read or write the value using the [] **operators**. For example, suppose that we had statements such as these to set the values of array elements:

```
Items.insert( nItems.end(), 1 );
nItems.insert( nItems.end(), 2 );
```

```
nItems.insert( nItems.end(), 3 );
nItems.insert( nItems.end(), 4 );
```

This sets up four elements in our array with the values 1 through 4. We could then modify the third element in the array using the **operator**[] and the index of the item (0 based):

```
nItems[2] = 5;
cout << nItems[2];
```

The previous two statements will assign the third element of the array to be 5 and will then print out (to the standard output stream) the value of that array element. This example should print the value 5.

Table 5.2 shows the most important methods of the **vector** class along with a description of what those methods do for you.

Table 5.2 Important **vector** class methods.

insert	Adds new data into the array
size	Returns the current number of entries in the array
operator[]	Indexes into the array to return individual entries for either reading or writing
operator=(vector)	Copies one vector into another
at	Same as operator[]
begin	Returns the beginning of the vector
end	Returns the end of the vector
capacity	Returns the allocated size of the vector. Can be different from size if reserve is used
reserve	Pre-allocates a fixed number of entries for the vector which can be changed at runtime
empty	Indicates if the vector does (FALSE) or does not (TRUE) contain data
erase	Removes entries from a vector
count	A utility function that counts the number of entries of a given type in the vector
max_size	Returns the maximum allowable size for this vector. Normally the total amount of memory available on the system for allocation
swap	Allows two vectors to swap their data quickly and efficiently
resize	Resizes a vector to a new fixed size, with an optional parameter to initialize the new values

The Replace Example

Now that we've examined the **string** and **vector** classes, it's fitting that we look at an example that uses both of them in order to understand how you work with the **vector** and **string** classes.

Create a new console application in CBuilder. To do this, select File|New and select Console Application from the first tab of choices. CBuilder will create a new project file and a main program file for the application called project.cpp. This program will only run in the console, or MS-DOS box, mode of Windows 95 and NT. Add the following code to the project.cpp source file:

```
#include <stdio.h>
#include <stdlib.h>
#include <string.h>
#include <vector>
using namespace std;

class StringReplacement
{
private:
    string strSearchText;
    string strReplaceText;

public:
    StringReplacement(void)
    {
    }
    StringReplacement( string search, string replace )
    {
        strSearchText = search;
        strReplaceText = replace;
    }
    void DoReplace( string& text )
    {
        int i=0;
        string strComplete = "";
        while ( i < text.size() )
        {
            if ( !strncmp(text.c_str()+i, strSearchText.c_str(),
                strSearchText.size()) )
            {
                i += strSearchText.size();
                strComplete += strReplaceText;
```

```
         }
         else
         {
            strComplete += text[i];
            i++;
         }
      }
      text = strComplete;
   }
};


vector< StringReplacement, allocator<StringReplacement> > strList;

int main(int argc, char **argv)
{
   if ( argc < 2 )
   {
      printf("Usage: repl <input-file> <definitions-file>\n");
      return -1;
   }

   FILE *fp = fopen(argv[1], "r");
   if ( fp == NULL )
   {
      printf("Unable to open file %s\n", argv[1] );
      return -1;
   }
   strList.insert( strList.end(), StringReplacement("$$Author$$",
     "Matt Telles") );
   strList.insert( strList.end(), StringReplacement("$$Program$$",
     "Matt's Test") );

   char szBuffer[ 256 ];
   while ( !feof(fp) )
   {
      if ( fgets(szBuffer, 255, fp) == NULL )
         break;
      string s = szBuffer;

      for ( int i=0; i<strList.size(); ++i )
        strList[i].DoReplace( s );
      printf("%s", s.c_str());

   }
```

```
    fclose(fp);
    return 0;
}
```

There are a couple of important points in this demonstration program. The program, by the way, will search for and replace all occurrences of a given set of strings in a file with another set of strings. We are using the vector here to store objects and the objects to maintain strings. You can see how we iterate through the vector, using the **size** and **operator[]** methods of the vector. In addition, you can see how the vector can store different kinds of data, even though that data is not derived from a common **base** class. If you're accustomed to working with other systems where the various data structures require a common derived base class to work with, you know how nice this can be.

To run the replace program, open an MS-DOS window and run the project1.exe program. You'll need to create two files, the first being a replacement file that contains entries of the form

```
oldvalue=newvalue
```

where **oldvalue** is the value you want to replace and **newvalue** is the value you want to replace the old value with. For example, to replace all occurrences of the string **$$Author$$** with the name Matt Telles you would write:

```
$$Author$$=Matt Telles
```

This program is nice as a template expander for documents, source files that require headers, and other cases. The code in it could be stripped out and placed into a utility function that could be used in your own applications to generate standardized headers for your files, to cite but one example. In the second file you would have text, such as:

```
The author of this program was: $$Author$$ and it was written on $$Date$$
```

Then, running it through the replace program, the output would become:

```
The author of this program was: Matt Telles and it was written on Today.
```

That's really all there is to talk about vectors. Like most of the STL, it's fairly easy to use and rather intuitive to work with. Think of vectors when writing any classes or components in CBuilder that require an array of indeterminate (or later modified) size.

Working With Lists

The next major component of the STL that we're going to look at is the **list** class. Lists are the infamous singly linked lists that everyone and their brother or sister has had to write for a basic computer science course. The general idea of a list is that you have a starting point to the list (usually called the head of the list) and then a series of entries in the list (called nodes of the list). Each entry contains a pointer to the next entry in the list so that the list can be traversed easily in one direction.

The STL version of the **list** class is quite rich in its implementation. It offers the ability to add entries to the end of the list, insert entries at the beginning of a list, and even insert entries in the middle of a linked list. In addition, the **list** class offers sorting and searching capabilities as well as tests for inclusion (whether or not a given entity exists in the list).

The advantage to the **list** class is flexibility. If you're going to access data in a sequential manner and have no idea how many entries you're likely to have, use a list. If you are going to create a data structure that requires entries to be inserted into the middle of the elements already present, use a list rather than a vector. Vectors require that all entries be stored in a single block with each entry immediately after the previous one in memory. Inserting an entry into a vector, therefore, requires that all entries be moved around after that entry. In a list, entries point at each other rather than occupying physically adjacent memory location. For this reason, inserting into a list is not an expensive operation. Appending and inserting at the front of the list are also quick operations for this reason.

In general, you need to know how to put things into a list and get them back. To put things into the list, you use the insert method. This is exactly the same method as we saw in the **vector** class, and you use it the same way. For example, to create a new list containing integers, we would write:

```
list<int, allocator<int> > intList;
```

The type of the elements in this list will be of type **int** or be integers. The **allocator<int>** argument to the list constructor gives the **list** class added flexibility by allowing it to allocate new integers in a dynamic fashion. The STL provides the allocator class to create new instances of a type, but you can provide your own allocation scheme if you would like. Normally, you would simply provide a templated instance of the allocator class.

A note about allocators: The **allocate** class requires that your object be able to be created with no arguments to the constructor. This means that for a class **Foo**, you must have a class definition like this:

```
class Foo
{
public:
    Foo(int x);
    Foo(void);
}
```

If you don't have a void constructor (as they are called), the compiler will complain about some esoteric statements within the list header file and your application will not compile. If this happens, add a void constructor. In addition, if your class requires special handling for copies, be sure to implement a copy constructor:

```
Foo(const Foo& aFoo);
```

You would need a copy constructor if your class contained other objects or pointers that were allocated by the class. The default copy constructor does a bitwise copy of each element in the class, which can lead to problems in the de-allocation phase of the class (the destructor).

In any case, to add a new element to the list you would use the insert method:

```
intList.insert( intList.begin(), 12 );
```

This statement would put the value 12 at the beginning of the list, pushing all other elements of the list back one place in the list hierarchy. Likewise, the following statement

```
intList.insert( intList.end(), 12 );
```

would place the value 12 at the end of the list following all other entries in the list. It's important to note that each time you use begin or end insert, you're changing the place of the former beginning or end value. Therefore, when you do:

```
intList.insert( intList.begin(), 11 );
intList.insert( intList.begin(), 12 );
intList.insert( intList.begin(), 13 );
```

You end up with a list containing the values: 13, 12, and 11, in that order.

With all of that in place, let's take a look at some of the available methods of the **list** class and what they can do. Table 5.3 lists the most important of the **list** methods and a description of what each method does.

The previous functions can be used with any list. They provide a powerful set of operations that allow you to do almost anything that you need to do with any given list. For your own classes, you can also derive a class from one of the lists for a specific type and then implement the methods you need for that type only.

Table 5.3   Important **list** class methods.

insert	Inserts a new element at a specified position in the list
push_back	A commonly used method that is the equivalent of an insert at the end of a list
push_front	A commonly used method that is the equivalent of an insert at the beginning of the list
splice	A way to insert one list (or pieces of one list) into another list
swap	A way to exchange one list for another in a very efficient manner
remove	This method will remove all entries in a list which fit a given value
remove_if	This method will remove all entries in a list with a given value which fit a given predicate
erase	This method removes a given entry in a list
unique	This utility operation will remove all but one entry in a list for each value
size	Returns the number of elements in the list
empty	Indicates if the list currently does (FALSE) or does not (TRUE) have any elements
resize	Forces the list to have a specified number of elements
front	Returns the first element in the list
back	Returns the last element in the list
sort	Sorts a list into ascending order. Can be used with a function to compare elements or by default sorting order
find	Returns the position of the first element in a list that matches requested criteria
reverse	This method will reverse the order of the list, making the last element the first and the first element the last and all of the other elements likewise swapped
for_each	This method will apply a given function to all elements in a list

Let's look at a complete example of how to use lists. Create another console application in CBuilder and add the following code to the project.cpp file:

```
#include <stdio.h>
#include <string.h>
#include <stdlib.h>
#include <list>
#include <string>
using namespace std;

int main(void)
{
    list<string, allocator<string> > listStrings;

    listStrings.insert( listStrings.end(), "First" );
    listStrings.insert( listStrings.end(), "Second" );
    listStrings.insert( listStrings.end(), "Third" );
    listStrings.insert( listStrings.end(), "Fourth" );
    listStrings.insert( listStrings.end(), "Fifth" );
    listStrings.insert( listStrings.end(), "Sixth" );

    list<string, allocator<string> >::iterator list_iterator;
    list_iterator = listStrings.begin();
    while ( list_iterator != listStrings.end() )
    {
        printf("String = <%s>\n", (*list_iterator).c_str());
        // advance( list_iterator, 1 );
        list_iterator++;
    }


    return 0;
}
```

This simple example illustrates several of the important features of using the list. First of all, you might notice that just below the include line for the list header file, you'll find the line:

```
using namespace std;
```

This line is essential for compiling STL applications with CBuilder. In the CBuilder system, Borland has chosen to wrap all of the third-party pieces, such as the STL, with **namespace** wrappers. This is good for you in that it means that the third-party libraries that you use in your applications will not conflict with other libraries for which you have no source code.

A **namespace** is simply a higher level of **scope**. For example, in the following simple program, there are three elements called **foo**:

```
class MyFoo
{
    int foo; // 1
public:
    MyFoo();
}

int foo; // 2

int main()
{
    int foo = 2; //3
}
int func()
{
    foo = 3;
}
MyFoo::MyFoo()
{
    foo = 4;
}
```

Depending on where you are in the program, the name **foo** means something differ-ent. Within the **main** function, the **foo** is the local variable **foo**. Outside of the **main** function, in another function **func**, the **foo** is the file level variable **foo** (shown with the comment // 2). Finally, within a **class** method, the **member** variable **foo** takes precedence as shown in the line marked with the comment // 1 and found in the **member** function **MyFoo** (the constructor).

A **namespace** is quite similar to the notion of **scope**, but it allows you to wrap only selected regions of the program. In the case of the STL, Borland has wrapped the functions within the **namespace** std. To access the members of the **namespace** std, you use the standard scoping operator ".". For example, to use the class **list** defined in the **namespace** std, we could write:

```
std::list< int, std::allocator<int> > intList.
```

In fact, the previous code will compile, link, and run perfectly in the CBuilder environment. Alternatively, if you don't like using the **std::** scope everywhere that you refer to one of the **STL** classes, you can use the other method, which is to tell the compiler that you're referring to things in the std **namespace**. This is accomplished by the using **namespace** <name> statement, which tells the compiler to look automatically in **namespace** <name> for any symbol that it doesn't recognize. The problem with this approach is that it eliminates the ability to keep third-party libraries separated. If I had another **namespace** that contained the **list** class and I wanted to use both of them, I would still be forced to fully qualify the classes from the second **namespace**. In short, **namespaces** are a good idea that still can lead to some work on the part of the programmer.

The Iterator

The second part of the example program that is important to note is the use of the **iterator** class. In the code lines that read

```
list<string, allocator<string> >::iterator list_iterator;
list_iterator = listStrings.begin();
```

we are defining a new object called an iterator, which refers to the beginning of the list. In the STL, an iterator is a way to walk through the elements in the list without modifying the order in which they occur in the list. You can also have multiple iterators referring to the same list and maintaining different positions in the list. For example, I could define two iterators and step forward and backward through the list at the same time by writing:

```
list<string, allocator<string> >::iterator forward_list_iterator;
list<string, allocator<string> >::iterator backward_list_iterator;
forward_list_iterator = listStrings.begin();
backward_list_iterator = listStrings.end();
```

To work with an iterator, you can either use the operators ++ and -- to move forward and backward. Iterators move sequentially, so there is no direct way to move from point A to point C if point B is in the way. Iterators are important because they provide a way to manipulate the data in a list (or other data structure) without working with the data structure directly. Therefore, you can use an iterator anyplace that you like without really knowing anything about how the underlying data structure is implemented.

Iterators can be of different types. Some move only forward, others only backward. Some can be used for reading only, while others can be used to modify the data structure that they work on. In all cases, however, the operator ++ will step through the data structure moving from the first element to the last. The operator -- will move backward through the data structure moving from the last element to the first. When an iterator is "pointing" at a given data element as seen in the example **forward_list_iterator** in the previous code, you can get at the underlying data type (in this case a string) using the operator "*". For example:

```
forward_list_iterator = listStrings.begin();
string s = (*forward_list_iterator);
```

Assuming that the list had elements, the string **s** would now have the same value as the first string in the list. Because the * operator returns the object itself, you can directly work with the list entry by manipulating the **iterator** object:

```
(*iterator).c_str()
```

If the iterator is pointing at a string element in the list, the previous code will return a character pointer that represents the string at that position in the list. In our previous example, therefore, the iterator steps though each element of the list, passing a character pointer representing the element to the **printf** function, which then prints the value to the standard output. The result of the output of this program should be:

```
First
Second
Third
Fourth
Fifth
Sixth
```

To test this theory, compile and link the program by doing a Build|Make in the CBuilder IDE. Open an MS-DOS command window and run the program by typing project1. You should see the output appear in the window, and it should look exactly like the output we just showed in the previous list.

That's pretty much all there is to say about lists and list iterators. When you need a list in your own application, just add it to the class and go. Lists are probably best suited for applications containing a variable amount of data, which normally step through the data in a sequential manner, and need the ability to remove and add data at any position in the list. Address books and inventory systems are good examples of list-based application types.

Working With Maps

The next thing we're going to consider in the STL discussion is that of maps. Maps are great. They tell you how to get from New York to Colorado in the shortest possible time, and where that wonderful road goes off the interstate. They'll keep you from getting lost and help you get to where you're going.

Okay, I didn't really mean that kind of map. The map is also a data structure in the STL that provides a convenient and powerful way to map one kind of data to another. Rather than trying to explain the map concept, it's easier to use an example to show what maps do for you (besides getting you across Interstate 80, I mean).

Table 5.4 lists the important methods of the **map** class in the STL.

Here is an example of a map:

```
#include <stdio.h>
#include <stdlib.h>
#include <string.h>
#include <string>
#include <map>

int main(void)
{
    map<string, string, less<string>, allocator<string> > stringMap;
    stringMap["Kirk"]   = "William Shatner";
    stringMap["McCoy"]  = "DeForest Kelley";
    stringMap["Spock"]  = "Leonard Nimoy";
    stringMap["Scotty"] = "James Doohan";
    stringMap["Sulu"]   = "George Takei";
    stringMap["Uhura"]  = "Nichelle Nichols";

    printf("Enter a character: ");
    char szBuffer[20];
    gets(szBuffer);
    if ( stringMap[szBuffer].length() )
        printf("That's really: %s\n", stringMap[szBuffer].c_str());
    else
        printf("I don't know that character!\n");
    return 0;

}
```

Table 5.4 Important **map** class methods.

empty	Indicates if a map does (FALSE) or does not (TRUE) contain data
count	Returns the number of elements presently found in the map
insert	Adds a new member to a map
erase	Removes an existing member from a map
find	Does a search for a given key to a map
operator[]	Finds an entry corresponding to a key value in the map
lower_bound	Returns the lower bound of the map. The lower bound is the first entry that matches a given key value
max_size	Returns the maximum allowable size of the map (usually the maximum memory available on the system for allocation)
rbegin	Returns the last entry in the map (beginning from the end)
rend	Returns the first entry in the map (starting from end of the map)
size	Returns the currently allocated size of the map, usually the number of entries in the map
swap	Exchanges the members in one map for the members of another map object
upper_bound	Returns the last matching item for a given key value
operator=	Assigns one map object to another, copying all data values from the first to the second map
operator<<	Streaming operator allowing a map entry to be written to an output stream
begin	Returns the first entry in the map
end	Returns the last entry in the map
key_comp	Compares two entries using the map comparison function
for_each	Performs a given action on each entry in the map

In this example, we're initializing a **map** object, using the key value as a string. The key value in this example is the last name (or in Spock's case, both names) of the character in the original Star Trek series (just in case you didn't recognize them), and the value assigned to each key is the name of the actor that played that character in the series. We then ask the user to enter a character name and print out the name of the actor. If the character name is not found, the returned string will be empty. We treat this as an error condition and tell the user that there is no character found by that name.

This example shows several interesting aspects of the **map** object. First of all, you really treat a **map** as an array, with potentially non-integer indices into the array. In this case we're using a string as the index. The second point that quickly becomes clear is that there can be only a single entry for each key value in a map, or otherwise you would be unable to determine which entry corresponded to a given array index. Imagine using an array of integers and getting two answers for the statement **array[0]**.

Maps contain ordered pairs of data. By ordering them we can make sure that the items are in a given alphabetical order, for example, for printing. In addition, we can treat a map as a dictionary, retrieving definitions for "words."

Why Use Maps?

There are numerous very good examples of using maps. In our vector example, for instance, we treated the search and replacement strings in the replace program as an array. We could have as easily created a map of search string keys with replacement strings as the values. Because maps are ordered, searching in a map for a given key value is quite fast. This makes the map an excellent choice for simple structures that need quick data lookups. Macro processors, dictionary lookups, and even spreadsheet grids can benefit from the structure and speed of a map.

Another class in the STL, **multimap**, allows multiple entries for a given key. If you have a situation that seems ideal for a map but cannot guarantee a single key for each entry in the system (say a telephone number lookup that doesn't necessarily store the area code, for example), you should consider the **multimap** class instead. In general, the methods and accessors for the **multimap** class are exactly the same as that of the **map** class.

The Almighty Set

The next class we're going to consider in our whirlwind tour of the STL is the **set** class. Sets represent the equivalent of the mathematical set type. Sets contain single entries of a given value. A set may not have multiple keys with the same value. In order to use the **set** class in your own application, include the **<set>** header file:

```
#include <set>
```

As I just mentioned, sets store a single entry for a given key. This makes sets perfect for things that require that you know whether an entry was included or excluded, such as an option list for a program. Other uses for sets might include a spellchecker, grammar checker, or a test program. Sets can be combined in either a union or an intersection. The union of two sets is a set containing all unique members of both sets, while the intersection of two sets is a set containing only the members common to both sets.

Suppose, for example, that you needed to keep track of all of the words that a user searched for in a program. This is a common situation for a search dialog, which normally contains a drop-down combo box that holds the last n search strings. You don't want to use up the n values with repeat searches, so you could use a set to store the data instead of simply using an array or list to store it and be assured that there would be only a single entry of each search string maintained.

Let's take a look at the available methods of the **set** class first, and then talk a little about how you use them. Table 5.5 lists the important methods of the **set** class of the STL.

Table 5.5 Important **set** class methods.

begin	Returns the starting position of the set (the first element in the set)
end	Returns the ending position of the set (the last element in the set)
count	Returns the number of elements in the set which match a given key
empty	Indicates if the set is (FALSE) or is not (TRUE) empty of elements
insert	Adds a new element to the set if possible. If the element already exists the insert will fail and the new value will not be added
erase	Removes an entry from the set if it exists. Otherwise the remove fails and there is no effect on the set
size	Returns the number of elements held by the set
find	Returns the first element matching a given key or an empty key if the element could not be found
lower_bound	For normal sets, same as find. For multisets, returns the first entry which matches a given key
upper_bound	For normal sets, same as find. For multisets, returns the last entry which matches a given key
rbegin	Returns the starting position of the end of the set (the last element in the set)
rend	Returns the starting position of the beginning of the set (the first element in the set)
includes	Tests if one set contains all of the elements of another set
set_union	Returns the union of two sets

(continued)

Table 5.5 Important **set** class methods (*continued*).

set_intersection	Returns the intersection of two sets
set_difference	Returns all elements in one set that are not in another set
accumulate	Reduce the set to a single value
count_if	Count the number of elements that satisfy a given condition
swap	Moves all elements from one set to another and vice versa
operator=	Copies the contents of a given set into another set, producing a copy of the first set

Here is an example of using a set. In this example, we allow the user to enter values and try to add them into the set. If the value cannot be entered, we print out an error message and continue. The process continues until the user enters a signal value (DONE), which indicates data entry is finished. At that point, we print out the complete set of values that were valid that have been entered into the set. To create this example, create a new console application in CBuilder and add the following code to the project1.cpp source file:

```
#include <stdio.h>
#include <string.h>
#include <stdlib.h>

#include <set>
#include <string>


int main(void)
{
    // Define the set object we will be using.
    std::set<std::string, less<std::string> > setString;

    // Loop through user input, checking for duplicate entries
    int bDone = FALSE;

    while ( !bDone )
    {
        // Get an entry from the user
        printf("Enter a value to search for (Enter DONE to finish):");

        // Store result in string
        char szBuffer[ 256 ];
        gets(szBuffer);
```

```
            // See if they wanted out
            if ( !stricmp(szBuffer, "done") )
            {
               bDone = TRUE;
               continue;
            }

            // Try to put it into the set
            int bOkToAdd = setString.insert( szBuffer );
            if ( bOkToAdd == FALSE )
            {
               printf("Unable to add: Duplicate Entry!\n");
            }

        }

        // When all done, print them out
        std::set<std::string, std::less<std::string> >::iterator setIterator;
        setIterator = setString.begin();

        // Loop through all entries
        while ( setIterator != setString.end() )
        {
           printf("Entry: %s\n", (*setIterator).c_str() );
           setIterator++;
        }
        return 0;

    }
```

There are a couple of interesting points in this example. First of all, the example does not use the **using namespace std;** statement that we have been using up to this point when working with the STL. There are several reasons for this. First of all, the **using** statement really isn't intended to be used in new code; it's simply an easier way to make things compile properly. You really should get used to working with **namespaces**, an issue that we'll discuss shortly.

The second point of interest is that the set is nothing but a normal data structure. You can insert into it and declare an **iterator** for it. This is important because too many people seem to have the idea that you use a set simply to check whether data values exist. The **iterator** class works with sets the same way that it works with any of the other STL data structure classes.

The final point of interest in the set is that this is one of the few cases where we actually use the data structure itself to validate input. In general, your normal data structure classes (**list, vector**, etc.) don't have any sort of built-in validation. The user could type in any old string and the **list** or **vector** classes would happily place that entry at the end of the list. In the set **class**, as in the **map** class we looked at previously, only unique entries can be stored. Similar to the **map** class, however, a **multiset** variant exists, which allows duplicate values to be stored in the set. This would be an extremely rare occurrence, as other ordered data structures such as the **list** are better suited to this job.

A Momentary Pause: Namespaces And C++

We've examined two ways of working with the **namespace** issue in the STL, but it's important to consider the underlying issue. A **namespace** in C++ is really just a superclass that contains nested classes. In the following, we are creating a superclass called **fred**:

```
namespace fred
{
    class A
    {
    }
    class B
    {
    }
}
```

The code contains two sub-classes defined as **class A** and **class B**. A **namespace** is just a class whose data members are all public. As a result, I can refer to the A class within **fred** as **fred::A** and the B class within fred as **fred::B**. Why is this important? Imagine that you have the previous class definition in your own library (try to ignore the fact that your manager wouldn't let you name a class A or B). Now, a third-party library is needed in your application. This third-party class library, which does not ship with source code, contains the following declaration:

```
namespace thirdpartylib
{
    class A
    {
    }
```

```
class B
{
  }
}
```

Obviously, you have a problem. There are two class A's and two class B's, and you'll need to go through all of your source code and change the name of all variables of these types, modify all classes that refer to these two classes, and change all functions and methods which use the classes to use some new name. Right? Wrong. The **namespaces** used in these two examples are different. For example, to use the class **A** in your code, you would have had to have written **fred::A**. To use the third-party class library class **A**, you would need to write **thirdpartylib::A**. These two names are different to the compiler, and therefore the whole thing works the way it's supposed to.

But wait, I can hear you screaming. Do you mean that all the way through the implementation of the **A** and **B** classes you have to write ugly things like:

```
// Void constructor for the A class in the fred namespace
fred::A::A(void)
{
}
```

The answer to this is no. A **namespace** encloses things, so you can accomplish this same job by simply wrapping the header and source files with the **namespace** declaration. We already looked at the header file case; the source file would look quite similar:

```
namespace fred
{
// Void constructor for the A class in the fred namespace
A::A(void)
{
}
}
```

Note that you can open and close **namespaces** in a file. All entries are just appended to the **namespace** area. For example, if you had two classes defined in a single source file that belonged to different **namespaces** (not that you should do something like this, but you can) you would write:

```
namespace fred  // Open namespace fred
{
  // Code for namespace fred
} // Close namespace fred

namespace george
{
  // Code for namespace george
} // Close namespace george

// More code.
```

There is one more issue involved in opening and closing **namespaces**. If you want to use a class declaration from another **namespace**, you might think that you could write something like this:

```
namespace fred
{
    class george::A;  // Import the A class from the george namespace

    class Foo
    {
        george::A aGeorgeA;
    }
}
```

It doesn't work this way. Although the **namespace** can generally be treated as a superclass-type structure, it really isn't one. A single **namespace** can be open at a given time, and forward class definitions cannot contain **namespace** qualifiers. How do you get around this? The answer is obvious once you think about it. You close the current **namespace** and open another one.

```
namespace fred
{
    // Fred stuff
}

namespace george
{
    class A;  // forward declare A in george
}

// Now you can write
```

```
namespace fred
{
    class A
    {
        george::A aGeorgeA;
    }
}
```

The previous code should compile and work with any ANSI standard C++ compiler, of which CBuilder is one. All of this leads up to what the **using** statement is and why you shouldn't be using it.

The Using Statement

The **using** statement in C++ literally strips away a **namespace** from a given block of code. If you have a bunch of classes defined using the **namespace** std, for example, the statement

```
using namespace std;
```

allows you to refer to any class in the std **namespace** without qualifying it with the std:: modifier. This change will also impact other classes and **namespaces** in the system. In our imaginary fred/george **namespace** issue shown previously, for example, suppose that we wrote:

```
using namespace fred;
using namespace george;

int func(void)
{
    A anAObject;
}
```

At this point, what is the A in the **func** function? Is it the **fred A** or the **george A**? The answer is that we don't know, so the compiler will choke all over it. It can be even worse if you have a class **A** outside of any **namespace**. Suppose, for example, that you wrote your own **list** class that did something other than what the STL **list** class implemented. Now, if the user puts a using statement for the std **namespace**, the **list** class is not directly accessible. You would still need to use the **scoping** operator to pick out the **list** class that you really wanted, which defeats the purpose of the whole **namespace** idea in the first place.

As a result of all of this discussion, I would recommend that you bite the bullet and use the **scope** resolution operator std:: to use the STL classes in your own applications. The **using** statement was intended not for new development but rather for existing bodies of code that work with header files that have been **namespace**-wrapped. If you had a program written several years ago using the STL, you could fix the problem of the std **namespace** by adding a **using** statement to it. For new development, however, you should respect the **namespace** issue by fully qualifying the class that you are using with the std:: **namespace** tag.

And now back to our regularly scheduled discussion on the STL classes.

Stacks And Queues

There is probably no more basic data structure in computer science than the stack. Computer operating systems are based around this simple data structure, and nearly every programmer has experienced the joys of having a stack overflow in a program at one time or another.

The STL offers implementations of both the stack and its close cousin, the queue. Put simply, a stack is a one-sided queue that allows operations of push (put an item onto the top of the stack) and pop (remove an item from the top of the stack). Queues, on the other hand, allow the programmer to add a new entry at the beginning of the list and remove entries from the end of the list. The stack is often called a Last In First Out structure (LIFO) because the last item added to the stack via a push is the first item removed from the stack via a pop. The queue, on the other hand, is a First In First Out structure: The first item added to the queue is eventually pushed to the other end and removed as the first item out.

A stack or queue is generally represented by a linked list in C++. Most programmers have written implementations of these data structures in early C++ programming courses, so a complete refresher would be a little bit silly in this book. By using the implementation in the STL, rather than writing your own, you gain two large advantages over the linked-list stack/queue of your own systems. First, the code in the STL has been thoroughly tested to this point and will continue to be worked on in the future. Any bugs in the STL implementation of the stack will be fixed and redistributed free of charge by the implementors of the STL and then picked up and incorporated into the offerings from the various compiler vendors (including Borland

Table 5.6 Important **stack** class methods.

empty	Indicates whether there are (FALSE) or are not (TRUE) items in the stack or queue
size	Returns the number of items in the stack
top	Return the topmost element from the stack but do not remove it (effectively a peek)
push	Adds a new element to the top of a stack or queue
pop	Removes the top element from the stack or queue
front	Returns the element at the front of a queue but does not remove it from the queue
back	Returns the element at the end of a queue (most recently added) but does not remove it from the queue
operator=	Copies a stack or queue into another of the same type of object
constructor	Allows the programmer to specify the type of data stored in the queue or stack and the underlying data structure to be used in storing the structure

and CBuilder). Secondly, and more importantly, the underlying data structure implementation can be modified in the STL so long as the interface (method signatures) doesn't change. This allows you to write code based on a stack or queue and not worry about whether the push and pop methodology will change in the future.

Let's take a look at the available methods of the **stack** and **queue** classes first, and then talk a little about how you use them. Table 5.6 lists the important methods of the **stack** class of the STL.

As you can see from the previous table, the stack and queue are not real data structures in the STL, but rather use the implementation of another data structure, such as a list or deque to implement the functionality of the container for the objects.

One important note about stacks and queues: There is no iterator defined for these data structures. You cannot use an iterator to move through a stack or queue and must use the push and pop methods to add or remove data from the container.

Let's look at a simple example of a stack-based program.

```
#include <stdio.h>
#include <string.h>
#include <stdlib.h>

#include <stack>
#include <string>
#include <list>
```

```
int main(int argc, char **argv)
{
    std::stack< std::string, std::list<std::string> > stringStack;

    // Push all of the elements that are given to us onto the stack
    for ( int i=1; i<argc; ++i )
    {
      stringStack.push(argv[i]);
    }

    // Now, remove all of them in reverse order
    while ( !stringStack.empty() )
    {
        std::string s = stringStack.top();
        printf("%s\n", s.c_str() );
        stringStack.pop();
    }

    return 0;
}
```

As you can see from the example code, this example simply accepts a command-line set of arguments and prints them out in the reverse order that they were entered. For example, if you opened an MS-DOS command box in Windows 95 or NT and ran the following command in the command box prompt

```
stktest Hello world how are you?
```

assuming, of course, that you saved the project as stktest, you would see as output from the program:

```
you?
are
how
world
Hello
```

Note that the removal of items from the stack is a two-step process. First, get the item using the top method of the **stack** class (which gets the item without removing it) and then remove the item from the stack using the pop method. This contrasts with the push method, which does it all in a single step.

A note on double angle-brackets: You may notice that using the STL requires that you often use expressions that result in two angle-brackets (>) that run into each other. An example of this is found in the **stack** class, which requires a templated class in the second argument. As a result, you might be tempted to write something like:

```
std::stack< std::string, std::list<std::string>> stringStack;
```

Don't do it. If you do, the compiler will complain and call you all sorts of nasty names. The problem lies in the fact that the >> symbol represents a right shift operator in C and thus in C++. When you get horrible errors for doing something like this, use a space between the two > symbols to fix it. This represents a bug in the design of the C++ template system, not a bug in any compiler reporting the problem.

Putting It All Together: Scribble Revisited

If you'll recall, way back in Chapter 2 we put together a complete implementation of the infamous Scribble program. Scribble, you might remember, is the Visual C++ tutorial that took hundreds of pages to implement. If you don't remember or don't want to remember, don't worry about it too much. We'll cover the salient points in this example.

The Scribble example allows you to draw on the surface of a form by using the mouse. Pressing the left mouse button will start the drawing process, and moving the mouse around while holding the left mouse button will draw on the form canvas. When we last left Scribble, it had several problems. The first big problem we faced was that we were limited (by design) to 100 points in the drawing process. Although this is not a particularly difficult problem to overcome, the program would still have been limited to a fixed number of points regardless of what we were using as the maximum. Using the STL, we can overcome this problem by using a **vector** object rather than a fixed array of points.

The second problem in the Scribble program might not have been apparent at the time, but is a problem nonetheless. When you drew a line in Scribble and released the left mouse button, the program quit keeping track of movements. Pressing the left mouse button a second time resulted in drawing a separate line. This is all well and good, but the problem comes in when we redraw the form in the paint routine. If, for example, you drew three or four lines and then minimized and maximized the form, only the last line would be displayed. This was caused because we quit recording when the mouse button was released and then started recording again (from scratch) when the mouse button was pressed a second or third time. In this example, we'll fix Scribble once and for all so that it works correctly.

> **Note:** You'll find the complete source code for this example on the accompanying CD-ROM in the Chapter5\ScribbleSTL directory. If you would prefer simply to open this source and follow along instead of typing in the code, please feel free to do so.

Rather than recap the entire development of the Scribble project, we'll simply start with the existing project and make the modifications that are needed to do this job. If you're particularly interested in how the whole thing was put together originally and didn't read Chapter 2, please consult that chapter for more information.

The first step in the process is to replace the existing point arrays with a vector containing the point. We would also like to modify the process to remember when the mouse is moved from point to point, as well as when the mouse button is released, so we're going to store the information in an object. This new C++ class will store the information for the X and Y positions of each point, as well as a mode indicator indicating whether the point was a move or a draw. A **move** mode indicates that the mouse button was not pressed at this point, while a **draw** indicates that the mouse button was pressed.

To do all of this we need to do a couple of things. First, the new class that contains this information needs to be added to the system. Next, we need to modify the parent MDI window class to use this new class in a vector STL object to store its information and to use that vector in the return of information. Finally, we need to change the drawing routine of the child MDI windows to use the new mode indicator to know whether they should draw or move the pen.

Modifying The Parent Window

As it turns out, all of the major changes for the parent window occur in the header file (MainForm.h). Let's start with the addition of the class for holding all of the data by taking a look at the code to accomplish this first and then talk about what's going on:

```
const int MoveMode = 1;
const int DrawMode = 2;

class TScribblePoint
{
    int FnX;
    int FnY;
    int FnMode;
public:
    TScribblePoint(void)
    {
        FnX = 0;
        FnY = 0;
        FnMode = MoveMode;
    }
    TScribblePoint( int nMode, int nX, int nY )
    {
        FnX = nX;
        FnY = nY;
        FnMode = nMode;
    }
    int GetMode(void)
    {
        return FnMode;
    }
    int GetX(void)
    {
        return FnX;
    }
    int GetY(void)
    {
        return FnY;
    }
};
```

As you can see, the **TScribblePoint** class is pretty simple. It holds three data members for the X and Y points of the event and the mode in which the event occurs. In addition to the class, we have added two constants for use in defining the two event types that can occur.

In addition to the member variables, the **TScribblePoint** offers accessor functions to get at the data, which is generally a good idea in C++ programming. Rather than giving the end user direct access to the internal data of a class, you control their access and whether they can read or write the data. This notion will occur a little later in the book as a property of a component and will be very important. If you get accustomed to working with internal data as only internal and providing only the access to the data that is needed, you'll have a giant step up on writing component properties.

That little lecture aside, we now need to move on to the second step of the procedure, modifying the main form class to use our new **TScribblePoint** class. Here are the changes you'll need to make to the class to support our new object:

```cpp
class TForm2 : public TForm
{
__published:      // IDE-managed Components
                TMainMenu *MainMenu1;
                TMenuItem *File1;
                TMenuItem *New1;
                TMenuItem *Exit1;
                TMenuItem *Update1;
                TMenuItem *AllWindows1;
                void __fastcall New1Click(TObject *Sender);
                void __fastcall AllWindows1Click(TObject *Sender);
                void __fastcall Exit1Click(TObject *Sender);
private:     // User declarations
   std::vector<TScribblePoint> FvPoints;

public:                   // User declarations
                __fastcall TForm2(TComponent* Owner);
   void ClearPoints(void)
   {
     FvPoints.erase( FvPoints.begin(), FvPoints.end() );
   }
   void AddPoint(int nMode, int X, int Y)
   {
     TScribblePoint point(nMode, X, Y);
     FvPoints.insert( FvPoints.end(), point );
   }
   int NumberOfPoints(void)
   {
     return FvPoints.size();
   }
   void GetPoint( int Index, int& X, int& Y, int& Mode )
   {
     X = FvPoints[Index].GetX();
     Y = FvPoints[Index].GetY();
     Mode = FvPoints[Index].GetMode();
   }
};
```

These changes will enable the main form to work with the vector. Notice that with the exception of adding the **Mode** parameter to the **GetPoint** method (which is needed to implement new functionality), none of the interfaces to the methods have changed. This is another important point about writing object-oriented code. If you write the **accessor** methods correctly, you can change the underlying data structure without directly affecting client programs that are using your object. If you've taken many computer science courses you've probably heard this point hammered home a hundred times but have never actually seen a case where it mattered. Well, now you have.

The advantage of using C++ over C or Visual Basic is really shown off in this example. If, for example, you had been using Visual Basic and had used variables to hold the data such as the points, you would need to find every occurrence of the point variables in the program and change them to new types and new names. Of course, if you were really writing in VB you wouldn't have this problem because the STL isn't supported in any language other than C++. In this particular case, this is a pretty major difference between CBuilder and Delphi as well. Delphi, written in Object Pascal, has many third-party implementations of vectors, sets, and so forth, but it does not and probably never will support the STL standard. End of soapbox.

The next change is found in the child windows. First, we need to add the new **Mode** parameter to the **AddPoint** call in the child windows. Modify the following methods in the Unit1.cpp source file in the project:

```
void __fastcall TForm1::OnMouseDown(TObject *Sender, TMouseButton Button,
                                    TShiftState Shift, int X, int Y)
{
    FbMouseDown = TRUE;

    // Move to this point initially
    Canvas->MoveTo(X,Y);

    // Now update the main form with the new
    // data.
    Form2->AddPoint( MoveMode, X, Y );
}
//-----------------------------------------------------------------------
---
void __fastcall TForm1::OnMouseMove(TObject *Sender, TShiftState Shift,
                                    int X, int Y)
{
```

```
            if ( FbMouseDown )
  {
     Canvas->LineTo(X,Y);

     // Update the main form with new data.
     Form2->AddPoint( DrawMode, X, Y );
  }
}
```

There are actually two changes made here. First, we have added the **Mode** parameter to the **AddPoint** call to the parent window. Secondly, we have removed the **ClearPoints** call that used to be in the **OnMouseDown** method. We now want to allow the user to draw multiple lines (a change in functionality for the application), so we no longer want to remove all existing points whenever the user releases the mouse and then puts it down again someplace else. That, after all, is what the whole **MoveMode** parameter is all about.

The final change in the child window is to add the drawing code needed to handle the move and draw cases that we've changed in the program. Modify the **OnPaint** method of the child window in Unit1.cpp:

```
void __fastcall TForm1::OnPaint(TObject *Sender)
{
   if ( Form2->NumberOfPoints() > 0 )
   {
     int X = 0, Y = 0, Mode=DrawMode;

     // Now, loop through each point, getting them
     // from the main form and drawing them.
     for ( int i=0; i<Form2->NumberOfPoints(); ++i )
     {
                 Form2->GetPoint( i, X, Y, Mode );
        switch ( Mode )
        {
           case DrawMode:
                            Canvas->LineTo( X, Y );
              break;
           case MoveMode:
                                     Canvas->MoveTo(X,Y);
              break;
        }
     }
          }
}
```

This change will now check the drawing mode and properly handle the difference between moving the mouse with the left mouse button down and moving the mouse without the button down. Notice also that we no longer need the special case code of handling the first point differently from the others. Now, it's the mode of the point that makes the difference, rather than the order of the points. We've brought a higher level of abstraction to the application.

That's all the changes needed to make the Scribble application use the new object, use the STL, and support an indefinite number of drawing points and lines. All that and we actually ended up with a smaller codebase than before. As I hope you can see, the STL can make itself quite useful in writing quality applications in less code.

One final bonus in this chapter for readers who have access to the CD-ROM that ships with the book: On the accompanying CD-ROM, you'll find a text-searching program, written using the STL, that supports relevance ranking as well as multiple keyword searching. This program, with the name "Search," is found in the Extras directory of the CD-ROM. To make the new program, just open it in CBuilder and compile it. Search is a console application, meaning that you need to run it in an MS-DOS command box under Windows 95 or NT.

What Did We Learn In This Chapter?

At the conclusion of each chapter, it's nice to look back and see what kinds of things you learned about in CBuilder. You should have come out of this chapter having at least a passing knowledge of the following subjects:

- The Standard Template Library can be used to make programs more modular, easier to use, and more flexible.

- The **vector** class implements a dynamic array in the STL.

- A console application can be created in CBuilder to use with command-line arguments in an MS-DOS command window under Windows 95 and NT.

- Using the STL, we can even make visual CBuilder applications easier to use and easier to code.

- The string class from the STL can be used in place of character arrays and does not suffer from the memory overwrite problems common when using these character arrays.

Working With ActiveX

HIGH PERFORMANCE

CHAPTER

6

- **ActiveX Controls**

- **Using ActiveX**

- **Dynamic ActiveX**

- **An HTML Viewer**

Working With ActiveX

Everywhere you turn these days, you hear about ActiveX. Everything is Internet-based with ActiveX controls, ActiveX Template objects for communicating among objects, ActiveX documents for displaying data, Active this Active that. In this chapter, we explore the uses and oddities of working with ActiveX controls. By the time this chapter is complete, you should understand how to install an ActiveX control into CBuilder, how to add one to your form, and how to work with it once it's inserted into your project.

Although you can't construct ActiveX controls directly in the current release of CBuilder, you can use ActiveX controls and objects constructed elsewhere. Delphi 3.0 can easily create ActiveX controls and documents, and you can bet that this feature will be in the next release of CBuilder as well. For the present, though, you can use other people's ActiveX controls in your CBuilder forms easily enough.

We'll explore ActiveX in CBuilder in three ways. First, we will take a quick overview of the ActiveX controls that ship with CBuilder and can normally be found on the ActiveX tab of the Professional edition of the software. Secondly, we'll add a new ActiveX control to CBuilder and see what new files are generated, what the process is for adding ActiveX, and how to find out what is available in a generated ActiveX control in CBuilder. The third and final aspect of the chapter includes the use of one of the ActiveX controls that ships with CBuilder (the HTML control) to build a simple, but fully functional, local HTML viewer that you can use on your own computer (no Internet needed). With more and more help files shipped in HTML format, this little utility program could be worth its weight in gold.

ActiveX And CBuilder Professional

If you look at the CBuilder component palette, you'll see one tab with the name ActiveX. This tab contains a variety of ActiveX controls that you're allowed to use and ship with your application. In general, these controls are stripped-down versions of complete Active controls from companies hoping to sell the more complete versions of their products to professionals.

In addition to the ActiveX tab, another complete set of ActiveX controls ships with the CBuilder Professional set. These controls are found on the Internet tab of the component palette and offer the programmer the ability to include Internet capabilities such as HTML, FTP, and other common Internet needs. The Internet controls are supplied as a subset of the full functional controls by NetManage, and although they do the job, they're really not the best choice if you're developing a full-functioned Web browser in your application.

The ActiveX Tab

If you're using the Professional edition (or higher) of the CBuilder Development system, click on the ActiveX tab. Let's examine the available controls shown here and how you would use each of them in your own applications.

The first control you'll find is the ChartFx control, which allows you to display various charts, line graphs, bar charts, and other things in a CBuilder form. In case you have an interest in using this control, you would probably like to view its help file. The file does not come up when you hit the F1 key in CBuilder because it's in a different directory than the normal help files. Find the help file in the CBuilder\OCX\Chartfx directory. You can either use it directly from that directory or you can add it to the Tools menu to be able to view it easily. The help file lists all available properties and methods of the control, which is a whole lot better than reading through the include file looking for a method and guessing at what the parameters mean.

The second control on the ActiveX tab of CBuilder is the VCFirstImpression charting control. This control, like the ChartFx control, allows you to view data in a variety of graphical means. This control supports line and bar charts and display of a variety of data comparisons. The help file for the VCFirstImpression control is found in the CBuilder\OCX\Vci directory.

The third control on the ActiveX tab is the VCFormulaOne spreadsheet control, a very nice spreadsheet with capabilities similar to Microsoft's Excel. You can use the spreadsheet anywhere that you might use a grid for input in CBuilder. The help file for the VCFormulaOne control is also found in the CBuilder\OCX\Vci directory.

The next control on the ActiveX tab, the VCSpeller control, is quite interesting in that it is an invisible ActiveX control shown to the user at runtime. The VCSpeller control allows the programmer to offer spellchecking in applications through a standard interface and dictionary. Once again, the help file for this control (like all of the VC controls) is found in the CBuilder\OCX\Vci directory.

The last icon on the ActiveX tab is the Graphics Server, which is used as an ActiveX server for graphics for CBuilder applications.

In addition to the controls found on the ActiveX tab, you can add your own controls as well. Let's take a look at the process of adding a new control and what happens when you do so.

Adding Your Own ActiveX Controls

Certainly one of the nicest features of the CBuilder environment is the ability to add new components and controls to the system. Components added after the fact to the Component Palette respond exactly as if they were there in the shipped version of the product. This extendibility insures that your system will never be out of date with respect to the available components in the world. Other systems offer similar extendibility, but never as easily as in CBuilder (except, for obvious reasons, Delphi).

To add a new component to the Component Palette, you follow the same basic procedure whether that component is a normal CBuilder or Delphi component or whether the component is an ActiveX control written in some other system. Here is the process you need to go through to add a new ActiveX component to the ActiveX tab of CBuilder.

For this example we're going to add the Internet Explorer ActiveX control (called WebBrowser). This component is automatically installed on your machine if you're running Internet Explorer, but if you're not running Internet Explorer you have two choices. You can download a free copy from Microsoft's Web site (http://www.microsoft.com), or you can simply use another ActiveX control in place of that one. The procedure for adding the control is the same regardless of what control you're installing, although the resulting files will be named differently.

The first step is to bring up the Install Components dialog (shown in Figure 6.1). Select the Component|Install menu item to display the dialog, which will allow you to modify the components installed in the system. From this menu you can add or delete normal CBuilder/Delphi components as well as ActiveX controls.

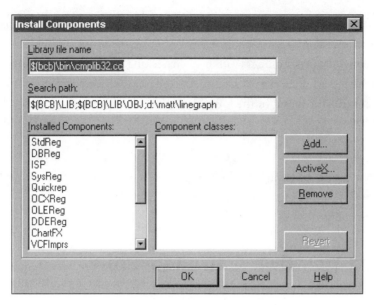

Install Components

Library file name
$(bcb)\bin\cmplib32.cc

Search path:
$(BCB)\LIB;$(BCB)\LIB\OBJ;d:\matt\linegraph

Installed Components:
StdReg
DBReg
ISP
SysReg
Quickrep
OCXReg
OLEReg
DDEReg
ChartFX
VCFImprs

Component classes:

Add...
ActiveX...
Remove
Revert

OK   Cancel   Help

Figure 6.1
The Install Components dialog in CBuilder.

Within the Install Components dialog, you'll see a button on the right side of the dialog labeled "ActiveX". Click on this button to bring up the Import OLE Control dialog (shown in Figure 6.2). This is the dialog we'll be using to select the actual ActiveX control installed on the system. In order to use the import dialog, your component (ActiveX control) must be registered with the system. This will normally happen by itself if the component is used in an application, because the installation program for the application will normally register the component as part of the installation process. If, for some reason, the control is not already registered, you can register it with either the Test Container application (found in most development environments) or by using the regsvr32.exe application found in Windows 95/NT. If you've developed the control yourself on another machine, you'll need to register it before trying to use it in an application on another system, including CBuilder.

In any event, we'll assume for the moment that you've installed the ActiveX control for our test (the Internet Explorer ActiveX control), and that everything is registered properly. If so, you should be able to select the Microsoft Internet Controls entry in the registered controls list and see a few entries change in the dialog. First, the Unit file name will change to SHDOCVW.PAS (all components are generated using a Pascal unit

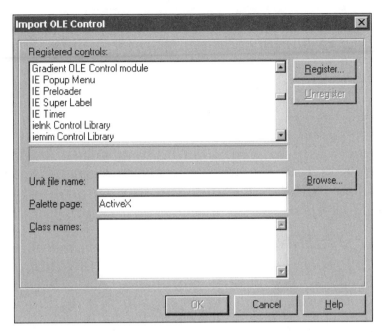

Figure 6.2
The Import OLE Control dialog.

for compatibility with Delphi). The Palette page entry will change to ActiveX, and the Class names entry will change to TWebBrowser.

While you can change any of these entries, it's probably best to leave them alone. The exceptions are the Palette page, which you can change to place the control wherever you want it, and the Class names, which you can change to something that reflects the use of the component better. In this case, all of the above are as good as we're going to get to reflecting the use of the control, so we simply leave them alone. Click on OK to close the Import OLE Control dialog. This will return you to the Install Components dialog. Click on OK in this dialog to indicate that you're finished making changes to the components in the system. If you wanted to, instead of clicking on OK, you could add another component or remove an existing component.

Once you close the component installation program, CBuilder leaps into action. The first thing that you notice is that the compiler will start and CBuilder will rebuild the component library. The unit file for the component(s) that you added will be compiled (SHDOCVW.PAS in our case), and the resulting library will be linked together. Once the compiling and linking process is complete, you'll see the familiar dialog box indicating that the make was complete by showing Done: Make.

At this point the component palette display will disappear for a few moments as CBuilder reloads all of the components by searching the library for the entries and putting them onto the proper tabs. Eventually, however, the Component Palette will be redisplayed. Move to the ActiveX tab of the palette and look carefully at the new entries. You'll find that the new TWebBrowser component is now showing at the end of the palette tab. The symbol for the component, by the way, will be the familiar file search icon that is stored in the file.

You can now drag and drop an instance of the TWebBrowser component onto a form and use it the same way that you use any other component.

> **Note:** A word of warning. Although ActiveX controls are treated exactly the same way as any other component in CBuilder, it takes considerably longer to drop an ActiveX control onto a form and have it appear. This is because creating an ActiveX control takes significantly longer than creating a new VCL component.

Looking At Files Generated For An ActiveX Control

When you use a regular component in the VCL, you include a header file for the component. The source file for that component resides in a PAS file, which you may or may not have on your system (depending on whether you bought the source to the VCL in your version of the CBuilder system). In either case, the library file contains the object file for the PAS file. How is it that CBuilder is able to use ActiveX controls as normal components when an ActiveX control is written in another system for which you very likely don't have the source code?

The answer lies in the wrapper that is generated for the ActiveX control. CBuilder is quite capable of using ActiveX; it just can't directly create it (actually it can, as any C++ compiler can; the issue is that it has no nice tools for working with ActiveX). So how is it working with the control? Remember that the component install generated a file called SHDOCVW.PAS? This file contains the source code for the wrapper class that contains the control. Here is a segment of that file:

```
procedure TWebBrowser.GoBack;
const
  DispInfo: array[0..7] of Byte = ($64,$00,$00,$00,$00,$01,$00,$00);
begin
  InvokeMethod(DispInfo, nil);
end;

procedure TWebBrowser.GoForward;
const
  DispInfo: array[0..7] of Byte = ($65,$00,$00,$00,$00,$01,$00,$00);
begin
  InvokeMethod(DispInfo, nil);
end;

procedure TWebBrowser.GoHome;
const
  DispInfo: array[0..7] of Byte = ($66,$00,$00,$00,$00,$01,$00,$00);
begin
  InvokeMethod(DispInfo, nil);
end;
```

The **InvokeMethod** call that you see in these Pascal functions is a base function that exists in the base class **OleCtrl** for the **TWebBrowser** class. All of these functions simply build an array of data that is needed to send to the underlying ActiveX control method and then invoke it indirectly. This is all accomplished via the underlying IDispInterface OLE interface built into the ActiveX controls.

A Few Words About ActiveX Controls

At this point it's appropriate to take a few minutes to talk about ActiveX controls and their structures. Like VCL components, ActiveX controls contain properties, methods, and events. Unlike VCL, ActiveX controls contain a dictionary of sorts that allows outside applications (called *container objects*) to learn which properties, methods, and events a given control supports. In truth, this last statement is a lie. VCL objects can be queried for the information stored in them. That ability, however, exists only in VCL systems like Delphi and CBuilder.

That notwithstanding, in ActiveX each property can be accessed via the **Set** and **Get** methods. These methods permit the ActiveX control to control the access to the actual underlying property. Similarly, the controls contain methods defined to accept a set number of arguments of fixed types. Does this sound familiar? It really should. This is the same basic system used by the VCL itself. VCL objects have properties that can have **Set** and **Get** methods and methods in parameters (usually). The biggest difference between VCL and ActiveX, in fact, is that while ActiveX objects can only have limited types passed to them, VCL objects can accept anything that the compiler can understand. In addition, of course, VCL objects are restricted to Delphi and CBuilder for now, while ActiveX controls can be used in nearly every development environment on Windows.

The ActiveX control uses a type library (TLB file) to define the information available to the system from the control. This library is what permits the system to know what the properties and methods are for a given control. CBuilder uses this information to generate the wrapper files for the ActiveX control and to make it look as much like a VCL component as possible.

If we take a look at parts of the header file for the generated wrapper file, you'll begin to see what I mean by making it look like a VCL component. Open the SHDOCVW.HPP file in the CBuilder editor and take a look near the top of the file. You'll see lines like the following:

```
namespace Shdocvw
{
//-- type declarations -------------------------------------------------
typedef void __fastcall (__closure *TWebBrowserBeforeNavigate)
  (System::TObject* Sender, const System::AnsiString
                URL, int Flags, const System::AnsiString TargetFrameName,
                  System::Variant &PostData, const System::AnsiString
                Headers, Word &Cancel);
```

There are a couple of interesting points to understand here. First, CBuilder generates a **namespace** wrapper around the component. This is good for you, because it this means that all of the classes, methods, and event types defined in this file are independent of anything else in the system.

The next few lines define an event for the **TWebBrowser** control. This particular event is called the **TWebBrowserBeforeNavigate** event. In the case of the real ActiveX control, this is the ActiveX event that is generated by the control just before the control navigates to a new location. You can add an event handler directly for this event using the Object Inspector. This is the first way in which the system makes working with ActiveX controls exactly like working with VCL components.

A bit further down in the file we come to the actual definition of the class. We'll look at some but not all of the whole class definition. Here are the parts of the class definition block we're interested in:

```
class __declspec(delphiclass) TWebBrowser;
class __declspec(pascalimplementation) TWebBrowser : public
Olectrls::TOleControl
{
               typedef Olectrls::TOleControl inherited;

private:
               TWebBrowserNewWindow FOnNewWindow;
               TWebBrowserTitleChange FOnTitleChange;
               TWebBrowserFrameBeforeNavigate FOnFrameBeforeNavigate;
               TWebBrowserFrameNavigateComplete
                 FOnFrameNavigateComplete;
               TWebBrowserFrameNewWindow FOnFrameNewWindow;
               TWebBrowserQuit FOnQuit;
               Classes::TNotifyEvent FOnWindowMove;
               Classes::TNotifyEvent FOnWindowResize;
               Classes::TNotifyEvent FOnWindowActivate;
               TWebBrowserPropertyChange FOnPropertyChange;

protected:
               virtual void __fastcall InitControlData(void);

public:
               void __stdcall GoBack(void);
               void __stdcall GoForward(void);
               void __stdcall GoHome(void);
               void __stdcall GoSearch(void);
               void __stdcall Navigate(const System::AnsiString URL,
                 System::Variant &Flags, System::Variant
                   &TargetFrameName,
                 System::Variant &PostData, System::Variant &Headers);
               HIDESBASE void __stdcall Refresh(void);
               void __stdcall Refresh2(System::Variant &Level);
               void __stdcall Stop(void);
               __property System::Variant Application =
                 {read=GetVariantProp, index=200};
               __property System::Variant Parent = {read=GetVariantProp,
                 index=201};
               __property System::Variant Container =
                 {read=GetVariantProp, index=202};
```

```
            __property System::Variant Document =
            {read=GetVariantProp, index=203};
            __property Word TopLevelContainer = {read=GetOleBoolProp,
            index=204, nodefault};
            __property System::AnsiString Type_ =
            {read=GetStringProp, index=205, nodefault};
            __property System::AnsiString LocationName =
            {read=GetStringProp, index=210, nodefault};
            __property System::AnsiString LocationURL =
            {read=GetStringProp, index=211, nodefault};
            __property Word Busy = {read=GetOleBoolProp, index=212,
            nodefault};

__published:

            __property TabStop ;
            __property DragCursor ;
            __property DragMode ;
            __property OnEnter ;
            __property OnExit ;
            __property OnStartDrag ;
            __property int Left = {read=GetIntegerProp,
            write=SetIntegerProp,
            stored=false, index=206, nodefault
                    };
public:

            /* TOleControl.Create */ __fastcall virtual TWebBrowser
            (Classes::TComponent* AOwner) :
            Olectrls::TOleControl(AOwner) { }
            /* TOleControl.Destroy */ __fastcall virtual
            ~TWebBrowser(void) { }

public:

            /* TWinControl.CreateParented */ __fastcall
                TWebBrowser(HWND ParentWindow) :
                Olectrls::TOleControl(ParentWindow) { }

};
```

The first section of the class definition defines all of the events for the control. These events will map one-to-one to the events in CBuilder defined in the Object Inspector for the control. You can add normal event handlers for these events through either the Object Inspector or by directly setting them as we saw a bit earlier in Chapter 4. Notice that the events fall into two categories. The first is the private events, which you cannot directly access. The public events come next and are allowed to be handled by your application programs.

Following the events, there are a number of methods declared. Methods are the same as they are in normal C++ objects. Given an instance of an ActiveX control component class, you can invoke any defined event (such as **GoForward**, **GoBack**) directly from the object:

```
TWebBrowser *pObject;
pObject->GoBack();
```

As you can see, there is nothing surprising about this access. It looks just like a VCL component, which is, of course, exactly the point of the exercise.

Similarly, properties are defined as actual properties just as if they were VCL properties. Properties of ActiveX controls can be either published or not, depending on how they're implemented in the ActiveX control. In addition, many properties are defined by the base ActiveX control automatically for the ActiveX control so they are automatically published by CBuilder. Properties of this type include **TabStop** and others. These properties are actually implemented by the VCL object in CBuilder, but appear to be implemented by the ActiveX control.

Events in ActiveX are really just properties. In the VCL, they're treated as events as well as looking exactly like properties. I hope you can see why things are so well translated between ActiveX controls and CBuilder. Components look almost exactly like ActiveX controls. This huge advantage is why the next release of CBuilder will almost certainly allow you to easily make components into ActiveX controls.

Using The ActiveX Control

Using an ActiveX control in CBuilder is just like any other control. You select the control from the ActiveX tab (or wherever else you put it) and drop it onto a form. Set the properties that you want to set, accepting whatever defaults you want to leave, and the control does the rest. The biggest difference between ActiveX and VCL comes at the installation time, when you must ship not only the application's executable file but all of the OCX files for the ActiveX controls. In addition, you need to register the new ActiveX controls with the system you're installing the controls on.

Creating Controls Dynamically

One of the more frequently asked questions about using ActiveX controls with CBuilder is how you can dynamically create an instance of an ActiveX control at runtime without using the form editor to add an instance of it first. You would think that this would be quite easy because ActiveX controls are treated just like VCL components in CBuilder, and you would be right.

> **Note:** The complete source code for this example can be found on the accompanying CD-ROM in the Chapter6\DynActive directory.

Let's take a simple example that creates an instance of the **VCFormulaOne** control when a form is first created. There are a couple of things you'll need to know to do this. First of all, you need to modify the header file for the form to contain the proper include files. Unlike VCL components, the ActiveX control header files are not automatically included by the compiler for your project. In addition to the header file, you need to define a pointer to the component to use for creating the control. Here is the modified header file showing all of the changes in highlighted print:

```
//-----------------------------------------------------------------
#ifndef Unit1H
#define Unit1H
//-----------------------------------------------------------------
#include <vcl\Classes.hpp>
#include <vcl\Controls.hpp>
#include <vcl\StdCtrls.hpp>
#include <vcl\Forms.hpp>
#include <vcl\VCFrmla1.hpp>
#include <vcl\OleCtrls.hpp>
//-----------------------------------------------------------------
class TForm1 : public TForm
{
__published:    // IDE-managed Components
private:    // User declarations
                TVCFormulaOne *VCFormulaOne1;
public:             // User declarations
                __fastcall TForm1(TComponent* Owner);
};
//-----------------------------------------------------------------
extern TForm1 *Form1;
//-----------------------------------------------------------------
#endif
```

Once you have all of the preliminary work done, the only thing left to do is create the control itself. Add an event handler for the **FormCreate** event for the form by double-clicking on the form. Add the following code to the **FormCreate** method for the form:

```
void __fastcall TForm1::FormCreate(TObject *Sender)
{
   VCFormulaOne1 = new TVCFormulaOne(this);
   VCFormulaOne1->Parent = this;
   VCFormulaOne1->Left = 10;
   VCFormulaOne1->Top = 10;
   VCFormulaOne1->Width = ClientWidth-20;
   VCFormulaOne1->Height = ClientHeight-20;
   VCFormulaOne1->Visible = true;
}
```

As you can see from the previous code, there is no difference between creating an ActiveX control and any other kind of component. You need to create an instance of the component using the new operator and then assign the **Parent** property of the component (which is automatically generated by CBuilder) to the form on which the control will reside. Once the control is created and the **Parent** property assigned, the rest of the properties are assigned normally. The **Left**, **Top**, **Width**, and **Height** properties are supplied by CBuilder automatically in the wrapper generation.

A Real-Life Example: An HTML Viewer

Now that we know everything that there is to know about working with ActiveX controls (namely, that it's the same as anything else), it's time to use an ActiveX control to build a somewhat real-world example to demonstrate the power of ActiveX and the Internet controls for CBuilder.

In this example, we'll build an HTML viewer that can be used to select an HTML file on your local machine to view. This is important given that the future of Windows Help files will be in HTML format (according to Microsoft). This simple viewer, then, could be considered a replacement for the Windows Help system. This is some high-powered example, then, isn't it?

> **Note:** The complete source code for the HTMLViewer example will be found on the accompanying CD-ROM in the Chapter6\HTMLViewer directory.

Figure 6.3 shows the form we'll be working with to build the HTMLViewer project. The form consists of a combo box, an HTML control (from the Internet Component Palette page), an edit box, and button and label controls. That's all there is to the problem solution.

The process that we'll use is pretty simple. When the user enters a URL (Web address) into the edit box at the bottom of the form and clicks on the Go! button, we will try to load the HTML document. If the given URL is not a Web address, we treat the HTML file as a local file on the disk. In order to do this you need to understand a little bit about how the HTML control works with files.

If the HTML control is passed a valid URL address, it first looks to see if an Internet connection already exists. If not, the user's default Internet connection attempts to load itself by displaying the ever-popular password connection box. If the Internet connection is already there, it uses the underlying Internet connection API in the

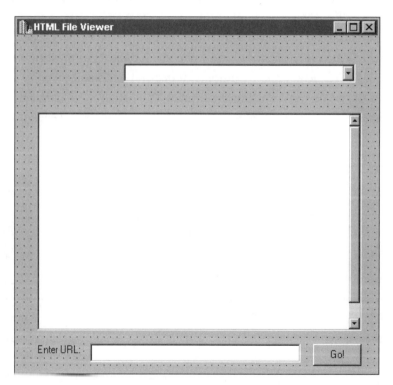

Figure 6.3
The HTMLViewer form.

Windows 32 API to make the connection to the Internet. At that point the HTML file is located and loaded into the viewer.

The more interesting case, from our perspective, is the case of looking at local HTML files, those residing on the user's hard-drive (or other storage mechanism). The HTML object supplied with CBuilder contains a way to request documents from a server (**RequestDoc**), but seems to have no direct way to load data from the local drive. Appearances can be deceiving, however. The **RequestDoc** method of the HTML control does, in fact, know how to load local files if you know how to do it. Fortunately, we do know how to do it.

Add an event handler for the button click event for the Go! button on the form and the following code to the button:

```
void __fastcall TForm1::Button1Click(TObject *Sender)
{
    AnsiString s = Edit1->Text;
    if ( strstr(Edit1->Text.c_str(), "//") == NULL )
        s = "File:///" + s;
    HTML1->RequestDoc(s);
    ComboBox1->Items->Add( s );
}
```

In our previous code, we first get the text from the edit control. Assuming that something was found, we check for the // string in the text. If found, this would indicate that the string contained a valid http address of the form http://xxx for an Internet address. If this string is not found, we make the assumption that the user really wanted to load a local file. In this case, we use the special device file: to access the local file system. When the HTML control finds the file: directive, it treats the remainder of the address as a local file path (or a network file path) and tries to open the file. To read the file HTML1.HTM on the c:\temp directory, for example, you would use the string file://c:\temp\html1.htm. It may look funny, but it works.

Once the file string is constructed, we add the file to the combo box at the top of the form and allow the user to go back to a previously loaded file by simply selecting it from the combo box entries in the form. In order to use that information, of course, we need to deal with the user selecting an entry from the combo box. To do this, add a handler for the **OnChange** event of the combo box. Add the following code to the **ComboBox1Change** method:

```
void __fastcall TForm1::ComboBox1Change(TObject *Sender)
{
    AnsiString s = ComboBox1->Text;
    HTML1->RequestDoc(s);
    Edit1->Text = s;
}
```

This method is simply going to get the requested string from the edit portion of the combo box and send it on to the HTML file. This will load the requested file into the control and display it for the user. Finally, the edit box is updated with the current text string so that the user can edit the address if necessary.

Figure 6.4 shows the program in use showing the HTML file supplied with the VC controls in the CBuilder\OCX\Vci directory.

That completes the HTML control showing you how you can quickly and easily use the HTML component in your own applications. Using ActiveX is easy in

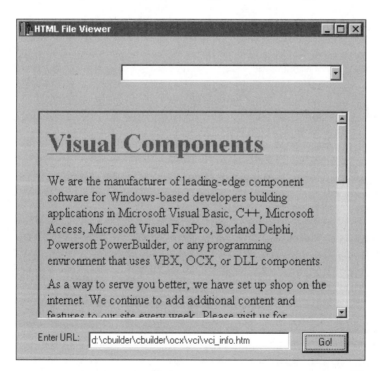

Figure 6.4
The HTMLViewer program in action.

CBuilder, probably easier than it is in the environments that actually allow you to create the controls in the first place.

What Did We Learn In This Chapter?

In this chapter you saw how quickly and easily you can add new ActiveX components to your CBuilder environment and to your CBuilder applications. ActiveX technology is quite prevalent in the Windows world these days, so the ease with which CBuilder handles the controls makes it even more wonderful to use these versatile components.

Specifically, these are the high points of this chapter:

- We learned how to add a new ActiveX control to the control palette and make it part of the system.

- We learned what files are generated by CBuilder when an ActiveX control is added to the system.

- We learned how to create dynamically an instance of an ActiveX control in our CBuilder forms.

- We learned how to use the HTML component supplied with the CBuilder Professional system to create a simple, yet powerful, HTML viewer, complete with history logging and automatic loading.

One last note concerning the ActiveX controls supplied with CBuilder. When the system was originally released, the ActiveX controls were only supplied with the Professional and higher environments. At the end of May 1997, Borland made the Internet controls available for download from its web site in a special arrangement. If you have the Trial edition or Beginning CBuilder edition of the software and would like these controls, check with the Borland web site to see if they're still available.

Working With Databases

CHAPTER

7

- **Understanding Database Internals**

- **Creating Databases From Scratch**

- **Database Event Handling**

- **Validating Data**

- **I'm Just Browsing!**

- **Working With Multiple Tables**

Working With Databases

One of the most important aspects of the new CBuilder system is the database functionality built into it. For the first time, C++ programmers have true drag and drop accessibility to databases, which CBuilder supports in a wide variety of formats. Borland standard database formats (directly supported by the Borland Database Engine) include dBase, Paradox, and InterBase. In addition, the latest versions of CBuilder ship with drivers that permit direct access to Microsoft Access databases. Any ODBC-compliant database can be used with CBuilder to give you access to nearly every database available in the Windows world.

Database functionality in CBuilder is much more than simply the wide variety of database formats supported. In addition, CBuilder's extensive VCL does nearly all of the important work for connecting with the database, maintaining the data in the database, and all other aspects of the underlying database tables. As we'll see in this chapter, you can build a complete database-viewing program that permits adding, deleting, modifying, and viewing data records in a database without writing a single line of code. Try that in another development environment (Delphi excepted, of course). If that were all the VCL offered, it would be an amazing system in and of itself. More than that, however, CBuilder offers complete control over the database functionality right down to the record modification level.

In this chapter, we do a little more than scratch the surface of working with the database objects in CBuilder. In addition to exploring connecting to ODBC connections, we will look at the internals of databases by creating a database field explorer that allows you to see the fields and field types that make up the database of your choice. We'll look at creating database tables on the fly from user requirements. We'll even build a database browser (as mentioned a little earlier) that can load arbitrary database records into a grid-like display. It will offer users the ability to select the database of their choice, display the fields they want to see, and even filter out records that they don't particularly want to see. All of this in only a handful of lines of code written by the programmer (me, in this case). In short, this is a power-packed chapter full of stuff that you'll probably want to use in your own applications.

Understanding Database Internals

Databases are complex. They are made up of tables, and the tables are made up of rows of data. The rows of data are stored on the disk and make up what we think of as the data in the database. There is more to the process than just the data, however. Each database needs to know how to convert the data on the disk into the format requested by the application program. For example, a date field is interpreted differently from a numeric field, even though both fields could be stored in the same way on disk. It's this internal manipulation that we're going to consider in this first example.

If you ignore the data in a database, what you're left with is called the schema. The schema represents the field definitions for each field that makes up a row in the database. Schema represents such things as the field data, the index data, and the number of fields for each database table. Most database classes in C++ tend to ignore this side of the equation, focusing instead (understandably, really) on the data side of the database. From time to time, however, you'll want to look at unfamiliar databases. Good examples of this are in data import applications, database publishing applications, and Web-based database display. All of these application types need to be able to load any sort of database that the user requests without really knowing anything about the data fields from which it's working.

In our first example, we'll build a database field browser. This browser will not display any data at all in a user-selected database, but will instead display the schema of the database at the field level. We'll show you how to inspect the fields of a database, determining not only the field names but also the field types and sizes. Given this information, it would be almost trivial in CBuilder to build a generic program to browse and input data into a database, regardless of the structure of the data fields.

Why would CBuilder have all of this information about fields and structures in hand? Actually, all database manipulation systems need the schema information. CBuilder needs it in order to support data-aware fields such as the **DBGrid** class. With the information already available, why not expose that information for the programmer to use as well? Why not indeed.

The Database Field Browser Example

In order to build a database field browser, you need to know a little bit about the internals of the database. To do this, you need to have a database to work with. For our example, we'll allow the user the ability to select a database from the drive. In this case, we're restricting the database type to dBase so that you'll not need to worry about any installed ODBC drivers, but the same process will work for any database type you could select that is supported by CBuilder.

Once the user has selected the database, the next step is to get the field information out of it. To accomplish this, we'll use a **TTable** object to open the specific dBase database file that the user selects. Within the **TTable** object you'll find information about the fields and indices that are contained in that table. In this example, we're not going to worry about the indices, just the field information.

Within the **TTable** object is a pointer to a **TFieldDefs** object. This object contains an array of field definition objects of type **TFieldDef** (one **TFieldDefs** object contains multiple **TFieldDef** objects). This object contains properties that represent the field information for each field. Within this object you'll find the field name, the field type, and the field size, among others. Given all of this information, we can then implement the browser using the form shown in Figure 7.1.

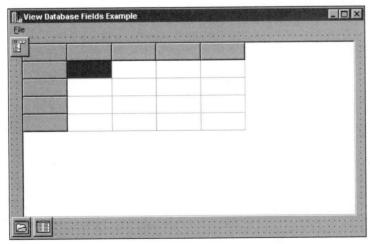

Figure 7.1
The database field browser form.

Building The Database Field Browser Example

Construct the form shown in Figure 7.1 by adding a **TStringGrid**, a **TMainMenu**, a **TOpenDialog**, and a **TTable** object to the blank form. In this example we'll not be directly setting any properties of the **grid**, **dialog**, or **table** objects. The **main menu** object should contain a main menu entry called File with menu items Open and Exit. The Open menu item will be used to select a database table to browse, while the Exit menu item will be used to close down the application.

The first step to displaying the information is to build a table of field types. Field types are stored in the database as numeric values of type **TFldType**. We would like to be able to display these fields in a more informative format for the user to be able to understand. Add the following code to the top of the Unit1.cpp source file to enable us to do this conversion:

```
typedef struct
{
    int  nCode;
    char *strDesc;
} DbFieldType;

DbFieldType sFieldTypes[] =
{
        {ftUnknown, "Unknown or undetermined"},
        {ftString, "Character or string field"},
        {ftSmallint , "16-bit integer field"},
        {ftInteger  , "32-bit integer field"},
        {ftWord  , "16-bit unsigned integer field"},
        {ftBoolean  , "Boolean field"},
        {ftFloat , "Floating-point numeric field"},
        {ftCurrency , "Money field"},
        {ftBCD, "Binary-coded decimal field"},
        {ftDate  , "Date field"},
        {ftTime  , "Time field"},
        {ftDateTime , "Date and time field"},
        {ftBytes , "Fixed number of bytes (binary storage)"},
        {ftVarBytes , "Variable number of bytes (binary storage)"},
        {ftAutoInc  , "Auto-incrementing 32-bit integer counter field"},
        {ftBlob  , "Binary Large OBject field"},
        {ftMemo  , "Text memo field"},
        {ftGraphic  , "Bitmap field"},
        {ftFmtMemo  , "Formatted text memo field"},
        {ftParadoxOle  , "Paradox OLE field"},
```

```
        {ftDBaseOle , "dBASE OLE field"},
        {ftTypedBinary , "Typed binary field"},
    {-1,""}
};
```

This table will simply do a match between the data types (the ftxxx symbols) and the string that describes that field type. The strings will be displayed in the grid for each field as the type of field displayed there.

In order to do the conversion between the field type and the description, we'll add a utility function to the form as well. We'll give the function the name **GetFieldTypeDescription**. This function will take a single argument, the database field type, and return a string which represents that field. Here is the code to add for the **GetFieldTypeDescription** method:

```
char *TForm1::GetFieldTypeDescription( int nIdx )
{
   for ( int i=0; sFieldTypes[i].nCode != -1; ++i )
      if ( sFieldTypes[i].nCode == nIdx )
         return sFieldTypes[i].strDesc;
   return "";
}
```

Once we have the field types mapped onto the strings that will be used to display them, the next step is to handle opening the database and loading the grid with the information for the table. Add a handler for the File|Open menu item. To the **Open1Click** method of the form, add the following code:

```
void __fastcall TForm1::Open1Click(TObject *Sender)
{
   OpenDialog1->Filter = "Dbase Files|*.dbf";
   if ( OpenDialog1->Execute() )
   {
      // Try to open the database given to us
      Table1->DatabaseName = ExtractFilePath(OpenDialog1->FileName);
      // Set the table
      Table1->TableName = ExtractFileName(OpenDialog1->FileName);
      // Make it active
      Table1->Active = true;
      // Load the grid with the pieces of the table
      StringGrid1->RowCount = Table1->FieldCount;
      StringGrid1->ColCount = 4;
```

```
// Set up the column widths
StringGrid1->ColWidths[0] = 30;
StringGrid1->ColWidths[1] = StringGrid1->ClientWidth / 3 - 10;
StringGrid1->ColWidths[2] = StringGrid1->ClientWidth / 3 - 10;
StringGrid1->ColWidths[3] = StringGrid1->ClientWidth / 3 - 10;

// Set up the titles
StringGrid1->Cells[0][0] = "Fld#";
StringGrid1->Cells[1][0] = "Field Name";
StringGrid1->Cells[2][0] = "Field Type";
StringGrid1->Cells[3][0] = "Size";


for ( int i=1; i<Table1->FieldCount; ++i )
{
    StringGrid1->Cells[0][i] = AnsiString(i);
    StringGrid1->Cells[1][i] = Table1->FieldDefs->Items[i]->Name;
    StringGrid1->Cells[2][i] = GetFieldTypeDescription(Table1->
      FieldDefs->Items[i]->DataType);
    StringGrid1->Cells[3][i] = AnsiString(Table1->FieldDefs->
      Items[i]->Size);
}


    }
}
```

What's Going On?

Some of the code above—like initializing the grid with the column headers and widths—is pretty straightforward. The confusing parts are dynamically opening the database and getting the information from the fields.

Two utility functions, defined in the sysutils.hpp header file in the include\vcl directory, are used to build the database name and the table name. The database name for a dBase file is simply the directory in which that file exists. The table name, likewise, is the name of the file you want to open.

The **TOpenDialog** object returns you the complete path to the user-selected file in the **FileName** property. We know that the file is of the correct type because we set the **Filter** property to only allow dBase (DBF) files. For this reason, we can use the **ExtractFilePath** utility function to get only the directory selected and the **ExtractFileName** utility function to retrieve the name of the table file that was selected. Once these two functions have been used, we "open" the database by setting the **Enable** property to true.

> **Note:** Although it's not shown in this example, the above code could lead to an exception being thrown. If you want to handle this exception yourself, wrap a **try .. catch block** around the setting of the **Enable** property. Do whatever you want in the catch block to indicate to the user that there was an error and abort the method. If you don't do this, CBuilder will automatically handle the exception and will stop the program

Once the database is open, we set the number of rows of the grid to be the same as the number of fields stored in the **FieldCount** property of the table. This property represents the number of fields defined in the table that you've access to. In the case of a dBase file, this is the same as the number of fields available in the table.

After the grid is initialized and the widths and headers are set, the fields are interrogated one by one and the data is loaded for each into the grid cells. If you've never used the **TStringGrid** class before, don't bother to look for the documentation in the online help. There is an updated help file on the Borland Web site that contains information on the grid, and several other classes inadvertently left out of both the online help and the paper documentation. In this case, we use the **Cells** property of the **TStringGrid** to set the individual row and column attributes of the grid. If these statements look a little funny, it's not your imagination; the **Cells** property works in a column, row format.

Within the **FieldDefs** object, the individual fields are stored in the **Items** property, much as everything else in the system is. Within the **Items** property, you'll find information about the field name (the **Name** property), the field type (the **DataType** property, which we convert into a string with our **utility** method) and the size of the field (the **Size** property).

> **Note:** For everything except a string (or character array) field, the **Size** property should be 0. All other field types have an implicit size based on their real implementation. For example, a 16-bit numeric field will be represented by a 2-byte integer, while a 32-bit numeric field will be represented by a 4-byte integer (or **long**). dBase already knows about all of this, so only character strings need to be defined by the **Size** property.

One last thing to notice in the code is the conversion of the field number to a string using the **AnsiString** class. Although we looked at the **string** class of the Standard Template Library earlier in the book, we really haven't talked much about **AnsiString**. This class implements most of the same methods of the **string** class and is used for any situation that requires a Pascal-style string. All VCL methods that work with strings accept an **AnsiString** argument.

The last step to completing the application is to close it down in response to a File|Exit menu selection. Add a new handler for the Exit menu item and add the following code to the **Exit1Click** method:

```
void __fastcall TForm1::Exit1Click(TObject *Sender)
{
    Application->Terminate();
}
```

That completes the Database Field Browser example. Compile and run the application and select a database table to view. Good examples will be found in the CBuilder\ Examples\Data directory in your installed CBuilder tree. Figure 7.2 shows one such file, the CLIENTS.DBF file, displayed in a running Database Field Browser form.

I hope you can see how powerful the CBuilder database functionality is and what a wide degree of latitude it affords you when working with databases. In other systems,

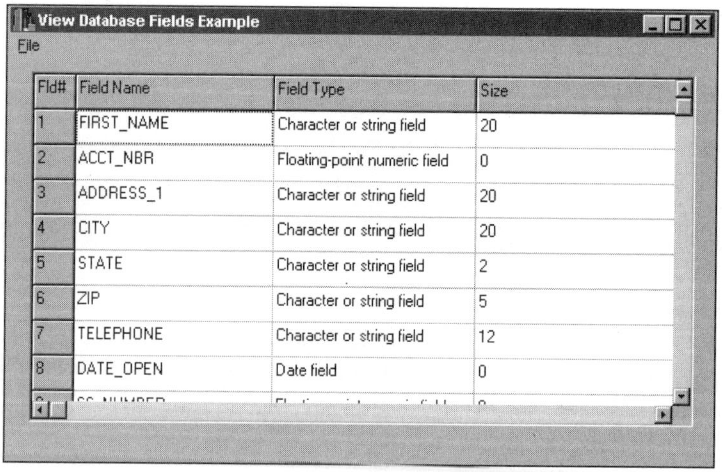

Figure 7.2
The client database displayed in the field browser form.

there is no direct way to access the kind of information that you get for free in the CBuilder **TTable** objects.

In our next example, we'll see just how powerful the **TTable** objects can be when we begin to explore how you can really manipulate the field definitions when we create a complete database on the fly from user-specified criteria.

Creating A Database From Scratch

Once you understand how the fields for a database are put together, the next logical step is to be able to assemble the fields together into a database, right? Well, of course that is what you would expect to do. After all, all you need to do is to slap the database directory and table name into place, add some fields, and set the **Enable** flag to true, right? Actually, the truth isn't very far from that. There will be times when you need to create a database from user requirements that are not known beforehand. Tracking bugs, note databases, and other kinds of applications requires that you allow the user to define the database in the fashion in which they want it to appear rather than the way some programmer (or worse, database designer) has decreed that it should appear. Of course, you still need to write the code that loads the fields with data later on, but at least for the creation process CBuilder can make the job a snap.

In this example, we build a form that allows you, acting in the user role, to define the schema of the database. The fields will be added to the table, the name and directory set, and the database will be created in a few dozen lines of code. Worse yet, many of those lines of code are more for the user interface than the creation process.

Figure 7.3 shows the form we'll be using for creating the database. Note a few things: First, there are no data-aware controls shown on the form (the grid shown is a TStringGrid in case you were wondering). That's because we won't be using the underlying database controls through the CBuilder form interface for this example. Everything we do will be low-level coding. Next, notice that there is no data table object on the form. We will be using a **TTable** object to do the actual creation process, but in this instance we'll create the table from scratch to show you how to do this job.

We need to add the same description/code table that we used in the previous example to the form code. In the last example, you might remember, the code from the **field definitions** object was used to map to a description for the user. In this example,

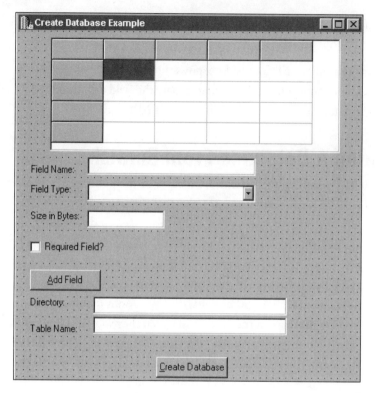

Figure 7.3
The create database form.

we are going to use the field description for the user to select the **field** type and then be able to remap that description back onto the **actual field** type for defining the field within the table. Add the following code to the top of the Unit1.cpp source file:

```
typedef struct
{
    Db::TFieldType  nCode;
    char *strDesc;
} DbFieldType;

DbFieldType sFieldTypes[] =
{
        {ftUnknown, "Unknown or undetermined"},
        {ftString, "Character or string field"},
        {ftSmallint , "16-bit integer field"},
        {ftInteger  , "32-bit integer field"},
```

```
        {ftWord  , "16-bit unsigned integer field"},
        {ftBoolean  , "Boolean field"},
        {ftFloat , "Floating-point numeric field"},
        {ftCurrency , "Money field"
        {ftBCD, "Binary-coded decimal field"},
        {ftDate  , "Date field"},
        {ftTime  , "Time field"},
        {ftDateTime , "Date and time field"},
        {ftBytes , "Fixed number of bytes (binary storage)"},
        {ftVarBytes , "Variable number of bytes (binary storage)"},
        {ftAutoInc  , "Auto-incrementing 32-bit integer counter field"},
        {ftBlob  , "Binary Large OBject field"},
        {ftMemo  , "Text memo field"},
        {ftGraphic  , "Bitmap field"},
        {ftFmtMemo  , "Formatted text memo field"},
        {ftParadoxOle  , "Paradox OLE field"},
        {ftDBaseOle , "dBASE OLE field"},
        {ftTypedBinary , "Typed binary field"},
};
```

In addition to the list, we also need to know how many entries there are so that we can add them to the combo box a little later in the code. We could simply use a constant value to represent the number of entries (22), but this leads to an error-prone future whereby entries are added to or removed from the list but the constant isn't updated. Fortunately, the C++ pre-processor has a helpful trick. Add the following line of code directly below the array of structure entries:

```
#define NumberOfFieldTypes (sizeof(sFieldTypes)/sizeof(sFieldTypes[0]))
```

You may have seen lines like this in code you've worked on. You might even have written something like it yourself. Put simply, the **sizeof** operator returns the size, in bytes, of the variable passed to it as the argument. In the case of the array of entries, each entry has a specific size (usually 8 bytes, depending on your compiler). The size of a specific entry, therefore, when divided into a multiple of that size, will yield the total number of entries. The formula looks something like this:

```
int nTotalEntries = (nNumberOfEntries * nSizeOfOneEntry) /
  nSizeOfOneEntry;
```

This code, as those of you with a math background will verify, factors out to the equality of **nTotalEntries = nTotalEntries**. In our **#define** above, this is all we're really doing, without knowing what the **nNumberOfEntries** or **nSizeOfOneEntry** factors are. Wonderful thing, the **sizeof** operator.

Next we need to do the following housekeeping for the system: We need to modify the constructor for the form to set up the new table object we'll be using for the creation process, and we need to clean out some things in the object so that we can use the object for creating the new table. Add the following code to the constructor for the **TForm1** object:

```
__fastcall TForm1::TForm1(TComponent* Owner)
                : TForm(Owner)
{
                Table1=new TTable(this);
                Table1->Active = false;
                Table1->FieldDefs->Clear();
                Table1->IndexDefs->Clear();

}
```

As you can, see we're creating the **TTable** object in this constructor. This allows us to then use the **table** object later on directly. Strictly speaking, the **Clear** calls to the field definitions array and the index definitions array are not necessary because these objects will have been initialized to the clear state. It is, however, a good practice not to assume anything about the objects you're working with. Likewise, the **TTable** object is created with the **Active** property set to false by default. Still, to be safe and not make assumptions that can come back to bite us (or byte us?), we'll force the setting to what we want here in the constructor. This is a good habit to apply in your own applications: initialize everything.

The next step in the process is to initialize the grid and the combo box so that they look correct to the user when the program starts up for the first time. To do this, add a new event handler for the **OnCreate** event for the form and add the following code to the **FormCreate** method:

```
void __fastcall TForm1::FormCreate(TObject *Sender)
{
   StringGrid1->ColCount = 5;
   StringGrid1->Cells[0][0] = "Field";
   StringGrid1->Cells[1][0] = "Name";
   StringGrid1->Cells[2][0] = "Type";
   StringGrid1->Cells[3][0] = "Length";
```

```
    StringGrid1->Cells[4][0] = "Required";
    StringGrid1->RowCount = 1;

    // Load the combo box
    for ( int i=0; i<NumberOfFieldTypes; ++i )
    {
        ComboBox1->Items->Add( sFieldTypes[i].strDesc );
    }
}
```

All we're doing is setting up the grid with the proper column headings, number of columns, and number of rows (1 for the top row). Next we add the descriptions for the field types to the field type combo box. This comes from the data stored in structure, which we added to the source file a little earlier in the example.

So, the user is now looking at the form that contains a blank grid with no entries in it and a combo box that contains the data for the field types allowed by the system. What we need to do now is to allow the user to add fields to the database (and display them for the user using the grid on the form).

Adding Fields To The Table

The process for adding new fields to the database table is as follows. First the user will fill in the field name and field size edit fields and select a field type from the field type combo box on the form. Then, the user will click on the Add button to add the new field to the table. Nothing is actually created in the database until the user fills in the database directory and table names and clicks on the Create button at the bottom of the form. Still, as we'll see, things are going on behind the scenes even as the user adds the individual fields for the new database.

To add a new field to the database, we need to wait until the user clicks on the Add button. Once this happens, we spring into action and add an event handler for the Add button, button-click event. Add the following code to the **Button2Click** method of the **form** object:

```
//-----------------------------------------------------------------
void __fastcall TForm1::Button2Click(TObject *Sender)
{
    char szBuffer[ 80 ];
    strcpy ( szBuffer, Edit2->Text.c_str() );
    unsigned short nSize = (unsigned short)atoi(szBuffer);
```

```
// Check if we need the size argument
if ( sFieldTypes[ComboBox1->ItemIndex].nCode != ftString )
   nSize = 0;

// Set up the field definition for this field
            Table1->FieldDefs->Add(Edit1->Text,
              sFieldTypes[ComboBox1->ItemIndex].
              nCode, nSize, CheckBox1->Checked);
// Set up the next row
StringGrid1->RowCount++;
              // Now, put that data into the grid
int nRow = StringGrid1->RowCount-1;
StringGrid1->Cells[0][nRow] = AnsiString(nRow);
StringGrid1->Cells[1][nRow] = Edit1->Text;
StringGrid1->Cells[2][nRow] = sFieldTypes[ComboBox1->
   ItemIndex].strDesc;
StringGrid1->Cells[3][nRow] = Edit2->Text;
if ( CheckBox1->Checked )
              StringGrid1->Cells[4][nRow] = "Yes";
          else
              StringGrid1->Cells[4][nRow] = "No";

}
```

In this code we first retrieve the information we need from the fields on the form. The field name edit field is simply used directly in the addition of the field. The combo box selection (the index of which is found in the **ItemIndex** property of the combo box) is used to find the actual field type in the structure we're using to hold the data for the field type mapping. Converting the size field does present something of a challenge, however.

Two things are important to note when working with the size field. First, you should never directly pass the text for an edit field directly to a function, even using the **c_str()** method of the **TEdit** object. It's not safe to modify the string directly in a **TEdit** field in this fashion. For this reason, we copy the buffer into a plain old character buffer and use that to get the length of the field.

The second important thing about adding the size of the field is whether the size is allowed or not. For fields other than the string type field, the size field is not only not used, it's not permitted. If you allow the user to enter a size for the field and then pass that size to the **Add** method of the **field definitions** object, you will get an error generated by the object and the add will fail. For this reason, we check the field type before we add the size, and, for non-string types, we set the size field (which is an unsigned short rather than an int, by the way) to 0 in this case.

Once the field is safely added to the database structure, the information is shown to the user in the grid and the user is ready to move on and add another field type.

Protecting The User

One nice thing that we can do for the user is to check to see whether or not the field type they have selected allows them to add a size for it. Let's check for this case and handle it appropriately by disabling the size box for non-sizable field types (numerics and such).

Add a new event handler to the form for the **OnChange** event of the combo box. Add the following code to the **ComboBox1Change** method of the form:

```
void __fastcall TForm1::ComboBox1Change(TObject *Sender)
{
   if ( sFieldTypes[ComboBox1->ItemIndex].nCode != ftString )
   {
      Edit2->Enabled = false;
   }
   else
      Edit2->Enabled = true;

}
```

Creating The Database

At this point the user has probably added several fields and is now ready to create the database on the disk directory and file that he or she has selected for the new table. Our moment is finally at hand—it's time to learn how to create the database within our application. I know that you waited with bated breath for the code, so I won't make you wait any longer.

Add the following code for the **Button1Click** method. This is the button that will be used for creating the database, the button appropriately labeled Create.

```
void __fastcall TForm1::Button1Click(TObject *Sender)
{
   // Set up the information for the database
   // and table names
```

```
        Table1->DatabaseName = Edit3->Text;
        Table1->TableName = Edit4->Text;

// Set the type to be a dBase field
        Table1->TableType = ttDBase;

// Go ahead and create the table
        Table1->CreateTable();

// And then delete the object
delete Table1;

// Let the user know
MessageBox1(NULL, "Created Database!", "Info", MB_OK );
// And close down the app
Application->Terminate();
}
```

Are you surprised at how little code is involved in the creation process? I certainly was when I first tried this in another real-life program. My own program was a bit longer, as I added quite a bit of error-handling because I couldn't afford to have the thing display an error message to the user. Still, the basic code was the same, and it worked like a champ the very first time it was run and every time since.

In the creation process, we first assign the database name and table name fields. These determine where the database file will actually be created on disk. You can enter any valid path and file names that you like, including network paths. After the names are assigned, we need to set the type of database we're creating. The CBuilder system knows by default how to create dBase and Paradox tables. With appropriate ODBC drivers you can create other kinds of tables as well.

Once the database is successfully created (note that nothing checks for the possibility of an error in this example, which you would certainly do in your own code), the **table** object is deleted to avoid a memory leak and the user is informed that the database was created. Finally, the application terminates. Theoretically, you don't need to end the program at this point. You could create and initialize a new **TTable** object and then allow the user to create multiple databases in a single run of the program. In this case, however, we're going to take the easy way out and just shut everything down.

That is all that is involved in creating a database from scratch in your application. Set up the fields, assign the path and file names, and let CBuilder's VCL objects do the rest of the job. Quick and easy like everything should be.

Database Event Handling

CBuilder ships with a wonderful tool called the Database Form Wizard. You can get to the wizard by selecting the Database menu and then selecting the Form Wizard menu item. This will bring up a simple database wizard which will allow you to select a given database file, pick the fields from the database you want to enter, and then set them up in the form style you want the user to see: horizontal, vertical, or grid format. At this point, the wizard goes off and generates a new form complete with a Form File (DFM), Unit File (CPP), and Header file (HPP). All of these files are added directly to your project.

CBuilder certainly isn't the first system to support this kind of automatic form generation, but it's one of the few C++ RAD products to produce a complete system that requires no further coding to add data. More importantly, CBuilder provides programmers with a wealth of programming events and hooks to use to validate, manipulate, or even modify the data before or after it's put into the database.

In this example, we look at some of the ways that you can hook into the database code for CBuilder and still allow the system to do the lion's share of the work in adding, modifying, and deleting records from a database table.

The first step toward making a data validation form is to start with a database. There are several approaches to this. You could either start with one of the existing databases shipped with CBuilder, work with an existing database on your own system, or create one from scratch. Let's use the database building program that we created in the previous example to create a database that you can use in this example. Think of it as inheritance of examples.

Create a new database (in whatever directory you like) and make it an address book style. To accomplish this, add the fields and types shown in Table 7.1.

Once you've created the table using our database creation program, use the Database Form Wizard to generate a new form for a new application. In my case, I selected all of the fields and vertical alignment for the form parameters. Your mileage may vary, of course.

The first change we're going to make to the form is to add a status bar to the bottom to display statistical information about the changes made by the user to our database table. Modify the form that was generated by the Form Wizard until it looks

Table 7.1   The format of the address book database.

Last Name	Character Field 40 characters
First Name	Character Field 40 characters
Address Line 1	Character Field 40 characters
Address Line 2	Character Field 40 characters
City	Character Field 60 characters
State	Character Field 10 characters
ZIP Code	Character Field 12 characters
Phone Number	Character Field 14 characters

like the one shown in Figure 7.4. As you can see from the status bar text, we'll be displaying the number of records added, modified, and deleted by the user during the course of a given application run.

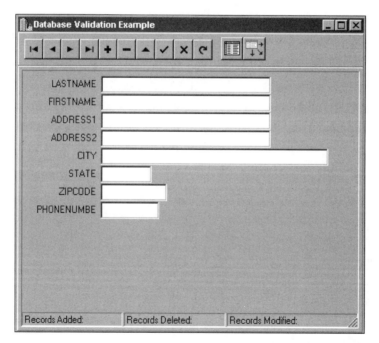

Figure 7.4
The database validation form with status bar.

Tracking The Changes

Once the status bar is in place, the next step is to track the individual changes made by the user to the database records. To do this, we need to know a little something about when things happen in the record's life.

When the user clicks on the + button of the **TDBNavigator** object on the database entry form, a new record will be added to the database. Modifying an existing record takes place when the user navigates to an existing record using one of the navigation buttons on the **navigator** object and changes it before rewriting it to the database. In either case, the event that occurs in the record is called a **Post**. A **Post** event occurs when the record is written to the database, whether for the first time or in an update mode.

If you look through the available events for the table object associated with this form, you won't find separate events for an update and an insert. Instead, you'll find an event for **AfterInsert** and one for **AfterPost**. The **AfterInsert** event is called when the user clicks on the Insert button after the new record is added to the database. We can't tell whether a **Post** comes from an insert or an update, so we'll keep track of whether the last thing they did was an **insert** or a **navigate**. To do this, we'll add a **status** flag to our form. While we're at it, let's add the needed counters for tracking the inserts, deletes, and modifies for the database during this session.

Modify the header file for the form to add the following variables to the form definition. While you're there, look at all of the variables already added by the Form Wizard. Saved you quite a bit of work, didn't it?

```
private:
               // private declarations
    int FnNumAdds;
    int FnNumUpdates;
    int FnNumDeletes;
    bool FbUpdateMode;

               void UpdateStatusBar(void);
```

In case you were wondering why **UpdateStatusBar** function is in there, we're going to use it to put all of the data into the individual status bar panels for the form.

The next step is to initialize all of the data in the constructor for the form. The counts, of course, initialize to 0, but the **update mode** flag is set to false. Why? Well, the first time that you come into the form, CBuilder will append a new record for you to enter new data into. If the user navigates to a different record and modifies it, we'll know as it happens. For this reason, we assume a new record insert. Here is the complete code for the constructor:

```
__fastcall TForm2::TForm2(TComponent *Owner)
                : TForm(Owner)
{
   FnNumAdds = 0;
   FnNumUpdates = 0;
   FnNumDeletes = 0;
   FbUpdateMode = false;
}
```

Once we have everything initialized, the next logical function to add is the update routine for the status bar. Here is that code, which simply assigns each panel of the status bar to contain the proper data for that information:

```
void TForm2::UpdateStatusBar(void)
{
   StatusBar1->Panels->Items[0]->Text = "Records Added: "
      + AnsiString(FnNumAdds);
   StatusBar1->Panels->Items[1]->Text = "Records Deleted: "
      + AnsiString(FnNumDeletes);
   StatusBar1->Panels->Items[2]->Text = "Records Modified: "
      + AnsiString(FnNumUpdates);
}
```

Okay, we have the count variables initialized and displayed. It's time to start handling the actual events that we need to update the display. First we'll handle the actual change of the record in the database, and then we'll move to editing a record or adding a new record. Assuming that you have a record that is edited or inserted and now written back to the database, the event that occurs is a **Post**. This event, as we mentioned earlier, happens regardless of whether this is an update or an insert. Why? When you do an insert into a table, a new blank record is created. An update is modifying a record that contains data in the database. In either case, we're really just updating an existing record, and the database doesn't know or care whether the previous change was an insert of a new record or an edit of an existing record.

To handle the **Post** event after the fact (which is all we need to do), add a handler for the **TTable** object's **AfterPost** event. Add the following code to the **AfterPost** event handler for the form:

```
void __fastcall TForm2::Table1AfterPost(TDataSet *DataSet)
{
   if ( FbUpdateMode )
      FnNumUpdates++;
   else
      FnNumAdds++;
            UpdateStatusBar();
}
```

If the user adds a new record to the database, the **AfterInsert** event is fired by the table object. There is, by the way, a corresponding **Before** event for each **After** event. Thus, if you wanted to handle the **BeforeInsert** or **BeforePost** (which we'll look at in a moment), you could add handlers for those events as well.

Add the following code to the **AfterInsert** event handler for the form to track when the user adds new records to the database:

```
void __fastcall TForm2::Table1AfterInsert(TDataSet *DataSet)
{
   FbUpdateMode = false;
}
```

There is not much going on here. All we need to do is remember that the last thing the user did was to insert a new record. Similarly, if the user modifies an existing record, the **AfterEdit** event is kicked off. We can trap this event to indicate to the form that we're now in **Update** mode. Here's the miraculous code for the **AfterEdit** event handler:

```
void __fastcall TForm2::Table1AfterEdit(TDataSet *DataSet)
{
   FbUpdateMode = true;
}
```

The final event we need to **catch** is when the user deletes a record from the database. Not terribly surprisingly, the event for this is the **AfterDelete** event. Even less surprisingly, here is the event handler for the **AfterDelete** event:

```
void __fastcall TForm2::Table1AfterDelete(TDataSet *DataSet)
{
   FnNumDeletes ++;
   UpdateStatusBar();
}
```

Notice that in the case of a delete we update the status bar. That is because there is no other change to the database that we can **catch** for a delete. Once it happens it happens, and you need to deal with it. In the case of an update or an insert, however, the action doesn't really occur until the user commits to the change, which triggers a **Post** event. In that case, we need to **catch** this **Post** event and update the status bar accordingly. Here is the code for the **AfterPost** event handler for the form:

```
void __fastcall TForm2::Table1AfterPost(TDataSet *DataSet)
{
    if ( FbUpdateMode )
        FnNumUpdates++;
    else
        FnNumAdds++;
                UpdateStatusBar();
}
```

That's all there is to updating the status bar. You can now add records, modify records, and delete records to your heart's content and watch the status bar rack up the changes you make to the database.

Validating The Data

In a perfect world, we would simply let users modify the data the way they would like it and let CBuilder handle everything else in the process. When you move into a perfect world, please let me know and I'll join you there. Unfortunately, the issue of data integrity and validation will always seem to rear its ugly head in any database form discussion.

Data integrity means that the data in your database is correct and in a valid format. For our database, for example, it really wouldn't do to allow the user to enter letters or punctuation marks into the ZIP code field. Even though the ZIP code field is stored as a character string, it really represents a numeric entry. For this reason, we need to be able to check the entry for the ZIP code field for validity. Other fields in your own databases might require their own checks.

In our discussions about database events so far, we've focused on the changes that occur after the user does something to the database. In the case of data validation, however, it's already too late to do something about it once the record is written into the database. *That* information we need before the record is written to disk. This is the purpose of the **Beforexxx** events (where xxx is the usual cast of **Insert**, **Delete**, or **Post**).

The **Post** event is fired when there is a change to the record in the database. CBuilder's database sub-system will fire the **BeforePost** event before the record is written to the database. This is your chance to validate the data in the record before allowing the process to proceed. If there are no problems, you just let the process continue with the default handling (which is to write the record back to the database file). If, on the other hand, there are problems with the processing of the record, you need to stop the process from going to completion by using the **Abort** method. Here is the code to add to your **BeforePost** handler for the database form:

```
void __fastcall TForm2::Table1BeforePost(TDataSet *DataSet)
{
   // First, verify that they put in a ZIP code
   if ( Table1ZIPCODE->Text.IsEmpty() )
   {
      MessageBox(NULL, "The Zip Code Field is Required!", "Error",
        MB_OK );
      Abort();
      return;
   }

   // Validate that the zip code is numeric
   std::string s = Table1ZIPCODE->Text.c_str();
   for ( int i=0; i<s.size(); ++i )
   {
      if ( !isdigit(s[i]) )
      {
         MessageBox(NULL, "The ZipCode field must be numeric!",
           "Error", MB_OK );
         Abort();
         return;
      }
   }

   // All is well, proceed

}
```

Just as a note, to make this compile you'll need to include **<string>** at the top of your source file to get the definition of the STL **string** class.

In any event (excuse the pun), the **BeforePost** handler checks each character in the ZIP code and verifies that it's a number. If it isn't, or if the ZIP code field is blank, the user is notified of the error and the **Abort** method is called.

Compile and run the application at this point. Assuming you didn't make too many mistakes in typing, it will run displaying the database form. Enter the string ABCDEF for the ZIP code field and click the check button to write the changes back to the record. You'll see a message box displayed telling you that the ZIP code field needs to be numeric. Following that, CBuilder will pop up an ugly display box indicating that something horrible has happened. What is going on here?

The answer is that CBuilder automatically throws an exception when you call the **Abort** function. It isn't that the exception isn't handled, which you can verify by telling the program to continue running. It's that you told it to break on exceptions. You don't remember doing this? Well, truth to tell, you didn't do it. CBuilder sets that flag by default. If you don't like this, and most of us don't, you can change it. Go to the Options|Environment menu item and look down in the Debugging section of the first tab of the property sheet. Turn off the checkbox for the entry "Break on exception" and re-run your program. It will no longer display the horrible exception message, and the program will run the way that you expect.

Any other fields that you need to validate can be done in the same fashion. Delete validations (checking for matching records and so forth) can be done in the quite similar **BeforeDelete** event handler.

That really finishes up the event handling example, and I hope you now understand quite a bit more about how the event handling system and the database system coexist within the CBuilder environment.

I Want To Do It Myself!

I have two young daughters who often tell me they want to do it themselves, often when I don't think they can. I am invariably wrong, and they usually handle the job better job than I could have. It's simply the life of a parent, I suppose. Borland faced the same problem when its programmers were writing the VCL database objects. Many programmers are a lot like my young daughters in that they don't really want the VCL doing all of the database changes, posting, deleting using the **DBNavigator** object. They themselves would prefer to handle the actual work of writing to the database for inserts, updates, and deletes. CBuilder lets you handle as much of this as you want to all by yourself.

Figure 7.5 shows the form we'll be using for this example. It was patterned after the form we generated from CBuilder's Database Form Wizard. The biggest difference is the

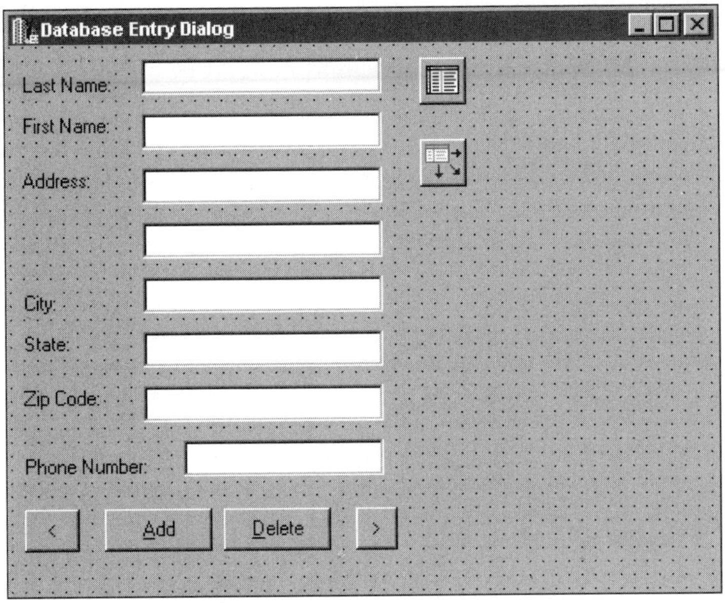

Figure 7.5
The database editor form.

addition of our own navigation buttons at the bottom of the form and the removal of the navigator component. In addition, of course, we aren't displaying a status bar in this example.

Implementing this form is easy. The edit fields are still tied into the data source, which is tied into the dataset (the table). The table itself points at our address book database file. The only implementation, therefore, is for the navigation buttons that we've added. Let's tackle them one at a time.

We want the user to start with a blank form in our own database editor form, so we need to add a blank record when the form is first displayed. Add a handler for the **FormCreate** event to the form and add the following line to that event handler:

```
void __fastcall TForm1::FormCreate(TObject *Sender)
{
    // Add a new record to the dataset.
    Table1->Append();
}
```

The **Append** method of the **TTable** object will add a new, blank record to the end of the database, which puts the database into edit mode and allows the user to add a new record. When they're finished entering data for the record, they'll then click on the Add button to add this record to the database and create a new one. Let's look at the handler for the Add button:

```
void __fastcall TForm1::Button1Click(TObject *Sender)
{
    if ( Table1->State == dsInsert ||
         Table1->State == dsEdit )
                    Table1->Post();
    Table1->Append();
}
```

The important consideration for us is whether or not the table is going to allow us to **Post** changes to the database before we add a new record. If the current record is not in edit mode (which it would be if we moved backward and didn't permit editing of records), the **Post** would fail, and a nasty error box would be displayed. In keeping with the VCL habit of fixing the problem when it can, the program will not bomb if you do this (VCL, unlike some other component systems, doesn't believe in **ASSERTing** on errors and stopping the program), but the program will not behave the way we want it to. Therefore, we check the state of the database by looking, appropriately, at the **State** property of the dataset. If the current state is either insert or edit mode, we allow the **Post**; otherwise, we skip the current record changes.

The Delete button is equally straightforward. Here is the code for the Delete button handler for the form:

```
void __fastcall TForm1::Button2Click(TObject *Sender)
{
    Table1->Delete();
}
```

In this example, there is no reason not to allow the user to delete a record, so we make no effort to stop it. In your own applications you might want to check with them via a message box ("Are you sure you want to delete this record?" with Yes and No buttons), but we have no need to do this. Note that we don't need to worry about the **Abort** method call in this example because we're controlling all of the operations, not the database.

The move backward (<) and move forward (>) buttons aren't complex either. They simply verify that the database is not at the beginning or the end of the database respectively. If those conditions are not true, then the database is moved in the appropriate direction to the record indicated. Here are the handlers for the buttons:

```
void __fastcall TForm1::Button4Click(TObject *Sender)
{
   if ( !Table1->Eof )
      Table1->Next();
}
//-----------------------------------------------------------------
void __fastcall TForm1::Button2Click(TObject *Sender)
{
   Table1->Delete();
}
```

Note the use of the **Bof** (Beginning of File) and **Eof** (End of File) properties of the database to check to see if we can accommodate the user's request.

That takes care of the complete example. It shows you how really easy it is to handle the level of work you want to handle in database forms. You could even remove the **DBEdit** fields and replace them with normal edits if you like. If you do this, you would then assign the fields of the database using the **FieldValues** property of the database:

```
Table1->Fields["LASTNAME"] = "Telles";
```

This would set the last name field of the current record to have the value Telles (a wonderful value to have). This is really all that the **DBEdit** component does. Similarly, to set the value of the edit field to be the same as the field value you would use:

```
Edit1->Text = Table1->Files["LASTNAME"];
```

That finishes up the process of editing databases. Let's move on to the problem of looking at the data in the database in a generic fashion.

A Generalized Database Browser

One of the most exciting features of the CBuilder database system is the ability to use a single set of code to interface with any set of data. The data-aware controls supplied with CBuilder do an amazing job of processing, displaying, and allowing modification of a wide variety of data stored in nearly any CBuilder-supported database (which is most of them).

In this example, we would like to create a generalized database browser. This browser will allow you to view any database by simply opening it up using a standard FileOpen dialog. In addition, we'll give the program the ability to filter out records unless they fit a given criteria that we'll define at runtime. Certainly the database desktop that ships with CBuilder can do all of these things, but sometimes all you want is a quick look without taking the time to load the desktop. In addition, if CBuilder is already running, the memory requirements become quite extensive. Our Database Browser example demonstrates the real power of the data-aware controls.

Figure 7.6 shows the form used in this example. In terms of either the controls used or the code written, there really isn't a lot to the example, but it does show the power of the underlying VCL database controls.

In this example, we allow the user to select a new database to open when the Open button on the form is clicked. To open the database, we use code that is quite similar to several previous examples. Here is the code to add for the **OnClick** event for the button on the form:

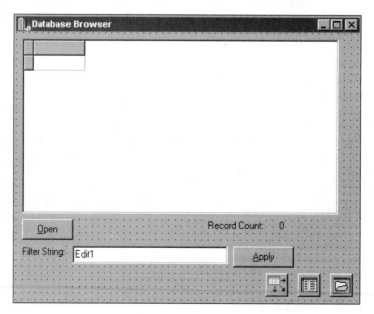

Figure 7.6
The database browser form.

```
void __fastcall TForm1::OpenClick(TObject *Sender)
{
   if ( OpenDialog1->Execute() )
   {
      if ( Table1->Active == true )
         Table1->Active = false;
      Table1->DatabaseName = ExtractFilePath( OpenDialog1->FileName );
      Table1->TableName = ExtractFileName( OpenDialog1->FileName );
      Table1->Active = true;
      RecordCount->Caption = AnsiString((int)Table1->RecordCount);
   }
}
```

In this case, we first check to see if the database is already open, because the user could have first opened one database and then decided to open a second. To keep CBuilder from getting annoyed if you change the database name and table name while the database is open, we close by setting the **Active** property to false. The code to set the database and table names is quite familiar, as we've used it before. We set the **Active** property to true to open the newly selected database, and then show the user the number of records in the database by interrogating the **RecordCount** property of the table.

> **Note:** Not all databases will support the **RecordCount** property. In some cases you'll need to traverse all records before the **RecordCount** property is correct. Most PC databases, however, will report the correct number here.

This code appears to do very little more than open the database. Why then, when you run the sample program from the CD-ROM, does the data grid automatically load itself from the database and show you all of the records? The answer is that you missed one step (or at least I didn't tell you about it, which is the same thing). The **DBGrid** object on the form has a property called **DataSource,** which represents the data source object on the form from which it will obtain its data. Likewise, the **DataSource** object on the form contains a property called **DataSet,** which represents the database table (or query) from which it will obtain its data. Set the **DataSource DataSet** property to be the **Table1** object. Set the **Enabled** property for the **DataSet** to true to allow it to load data. Next, set the **DBGrid DataSource** property to be **DataSource1,** which is the name of the **DataSource** object. This completes the circuit betwen the database and the data grid.

At this point, opening a database will load the data from that database into the grid and will display the number of records in the database in the static text field on the form. The next step is to enable that filtering mechanism at the bottom of the form.

To filter the data, the user will first enter an expression in the edit field at the bottom of the form, which represents a valid filter criterion. Criteria for filters are of the form field expression value. Field is the name of one of the fields displayed in the data grid. Expression is a comparison operator such as =, <> (not equal), <, >, >=, <=, or like. Finally, value represents the value you want to compare. If you were working with the address book example and wanted only those people who did not live in the state of New York (obviously a cultural bias), you would use:

```
State <> 'NY'
```

This code uses the **State** field of the database and uses the comparison operator not equal <> and the string **NY**. Note that because the string eventually has to be embedded in double quotes, if you're using a string (in this case, **NY**), you must put it into single quotes.

Here is the complete code for the filter button on the form to add to the event handler for the **OnClick** method:

```
void __fastcall TForm1::Button1Click(TObject *Sender)
{
    if ( Table1->Active == true )
    {
        Table1->Filtered = true;
        Table1->Filter = Edit1->Text;
        RecordCount->Caption = AnsiString((int)Table1->RecordCount);
    }

}
```

This code simply sets the filter into the table and tells the table to use the **Filter** property by setting the **Filtered** flag to true. This will force the database to filter out all records that do not have the corresponding fields with the proper values. In addition, we reset the number of records shown when the filter is applied. The neat thing about the filter is that it automatically updates the database record count according to the number of records that pass the filter criteria.

That's really all there is to the database browser: a dozen or so lines of code, a couple of drag and drops, and there it is. This example, more than any other in this chapter, shows off the real power already built into the database components of the VCL for CBuilder.

Multi-Table Viewing

This ability to view the contents is all very nice, but very few applications work with a single database file. It's much more likely that data for an application is stored in multiple tables of a database and then joined together in whatever way is needed for any given piece of information. One table in your database might contain customer information, another might contain sales information, while another table might have information about the bug reports made by that company. The tables are most likely connected to each other by a common field. In this example, we explore using multiple tables in a viewable format on a form.

Figure 7.7 shows the form for displaying multiple tables on a single form. The user will be allowed to select two tables and then select one field in each table on which

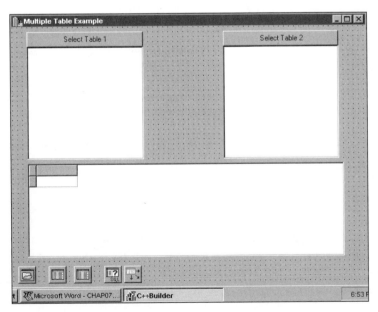

Figure 7.7
The multi-table viewing form.

to build the relationship for the two tables. When the user has selected one field in each database table, we'll try to link the two fields.

The problem basically breaks down into three stages. First, we need to allow the user to open a given database table. We've done this several times, so that part isn't particularly difficult. The second stage is to load the list boxes with the field names from each selected table. Once again, this isn't difficult; it's just a variation on the database field browser example from a bit earlier in the chapter. Finally, the last step is to display in the data grid the records that contain all of the information from both tables. This is a bit more complex. Let's tackle the easy stuff first.

To allow the user to open the first database file, add the following code to the Select Table 1 button **OnClick** handler for the form:

```
void __fastcall TForm1::Button1Click(TObject *Sender)
{
    OpenDialog1->Filter = "DBase Files|*.dbf";
    if ( OpenDialog1->Execute() )
    {
        // Try to open the database given to us
        Table1->DatabaseName = ExtractFilePath(OpenDialog1->FileName);
        // Set the table
        Table1->TableName = ExtractFileName(OpenDialog1->FileName);
        // Make it active
        Table1->Active = true;

        for ( int i=0; i<Table1->FieldCount; ++i )
        {
            ListBox1->Items->Add(Table1->FieldDefs->Items[i]->Name);
        }

    }
}
```

This code not only opens the table that the user selects but also does the second job of loading the field names into the list box. The code for the Second Table 2 button handler looks almost identical. Add the following code to the handler for the button in the form:

```
void __fastcall TForm1::Button2Click(TObject *Sender)
{
    OpenDialog1->Filter = "DBase Files|*.dbf";
```

```
if ( OpenDialog1->Execute() )
{
  // Try to open the database given to us
  Table2->DatabaseName = ExtractFilePath(OpenDialog1->FileName);
  // Set the table
  Table2->TableName = ExtractFileName(OpenDialog1->FileName);
  // Make it active
  Table2->Active = true;

  for ( int i=0; i<Table2->FieldCount; ++i )
  {
      ListBox2->Items->Add(Table2->FieldDefs->Items[i]->Name);
  }


}


}
```

Here's a quick tip: If, like me, you work in a small-screen resolution, you will find that it's difficult to move between the larger forms like this one and the code editor. You can do this directly from the IDE by pressing the F12 key while on the form, which will move you to the code editor directly.

That takes care of Steps 1 and 2. Step 3 is accomplished when the user has selected something from both table 1 and table 2. To do this, add handlers for both of the list boxes' OnClick events. Add the following code to both handlers (only one code block is shown; they're both the same) or use a single handler for both list box events:

```
void __fastcall TForm1::ListBox1Click(TObject *Sender)
{
    if ( ListBox1->ItemIndex != -1 &&
         ListBox2->ItemIndex != -1 )
         DoSQLProcess();
}
```

The last step is to implement the **DoSQLProcess** method. This method is going to build a dynamic SQL statement and assign it to the **TQuery** object that we're using to load the data into the grid. Let's first look at the code for the **DoSQLProcess** method of the form and then we'll talk about how it works:

```
void TForm1::DoSQLProcess(void)
{
    int nList1Idx = ListBox1->ItemIndex;
```

```
AnsiString s1 = ListBox1->Items->Strings[nList1Idx].c_str();
int nList2Idx = ListBox2->ItemIndex;
AnsiString s2 = ListBox2->Items->Strings[nList2Idx].c_str();

AnsiString s = "SELECT * FROM \"";
s += Table1->DatabaseName.c_str();
s += Table1->TableName.c_str();
s += "\" as T1";
s += ",";
s += "\"";
s += Table2->DatabaseName.c_str();
s += Table2->TableName.c_str();
s += "\" as T2";
s += " WHERE ";
s += "T1." + s1 + " = T2." + s2 ;

// Assign the SQL string.
Query1->SQL->Add( s );
Query1->Active = true;
}
```

How Does It All Work?

The **SQL** property of the **TQuery** object is a list of strings intended to represent the SQL command you want to send to the database. The SQL language itself is beyond the scope of this book, but the particulars of this example are interesting. First, we build a string consisting of the standard **SELECT** statement for SQL

```
SELECT * from db1, db2
```

where **db1** is the name of the first database table and **db2** is the name of the second database table. The only problem is that we don't use anything as easy as db1 and db2. Instead, our table names are of the form d:\directory\tablename.dbf. This makes it a little harder to work with the database names. SQL tends to choke on things like this, so we enclose the name of the database in quotes. That makes the first part of the statement of the form

```
SELECT * from "d:\directory1\table1.dbf", "d:\directory2\table2.dbf"
```

which is a standard enough looking SQL statement. The next part of the statement is normally the **WHERE** clause, something like db1.field = db2.field. This kind of a clause would retrieve all records where the field in db1 was equal to the field in db2. The problem here is that SQL rolls over and dies looking at a statement like:

```
WHERE d:\directory\table1.dbf.field = d:\directory\table2.dbf.field
```

To get around this problem, we use the SQL alias statement (AS), which allows us to refer to the table name by a shorter name. In this case, we refer to table 1 as t1 and table 2 as t2. This allows us to then refer to the fields as t2.field and t1.field.

Once the SQL string is built, we add it to the **Strings** field of the **TQuery** object and then make the query active. This selects the given records we want from the tables and loads them into the grid. Easy, isn't it? Well, it is once you know how to do it.

Using An ODBC Source With CBuilder Database Objects

One of the most commonly asked database questions on the Internet is how to use an ODBC database with CBuilder. The database in question is often a Microsoft Access database, but the procedure remains the same for all similar ODBC databases.

First, locate and open the ODBC Administrator, which is usually found in the Control Panel applet in Windows 95 or Windows NT. To get there, open the Control Panel (Start | Settings) and double-click the ODBC icon in the Control Panel main screen.

From the ODBC Administrator, select the Add button. You'll be presented with a list of database types in a dialog labeled "Add Data Source". Select the type of database product you want to open. In the case of Microsoft Access files, select "Access Data *.mdb".

Click the OK button in this dialog, and you'll be presented with a dialog entitled "ODBC Microsoft Access Setup". Enter the name you want to use as the source of the database in CBuilder. For example, type in the name CBuilderAccess.

Click on the Select Database button and navigate to the database file you want to use in CBuilder. Click on the OK button, and the database name will appear in the Setup dialog. Click on the OK button in the Setup dialog and then the Close button in the Add Data Source dialog. This will close down the ODBC Administrator.

Next, open the Borland Database Configuration Utility, which ships with CBuilder. You'll find this utility in the Borland menu of the Start menu in Windows 95. In the main window of the Configuration Utility screen, click on the New ODBC Driver button. In the SQL Link Driver: field, enter the string **ODBC_ACCESS**. From the default ODBC Driver list, select the Microsoft Access Driver (*.mdb). Set the name of the default data source to **CBuilderAccess** as you did in the ODBC Administrator screen.

Click on the Aliases tab at the bottom of the Configuration screen. Click on the New Alias button and name the new alias whatever you would like it to appear in CBuilder. Choose **ODBC_ACCESS** as the database type.

Close the Configuration program and be sure to save the changes. When you next bring up CBuilder, the new database will appear in the list of available databases in the **Database** property for a new **TTable** or **TQuery** object.

What Did We Learn In This Chapter?

This has been a fairly in-depth chapter analyzing the ins and outs of database programming using CBuilder and the VCL. In this chapter, you should have gotten at least the following:

- Viewing the field structure of a database at runtime.

- Understanding how to create a database from your own or user-defined criteria.

- Working with the data-aware controls to speed database manipulation.

- Connecting to an ODBC source with CBuilder.

- Working with the **TQuery** object to connect to multiple tables at the same time.

- Filtering data that you don't want to see out of a database.

- Browsing the data in a database using the data-aware grid.

Interlude: The CBuilder Tools

CHAPTER

8

HIGH PERFORMANCE

- **Command Line Tools**

- **Working with Resources**

- **Importing DLLs**

- **What's a grep?**

- **Going to the Library**

- **Working with BDE**

Interlude: The CBuilder Tools

The Integrated Development Environment (IDE) is the most visible aspect of the CBuilder system, but there is much more to CBuilder than that. Most of the tools that make up the IDE can be used separately to accomplish simpler tasks, and in this chapter we'll take a look at some of them, including the compiler, the linker, and the resource compiler. In addition, we'll look at how to utilize some of the utilities that come with the system: grep, tlib, IDEToMak, and tdump. I should warn you that most of the tools in the CBuilder system run best under a command-line (MS-DOS Command Window) interface, so if you're not comfortable dropping into that mode, you'll find it difficult to work with some of the tools.

Working With The Command-Line Compiler

The very first command-line tool we'll examine is the command-line compiler, BCC32.EXE. This tool can be used to work with simple test programs that you want to hack together in the command-line environment to test little algorithms or write simple utility programs. This is an industrial-strength compiler, but it's unlikely at this juncture that you'll be writing extensive programs in the command line. To use the command-line compiler, you first create your program source code using some sort of editor. Then, you simply type at the command-line the command

```
bcc32 mysource.cpp
```

where, of course, mysource.cpp is the name of the source file you want to compile. The compiler will automatically compile the source and, if there are no errors in the compilation, link it into a console application. Nearly any kind of C++ source code can be compiled this way, from utility programs to complete Unix utilities ported to Windows95/NT.

Let's look at some of the options available as command-line arguments to the compiler. Most of the options are unlikely to come up in any simple programs you're writing. Some might, depending on whether you're writing new code or porting older C++ applications from another environment. Table 8.1 lists some of the more common command-line arguments to the compiler and what they do.

A Simple Example

Here's a simple example of using the compiler in the environment. Suppose that you had an algorithm that calculated the factorial of a given number. If you sus-

Table 8.1   Common BCC32.EXE command-line arguments.

-C	Allows nested comments in the source file.
-I	Allows you to define added include file directories to search for include (.h) files for this compile only.
-L	Allows you to define added library file directories to search for library files (.LIB) for this link only.
-N	Checks stack overflow. If you don't include this, your program may crash the MS-DOS box it's running in.
-P	Forces C++ compile. This option is useful if your source files do not contain an extension of .cpp.
-c	Compiles only. Nice for syntax checking or finding out why the IDE choked on your source file.
-e	Changes the executable file name of the finished product. Normally this name is the same as the first module that is compiled.
-tW	Creates a Windows application. Generates correct prologue/epilog code for Windows applications.
-v	Enables source-level debugging.
-x	Enables exception handling.
-H	Uses pre-compiled headers in the compilation process. Can speed things up a lot if you have several modules in your program.
-u	Generates underscores (_) on externs. Very useful if you're creating DLLs to use with other systems such as Delphi or Visual Basic.
-w	Allows you to suppress certain warnings that you might not want to see.
-U	Undefines a given macro. Nice if you want to replace a macro with a function or remove certain #ifdef code.

pected that your code contained an error and wanted simply to test it, you could create a small test program to look at the thing and then run it in the command line. For example, suppose we had a program such as this:

```
#include <stdio.h>
#include <stdlib.h>
#include <string.h>

double fact(int nNum)
{
    double dFact = 1.0;

    for ( int i=1; i<=nNum; ++i )
        dFact *= (double)i;

    return dFact;
}

int main(int argc, char **argv)
{
    if ( argc < 2 )
        return -1;

    int nNum = atoi(argv[1]);

    printf("Factorial of %d = %lf\n", nNum, fact(nNum));
    return 0;
}
```

This program calculates the factorial of a number input by the user. To compile it at the command line, you would type bcc32 fact.cpp. The output from this compile would look like this:

```
d:\test>bcc32 fact.cpp
Borland C++ 5.2 for Win32
Copyright (c) 1993, 1997 Borland International
fact.cpp:
Turbo Link  Version 2.0.68.0
Copyright (c) 1993,1997 Borland International
```

In this case there are no warnings or errors, and the program is therefore compiled and linked. To run the program, you would type

```
fact 5
```

which would calculate the factorial of the number 5. The output from this program at the command line would be:

```
D:\test>fact 5
Factorial of 5 = 120.000000
```

The command-line compiler is also nice for testing for the "Unknown Error #1" that occasionally pops up in CBuilder. Although this problem is usually removed by deleting the incremental compile and link files (*.il?), it can sometimes be caused by the compiler not understanding something in your source code. Dropping into a command box and compiling the module in question may give you a clue as to how to fix it.

The Resource Compiler

Resources are the backbone of most Windows applications, and CBuilder allows you to import them into CBuilder applications quite nicely, as we'll see a little later in the book. Generally, you can get any resource file into your application directly by including it in the project and then letting the IDE do the rest. Sometimes, however, you'll want to pre-compile resource files and only distribute the compiled version (res files) to other programmers. For this, Borland provides two different programs for working with resource files.

BRC32.EXE is a 32-bit resource compiler and linker. This program will compile a resource file and then link it into the executable file you supply. BRC32 is a good way to work with older Windows applications you might have inherited that require a separate resource compile and link step. To run BRC32.EXE, use this syntax: BRC32.EXE filename, where filename is the name of both your resource file (.rc) and executable application file (.EXE). Table 8.2 lists the common options to the resource compiler:

Table 8.2 Common resource compiler (BRC32.EXE) options.

-r	Compile the file only, do not bind. This is the same as running the BRCC32.EXE program.
-fo<filename>	Specifies <filename> as the name of the output res file, the default io tho same as the input file with the extension .res.

(continued)

Table 8.2   Common resource compiler (BRC32.EXE) options *(continued)*.

-fe\<filename\>	Specifies \<filename\> as the name of the output executable file. The default is the same as the input file with the extension .EXE.
-I	Allows you to specify an include file path for searching for include files.
-x	Tells the compiler to ignore the environment variable INCLUDE and use only what you specify.
-Vd.d	Allows you to mark the resulting executable as a Windows version d.d (4.0 is default) file for running in Windows 95/NT.

To use the resource compiler, you must first have a resource file. If you wanted, for example, to add a stringtable to your executable file to allow for user-customized messages, you might create a resource like this:

```
///////////////////////////////////////////////////////////////////////
//
// String Table
//

STRINGTABLE DISCARDABLE
BEGIN
    101            "This is the first string."
    102            "This is the second string"
    103            "This is the third string."
END
```

This resource file would allow you to use the **LoadString** function in your application to get at certain strings in the resources. To compile this file, you would use the syntax brc32 -r strings.rc. Alternatively, you could simply type brcc32 strings.rc. Both of these cases will generate a new compiled resource file strings.res that can be included in your application and used to load strings. Running this command will result in the following display in your command box window:

```
D:\test>brcc32 strings.rc
Borland Resource Compiler  Version 5.02
Copyright (c) 1990, 1997 Borland International.  All rights reserved.
```

Using the resource compiler isn't difficult and can be quite rewarding, depending on your application. Rather than using the compiler directly, though, you're most likely to simply include the .rc file directly in the IDE project in CBuilder and allow the IDE to call the BRCC32 executable by itself.

Using Implib

The implib program is used to generate import libraries for Dynamic Link Libraries (DLL's) you would like to include in your application. It's important that you use the Borland CBuilder version of the Implib program to generate import libraries for use with CBuilder applications. Older Borland versions of implib and other companies' programs will create incorrect libraries and result in strange error messages in your code. We will look at using DLLs in CBuilder as well as generating DLLs with CBuilder for other applications in a future chapter. For now, let's simply examine the steps you would take to generate an import library for use in your basic CBuilder application.

Suppose, for example, that you had a DLL that you wanted to use in your application. This DLL might have been created by CBuilder, by Visual C++, by Delphi, or by any other system that can create DLLs. There are two basic things that you would want to do to use this DLL. The first is to generate an import library (.lib) file for this DLL that could link into your executable. This is accomplished by the **implib** command. The second thing that you would want to know is what functions are available to call in the DLL. This is accomplished by taking the import library that you just generated using implib and running it through the **tlib** command to generate a listing file for the library. Using these two programs, you can generate library listings for any standard DLL file in the Windows system.

Let's use the implib program to generate an import library for one of the DLLs found in your Windows directory (WinNT in the case of WindowsNT 4.0) and look at what is available in that library for use in your application. The Winsock.DLL file is probably in your Windows directory. Winsock is the Windows implementation of the Sockets communication library found in Unix and other systems and can be used quite nicely to create effective Internet communication programs.

First, run the implib program on the WINSOCK.DLL program by typing in the following command at the command line:

```
C:\WINDOWS>implib winsock.lib winsock.dll
```

```
Borland Implib Version 2.0.140.1 Copyright (c) 1991, 1997 Borland International
```

When you've finished typing in the command and the program has done its work there should now be a file in the C:\Windows directory (in this case) called Winsock.LIB. You can now examine this file by using the tlib program (which we will look at a bit later) by typing:

```
C:\WINDOWS>tlib winsock.lib, winsock.lst
TLIB 4.00 Copyright (c) 1987, 1997 Borland International
```

As we'll see in a little while, this command creates a listing file for the library showing all public symbols found in the library. A public symbol is an exported function or object that you can use in your own applications by linking to this import library. Here is a small snippet of the file showing some of the functions that you can import from the WINSOCK.DLL file:

```
Publics by module

ACCEPT                         size = 0
                ACCEPT

BIND                           size = 0
                BIND

CLOSESOCKET                    size = 0
                CLOSESOCKET

CONNECT                        size = 0
                CONNECT

GETHOSTBYADDR                  size = 0
                GETHOSTBYADDR

GETHOSTBYNAME                  size = 0
                GETHOSTBYNAME

GETHOSTNAME                    size = 0
                GETHOSTNAME

GETNETBYNAME                   size = 0
                GETNETBYNAME
```

You will see the functions shown previously in a Winsock manual. For example, **GetHostName** is a function that will tell you the name of the currently connected host. The implib program, combined with the tlib program, can provide a wealth of information about available functions in a DLL. More than a few of the undocumented functions in Windows have been found by running the implib program on some of the system DLLs in Windows and looking at the resulting output from the library program. (USER.EXE, for example, is nothing more than a disguised DLL.) Try it by running the implib program on the USER.EXE file found in your \Windows\System directory. Run tlib on the resulting USER.LIB file and look at the output in the USER.LST file. If you look hard enough, I'm sure that you'll find at least one function that isn't in the official Win32 documentation.

Working With IDEToMak

If you're a former (or current) user of the Borland C++ compiler (currently at version 5.02), you might want to take some existing projects and load them into the CBuilder environment. Why should you do this? To make working with forms easier and for converting DLLs to use the new VCLs, just to name two reasons that come to mind immediately.

Unfortunately, the Borland C++ compiler uses a proprietary IDE file to hold project information, and this IDE file is not compatible with CBuilder. After all, wouldn't you expect different versions of different compiler environments to be compatible? Well, in the Windows world you probably wouldn't, but in Borland's world you can.

The IDEToMak program will convert an existing Borland C++ IDE file into the equivalent project (MAK) file in the CBuilder system. To run the IDEToMak program, simply move to the directory that contains the IDE file and enter:

```
IDEToMak <IDEFile>
```

If you had a project in Borland C++ called Test, for example, you would enter the command:

```
IDEToMak Test.IDE
```

The resulting project would be called Test.MAK in the Test directory under the project. There are no options for the IDEToMak file, it's a simple utility that does a straight conversion.

Using The Pre-Processor

Like most C++ compilers, Borland CBuilder ships with a pre-processor program. In CBuilder it's called CPP32.EXE. The pre-processor is responsible for expanding all the pre-processor symbols into a complete application source file before the compiler is called to compile it. Pre-processors work with statements like **#include**, **#define**, **#ifdef**, and so forth. As an example, suppose you had an application file like this:

```
#ifdef WORKING
int x = 1;
#else
int x = 2;
#endif

#define X_WORD 32

int main(void)
{
    int z = X_WORD + 99;

    // Do something here with z

    return 0;

}
```

This simple application contains several pre-processor commands (**#ifdef**, **#else**, **#endif**, **#define**). If you were to run the application through the pre-processor by typing

```
C:\test>cpp32 test.cpp
Borland C++ Preprocessor 5.2 for Win32
Copyright (c) 1993, 1997 Borland International
TEST.CPP:
```

you would find that the resulting output is stored in a file called test.i. Here is what that file looks like for the previous source file:

```
/* TEST.CPP 1: */
/* TEST.CPP 2: */
/* TEST.CPP 3: */
/* TEST.CPP 4: */int x = 2;
/* TEST.CPP 5: */
/* TEST.CPP 6: */
```

```
/* TEST.CPP 7: */
/* TEST.CPP 8: */
/* TEST.CPP 9: */int main(void)
/* TEST.CPP 10: */{
/* TEST.CPP 11: */int z = 32 + 99;
/* TEST.CPP 12: */
/* TEST.CPP 13: */
/* TEST.CPP 14: */
/* TEST.CPP 15: */return 0;
/* TEST.CPP 16: */
/* TEST.CPP 17: */}
/* TEST.CPP 18: */
```

As you can see, the pre-processor does two things. First, it converts all of the symbols that it finds as directives into resulting output. Second, it generates a file and line number map that shows you the genesis of each of the generated lines in the result file. Should you care where the result of some strange include file ends up? Well, you just might. Suppose, for example, we modified the example program to look like this:

```
#include <vector>

#ifdef WORKING
int x = 1;
#else
int x = 2;
#endif

#define X_WORD 32

vector<int> intArray;

int main(void)
{
   int z = X_WORD + 99;

   // Do something here with z

   return 0;

}
```

Again, there is nothing amazing here. We just added an entry from the Standard Template Library, but you'll probably be as surprised as I was to find out that the resulting test.i is more than 6MB in size. This will tell you why compiling something using the Standard Template Library is certainly a lot slower than not using it. Looking at the generated output could take you weeks. The amazing part of the whole thing is that it only takes the pre-processor a few seconds (perhaps 30) to generate all that code, and it takes the compiler only a few more (maybe less than a minute) to compile the result into a fully working executable. Now that should give you a pause to reflect.

One of the most important uses of the pre-processor is to see why something isn't working properly even though it appears to be in the source code. If, for example, you have two definitions of a single #**define** scattered among all of the include files for your application, you can find them using the pre-processor. If you've removed code by using the #**ifdef** pre-processor command, you can likewise find out what is going on by looking at the pre-processor output.

Because of the sheer size of the output file from the pre-processor, this should be avoided unless absolutely necessary. Still, it's nice to know that it's there in case you ever need it.

What Is This Grep Thing Anyway?

By far the most useful of the utility programs supplied by Borland in the CBuilder package is the GREP.EXE utility. Grep stands for "Generalized Regular Expression Parser." The grep program has been a standard in the Unix environment for years, and has been emulated in the MS-DOS and MS-Windows environment for almost as long. Put simply, grep is a search tool that can look through text files (and some others) to find strings that match a given search string. The most common alternative to grep is the Norton Text Search utility or the Windows Find command in Windows Explorer. Neither, however, has grep's options or its power.

To use grep, you must supply two things: a search string and a file mask to search. Grep can search within a directory, within a directory and all subdirectories, or within an entire drive for files that match the specified search string. It's amazingly fast and incredibly accurate, and in fact the only reason to not like grep is its ugly name!

Table 8.3 shows some of the more common options that you can use with the **grep** command:

Table 8.3   The options for grep.

-r	Use regular expression parsing (see below).
-c	Return a count of the number of files found, rather than printing them out.
-v	Show all lines that do NOT match rather than those containing a match to the search string.
-d	Recurse through the subdirectories to find matching files.
-l	Display only the file names of files containing matching lines.
-n	Display the line number of the line the text is found on to match the search string.
-I	Case insensitive search.
-z	Display in verbose mode.

Using Grep To Search Files

In order to actually use the **grep** command, you need to know a little about regular expression parsing. As a novice user of the program, you need only worry about a few of the commands:

. (period) matches any character on a line, therefore H.t will match any of the following:

- Hot
- Hat
- Hut
- Hit

^ (carat) will match only things at the beginning of the line. Therefore, if you have the following lines of text:

This is a test
Why is This happening?
There is This There is That

And you search for ^This, only the first line will be reported. The * (asterisk) and + (plus) are used for multiple characters. A* matches zero or more A's in a text string; therefore, all of the following would match the string:

AAA
AA

A

B

The last line matches because it has 0 A's. The asterisk is a very powerful command and should be used carefully. Used haphazardly, it will return many more search hits than you might like.

The plus, on the other hand, will match only one or more occurrences of the letter, so searching the previous list of lines for A+ will return all but the last line, which does not contain any A characters at all.

If you want to search for multiple characters in a block, use the [and] commands. If you search for [aeiou] you'll find any line that contains a vowel in the search text. The complement to this is to search for [^aeiou], which will find any line without vowels.

Let's look at a couple of examples of using the **grep** command to search a file or multiple files.

First, let's consider a simple search. All I want to know is what line the word "attack" occurs on in the file "fred.txt". To use grep to run this search, I would enter this:

```
grep -n attack fred.txt
```

The command would return me the text lines containing the word "attack" along with the line number of that text line in the file fred.txt. Next, consider a search for all occurrences of the word "main" in source files (.cpp) in a CBuilder project directory. To search for this group of entries, I would use:

```
grep -d main *.cpp
```

This command would return me all of the text lines containing "main" in any file that ends in .cpp in either the current directory or any subdirectory (remember that the -d command recurses) of the current directory. Finally, let's search for all functions that return an integer in the current directory. How do you do this? Easy. Functions almost always start as the first thing on a line. The return type of the function is the first thing that you'll find. Therefore, we tell grep to search for all start of lines that begin with the word "int". Here is the command we would use:

```
grep ^int *.cpp
```

If you run this on the source code in any of your project directories, you'll find that it probably picks up all of the functions that return an integer. Although grep is certainly not perfect, it's amazingly fast and wonderfully small—as close to perfect as a computer program is likely to get.

Going To The Library

The next utility program we're going to look at is the **tlib** command. As we saw a little earlier, the **tlib** command can be used to view the contents of a library and produce a list file with all exported functions in that library. In addition to that simple task, however, tlib can also create new libraries, add modules to a library, and remove modules from a library.

What exactly is a library? Simply put, a library is a collection of modules called object files. Every time that you compile a C++ file (.cpp file) in CBuilder, an object file (.obj) is produced. These object files can be gathered together and placed in a library file (.lib) in order to re-use them in other programs. In general, you would put things into a library that you needed to use in other programs. Examples might include functions, forms, and other modules in CBuilder.

Table 8.4 lists the available options for the **tlib** command in CBuilder.

Using the **tlib** command is pretty easy. To add a file, such as FOO.OBJ, to a library such as FOO.LIB, you would type the command:

```
TLIB FOO.LIB +FOO.OBJ.
```

Table 8.4   Available tlib commands.

+<fileName>	Adds the object file <fileName> to the library.
-<fileName>	Removes the object file <fileName> from the library.
*<fileName>	Extracts the object file <fileName> from the library to an obj file without removing it from the library file.
-+<fileName>	Replaces the object file <fileName> in the library.
+=<fileName>	Same as -+.
/C	Creates a case-sensitive library.
/E	Creates an extended library.
/P<SIZE>	Sets the library page size to <SIZE>.

Similarly, to remove the file FOO.OBJ from the library FOO.LIB, you would enter the command:

```
TLIB FOO.LIB -FOO.OBJ
```

Finally, to get a listing file of a library, just append the ,<listFile> option to the end of the command such as:

```
TLIB FOO.LIB -FOO.OBJ, FOO.LST
```

This command will create the library file FOO.LIB if it doesn't already exist and remove the FOO.OBJ file from it if it's present (tlib will warn you if the file you're removing doesn't exist). It will then create a listing file that contains all of the public exports of the FOO.LIB library file and place that information in the FOO.LST file. That's really all there is to the tlib program.

Feeling In The tdump

The tdump program in CBuilder is another useful little utility that can be used in a variety of ways on files in your system. Basically, tdump allows you to break a file down into its component parts to look at how the structure of the file is maintained. When applied to executable files, tdump can present you with a list of the modules, exports, and, most importantly, the imports for that executable.

The tdump program can also be used as a quite literal "dump" program that will present a file in its hexadecimal (hex) format. If you run it on a simple binary file, you can look at a hex dump of the file format, which can be useful during debugging to find out why your file isn't storing what you think it should be storing or when that database file refuses to open.

In short, tdump is a programmer's tool that allows programmers access to the internals of files. It's a throwback to the days when programmers wanted complete access to how their programs were put together and what they output. With all of the complexity that Windows 95 and NT programs support these days, a program like tdump can be worth its weight in gold.

Table 8.5 shows some of the more common options for tdump, options that you can invoke at the command line when running the program. In general, the syntax for running tdump is to type the code that follows the table.

Table 8.5 Common tdump options.

-a	Display output in ASCII. This will display all ASCII characters in a file. Very useful for finding strings in an executable.
-a7	Like -a but only displays 7-bit ASCII characters.
-b#	Starts displaying input at byte offset #. Useful when you need to look at something in the middle or end of a file.
-e	Force executable file display. Regardless of the extension of the file, this command displays the input as an executable file.
-el	Don't display line numbers in the output. Default is to display line numbers.
-h	Force hexadecimal display. For types that tdump does understand, such as EXEs, the output is normally a record-based display.
-m	Disable C++ name mangling.
-oc	Check CRCs on OBJ file records. Basically see whether this OBJ file record is valid.
-xID	Don't display debug records of type ID.
-r	Do a raw dump of selected record contents.
-R	For PE files, dump relocatable entries table.
-v	Use verbose mode.
-o	Force tdump to dump this record as an object file (OBJ).

```
tdump [options] InputFile [Listing]
```

where **options** is zero or more of the options shown in Table 8.5, **InputFile** is the binary file you want to look at, and **Listing** is the output listing file for the program. If you don't supply a listing file, the tdump program will dump its output to the console.

As you can see, the tdump program can show you quite a bit about the file you run it on. Let's look at two simple examples of using the program to see what kind of output it can produce.

First, select an executable file on your system and run tdump on it. This file can be anything in the Windows directory that ends in an .EXE extension. In this example, I selected the Explorer.EXE program to dump. When you run tdump on this program you get an output display that looks something like this:

```
Turbo Dump  Version 5.0.13.1 Copyright (c) 1988, 1997 Borland International
                  Display of File EXPLORER.EXE

Old executable Header

DOS File Size                                  31E00h  (204288. )
Load Image Size                                  450h  (  1104. )
Relocation Table entry count                    0000h  (     0. )
Relocation Table address                        0040h  (    64. )
Size of header record       (in paragraphs)     0004h  (     4. )
Minimum Memory Requirement (in paragraphs)      0000h  (     0. )
Maximum Memory Requirement (in paragraphs)      FFFFh  ( 65535. )
File load checksum                              0000h  (     0. )
Overlay Number                                  0000h  (     0. )


Initial Stack Segment  (SS:SP)                        0000:00B8
Program Entry Point    (CS:IP)                        0000:0000



Portable executable (PE) File

Header base: 00000080

CPU type             80386
Flags                10E [ executable backwards 32bit ]
DLL flags            0000 [ ]
Linker Version       2.32
Time stamp           2FF35DC9
O/S Version          1.0
User Version         0.0
Subsystem Version    4.0
Subsystem            0002 [ Windows GUI ]
Object count         00000005
Symbols offset       00000000
Symbols count        00000000
Optional header size 00E0
Magic #              10B
Code size            00021800
Init Data size       00010200
Uninit Data size     00000000
Entry RVA            0000DEF1
Image base           00400000
Code base            00001000
Data base            00023000
Object/File align    00001000/00000200
```

```
Reserved                  00000000
Image size                00035000
Header size               00000400
Checksum                  00034598
Stack reserve/commit      00100000/00001000
Heap reserve/commit       00400000/00001000
Number interesting RVAs   00000010
```

All of this information tells you something about the file: code size, data size, and the load image size. The more exciting things, though, look more like this entry:

```
Imports from USER32.dll
    DispatchMessageA(hint = 0086)
    RedrawWindow(hint = 0194)
    RegisterWindowMessageA(hint = 01a0)
    SetScrollPos(hint = 01de)
    ScrollWindowEx(hint = 01ac)
    RegisterClassExA(hint = 0196)
    GetClassInfoExA(hint = 00c7)
    SendNotifyMessageA(hint = 01b5)
    IsWindowEnabled(hint = 0151)
    UnionRect(hint = 0212)
    GetMenu(hint = 00f3)
    SetWindowTextA(hint = 01ee)
```

Entries of the form Imports from tell you the DLLs that this module needs to run. You can therefore use the tdump program to tell you all of the DLLs that need to be on the system that the program is running on for it to work. More interestingly, you can get an idea about where the program is getting some of its functionality by looking at the kinds of functions it imports. Finally, you can learn a bit about the Windows API by looking at the imports from such Windows system DLLs as USER32 and GDI32. Sometimes you find functions that you didn't even know about buried in one of these DLLs and exported.

The second use of tdump is as a hex dump for a program. Instead of doing an export list for explorer, we can actually look at some of the strings buried in the file by using the command:

```
tdump -a explorer.exe
```

This will lead to a display that looks something like this:

```
C:\WINDOWS>tdump -a explorer.exe
Turbo Dump  Version 5.0.13.1 Copyright (c) 1988, 1997 Borland International
                    Display of File EXPLORER.EXE

000000: MZÉ..............+.......@.......................................Ç...
000040: ..|..|.-!+.L-!This program cannot be run in DOS mode....$.......
000080: PE..L...+]./...............2............._.......0....@........
0000C0: ................P.....ÿE...............@......................
000100: .@.._$...p..tº................. ..$*..........................
000140: .............................................text...
000180: ......................... ..'.data........0...............
0001C0: ....@..+.idata.._$...@...&... ............@..@.rsrc...tº...p..
000200: .¿...F.............@..@.reloc..d.... ...0..._...........@..B
000240: .............................................................
000280: .............................................................
0002C0: .............................................................
000300:^C
000300: .......................................,.............
```

What you can see from this display is the actual header for the executable file, the "stub" that is loaded when the executable file is run. In this case, we see the infamous "This program cannot be run in DOS mode" error message displayed when you try to run the explorer program in a non-Windows environment. If you dumped the whole file you would see error messages that are displayed for other purposes, as well as the default names of files, directories, and so forth.

The tdump program is most often used for displaying the import and export information for a program, but as we have seen, it can be used for much, much more.

What The Heck Is A Trigraph?

If you look through the bin directory in the CBuilder install tree, you'll find a program called trigraph. For most people, trigraph is a silly program that can be ignored. For people with European keyboards, though, the trigraph program can be a necessity. Some keyboards shipped in certain countries don't have all of the "standard" keys that are needed to program in C++. Just a few of these keys include the pound key (#), the square brackets ([and]), and the backslash key (\). The ANSI C++ committee recognized that these keys would not always be available, so they invented a way to emulate them on all keyboards.

The # key, for example, can be represented by the three-character symbol, ??=. For example, if you had a source file with the following code in it

```
??=include <stdio.h>
```

the standard C++ compiler would convert the previous line into the standard C++ code:

```
#include <stdio.h>
```

Unfortunately, putting this code into the compiler slows it down quite a bit. For this reason, Borland ships a separate product called trigraph to do this conversion for you. For example, we could create a file called tritest.cpp containing the following lines of text:

```
??=include <stdio.h>
??=include <stdlib.h>

int array??(20??);

int main()
??<
    return 0;
??>
```

Running the tritest command on this file using the command trigraph tritest.cpp will copy this file into a new file called tritest.bak. In its place, under the name tritest.cpp, will be the new file, which contains the more familiar text:

```
#include <stdio.h>
#include <stdlib.h>

int array[20];

int main()
{
    return 0;
}
```

This file will be directly compilable with the C++ compiler. I can't really imagine anyone actually using the trigraph compiler unless absolutely forced to, but if, however, your # key or {} keys were to suddenly break, you would have a simple alternative to shooting yourself in the head.

Looking At The BDE

The next piece of our overall tool discussion concerns the BDE, the Borland Database Engine, which represents an interface to the databases of the world. BDE can work directly with dBase and Paradox files as well as Interbase files. In addition, in some editions of the CBuilder product (Professional and above), the BDE can be used with ODBC files as well.

Installing the BDE is something that you normally do at the initial product installation time. If, for some reason, you didn't install the BDE product at the initial product installation time, you can install it later by running the setup program in the BDE directory of the CD-ROM for the CBuilder system.

If your program uses BDE and you need to install the system on a user's computer, I highly recommend using the InstallShield product that ships with the Professional Edition (and higher) of Borland CBuilder. Put simply, this product is a wonder. In general, all you need to do is to select the executable file that represents your program and then select any other files that you want shipped with your program. InstallShield will do the rest, including installing all of the allowable redistributable files for the BDE and the IDAPI systems that will allow your program complete database access.

BDE Configuration

What the BDE gives you most is the ability to provide database independence to your applications. Your program doesn't need to know where a database is or what machine it lives on in order to use it. Instead, you work with something called an alias.

In general, you will work via aliases in your database code in CBuilder, not worrying about the type or location of your database table files. Your code will generally work the same way regardless of whether you're working on an Oracle database located somewhere on the corporate LAN or a Paradox database located on the local hard drive. The BDE takes care of making all of the connections and working with the translations across the network. This is why you'll want to work with BDE.

There are two tools in the BDE system that are worth talking about briefly: the BDE Configuration program and the Database Explorer that ships with CBuilder. Let's give each one of them a brief once-over to familiarize you with their capabilities.

The BDE Configuration program allows you to define aliases, modify their properties, and work with the locations and permissions for databases in the system. Once you define the alias for a database in the BDE Configuration screen, you'll be able to use that alias directly in all database fields in the CBuilder Object Inspector. Figure 8.1 shows the first page of the BDE Configuration program, which you'll use to define aliases for the databases.

On the first page of the configuration screen you'll be able to define your driver of choice. This is known as the active configuration. Once you've selected a database to work with, you can move to the second tab of the window, the Alias page. Here you define a new alias for your data. Think of an alias as a database name. It's treated like a database in CBuilder. Depending on the type of database you're working with, you may have multiple tables within an alias.

The System, Date, Time, and Number tabs of the configuration screen contain information about how these types of data are displayed and manipulated in the system. For example, on the Number tab you'll see displayed a separator, decimal point, and number of decimal digits. If a number in the database is represented as 1000, using the default settings will result in a number of 1,000.00.

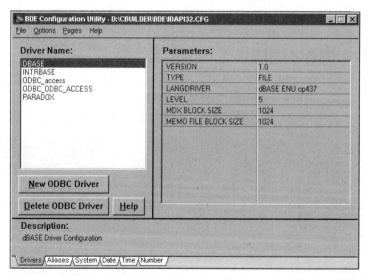

Figure 8.1
The BDE Configuration program.

Usually you'll simply use the BDE Configuration program to access databases you set up in the system. As you saw in the previous database chapter, you can also use it to define ODBC interfaces (if you're using the Professional edition or higher) and connect to all sorts of databases, such as Oracle and Access.

The Database Desktop

Again and again you'll need to test your code in a test database while the wondrous database designers are working on the "formal" design. The Database Designer is most definitely the way to develop new databases, test queries, write SQL statements, and view the data that you enter into the system.

The Database Desktop is found in the CBuilder menu item. The main screen of the desktop is shown in Figure 8.2.

Mostly you will use the desktop to create new databases and view data in current ones. The likely commands that you'll use are the File|New|Table command, which will allow you to define any kind of table that the desktop knows how to work with, and the File|Open|Table command, which will allow you to view data. In addition, to create a new query, use either the File|New|QBE Query or the File|New|SQL File commands either to directly query a database by selecting fields or to define an SQL command for later use in CBuilder.

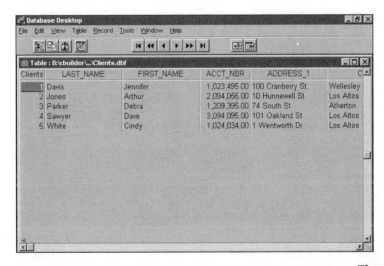

Figure 8.2
The Database Desktop.

There isn't a lot to say about the desktop program that isn't well covered in the on-line help or by simply trying the program. It's well laid out and quite easy to use.

Database Explorer

The very last utility that we're going to look at in this chapter is the Database Explorer. This utility, shown in Figure 8.3, allows you to quickly and easily view ODBC databases, Paradox databases and dBase databases. It allows you to view the structure of the database, including all table names, as well as the indices, fields, validity checks, referential integrity checks, and much, much more.

I strongly recommend that you become accustomed to working with the Database Explorer. It's a wonderful tool that gives you much more access and control over a database than the clunky tools shipped with most database products.

What Did We Learn In This Chapter?

To be honest, this chapter really wasn't intended to teach you a lot about the programming of the CBuilder system. I hope that you now understand considerably more about the utilities and other tools that ship with the system. One of the biggest complaints that most programmers have about development environments is

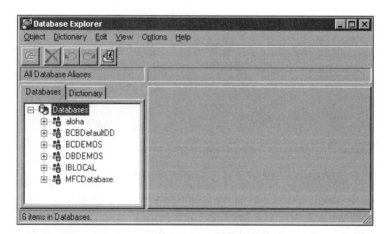

Figure 8.3
The Database Explorer.

that the system doesn't let them do the things they need to do. CBuilder most certainly will let you do whatever it is that you need to do as easily as possible.

In the end, the utilities that ship with CBuilder are worth almost as much as the IDE is. How much you get out of the product depends quite a bit on the amount you're willing to learn about the tools that are provided to help you do your job.

In the next chapter, we'll get back to more programming. I promise.

Working With The Windows API

HIGH PERFORMANCE

HIGH PERFORMANCE

- **Finding The Right API Function**

- **Stopping The Second Program Run**

- **Dragging And Dropping Files**

- **File Attribute Viewing**

- **Round Windows?**

Working With The Windows API

The Windows API lies underneath all the glitz of the VCL and the wonders of the drag and drop environment of the CBuilder IDE. There is nothing in the VCL that can't be done in the Windows API, and for a very good reason. Everything in Windows was written around the API. The operating system itself supports it and uses it in all of its utility applications. No matter how complex the code might be, sooner or later the whole thing rests on the back of API calls.

The Windows API contains several thousand different functions with dozens of different main categories. If you wanted to learn all of the API functions, couldn't you easily sit down with a manual and read until you found the ones required to create your application? Well, probably not. The interaction among the API functions would take years to learn, and writing a program would take decades, and the whole point of using the VCL and CBuilder is to avoid having to deal with all that icky stuff anyway.

Avoiding the Windows API is a worthy endeavor, and I highly recommend it. There are times, however, when the VCL can't do what you need to do and forces you to dip into the arcane knowledge of the Windows API to get the job done. If you're a Delphi or Visual Basic programmer, you're probably already shuddering in horror. Dealing with API functions in those languages can be a nightmare if the particular function you want requires data types that you don't have.

Fortunately for you, CBuilder isn't written in Basic or Pascal, it's written in C++. Dealing with the API from C++ is no harder than it was to deal with it in the original programming language of the API: C. Your job is getting easier by the moment. This is the only question left: When is the API needed to get the job done?

In this chapter, we examine a number of things that require the API to work. There is no direct way in CBuilder, for example, to determine whether the user has already launched a copy of your application. If your program expects to have sole control of a file on disk (say, a database) and there are two copies of the program running, well, let's just say the results would be ugly. Tracking down problems caused by multiple copies of a program can be a horrendous job. It's often simply easier not to allow the user to launch two copies. This doesn't work quite as well for simple utilities where the user might well want to launch two, but it works perfectly for corporate applications.

Another job that is tailor-made for the Windows API functions is that of determining how much disk space is left, volume names for disks, file attributes, and other information stored in the operating system file information. We'll explore how to use the API functions to pry this information loose from the operating system for use in your application.

Dealing with files dropped onto your application is one of the most common problems in dealing with the Windows 95/NT operating system. You might want to allow the user to select a bunch of files to process in a report writer, for example. Other programs might need a dropped list of files to send to an Internet address, perhaps. Whatever your need, the VCL comes to your rescue—er, not! While it's trivial to add a handler for the message you receive when getting dropped files, it's not possible within the VCL to inform the operating system that you can drop files in the first place. In this chapter you'll find out exactly how to do it with a minimum of fuss and effort.

The last problem for the application writer is handling all those silly user requests for odd-shaped windows. How, precisely, do you tell the VCL that you want your buttons to be round? The answer lies—you guessed it—in the WIndows API. Again, this is something we'll tackle in this chapter.

Finding The Right API Function

With several thousand alternatives, the biggest problem in working with the API functions isn't calling them, but finding the one you need. The Win32 SDK Help files can really be of assistance here. Although it's not obvious, Borland does ship copies of the Win32 SDK help files along with the CBuilder system. If you move to the CBuilder\Help directory, you'll see another directory below it labeled MSHelp. Within that help directory you'll find a number of help files, including the KnowledgeBase help file (KBase.hlp) and the Win32 SDK help file (Win32SDK.hlp). You can either add these help files to your Borland OpenHelp environment or simply add them to the Tools menu of the IDE.

The KnowledgeBase help file is useful if you're trying to figure out exactly how to accomplish a common programming task. A quick glance through the help file gave me information about such tasks as these:

- Getting Floppy Drive Information

- Getting the File Name Given the Window Handle

- GLLT.EXE: SAMPLE: Demonstrates Simple Lighting in OpenGL

These entries are just a few of the hundreds of separate KnowledgeBase articles that are supplied by the help file to aid in writing and debugging Windows applications. For obvious reasons, this help file does not contain information about CBuilder (it's not a Microsoft product, after all), but knowing the API function to use for a given task can often help you write what you need to write in CBuilder.

The Win32SDK.hlp file is the second help file in this directory that you'll find yourself turning to on a regular basis. This help file contains the complete Win32 SDK Function Listing in Help format. You can search for the function you need by name to see what parameters it requires, look at the overall groups of functions, and check the structures used by given API functions in the help file.

To find a specific function, use the Win32SDK.hlp file because it's optimized for individual functions. To find out how to handle a specific task, use the KnowledgeBase help file because it is more task and problem oriented than the SDK file.

So, how exactly do you locate a function to do something that your application requires? The answer generally is search through the help file for a function that sounds right or ask someone else who has done it before. This is the purpose of the Internet News Groups (USENET) or in picking up books like this. You generally learn by doing, and those of us who have been doing it since the SDK was the only answer will tend to simply know which function to call. People who start out only in CBuilder are at a definite disadvantage in this area. I strongly recommend that you pick up a good book on the fundamentals of Windows programming and read it cover to cover. You may never have to do any low-level C programming while using the SDK, but it certainly won't hurt to understand it. It will also give you an enormous appreciation for what CBuilder and the VCL are doing for you automatically.

Rather than beat the issue into the ground, let's start by looking at a very simple example of the power of the underlying API. The problem we're trying to solve is how to stop the user from launching a second copy of our application. What we would really like to do, of course, is stop the user from launching a second copy of the program and bring the first copy of the program to the front of the user's display so it can be seen. Often the problem is not that the user wants to run two copies of the program but rather that they have "lost" the second copy behind other windows.

The "OnlyOnce" Application

Figure 9.1 shows the form we'll use for the OnlyOnce application. As you can see, there is nothing special about the form; it has a single label telling the user not to run a second copy. Remember this form carefully, because we won't look at it again to make the program work.

Once you've created a new application in CBuilder and set up the form to look like the one in Figure 9.1, close the form. The work we need to do is not in the form itself, but rather in the application source code. This is your first chance to look at the application source code.

Select the View|Project Source menu item from the main IDE menu in CBuilder. The editor will load a copy of the project source file (project1.cpp). Take a look at this code, shown in the listing that follows Figure 9.1.

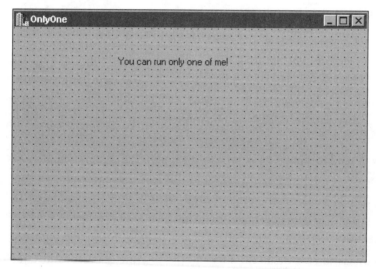

Figure 9.1
The OnlyOnce application form.

```
//-------------------------------------------------------------
#include <vcl\vcl.h>
#pragma hdrstop
//-------------------------------------------------------------
USEFORM("Unit1.cpp", Form1);
USERES("Project1.res");
//-------------------------------------------------------------
WINAPI WinMain(HINSTANCE, HINSTANCE, LPSTR, int)
{
        try
        {
            Application->Initialize();
            Application->CreateForm(__classid(TForm1), &Form1);
            Application->Run();
        }
        catch (Exception &exception)
        {
            Application->ShowException(&exception);
        }

        return 0;
}
```

There isn't much to this routine. **WinMain** is the entry point for all Windows applications in any version of the Windows operating system, and it will be called when the program starts. There is actually a bit of global code that runs before this in the startup code for the application. This startup code is responsible for creating the **Application** object. After that, everything happens here.

There are three steps to running the CBuilder program. First, the **Application** object is initialized. This is only important if your program is an OLE automation server. If your program is not a server, you can delete this line from the application source if you like.

Once the object is initialized, any auto-create forms are built. Auto-create forms are listed in the Project Manager for the CBuilder system. Normally, unless you specify otherwise, all forms that you add to a project are labeled auto-create in the system.

Why would you want your forms not to be created automatically? You may be writing an MDI application and don't want the child window to be created when you start the application. Or you may not want the form to be present in the application if a dialog is used only occasionally or a set of forms are mutually exclusive during an application run.

The final step of the application process is to run it. This is accomplished via the **Run** call in the startup code. This call will not return until the main form of the application is closed or the **Application->Terminate()** function is invoked.

Preventing The Second Copy From Running

In order to stop a second instance of the application from running, we need to stop the forms from being auto-created and the **Run** method of the application from being called. To do this, we first need to find out whether a second instance of the application is already running when we start up the program.

The Windows API does not have a direct method for finding a program. In the old days of Windows 3.1, there was a parameter passed to your **WinMain** function called **hPrevInstance,** which could be checked to see whether a prior instance of the application was running. In Windows 95/NT programs, that instance handle will always be **NULL.** There is a way, however, to search for a window that contains the same title as the program you're trying to run. This function is called **FindWindowEx.**

The **FindWindowEx** API function takes four parameters: a window class name, and a window title as well as two window handles identifying the parent and child windows. Either or both of the window class or title parameters can be **NULL.** Either or both of the window handle parameters can be **NULL.** If the parent window handle is **NULL,** all top-level windows will be searched.

What we want is all top-level windows that contain a window name that is the same as our program. Add the following code to your **WinMain** function above the **try {** statement that runs all of the **Application** object code:

```
            HWND hWnd;

            hWnd = FindWindowEx(
                NULL,    // handle to parent window
                NULL,    // handle to a child window
                NULL,    // pointer to class name
                "OnlyOne"         // pointer to window name
    );
    if ( hWnd != NULL )
    {
        BringWindowToTop(hWnd);
        return 0;
    }
```

This code will search for a top-level window that contains the text "OnlyOne", which is the same caption we gave the main form for our application. If the **FindWindowEx** API function finds such a window, it will return the handle of that window (much like the CBuilder **Form Handle** property). In this case, we use a second API function, **BringWindowToTop**, to redisplay that window as the topmost window in the system. **BringWindowToTop** takes a single parameter, the window handle, to move.

Once we've brought the old one to the top, we need to prevent the new program from running. The program terminates when the **WinMain** function exits, so the simplest way to do this is simply to return at this point. The value you return is traditionally the return code from the program, but it's rarely used, so we'll just return 0.

> **Note:** *Do not try running this application in the CBuilder IDE. Shut down CBuilder and then try to launch the program from Windows Explorer. The CBuilder IDE seems to keep a hidden form around with the title of the form we are working on. This is the form editor at work, it seems. When* **FindWindowEx** *locates that window, it will tell you about it, and your program will never launch.*

That's all there is to stopping a second run of your application. Now, you can simply add this code to all of your programs and not worry about the program running twice.

Dragging And Dropping Files

When programmers talk about Windows 95 or Windows NT, they often talk about drag and drop, and earlier in this book we looked at an example of dragging and dropping data between two list boxes on a form. Drag and drop, though, has quite another meaning as well. The Windows Explorer program, among others, has the capability to drag and drop files onto other programs. Sometimes, as with dragging and dropping a file onto a program icon, this action simply starts up the program with these files as arguments to the program. In other cases, the action allows you to process files by dragging them from the Explorer and dropping them onto a running program. In this example we'll look at the latter case.

Handling the drag and drop case is a matter of dealing with three conditions. First, telling the Windows system that you'll allow files to be dragged over your program and dropped onto them. Second, handling the notifications that Windows sends you when a file is dropped onto your program window. Finally, doing something with those files after they've been dropped onto the window.

The CBuilder system does support some forms of drag and drop, but only within the form system. If you wish to handle drag and drop in the CBuilder system, you'll have to delve briefly into the Windows API (which is of course why it's in this chapter). Let's look at each piece individually to see what is involved.

Informing the Windows system that your program accepts drag and drop files is a pretty simple affair. All you need is a single API function call, **DragAcceptFiles**. This API function takes two parameters, a window handle and a boolean flag. The window handle is simply the handle of the window that you want to allow dropping of files onto. The boolean flag indicates if this window will (true) or will not (false) accept dropped files. Obviously, by toggling the flag you can either accept or reject dropped files while the application is running. I personally have never encountered a case where you would want to stop accepting dropped files, but I suppose it's possible.

Once you've told the system that you're going to accept files, the next step is to wait for Windows to notify your application window that you're going to get a file. This comes in the form of a WM_DROPFILES message sent to your window handling procedure. In a CBuilder form, you can add a message handling function to process this message. The WM_DROPFILES message notifies you that the system is dropping one or more files onto your window, but it doesn't tell you what those files are. Your job as the programmer of the window is to inquire what each file is and process it appropriately.

The third step, processing the file, is application-dependent. You may want to open the file and read data from it. You may want to delete the file or copy it to some other device. Whatever it is that you want to do, you'll have the file name to work with. Your wish is your own command to execute.

Figure 9.2 shows the form we're going to use for the **DragDropFiles** example. This form contains only a single label (Files Dragged Here:), a button to close the form, and a list box to display the files that are dropped onto the form. In this example we don't do anything with the data except display it for the user.

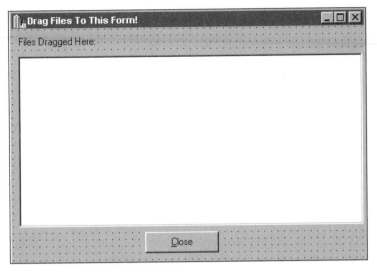

Figure 9.2
The DragAndDropFiles form.

The first step, as mentioned earlier, is to tell the system that this form window will allow files to be dragged and dropped onto it. Add a handler for the **OnCreate** event for the form, and add the following line to the **FormCreate** method of the form:

```
void __fastcall TForm1::FormCreate(TObject *Sender)
{
    // Allow our form to accept files
    DragAcceptFiles (Handle, TRUE);
}
```

In this case, we're notifying the operating system that we'll accept all files dropped onto the form (the **TRUE** argument to the function indicates this).

Handling Dropped Files

Once we've notified Windows that we'll handle dropped files, the next step is to sit back and wait for files to be dropped onto us. The message we're going to receive for the event will be WM_DROPFILES. There is no direct handler in the **TForm** class to handle this message, so we need to add a message map handler to the form as we did in previous examples.

Add the following lines to the header file for the form class. These entries will define a new handler for a standard Windows message and then link that new handler method to the WM_DROPFILES message:

```
class TForm1 : public TForm
{
__published:    // IDE-managed Components
                TListBox *ListBox1;
                TLabel *Label1;
                TButton *Button1;
                void __fastcall Button1Click(TObject *Sender);
                void __fastcall FormCreate(TObject *Sender);
private:    // User declarations
                void __fastcall HandleDropFiles(TMessage& Msg);
public:             // User declarations
                __fastcall TForm1(TComponent* Owner);
BEGIN_MESSAGE_MAP
MESSAGE_HANDLER(WM_DROPFILES,TMessage,HandleDropFiles)
END_MESSAGE_MAP(TForm)
};
```

Now that we've defined the procedure to do the job, all we need to is to add the code to do the job. Let's look at the code first and then figure out how it works:

```
void __fastcall TForm1::HandleDropFiles(TMessage& Msg)
{
   // Get the drop information from the message
   HDROP hDropInfo = (HANDLE)Msg.WParam;
   char szFileName[_MAX_PATH];

   int iFiles = DragQueryFile (hDropInfo, (DWORD)(-1), (LPSTR)NULL, 0);

   // For each one dropped, put it into the list
   // box strings array.
   for ( int nIdx = 0; nIdx < iFiles; ++nIdx )
   {
                DragQueryFile (hDropInfo, nIdx, szFileName, _MAX_PATH);
      ListBox1->Items->Add( szFileName );
   }
}
```

The first thing that we do is obtain a **HDROP** object by casting the **WParam** in the message to this structure. The **HDROP** structure is really just an index into the list of returned files from the system. Use the **HDROP** handle to retrieve each file in the block of dropped files.

The **DragQueryFile** API function has two separate uses (don't you just love functions like that?). First, if you call it with an index of -1 and a **NULL** pointer, it will return the number of entries in the drop list. This is the number of files that the user selected from Windows Explorer and then dragged onto your window. If you don't want to allow multiple files to be dropped at one time, you should add some processing code at this point to stop the process if the number of files is greater than 1. Note that you should never receive this message if there are no entries in the list.

Once we have the number of files in the drop list, the second use of the **DragQueryFile** function comes into play. If you pass a valid index number (the second argument to the function) and a buffer to hold the returned file name, the function will return each file in the drop list. Remember that Explorer deals in long file names, so we need to make the buffer large enough to handle any size file name that is dropped onto the window. The **_MAX_PATH** define found in the system header files is guaranteed to be large enough to handle any file name (up to 256 characters, as it happens) that is used in the Windows system. As a safety check, however, we pass this length to the API function so that in the case of future incompatibility (if file names get larger), the program will not crash unexpectedly.

In our case, all we need to do with the file names is add them to our list box. The user could then select several of these files and apply some function to them or whatever your program needs to do with them. This example is quite simple and doesn't do anything with them except put them on display.

The last step in this program is to handle the Close button at the bottom of the form. Add a handler for the button and add the following code to the **Button1Click** event handler for the form:

```
void __fastcall TForm1::Button1Click(TObject *Sender)
{
    Application->Terminate();
}
```

As you can see, handling the drag and drop of files from Windows Explorer is pretty simple. To see how it works, fire up the program and bring up an instance of the Windows Explorer. Select several files from a directory on your system and drag them (holding the left mouse button down on a selected file and moving it out of the window) over to the running application. Release the left-mouse button and observe how the file names appear in the list box.

Figure 9.3 shows the application running with several files dropped from the Explorer window. As you see, the full path names of the files appear in the list box for the application showing you exactly which files were selected by the user and dropped onto the form.

A More Complete Example: The File Attribute Viewer

The short examples you've seen presented in this chapter up to this point have shown how to do a job or two, but really haven't presented a fully rounded use of the Windows API. In this example, we look at not only one or two API functions, but a complete group of functions designed for the Windows file system. The example we'll be building is a simple file-attribute viewer. It will allow us to select a drive and directory and then display a set of information about that drive, directory, and files found in the directory.

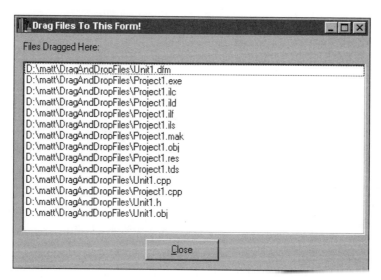

Figure 9.3
The DragAndDropFiles form in action.

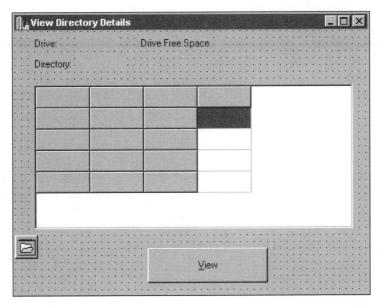

Figure 9.4
The FileAttributeViewer application form.

The Windows API provides a rich set of functions that work specifically with the file system. There are functions to retrieve all of the files that match specific criteria (such as a file mask), functions to retrieve disk free space, and functions to get volume names. In this example, we explore all of these functions to display information about them to the user.

Figure 9.4 shows the form we'll be working with for this example. You can see the kinds of information we'll be displaying based on the controls displayed here. Several labels are used to hold disk/drive information, while the string grid control will be used to display information about individual files found in the directory selected by the user. The View button is used to start the process, and the OpenDialog is used to get the selection of where to view information from the user.

The very first thing we need to do is to initialize the grid to have the correct column headers so that the user knows what he or she is looking at. Add the following code to the **FormCreate** method (the handler for the **OnCreate** event for the form):

```
void __fastcall TForm1::FormCreate(TObject *Sender)
{
    StringGrid1->Cells[0][0] = "File Name";
```

```
    StringGrid1->Cells[1][0] = "Attributes";
    StringGrid1->Cells[2][0] = "Size";

    StringGrid1->ColWidths[0] = StringGrid1->ClientWidth / 3;
    StringGrid1->ColWidths[1] = StringGrid1->ClientWidth / 3;
    StringGrid1->ColWidths[2] = StringGrid1->ClientWidth / 3;

    StringGrid1->RowCount = 1;
}
```

The first thing the user is going to do is to select a file by bringing up the Open File Dialog using the View button. Add a handler for the View button **OnClick** event to the form and add the following code to the handler:

```
void __fastcall TForm1::Button1Click(TObject *Sender)
{
   if ( OpenDialog1->Execute() )
   {
      // First, save the drive and directory
      AnsiString strDrive = ExtractFileDrive( OpenDialog1->FileName );
      AnsiString strDirectory = ExtractFileDir( OpenDialog1->FileName );

      // Get the volume name
      char szVolName[ _MAX_PATH ];
      DWORD dwVolumeSerialNumber=0;
      DWORD dwMaxVolumeLength = _MAX_PATH;
      DWORD dwFileSystemFlags = 0;
      char szFileSystemNameBuffer[ _MAX_PATH ];

      strDrive += "\\";
      GetVolumeInformation( strDrive.c_str(),
        szVolName, // address of name of the volume
        _MAX_PATH,  // length of lpVolumeNameBuffer
        &dwVolumeSerialNumber,     // address of volume serial number
        &dwMaxVolumeLength,  // address of system's maximum file name
                             // length
        &dwFileSystemFlags,  // address of file system flags
        szFileSystemNameBuffer,    // address of name of file system
        _MAX_PATH   // length of lpFileSystemNameBuffer
      );

      // handle the drive free space label
               char szBuffer[ 80 ];
                    DWORD dwSectorsPerCluster, dwBytesPerSector;
                    DWORD dwFreeClusters, dwClusters;
                    DWORD dwFreeSpace;
```

```
GetDiskFreeSpace(strDrive.c_str(),
    &dwSectorsPerCluster,
    &dwBytesPerSector, &dwFreeClusters,
    &dwClusters);

dwFreeSpace =
    dwSectorsPerCluster * dwBytesPerSector *
    dwFreeClusters;

sprintf(szBuffer, "%ld", dwFreeSpace );
DriveFreeSpaceLabel->Caption = szBuffer;

// Put them in the labels
DriveLabel->Caption = strDrive + "  [" + szVolName + "]";
DirectoryLabel->Caption = strDirectory;

AnsiString strAll = strDirectory + "\\*.*";

// Now, get all of the files in the directory using the
// FindFile API functions
            WIN32_FIND_DATA FindFileData;
        HANDLE hFirstFileHandle = FindFirstFile( strAll.c_str(),
        &FindFileData );
            int nRow = 1;

        while ( hFirstFileHandle )
            {
    // Increment the number of rows displayed
    // in the grid.
                StringGrid1->RowCount++;

    // Get the file size.
            long lFileSize = (FindFileData.nFileSizeHigh *
                MAXDWORD) + FindFileData.nFileSizeLow;

    // Get the file attributes
    AnsiString strArchive = "";
                        if ( FindFileData.dwFileAttributes &
                        FILE_ATTRIBUTE_ARCHIVE )
    strArchive += "A";
                        if ( FindFileData.dwFileAttributes &
                        FILE_ATTRIBUTE_COMPRESSED )
    strArchive += "C";
                        if ( FindFileData.dwFileAttributes &
                        FILE_ATTRIBUTE_DIRECTORY )
    strArchive += "D";
```

```
                                    if ( FindFileData.dwFileAttributes &
                                        FILE_ATTRIBUTE_HIDDEN )
                    strArchive += "H";
                                    if ( FindFileData.dwFileAttributes &
                                        FILE_ATTRIBUTE_READONLY )
                    strArchive += "R";
                                    if ( FindFileData.dwFileAttributes &
                                        FILE_ATTRIBUTE_SYSTEM )
                    strArchive += "S";
                                    if ( FindFileData.dwFileAttributes &
                                        FILE_ATTRIBUTE_TEMPORARY )
                    strArchive += "T";

                // Put the data into the grid.
                StringGrid1->Cells[0][nRow] = FindFileData.cFileName;
                StringGrid1->Cells[1][nRow] = strArchive;
                sprintf(szBuffer, "%ld", lFileSize );
                StringGrid1->Cells[2][nRow] = szBuffer;

                    if ( FindNextFile( hFirstFileHandle, &FindFileData ) ==
                        FALSE )
                {
                    if ( GetLastError() == ERROR_NO_MORE_FILES )
                        break;
                }
                        nRow ++;
            }
        }
    }
```

This is an awful lot of code to digest in one sitting. Let's tackle it one piece at a time to try to gain an understanding of what is going on here. The first thing that happens is that the user selects a specific file in a given directory using the Open File Dialog. Once they've successfully selected a file, the code then gets the drive letter and directory of the file using the utility functions **ExtractFileDrive** and **ExtractFileDir**. These functions, found in the vcl\sysutils.hpp include file in your CBuilder install tree, will return to you the drive and directory portions of the full pathname of the file. In the case of the directory, this information already includes the drive (i.e., the directory is D:\dir\), which we can then use to search for all of the files.

Once we have the drive letter of the file selected, our next step is to get the volume name of the drive where the file exists. The volume name is the name of the drive that appears in the directory list for the drive. For example, in most cases your C:

drive will appear as C: (Windows95) in the Windows Explorer and other directory listings. The volume name is the name that appears next to the drive letter, in this case Windows95. Although not particularly informative for hard drives such as C:, the volume information can be used to directly identify CD-ROMs or other removable media on your system.

Following the volume information, the next thing the program does is to get the amount of free disk space on the drive. You would think that something as simple as the free space of the drive would have its own API function, wouldn't you? After all, this information appears in all directory listings and Explorer windows. It must be as simple as calling an API function called something like **GetDriveFreeSpace**, right? Wrong. Getting the drive free space involves getting three different values from the API function and then combining them to form the total amount of drive space available on the disk. The information we retrieve includes the Sectors Per Cluster, which is the number of sectors found in a single cluster of the hard drive, the Bytes Per Sector, which represents the number of usable bytes on the hard drive for a single sector (one rotation of the disk), and the number of free clusters. This, by the way, is a factor of the hard drive. Some drives allow you to get space down to the individual byte, while others limit it down to the nearest cluster. The larger the number of the smallest unit, the more space that is used by each file on the disk. This is why the amount of space taken by a file on a hard disk doesn't really represent the amount of space used for that single file.

The three numbers are multiplied together and the result stored in the **DWORD** value **dwFreeSpace**. This information is then formatted for display and placed in the label for the disk free space.

In addition to the disk free space label, the directory, drive, and volume name are also placed into label captions at this point. The next step is to display the individual files found in the directory for the selected file.

To find all of the files in a given directory, you use the **FindFirstFile** and **FindNextFile** API functions. These functions will return you files that match a given criteria, such as all files (*.*), all source files (*.cpp), or all library files (*.lib). In addition, because you can use wildcard matching for the files, you could look for all files that begin with the name "Fred" by using the mask Fred*.* or even all files with the name Fred in them by selecting *Fred* as the file mask. The file mask is not case-sensitive, so all files that match the text in any case will be selected.

The **FindFirstFile** API function takes as arguments the file mask you want to find files to match and the address of a structure of type **WIN32_FIND_DATA**. Among other things, the **WIN32_FIND_DATA** has the file name of the file stored in the **cFileName** attribute of the structure. If successful, the **FindFirstFile** API function returns a handle to a search process that can be used with the **FindNextFile** API function.

Determining The State Of A File

One of the things that the **FindFirstFile** and **FindNextFile** API functions return is a pointer to a **WIN32_FIND_DATA** block, as I mentioned. This structure has a wealth of information about the file. Not only the full file name, but also the alternate file name, is found here. In addition, you'll find the size of the file (stored for unknown reasons in a high-word, low-word format) and the attributes for the file, which is what we were looking for in the first place.

The size of the file is stored in two separate **DWORD** pieces. Multiplying the high word of the size by the constant **MAXDWORD** results in the high end of the size. Adding to that the low-word size of the file results in a complete value representing the file size in bytes.

After the file size, we tackle the file attributes. The file attributes are a bitset of values that represent the state of the file. File attributes indicate whether the file is writable or not, whether it has changed since the last backup (archive bit), whether the file is a temporary file in the system and will be deleted upon reboot, and many other things. Table 9.1 shows the available file attribute bits and what they mean.

The file attributes of the file are examined to see whether each of the individual attributes applies to the file. Although there are a few combinations that will not occur naturally in the system (TEMPORARY and SYSTEM, for example), all of the attributes can be assigned to any file in the system if you so desire. The attr.exe program can be used to modify the attributes of a file in the command window, or the Windows Explorer program can be used to modify some of the attributes.

Once we've determined the attributes of a file and built the results into a displayable string, the information for the file is placed into a row of the string grid. The next file is obtained using the **FindNextFile** API function, and the process continues. The loop will exit as soon as the **FindNextFile** method returns false. Note that we then check the **GetLastError** API function to see if we're really done. If the last file has been

Table 9.1 File attributes for Windows files.

FILE_ATTRIBUTE_ARCHIVE	Indicates that this file has changed. Normally, the backup program you use clears this bit to indicate that it does not need to be resaved on the next save.
FILE_ATTRIBUTE_COMPRESSED	Indicates that this file is stored in compressed format and needs to be expanded to be used by the system.
FILE_ATTRIBUTE_DIRECTORY	Indicates that this file is really a directory and may contain sub-files within it.
FILE_ATTRIBUTE_HIDDEN	Indicates that this file is hidden. By default, hidden files do not appear in the directory or Windows Explorer file views. This can be changed by the user.
FILE_ATTRIBUTE_READONLY	Indicates that this file is read-only. Read-only files may not be modified by the user or application programs. In addition, you cannot delete a read-only file directly.
FILE_ATTRIBUTE_SYSTEM	Indicates that this file belongs to the operating system. Although this is really only a warning, modifying system files can have terrible repercussions on the system.
FILE_ATTRIBUTE_TEMPORARY	Indicates that this file is a temporary file. Temporary files will be removed from the system on the next system reboot.

processed, the **GetLastError** API function will return ERROR_NO_MORE_FILES. Any other error simply indicates that the file could not be processed (because it's currently being modified, for example).

Figure 9.5 shows the application running with a selection of files displayed. You can see the CD-ROM volume label in this case, as well as the individual files. Each of the files on the CD-ROM is shown with its individual attributes, file names, and file sizes displayed.

In this example, we've seen how to use quite a few of the API functions of the Windows SDK system. The good news is that this is easier to implement in CBuilder than in Visual Basic or Delphi because the types of data that you send to the API functions are compatible with the kinds of data that the C++ language supports directly. Aren't you glad that it is this easy? Don't you wish everything was this easy to implement?

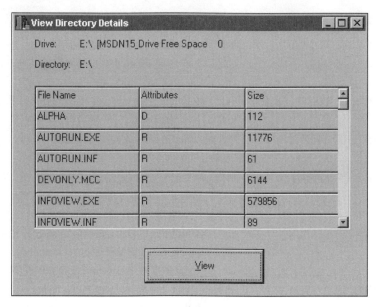

Figure 9.5
The FileAttributeViewer application in use.

The Infamous Round Window

The last example we're going to explore in this chapter is a really nice example of why you might want to use the Windows API to work with your programs. The ability to support windows that are not rectangular is one of the more exciting features added to the Windows API in Windows 95 and NT. In previous versions of the Windows operating system, it was not possible to have true non-rectangular windows. You could draw one that was oval or circular, but the actual window rectangle was still just that, a rectangle.

With the release of Windows 95 and NT, however, Microsoft added support for the concept of window regions. A window region is a shape that defines what the window looks like. They've been used for years to define the paintable area of a window. Only in the latest releases of the operating system, however, can the window region be used as the actual bounding region for the window. Window regions define not only the drawable area of the window, but also the area hidden under the window and the area of the window that responds to mouse clicks. In previous versions of the operating systems, the window might appear to be round, but a mouse click anywhere in the rectangular region of the window would activate it. In addition, the area behind the window was not updated when the underlying window changed, because Windows thought that the area was still covered by the top "circular" window.

As I mentioned, all of that has changed with the latest release of Windows. Today you can have true circular windows and you can even have windows with holes in the middle. This leads to all sorts of interesting possibilities for your application programs. Wonderful new effects to waste even more time can be presented to the user (just kidding).

In this example you'll see how to make a form with a round button in it and then add the ability to make the form itself round.

The RoundWindow Form

In the quest for more imaginative forms, a round form with a round button certainly would appear to be an innovative creation. There are problems with the approach, as we'll see as we explore the issue, but nothing that cannot be solved with the proper approach (read: a lot of programming).

Figure 9.6 shows the program we'll be developing. The form is not round, of course; it's actually elliptical. The button, likewise, is elliptical. An ellipse is just a circle with

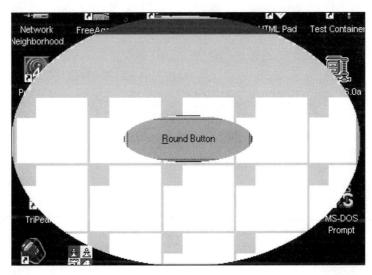

Figure 9.6
The RoundForm window.

one of its axes longer than the other. If you want the button to be perfectly round, all you need to do is make the button displayed on the form into a square. Likewise, if the form needs to be a circle, make the height and width parameters the same.

Figure 9.7, on the other hand, shows the form we'll be working from. As you can see from the figure, the shape of both the button and the form is set at runtime rather than design time because the technique we'll be using to set the shape of the windows can only be applied at runtime.

Implementing A Round Button

In order to implement a round button, you need to understand how the API works with windows. There are two steps needed to change the shape of a button, and there are two API functions involved in the process. The first step is to create a shape to apply to the window. You can think of this step as creating a cookie cutter. You create the cookie cutter shape any way you want to and then smash it down on the cookie dough to create a shaped cookie (well, in the case of my children you end up with a slightly eaten cookie dough shape, but that's another story). The second step of the procedure is the smashing down of the cookie cutter shape onto the window.

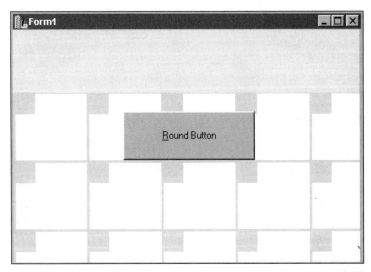

Figure 9.7
The design time view of the RoundForm window.

The first step is implemented by the **CreateEllipticRgn** API function. This function is a variant of the **CreatePolygonRgn** function. There are actually quite a few region-creation functions: **CreateRectRgn**, **CreateEllipticRgn**, **CreateRoundRectRgn**, and **CreatePolygonRgn**. Each of these, which you can look up in your Win32SDK.hlp help file, creates a different type of region display. If you want a complex region shape you can use the different region functions to create different regions and then combine them using the **CombineRgn** API function. This would allow you to implement a round region with a hole in the middle, for example. Once you've used the region functions to create a new region display, you apply the region to the window (the smashing of the cookie cutter) by using the **SetWindowRgn** function.

The best time to implement the region for the window is when the form is first created. Add a new handler for the **OnCreate** event for the form and add the following code to the **FormCreate** method of the form:

```
void __fastcall TForm1::FormCreate(TObject *Sender)
{            HRGN hRgn = CreateEllipticRgn(
        0,       // x-coordinate of the upper-left corner of the
                 // bounding rectangle
          0,     // y-coordinate of the upper-left corner of the
                 // bounding rectangle
        Button1->Width,   // x-coordinate of the lower-right
                          // corner of the button
        Button1->Height   // y-coordinate of the lower-right
                          // corner of the button
    );

    SetWindowRgn( Button1->Handle,     hRgn,  TRUE );
}
```

This code will create an elliptic region within the boundaries of the button and then assign it to the button as the new window region. Notice that the region has to be defined in terms of the coordinates of the button rather than in screen coordinates. The 0,0 point is the top left corner of the button, while the Width,Height point is the bottom right corner of the button.

> **Note:** It's extremely important that you do not do anything with the region handle once you've assigned it to the window. The best result of modifying or deleting the handle once you've assigned it to a window is a program

*crash; the worst is a system crash. At this point you have a form button that displays itself as an ellipse, and the next step is to add the code that does the same for the form. Before you do so, however, modify the border style property of the form to be **bsNone**. If you don't do this you'll see portions of the form border through the ellipse, and it will look ugly. You should notice that the background image control set onto the form is also affected by the round window. It will not draw itself over the window underneath the form.*

Add the following code to the bottom of the **FormCreate** method (below the code you just added for the button) to make the form elliptical.

```
HRGN hRgn1 = CreateEllipticRgn(
                0, // x-coordinate of the upper-left corner of the
                   // bounding rectangle
                0,    // y-coordinate of the upper-left corner of the
                   // bounding rectangle
                Width,    // x-coordinate of the lower-right corner of
                   // the bounding rectangle
                Height    // y-coordinate of the lower-right corner of
                   // the bounding rectangle
);

SetWindowRgn( Handle,
            hRgn1,
    TRUE );
```

This code looks almost exactly the same as the code for the button. The only difference is that the **Button** parameter is left off the properties. This is not a real surprise. All windows are treated exactly the same way in terms of window regions. You could, in fact, create a round list box, tree view, or dialog box if you so desired. It might look strange, but it's certainly possible.

You'll probably notice that the button looks strange when it's displayed in elliptical form. This is because of the border for the button. It's not directly possible to modify the button border without creating a new component based on the **button** class. This can certainly be done, but it's not quite as simple as just making the button round.

That completes the round form. All it took to make the whole thing work was four function calls of two different Windows API functions. Now do you see why learning what is possible with the Windows API is so important? Imagine what it would have taken to implement a round form without these functions.

What Did We Learn In This Chapter?

This chapter was a rather brief introduction to the Windows API. You could probably spend several years learning all of the API functions, at which point Windows would have added several thousand more to support all the new things that were going on in new releases. By staying with the CBuilder interface, you're assured that at least you'll stay current on the most basic issues of Windows programming.

Here are some of the things you should have gleaned from this section:

- The Windows API can be used directly from CBuilder with no modification of functions or parameter types (unlike Delphi or Visual Basic).

- Drag and drop of files from Windows Explorer or other Windows applications is easily handled in CBuilder by notifying the system you want to receive files and by processing the WM_DROPFILES message.

- The API functions for the file system can aid you in locating files, finding files using a wildcard, reading file attributes, and finding disk information.

- By using the **FindWindow** API function, you can prevent multiple instances of your applications from running.

- The shape of a window or form can be changed by a simple call to the Windows API function, **SetWindowRgn**.

That concludes our discussion of the Windows API. It's hard to overemphasize the need for professional programmers in Windows to understand something about the underlying system and the API functions that implement what is going on. By understanding something about what functions do and which functions are available, you'll make yourself a better CBuilder programmer as well.

Working With Resources

HIGH PERFORMANCE

CHAPTER

10

- **Why Use Resources?**

- **Working With Strings**

- **Dynamic Menus**

- **Working With The Resource Compiler**

- **The Dynamic Link Library**

Working With Resources

Resources are at the heart of everything that you do in CBuilder, whether you realize it or not. All form data, such as properties and event handlers, are stored as attached resources for the applications you write in CBuilder. The strings, menus, controls, and other information is all available to the underlying VCL classes via resources bound to your program at link time.

In this chapter we explore some of the other uses of resources in your applications. What is a resource? Basically, it is data attached to your program. Resources cannot directly contain code, but they can contain information used by code in your application. Normal examples of resources would include strings, menus, and bitmaps. This information is carried along with your executable or can be stored in a Dynamic Link Library (DLL).

We'll explore some of the lesser-known examples of how to use resources. We'll build a resource-only DLL in CBuilder and in another development system (in this case, Visual C++) and show you how to load information from that DLL at runtime. (A resource-only DLL has resources that can be dynamically loaded at runtime by the application.)

In addition to the resource-only DLL, we'll explore how to load menus dynamically at runtime in your application. CBuilder has no direct way to load a menu from a resource or external file, but you can easily configure a menu at runtime based on a selected menu from a resource.

Of course, you'll learn how to build resource files. Although most of the time you'll simply build a resource file using Borland's Resource Workshop (shipped with the Borland C++ product) or another environment (such as Visual C++'s Resource Editor), you can also build a fully functional resource file from scratch by entering it by hand. It isn't nearly as hard as it sounds, and you'll see how to do it.

The last example we'll examine in this chapter is a different kind of resource. You'll learn how to load actual code (functions) from an external DLL at runtime without linking to the DLL at compile time. This extremely powerful technique, known as dynamic loading of functions, can be used to extend existing programs without having the source code to them. With proper design, you can insure that your programs live on into the future by loading critical data from external DLLs.

Why Use Resources?

The first question in your head is probably why we use resources in the first place. After all, CBuilder already loads most of its data from resources, so why try to beat the system at its own game? The answer is that resources have more uses than CBuilder puts them to. CBuilder stores its data statically in resource files. You can store strings in the resource file and then recall them at runtime based on your own criteria. You can even change the display of labels based on the data stored in resource files.

Why would you want to do something like this? In a word, *internationalization*. The ability to store information for each language separately in string tables in the resource file lends itself nicely to defining separate tables for each language. This will become more and more important as software becomes more and more global in scope. You'll need to worry about versions of your code running not only in the United States and the United Kingdom, but also in France, Spain, Germany, Israel, Russia, and a host of other countries. Keeping the code itself in a single version is the only way to stay sane.

If you're able to load the different parts of the system that do change for different languages in a single place, you minimize the amount of work needed to convert your software for use in other countries. Although there are still some environments that simply won't work this easily (Chinese, for example, has other requirements that make this approach impossible), most will. With the power of resource files, you need only worry about loading the correct set of strings for a given environment rather than shipping separate products for each country.

Another huge advantage to resources is in customization. Suppose that your program has three different modes. The first mode supports those who have rarely used a computer and know nothing about working with Windows (your vice president is probably one of these people at your company). For them, you need more verbose error messages, simple screen prompts, and a short menu system that covers the most commonly used commands.

More advanced users want more options, more control over the system, and less verbiage in displays and error messages. They want to do the things that they need to do with the system and still have the ability to extend their control over the system in the future.

The final kind of user you're most likely to run across is the so-called power user, who will want complete control over everything. They want hot keys that let them quickly execute common controls, tight error messages that display only the information they need, and menus that can be configured to show the parts they want and leave off the fluff (like help, for example).

The only way to satisfy all three groups is to use resources. The only other alternative is to ship three separate products or have so much decision logic code in your program that it eventually implodes under its own weight. Let's explore how you can use resources to solve your problems in a little easier fashion without rewriting the same code three times in different ways.

String Resources

By far the most common use of resources is in storing and loading strings (text characters) from an external source. As mentioned previously, string resources are most commonly used for internationalization, but there are other, not quite as obvious, uses for string resources. If you want to change the error message displayed in response to some action, you normally use the **MessageBox** function to inform the user of what has gone wrong. The text that appears in the message box is normally hard-coded into the program. What, though, if you want to change that message later on, in response to user feedback about the problem? You would need to change the text, recompile, and redistribute the entire program. In addition, the testing people would insist that a new release requires new testing. It can be a nightmare to make a simple change like this in an application.

Suppose, instead, that the strings for your message boxes were stored in an external file. The length of the strings stored in the file would not change, so the testing people wouldn't require a complete systems test if you needed to change one. The documentation people would be happy because they would understand that text can change and would write the user instructions accordingly. Finally, you would be happy because the code for the test wouldn't change, the program wouldn't need to be recompiled, and your boss wouldn't yell at you. All this for changing the string in the external file and shipping that one file to the users.

This is the concept behind string resources. They're stored in either the program in which they're used or in an external DLL. In this example, we'll use a simple resource-only DLL, created in another system, to load data into our application at runtime.

Building The String DLL

We've established that creating a DLL containing our string resources is a good thing, so the next step is to actually build one. Creating a DLL in CBuilder is not difficult, nor is creating the strings that go into it. Let's do that first.

Create a new project in CBuilder by selecting File|New. In the Projects tab of the new item dialog, select DLL from the available object types. Click on the OK button, and CBuilder will generate the skeleton for a DLL, including the prolog code. We aren't going to work with this code at all in this example because this DLL will contain no extra code.

Create a new text file in CBuilder and add the following lines to it. This is going to be our string resource file for the DLL.

```
STRINGTABLE DISCARDABLE
BEGIN
    1001 "Hello"
    1002 "Aloha"
    1003 "Shalom"
    1004 "Hola!"
END
```

If you've never worked with string tables before, the concept is pretty simple. The string table resource is defined by the line **STRINGTABLE DISCARDABLE**. The **STRINGTABLE** keyword indicates to the resource compiler that the lines which follow define a string table resource. The **DISCARDABLE** flag indicates that this block need not be fixed in memory and can be swapped out to disk if needed. Following the definition of the block is the **BEGIN** statement, which indicates that we're now starting to define strings for the table.

Each string in a string table is a pair of integer values and string values. The integer values are used to identify each string in the table with a unique number. When you refer to a string by resource identifier, you'll use this number. When the string table is complete (it may have any number of entries), you terminate the string table definition with the **END** statement.

Save this file as strings.rc in the CBuilder project folder containing your new project. Add the new resource file to the project by selecting the Project|Add to Project menu item and then selecting the strings.rc file. CBuilder already knows what to do with resource script files (RC files), so there is no need to do anything more. Close the file and build the project in the usual fashion by selecting Project|Make or pressing F9. The resource file will be compiled and, if there are no errors, the DLL file will be generated for the project. That's all there is to creating a DLL in CBuilder.

The Dynamic String Load Example

The next step in our example is to build a form that takes advantage of the string DLL that we so laboriously just finished building. In this example, we'll pretend that the strings contained in the DLL represent different language displays for a given label on a form. In fact, if you look at the data you'll see that the strings represent the word Hello in several different languages (although all are using the English alphabet to display in this case).

Figure 10.1 shows the form we'll use to display the data for this form. As you can see, the form consists of one label and four radio buttons. These are the only controls we'll need to implement this example.

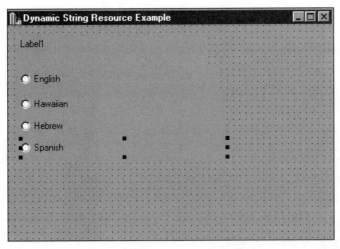

Figure 10.1
The dynamic string load example form.

After building the form, we need to worry about loading the data from the DLL. To do this, you need to understand two different Windows API functions. We talked quite a bit about API functions in the previous chapter, and these particular functions are two new ones.

The first API function to understand is the **LoadLibrary** function, which will allow you to open and extract data from a dynamic link library on disk. In order to use our DLL in the rest of the code for the form, we need to open it when the form starts up. Therefore, we'll use the constructor for the form to initialize the library handle. Add the following code to the constructor for the form:

```
__fastcall TForm1::TForm1(TComponent* Owner)
                : TForm(Owner)
{
   hLibHandle = LoadLibrary("project1.dll");
}
```

In addition, you need to add a definition for the hLibHandle variable to the form header file. Add the following line to the user private section of the form header:

```
private:    // User declarations
   HINSTANCE hLibHandle;
```

These two changes give you full access to the contents of the DLL called "project1.dll," which we built in the previous section. The **LoadLibrary** function gives you a handle to the instance of the DLL. Why an instance handle? A DLL can be loaded by multiple applications running in Windows. This is why they're useful. If a dozen different applications use code or resources in a DLL, they can all share the same DLL loaded into memory. When you use the **LoadLibrary** API function to get the handle to the DLL, you'll increment the instance count on the DLL. The DLL will only be unloaded from memory when all of the applications referencing it are unloaded from memory (for when the handle for the library is released).

Once you've loaded a library via the **LoadLibrary** function, you should always remember to unload it when you're finished. If you don't, it will hang around in memory and waste resources until Windows gets around to getting rid of it. Add a handler for the **OnClose** method of the form and add the following code to the **FormClose** method:

```
void __fastcall TForm1::FormClose(TObject *Sender, TCloseAction &Action)
{
   if ( hLibHandle != NULL )
   {
      FreeLibrary( hLibHandle );
   }

}
```

Note the check to see if the handle was NULL. If the **LoadLibrary** function fails to find the library or it's unable to load it into memory for whatever reason, the returned handle from the function will be NULL. It's not a good idea to pass NULL handles to functions or methods that expect valid handles, so we put in a check to be sure that the handle is valid before we try to release it. The same is true for any other use of the function, as you'll see shortly.

Okay, the library is loaded and the form displayed. The next step is to get the strings when the user requests them. Let's tackle the first one first, the English radio button. Add a new handler for the radio button and add the following code to the handler:

```
void __fastcall TForm1::RadioButton1Click(TObject *Sender)
{
   if ( hLibHandle != NULL )
   {
      char szBuffer[ 256 ];
                  LoadString( hLibHandle,
                        1001,
                      szBuffer,
                        256          // size of buffer
                );
      Label1->Caption = szBuffer;
   }

}
```

This handler first checks to see if we've successfully loaded the library by examining the handle. If it's not NULL, the method then calls the **LoadString** API function to retrieve a specific string from the DLL. The **LoadString** API function has the following syntax:

```
int LoadString( HINSTANCE hInstance, int nResourceID, LPSTR strBuffer,
                int nSizeOfBuffer);
```

In our case, the instance handle (**HINSTANCE**) is the handle of the library we loaded via the **LoadLibrary** function. The resource ID is the same as the string ID that we defined in the string table of the resource file. **LoadString** will look in the string table for a string containing the same ID as the one we set. Therefore, looking at the string table definition a bit earlier in the chapter, you'll see that string **1001** maps to the English entry "**Hello**".

The **szBuffer** and **256** entries are the buffer in which we want to contain the returned string and the length of that buffer, respectively. If **LoadString** finds a string longer than the maximum length allowed, it will only return the first 256 bytes of the string and thus not crash the program.

To handle the other radio buttons, we just change the ID of the string we want to retrieve from the DLL. Here are the handlers for the other three radio buttons on the form that you can add at your leisure:

```
void __fastcall TForm1::RadioButton2Click(TObject *Sender)
{
   if ( hLibHandle != NULL )
   {
      char szBuffer[ 256 ];
                  LoadString( hLibHandle,
                           1002,
                        szBuffer,
                           256        // size of buffer
               );
      Label1->Caption = szBuffer;
   }


}
//-------------------------------------------------------------------
void __fastcall TForm1::RadioButton3Click(TObject *Sender)
{
   if ( hLibHandle != NULL )
   {
      char szBuffer[ 256 ];
                  LoadString( hLibHandle,
                           1003,
                        szBuffer,
                           256        // size of buffer
               );
```

```
         Label1->Caption = szBuffer;
   }
}
//--------------------------------------------------------------------
void __fastcall TForm1::RadioButton4Click(TObject *Sender)
{
   if ( hLibHandle != NULL )
   {
      char szBuffer[ 256 ];
                  LoadString( hLibHandle,
                          1004,
                        szBuffer,
                          256          // size of buffer
               );
      Label1->Caption = szBuffer;
   }


}
```

As you can see, the process is exactly the same in each case. In fact, we could move all of this code into a single routine that simply retrieves data from a DLL and encapsulate the whole process in one place:

```
void GetString ( int nID, AnsiString& strLang )
{
   // First, load the DLL
   HINSTANCE hLibHandle = LoadLibrary("project1.dll");
   if ( hLibHandle )
    {
        char szBuffer[256];
        LoadString( hLibHandle, nID, szBuffer, 256 );
        s = szBuffer;
       FreeLibrary( hLibHandle );
    }
}
```

Then all of the previous code could use the single function **GetString** to retrieve the data each method needed to display the text. Notice that we also used the **AnsiString** object, which supports better string handling, to retrieve the data. An AnsiString can also be directly assigned to the **Caption** property of the label.

You have now mastered the art of loading language-dependent strings from a DLL. There is really nothing else to it. It's probably worth mentioning, however, that the same process can be applied to bitmaps and icons in resources as well. If you have a bitmap object (**TBitmap**) on your form, you can assign it to the loaded bitmap by getting an HBITMAP handle from the resource file and then assigning it to the **Handle** property of the **TBitmap** object. This works quite well for everything, as it happens, except menus. Let's explore why that is so.

Loading Dynamic Menus

After the last discussion, you would think that loading a menu from a resource file would be quite easy. Menus have their own handles, called HMENU handles, and can be loaded from a resource file using the **LoadMenu** API function. You would think, therefore, that loading a menu from a resource file would be as simple as writing a line of code like this:

```
MainMenu1->Handle = LoadMenu( HInstance, MAKEINTRESOURCE(ID_MY_MENU));
```

You would think this, but the truth is that it doesn't work. Menus are handled differently by the underlying Windows API than bitmaps, icons, or strings because the menu is really a part of the window, while the other pieces are discrete entities that don't interact with anything else. I was a little surprised, actually, that Borland did not wrap the menu functionality the same way it did everything else, but then you can't expect to have everything done for you.

Why can't you write the previous code? The answer is quite simple. The **Handle** property of the **TMainMenu** object is a private member of the class, and you won't be able to get at it from within your form object directly. Instead, you can only access the menu properties indirectly by subtracting or adding menu items to the menu.

It turns out, though, that we can emulate the loading of the menu items dynamically by doing it ourselves. To accomplish this, place a TMainMenu item on a form by itself with no menu items defined for it. The form we'll be using, in fact, is shown in Figure 10.2. As you can see, it's nothing more than a form with a main menu and no defined items.

Given the previous form, we're going to load a menu from a resource file attached to the program. First, create a resource file and add it to the project. All you need to create a resource file is a text file that contains the resource definitions (like our

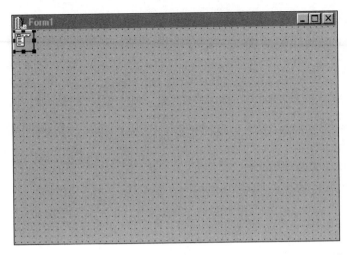

Figure 10.2
The dynamic menu form.

string table in the previous example) and then add that resource file to the project.
For our project, the resource file will look like this:

```
1001 MENU PRELOAD DISCARDABLE
BEGIN
    POPUP "&File"
    BEGIN
        MENUITEM "&New\tCtrl+N",                101
        MENUITEM "&Open...\tCtrl+O",             102
        MENUITEM "P&rint Setup...",              103
        MENUITEM "Recent File",                  104
        MENUITEM "E&xit",                        105
    END
    POPUP "&View"
    BEGIN
        MENUITEM "&Toolbar",                     106
        MENUITEM "&Status Bar",                  107
    END
    POPUP "&Help"
    BEGIN
        MENUITEM "&About...",             108
    END
END
```

Adding the resource file to the project is easy enough. Select the Project|Add To Project menu item and select the resource file from the file list. Set the file mask to either all files or resource scripts (*.rc). CBuilder knows enough about resource files to compile the resource script automatically and then bind it to the executable when it's finished linking.

We now have some resources attached to the project. The one that we care about, of course, is the menu in the resource file. It's now time to be able to load that resource from the executable at runtime. If you had multiple menus, you would simply select the one you want based on some criteria of your own and then load it in the same fashion. Let's look at the actual code that loads the menu from the resource and builds it on the form:

```
void __fastcall TForm1::FormCreate(TObject *Sender)
{
    // Load a menu resource from the rc file
    HMENU hMenu = LoadMenu((HINSTANCE)HInstance, MAKEINTRESOURCE(1001));

    // Get the number of sub-menus in this menu
    int nCount = GetMenuItemCount(hMenu);

    // Loop through each one, getting the
    // information we need
    for ( int i=0; i<nCount; ++i )
    {
        // Get the sub-menu
        HMENU hSubMenu = GetSubMenu( hMenu, i );

        // How many sub-menu items in this menu?
        char szBuffer[80];
        int nSubCount = GetMenuItemCount( hSubMenu );

        GetMenuString( hMenu,i,szBuffer,80,MF_BYPOSITION );
        TMenuItem *pMenuItem = new TMenuItem(MainMenu1);
        pMenuItem->Caption = szBuffer;
        MainMenu1->Items->Add( pMenuItem );

        // Get the information for the sub-menu
        for ( int nSubPos = 0; nSubPos<nSubCount; ++nSubPos )
        {
            GetMenuString( hSubMenu,nSubPos,szBuffer,
                80,MF_BYPOSITION );
            TMenuItem *pSubMenuItem = new TMenuItem(pMenuItem);
```

```
                    pSubMenuItem->Caption = szBuffer;
        pMenuItem->Add( pSubMenuItem );
    }
            }
}
```

Dynamic Loading Of A Menu

In order to load a menu resource from the resources in an executable (or any other kind of resource, for that matter), you need to know the identifier of the resource. This is the ID that we created with the **MENU** statement in the resource file. This identifier is passed to the **LoadMenu** API function to get back a handle to the menu resource. This is where the magic begins.

Once we have a menu loaded, we need to know how many main menu entries (the top line of the menu) will appear on this menu. This is obtained via the API function **GetMenuItemCount**, which takes a single argument, the handle of the menu you're working with. It works with either main menus or sub-menus. In this case, by passing the main menu handle to the function, we obtain the number of sub-menus in the menu.

In order to add the menu items, we loop through all of the sub-menus for the defined menu resource. Each one is added to the main menu by creating a new TMenuItem for the sub-menu and then setting the caption to the proper setting for this menu item. Within each sub-menu, we then repeat the process for the sub-menu. We get the count of the items within the sub-menu and then create each one of them.

The important function in the bunch is the **GetMenuString** API function. This method will return you the caption of the menu item in the menu by its position in the sub-menu (or main menu). Given this information, we can then add the menu item to the proper place with the proper string.

> **Note:** *This example does not retrieve the menu command identifiers from the menus and assign them. This is easy but rather pointless to add unless you really want to work with command identifiers. It's just as easy to assign a new event handler directly to the menu items as you create them and allow CBuilder to assign menu command identifiers automatically as it creates the menu items.*

The only thing that this example doesn't show is handling separators properly. It isn't hard to get this information from the menu resources you load from the resource file (use the **GetMenuState** API function and check the flags to see if this is a separator). I left this out of the example to make it a little easier to understand.

Removing The Menu Items

This is all well and good, I can hear you saying, but if I want to be able to load a menu dynamically, how do I remove the existing menu items? Well, if you'll just hang on a second, I'll show you how you do just that.

Let's add the ability to delete all the menu items from the form at runtime. Then, if you wanted to, you would be able to re-add the new menu items. I'll even show you how to re-add the items dynamically.

First, modify the form to add two new buttons with the captions "Delete All" and "Add Items". The new form is shown in Figure 10.3. The first button will be used to remove all existing menu items from the main menu, while the second button will be used to simply redo what we were doing in the creation process of the form—adding the menu items dynamically.

Rather than retyping all of the code for the Add Items button handler, just create a new function called **AddMenuItems**. Move all of the code that used to be in the

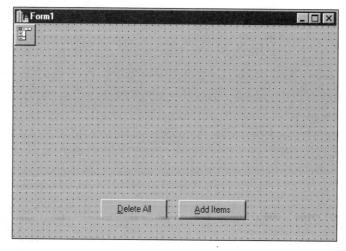

Figure 10.3
The updated dynamic menu form.

FormCreate method into the **AddMenuItems**. Then modify the **FormCreate** method to be a simple call to this new function:

```
void __fastcall TForm1::FormCreate(TObject *Sender)
{
    AddMenuItems();
}
```

The next step is to handle the deletion of the menu items. This is as easy as you might think it would be. The menu items, after all, are held in the **Items** property of the **TMainMenu** object. The **Items** property, like all **Items** properties in the VCL, has a set of functions to add or remove items. In this case, however, rather than using the **Remove** method (which is the normal way to remove items from the list) we use the **Delete** method. This method will remove the menu and all sub-menus from the list as well as de-allocating the memory associated with those items. **Remove** does not free up the memory and would result in a memory leak in your application. Here is the code for the Delete All button handler:

```
void __fastcall TForm1::Button1Click(TObject *Sender)
{
    while ( MainMenu1->Items->Count > 0 )
        MainMenu1->Items->Delete( 0 );
}
```

The handler for the Add Items button is, of course, simply another call to the **AddMenuItems** function:

```
void __fastcall TForm1::Button2Click(TObject *Sender)
{
    AddMenuItems();
}
```

So, there you have it: a complete method for dynamically loading menu items from a resource and removing existing menu items from a menu on the screen. All in one tight little package that you can easily liberate and move to another program. Pretty neat, huh?

A Word About Resource Files

Although you usually define resource files using some sort of automated process like the Resource Workshop in Borland C++ or Visual C++'s Resource Editor, you can certainly define a resource file by hand. There are a number of entries permitted in resource files that make sense in a CBuilder application and a few that make very little sense. Let's take a quick look at the kinds of things you might put into a resource file and things you probably wouldn't.

A string table is the first entry that is likely in a resource file. As we've seen, the string table resource is great for storing internationalization data and for being able to modify the string entries on a form on the fly. String tables have the following syntax:

```
STRINGTABLE DISCARDABLE
BEGIN
    id  string
END
```

where the **id** is the number you want to associate with the string. The string in the listing represents the actual string you want to add to the table.

Another kind of resource that is quite popular to use is the Bitmap resource. This resource allows you to define bitmaps that can be loaded at runtime from the program but are stored within the application. Bitmap resources have the following syntax:

```
id BITMAP DISCARDABLE "bitmapfile"
```

where the **id** represents the number to assign to this bitmap and **"bitmapfile"** is the actual file name of the Windows file containing the bitmap. For example, if you wanted to add the bitmap "clouds", which is found in the Windows directory, and assign that bitmap the identifier 102, you would use the following syntax:

```
102 BITMAP DISCARDABLE "c:\windows\clouds.bmp"
```

The **DISCARDABLE** flag indicates that Windows can move the bitmap memory out onto disk if it needs to when swapping is needed by the system. In general, there is no good reason not to include this flag for bitmaps.

The menu resource, which we looked at briefly in the previous example, can also be used in your application resource files. The menu resource has the following general syntax

```
menu-id MENU PRELOAD DISCARDABLE
BEGIN
    POPUP main-menu-name
```

```
    BEGIN
        MENUITEM sub-menu-string,              sub-menu-id [,GRAYED]
        MENUITEM SEPARATOR
    END
END
```

where the **menu-id** parameter represents the identifier to use when loading this menu resource into your application. The **main-menu-name** entry represents the top-level menu string to use when displaying the menu. A good example of this string is the File menu, which appears in nearly all Windows applications. Any of the menu names may contain an optional & (ampersand) character, which will cause the character following it to be underlined in the final display of the menu.

The **sub-menu-string** is the caption of the sub-menu that is displayed when the main menu is displayed in its dropped down position. This would be similar to the Exit command under the File command. Using our normal notation for menus, given the command File|Exit, the File part is the **main-menu-name** parameter and Exit is the **sub-menu-string** parameter. Similarly, the **sub-menu-id** represents the identifier command to be associated with this menu item. This is the command that is fired when the menu item is selected by the user. The optional parameter **GRAYED** indicates that this menu item is to be displayed initially disabled.

Another kind of menu entry is the **SEPARATOR** menu item. This entry will draw a horizontal line across the entry to allow you to separate items and group like menu commands together.

You are unlikely to use the DIALOG entry resource. This entry represents a dialog box template. You need not define templates to use for dialogs in your application because CBuilder already does dialogs for you in the form of the forms used in a project.

The final kind of resource that you may define in your application is a user resource. User resources are used to define any kind of data your application might need to store that is not covered by one of the other resources. Because there is no definite form to a user resource, it's kind of hard to show you one. It's important to note that all data for CBuilder forms is stored in the executable in the form of user resources. This information will contain such things as property values, menu callbacks, and event handlers for the form. You can look at the information stored in the form resource by viewing a form in text format. You can see this by right-clicking on a form and selecting the "View as Text" menu option from the speedmenu that is displayed.

Working With The Resource Compiler

If you want to add resources, like version information, to an executable later on outside of the CBuilder environment, you need to work a little bit with one of the two versions of the resource compiler. The first version simply compiles the resource file, and the second compiles the resource file and binds the resulting compiled resource file into the executable. You'll generally use the first form of the resource compiler to test your resource file and then use the second form after that.

To add a version resource to your executable, you need to first create a new resource file that contains the version information. Create a new file in CBuilder and add the following lines to it:

```
VS_VERSION_INFO VERSIONINFO
 FILEVERSION 1,0,0,1
 PRODUCTVERSION 1,0,0,1
 FILEFLAGSMASK 0x3fL
FILEFLAGS 0x0L
FILEOS 0x4L
 FILETYPE 0x1L
 FILESUBTYPE 0x0L
BEGIN
    BLOCK "StringFileInfo"
    BEGIN
        BLOCK "040904B0"
        BEGIN
            VALUE "CompanyName", "\0"
            VALUE "FileDescription", "Test Application\0"
            VALUE "FileVersion", "1, 0, 0, 1\0"
            VALUE "InternalName", "Test\0"
            VALUE "LegalCopyright", "Copyright (C) 1997\0"
            VALUE "LegalTrademarks", "\0"
            VALUE "OriginalFilename", "Test.EXE\0"
            VALUE "ProductName", "Test Application\0"
            VALUE "ProductVersion", "1, 0, 0, 1\0"
        END
    END
```

The version information block will contain information that can be read by programs such as the resource editors, which can tell the user what the program version number is, who created it, and so forth.

To compile the previous block, add it to a file called project1.rc and then type the following command in a command window prompt:

```
brcc32 project1.rc
```

You should then see the following output (if there are no errors):

```
C:\book\LoadMenu>brcc32 project1.rc
Borland Resource Compiler  Version 5.02
Copyright (c) 1990, 1997 Borland International.  All rights reserved.
```

This command will simply compile the resource file and check it for syntax errors. To actually compile and bind the resource file into your executable, type the command:

```
brc32 project1.rc
```

This will result in the resource file being compiled, and then the resulting RES file being added to the executable file. Once you've done this, a user can retrieve information about the program if you include version information in something like your Help|About command.

Working With Dynamic Link Libraries

Earlier in the chapter, we looked at storing resource information in dynamic link libraries. Besides resources, though, you can store other things in DLLs, the most important being program code. DLLs are one of the most useful and powerful features ever added to the Windows operating system. By using DLLs, you solve two major problems inherent in application development: memory constraints and version problems.

Memory constraints in multi-tasking operating systems are caused by many programs being loaded into memory at the same time. Each of these programs probably does many similar tasks, yet each contains code to do the job itself. If, however, all that code were factored out of the executable code and put into a single module shared among all of the running programs, there would be that much more space in memory for the running programs. This is the concept behind DLLs. The best example of a DLL is in the operating system itself. All of the Windows components that you call from within your application (drawing code, file system code, and so forth) reside in a set of system DLLs that are shared among all running applications. This ability to share code means that your program doesn't need to have all of that code linked into it.

When your program loads a DLL, either dynamically or statically, memory is searched to see if that DLL is already loaded. If the DLL is found, rather than loading another copy, the operating system simply returns a pointer (called a handle) to that DLL already loaded and increments the reference count for the DLL. You've seen this before in our string table example.

What is remarkable, though, is that not only can you load information such as resources from a DLL, but also you can use the functions that are stored there. In this example program, we'll create a DLL and then use a separate program to load a function from that DLL into our application. We can use the DLL functions to display a message, calculate a result, or anything else that can be done in a normal application. There are a few limitations to DLLs, most notably in the area of memory management, but that discussion doesn't apply to our usage in this example.

Creating a DLL With CBuilder

The first thing you need to be able to use code in a DLL is a DLL with code in it, right? Right. Let's create such a beast using CBuilder. Later on in the book we'll explore how to use a DLL created in CBuilder in another system, but for now we'll load the DLL into CBuilder.

One note. There are really two different ways to use functions in a CBuilder DLL. The first is to create an import library using the implib tool that ships with CBuilder. This import library can then be linked directly into the program, and Windows will do the job of loading the DLL at runtime for you. You need to remember to use the implib program that ships with CBuilder and not an older version from a different system, because CBuilder libraries have a different format than older ones and require the newer programs to generate them from DLLs. Once you have an import library defined for your DLL, you can just prototype the functions you want and call them directly, as if they were defined in your application. In our example, we're more interested in the mechanics of dynamic loading, so we'll do the work ourselves.

In this example we'll be creating the DLL in another environment, namely Visual C++. I made this selection partly because I know VC pretty well, but primarily because you'll generally be using third-party DLLs in your own application code rather than ones created in CBuilder. In any case, the steps involved are the same, so why not show you a little more for the same price?

Unlike CBuilder, Visual C++ (VC) is not quite nice enough to generate a DLL for you. Instead, it will create a makefile and leave it empty of source files. One more good reason to make the switch, I guess. Anyway, if you're in Visual C++, create a new file and add the following code to it. If you don't have Visual C++ or don't feel like writing all this code and loading the environment, there is a complete DLL shipped with this example source code on the accompanying CD-ROM.

```
#include <windows.h>
#include <stdlib.h>
#include <string.h>
#include <stdio.h>

BOOL WINAPI DllEntryPoint (HINSTANCE hinstDLL, DWORD fdwReason,
    LPVOID lpReserved) {

    BOOL fSuccess = TRUE;

    switch (fdwReason) {
        case DLL_PROCESS_ATTACH:
        case DLL_THREAD_ATTACH:
            break;

        case DLL_PROCESS_DETACH:
        case DLL_THREAD_DETACH:
            break;
    }
    return(fSuccess);
}

extern "C"
{
__declspec( dllexport ) int CallFunction1( void )
{
                MessageBox(NULL, "You called function 1", "Info", MB_OK
);
                                        return 0;
}
__declspec( dllexport ) int CallFunction2( const char *str )
{
                MessageBox(NULL, "You called function 2", str, MB_OK );
                                return 0;
}
```

```
__declspec( dllexport ) void CallFunction3( int nValue )
{
            char szBuffer[20];
            sprintf(szBuffer, "%d", nValue );
            MessageBox(NULL, szBuffer, "Value", MB_OK );
}
}
```

All of this code is nice in its own right, but the important things are the three functions. For now you can ignore the funky-looking **declspec(dllexport)**. This is simply a way of telling VC to export these functions in the DLL so that other programs can use them. You would think exporting the functions would be the default, but then a lot of things about Windows programming aren't quite what you'd expect.

There are three functions declared in the DLL, **CallFunction1**, **CallFunction2** and **CallFunction3**. They vary in the return value and the number of parameters accepted by the function. We'll be using all three functions in our example.

> **Note:** You'll notice that the functions are declared as **extern "C"** in the previous source code listing. Visual C++ and CBuilder use different mangling schemes to generate the names of their functions. To avoid having to look through the export listing and reproduce the actual names of the functions in mangled form, we're allowing the compiler to use the C calling conventions and naming scheme. This means that the resulting functions in the export format are called simply **CallFunction1**, etc.

Once we have the DLL defined, the next step is to create a CBuilder project to actually use the DLL functions that we've created and exported from the DLL. You should know that only exported functions can be dynamically loaded from a DLL or even linked into your application via an import library. Non-exported functions are effectively invisible to the outside world and can only be used by other functions in the DLL. We'll exploit this ability later in the book when we look at the other side of this equation: using CBuilder DLLs in Visual C++.

Creating The Dynamic DLL Form

In order to use our DLL from a CBuilder project, we need to create a form to view our display and allow the user to call from. Figure 10.4 shows the form we'll be

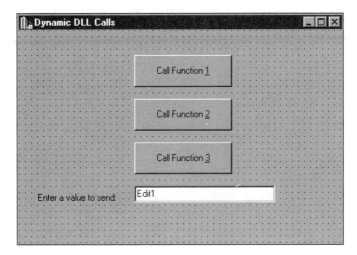

Figure 10.4
The dynamic DLL form.

using for the Dynamic DLL project. As you can see, we built this form using three buttons, a label, and an input edit field for sending data to the DLL functions.

The first step in the process of loading information from the DLL is exactly the same as for getting resources from the file, namely that we need to obtain a handle to the library file using the **LoadLibrary** API function. Add the following code to the constructor for the form to accomplish this task:

```
__fastcall TForm1::TForm1(TComponent* Owner)
              : TForm(Owner)
{
    hLibHandle = LoadLibrary("vcdll.dll");
}
```

Likewise, we need to make sure that the library handle is released when we're finished with it. This is accomplished in the **OnClose** event handler for the form, **FormClose**. Add the handler to the form and add the following code to the new handler:

```
void __fastcall TForm1::FormClose(TObject *Sender, TCloseAction &Action)
{
    if ( hLibHandle )
        FreeLibrary( hLibHandle );
}
```

At this point at least, the process we're following is exactly the same as the one we pursued to load the strings from the DLL. This is the point in the development process where the two examples diverge. Let's look at an example of this as we add a handler for the first button (**CallFunction1**) to the form. Here is the code to add to the new handler for the **Button1Click** event:

```
void __fastcall TForm1::Button1Click(TObject *Sender)
{
   if ( hLibHandle )
   {
               // Try to load the function from the library
                  pfivFunc pFunc = (pfivFunc)GetProcAddress(
                        hLibHandle,
                        "CallFunction1");
               if ( pFunc )
               (*pFunc)();
   }
}
```

In addition to the previous code, you need to add one more line to the file to make it compile. Add the following line right above this function, and then we'll talk about what's going on in this segment of the code:

```
typedef int (*pfivFunc)(void);
```

First things first. The line directly above this (the **typedef**) is a way of creating a new type in C and C++. Although it looks different than any other kind of type definition statement you might have seen in your code, it's really just a special case of the **typedef** statement.

The basic form of the **typedef** statement, which simply redefines a type as a simpler string for the compiler, is **typedef** old-type-definition new-type-definition. Here's a simple example to show you how the thing works. Suppose you wanted to define a new type called **IntBool** to represent a boolean number as an integer. This type is no different than an integer, but we want to make it clear to the programmer reading the code that this variable is intended to hold only boolean values (true and false) in an integer storage. We would write:

```
typedef int IntBool;
```

Then in the code that used the new type we would just treat the **IntBool** as a type to use in variable definition:

```
IntBool bMyInteger;
```

To the compiler, there is no difference between using the types **int** and **IntBool**. It simply substitutes one for the other. In our **pfiv** type above, we're really writing that **pfiv** is a symbol representing a function, which takes no parameters (the **void** between the parenthesis) and returns an integer value. The general form of a function-based **typedef** is

```
return-type (*function-name)(parameter types)
```

where **return-type** is the type of value the function will return (**int**, **void**, **bool**, etc.) and **function-name** is the name of the **typedef**. This is the symbol we'll be using as the new type, just as we used **IntBool** earlier.

parameter types is a list of valid C++ types (including **typedefs**). If your function took three types, say, an integer, a float, and a reference to an object of class **Foo**, this would read: (**int**, **float**, **Foo&**).

Once the strangeness is out of the way for the **typedef** statement, the rest of the code is just as weird. We're using the **GetProcAddress** API function to retrieve a pointer to a function found in the DLL, for which we've obtained an instance handle. This function will be returned as a **FARPROC**, which is simply a pointer to a function. We need to be able to call this function with arguments and check the return value, so we need the compiler to understand that this function takes such arguments. Because we have this wonderful **typedef** just lying around defining the exact prototype of our function, we cast the returned **FARPROC** into one of these new function pointers and call it indirectly by de-referencing the pointer and passing arguments (if any) to it.

> **Note:** It's very important to make sure that the types match exactly the numbers of parameters that you pass to a function in this way. Failure to do this can result in horrible consequences, including crashing the Windows operating system.

As you might recall from the DLL construction, the first function (**CallFunction1**) in the DLL was simply a function that displayed a message box. Our **GetProcAddress** function extracts the **CallFunction1** function from the DLL by matching the name we pass to the exported name in the DLL. This is why it's important to use the **extern "C"** statement in the DLL definition. If we did not, we would need to call the mangled (sometimes more nicely called decorated) name in the DLL and would end up calling something like "CallFunction1@iv1". This way we just refer to it directly by name.

> **Note:** You might be wondering if you could use the **GetProcAddress** to extract functions from within your own application and use them for an implementation like a scripting language for your program. The answer is yes. As long as the functions are available by name and you can match them, you can call them from any program to which you can get an instance handle. Theoretically, if you could get the instance handle of a running program, you could call functions in it as well.

For the second button, we need a function that takes an argument that accepts a string (**const char** *) and returns an integer value. To define a **typedef** that represents this kind of a function, we would add the following line to the source file:

```
typedef int (*pficsFunc)(const char *);
```

Likewise, we can now add the handler for the second button on the form to call the second function in the DLL (**CallFunction2**). Add a new handler for the second button and add the following code to the handler:

```
void __fastcall TForm1::Button2Click(TObject *Sender)
{
   if ( hLibHandle )
   {
                // Try to load the function from the library
                   pficsFunc pFunc = (pficsFunc)GetProcAddress(
                       hLibHandle,
                       "CallFunction2");
                if ( pFunc )
                (*pFunc)(Edit1->Text.c_str());
   }
}
```

The load process isn't much different. We simply extract the **CallFunction2** function from the DLL and then invoke it indirectly through the returned pointer. In this case, we need to send the function a string to display, so we use the edit component's current text to display.

One thing to note about the previous code is the defensive posture of it. There are several possible problems with the system around it, so the code tries its best to defend against errors that would cause catastrophic errors. First, we check the handle to the DLL to make sure that it's not NULL. This would cause serious problems in the **GetProcAddress** API function. Once we have verified to the best of our knowledge that the handle is valid, the next check is on the returned pointer from the **GetProcAddress** API function. If the function fails to find the requested function in the DLL or fails for some other reason, the returned value from the API function will also be NULL (most API functions that return handles or pointers return NULL in case of an error). In this case we won't call the function by indirection because that would cause a General Protection Fault or worse.

The third and final button calls a function that takes an integer value and returns nothing at all (**void**). The prototype for this function in a C++ **typedef** looks something like this:

```
typedef void (*pfviFunc)(int);
```

We can then use this **typedef** to send the data to the function by adding code to the handler for the third button. Add that handler to the third button and add the following code to the handler:

```
void __fastcall TForm1::Button3Click(TObject *Sender)
{
    if ( hLibHandle )
    {
                // Try to load the function from the library
                    pfviFunc pFunc = (pfviFunc)GetProcAddress(
                        hLibHandle,
                        "CallFunction3");
                if ( pFunc )
                (*pFunc)(atoi(Edit1->Text.c_str()));
    }
}
```

Once again, we're extracting the function from the DLL, this time to pass it an integer argument. Although I said earlier not to pass the **Text** property to a function such as **atoi**, this is not strictly true. It's generally a bad idea to pass the **Text** property as a string to anything that might change that string. Unpredictable results will occur in these cases. In the case of **atoi**, which promises not to modify the passed-in argument, this is a relatively safe maneuver.

If you compile and link the application now, you'll be able to see the results of all of your hard work. First of all, make sure that the VCDLL.DLL file is in the same directory as the program (project1.exe). This will insure that Windows can find the file and load it. If you don't put it into the same directory as the executable, Windows follows a simple process to try to locate it. First, it looks for a file with that name in the Windows and Windows\System directories (for NT, these are WinNt and WinNt\System). If they aren't found there, Windows then looks down every DLL found in the path statement for the machine (WinNt has a special environment variable which defines the DLL search path). Finally, if the file is not found, the **LoadLibrary** function returns NULL, indicating that the DLL was not found.

Assuming that you have, in fact, put the DLL file where Windows can find it, the form will start up and display the buttons for you to choose from. Enter some text in the edit field at the bottom of the form and click on the second button (Call Function 2). You should see a message box displayed with the text you entered as shown in Figure 10.5. This indicates that the function was, in fact, found and the text was passed correctly to the DLL function to display.

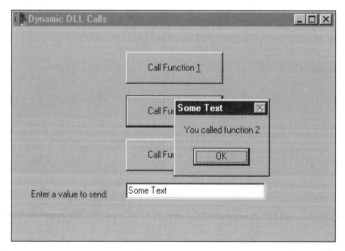

Figure 10.5
The dynamic DLL form in action.

That more or less concludes our discussion on working with dynamic DLLs. This very powerful technique allows you to move a bunch of your business logic out of the static application and into shareable libraries that can be loaded at runtime. This has two distinct advantages. First of all, the code will only be in one place even if you have multiple applications using it. This saves space and memory. Secondly, using DLLs to store your logic will allow you to make changes to the code that implements the business logic without the need to reship the entire application. If a specific function develops a bug, you just reship the DLL containing the function rather than a whole new executable.

What Did We Learn In This Chapter?

In this chapter, we explored the wide world of resources and their uses in CBuilder applications. Since most of the Windows world is concerned with resources and their uses, it behooves you to learn as much as you can about resources and their uses in applications. Here are the major points you should have picked up from this chapter for use in your own applications:

- All form data (properties, event handlers, controls, etc.) are stored in resource files for your executable by the CBuilder system.

- Resources can be used to store language-dependent information, a must for internationalizing your own applications.

- Using an attached menu resource, you can add customizable menus to your application for the user. Using the Windows API menu functions, you can add or delete menu items at runtime from a menu on the form.

- Dynamic Link Libraries (DLLs) are one of the most important aspects of the Windows programming system. DLLs can be used to store data or code and then used at runtime by your application to make your program more flexible and extensible.

- You can store version information along with your application to make the program more easily identifiable to the user, which will make tech support happy.

Working With Delphi

CHAPTER

11

HIGH PERFORMANCE

- **Using Delphi Forms In Builder**

- **Using Delphi Units**

- **The Hidden Pascal Compiler**

- **Rotating Text With Delphi**

Working With Delphi

As you've heard over and over, CBuilder is simply Delphi using C++ instead of Object Pascal as the development environment programming language. If this is really true (and it really is), shouldn't you be able to use Delphi objects in CBuilder? Wouldn't it be great if you could just take existing Delphi forms and programs and reuse them in CBuilder? Wouldn't it be the ultimate in code reuse, not only to use older existing application code, but also to reuse code developed in another development environment?

As it turns out, it is, with a few restrictions that we'll talk about in this chapter, entirely possible to reuse nearly all of the elements of your Delphi applications in your CBuilder applications. CBuilder can directly use Delphi forms, components (usually), and even code in CBuilder applications with no modifications necessary. In fact, you'll see that you can even mix Pascal and C++ functions in your applications. Pretty neat stuff, this CBuilder.

Everything Old Is New Again

Years ago, when I first started developing for the Windows environment, I was shocked and annoyed that everything I had developed in other operating systems (MS-DOS and Unix) wouldn't compile with the new Windows compilers. There were restrictions on what I could and couldn't use (the sprintf, for example, was not okay, but wsprintf, a stripped-down clone, was okay). None of my code would compile, and even code that did compile didn't work the way it was supposed to. It was my first real introduction to the concept of portability, which is to say not at all portable. Responses from compiler vendors reminded me of the old joke about the guy who goes to the doctor and says, "Doctor, it hurts when I do this," and the doctor looks him over and says, "Don't do that." Windows programming was quite similar.

The whole thing repeated itself when I started working with Visual Basic. I couldn't reuse my C and C++ code unless I created strange DLLs with exported functions to call them. I found that annoying, because there are some things VB just doesn't do well, and I wanted the ability to use the best of my C/C++ code along with the things that VB really does well (like string manipulation and form layout). All along, my co-workers told me that I was crazy and told me I couldn't mix languages. They were right, of course, and I eventually accepted the fact that I could only write code in one language at a time.

Along comes CBuilder, and suddenly I really can write applications in two languages, Object Pascal and C++. Even more stunning, I can simply reuse the code that I wrote for the last few years in Pascal without rewriting it in C++. I feel like I must be dreaming.

In this chapter we explore that dream. You'll see how to reuse a lot of existing Delphi work in CBuilder, which opens you to the wide world of components written for Delphi that you can simply install in your CBuilder environment and use in your own applications. In addition, given the number of books, magazines, and Web sites devoted to Delphi, you gain instant access to a huge base of code to use directly in your applications. It's like having a brand new product with five years' worth of debugging and support built into it. If you're accustomed to the typical version 1.0 products released for the Windows development world these days, this will probably come as a great relief to your development team.

The first example we're going to explore in this chapter is the ability to reuse a Delphi form in your CBuilder application. If you don't have Delphi (I used Delphi 3.0 for the example, but it would work just as well in 2.0), you can simply use my forms on the accompanying CD-ROM.

Reusing Delphi Forms

When Visual C++ 4.0 was released, Microsoft loudly touted the ability to import Visual Basic forms directly. After a few months, it stopped touting that ability and actually stopped talking about it. It wasn't that the import didn't work; it actually worked quite well. Nor was it the limitations of the import (it didn't understand the Visual Basic code very well, if at all). The metaphors just didn't work. Visual C++ used a document view architecture built around MDI or SDI windows with menus and status bars, but Visual Basic, like Delphi and CBuilder, is a form-based architecture with independent form windows. Visual C++ programmers (including myself) just couldn't make the two systems work together.

Delphi and CBuilder, on the other hand, share everything except a common language. Both are form-based systems, use the component model and event handling, and the Pascal-based VCL system. In short, the two development environments are perfectly compatible. It's no surprise, therefore, that many companies using Delphi were starting to use CBuilder. The ability to import work from both sides of the company was a major advantage over other tools. In this example, we explore the first and easiest aspect of the compatibility: form level code reuse.

Figure 11.1 shows the form that I developed in Delphi (3.0) to test the compatibility between the two systems. There is nothing monumental about it. The point is that any form will work, whether simple or complex. All forms are created equal.

This simple form contains a label, an edit box, and a button with the caption "Close". We will use these elements to create a complete form that can be used by the CBuilder system. The point of this example is not to create wonderful Delphi forms, but to show how to use the combination of CBuilder and Delphi.

To create the form, start your copy of Delphi (2.0 or 3.0, it doesn't matter) and add the components shown to the form. The one important aspect of this whole program is that you need to save the form with a unique name because CBuilder (as well as Delphi)

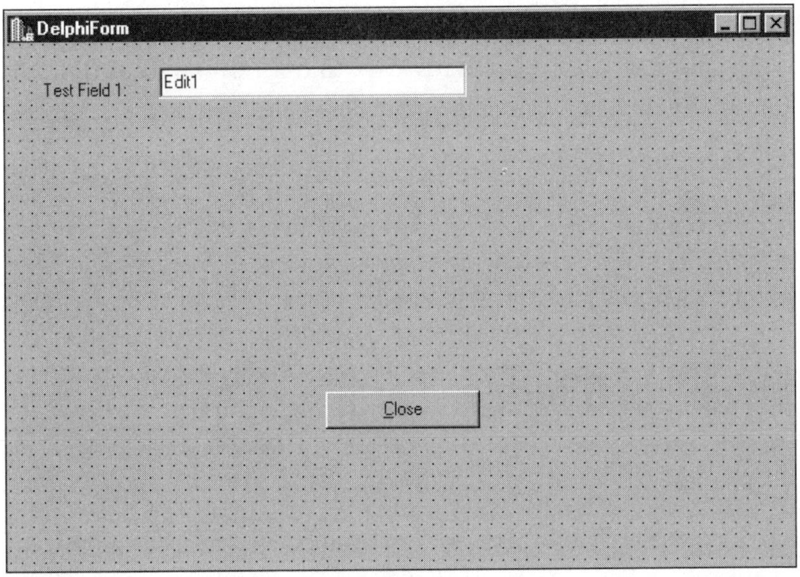

Figure 11.1
The Delphi form.

does not allow two forms with the same name in a project. This is not an unreasonable restriction, given the fact that you can't have two functions of the same name and arguments in C++ and you can't define two classes in the same namespace with the same name. As CBuilder and Delphi both use the same default name for forms (Form1, Form2), chances are that if you don't save a Delphi form with a unique name, it will likely interfere with an existing CBuilder form in a project. This is the form that we're going to import into our CBuilder application. Name it DelphiForm.

Mostly to show that it works, let's add a handler to the form for the Close button. We won't go into excruciating detail on the Pascal code, this being a C++ book and not a Pascal book, nor will we add much Pascal code. Add a single handler for the button and add the following code to the button handler:

```
procedure TDelphiForm.Button1Click(Sender: TObject);
begin
    Close;
end;
```

Note that you're writing this in Pascal, not C++. Remember not to add the parenthesis to the **Close** function call by writing Close(). We have to make some sacrifices in the name of progress. Once you've added the new code to the form, save it with its new name. Remember where you put the form, because we'll need it for the next step of the process. Once the project is saved and the form renamed, it's time to move on to the next step: creating the CBuilder application.

> **Note:** Once again, if you don't have Delphi or don't want to fire it up while reading along, please feel free to grab the existing Delphi form from the accompanying CD-ROM. Like all of the code for this book, you'll find the complete CBuilder project there as well.

Building The CBuilder Form

The next step in our development process is to create the actual CBuilder program to use the Delphi form. This is what you've been doing up to this point in the book.

Figure 11.2 shows the simple form with two components and a button that we'll use in the development of this example. We'll use the button to connect to the Delphi form from our form, and use the **Label2** component to display the text that the user enters into the edit field on the Delphi component.

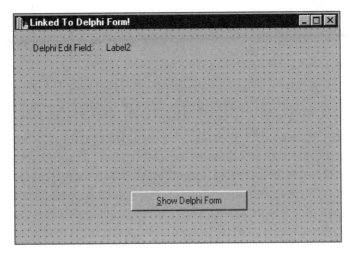

Figure 11.2
The CBuilder form for interfacing with Delphi.

In this example, we're going to display the Delphi form in modal format, which is like using the form as a dialog box rather than a "regular" form that is open at the same time as other forms and allows you to move back and forth among the forms. The reason for this selection is twofold. First of all, we haven't created any modal forms in this book up to this point, so it's kind of a nice change. Secondly, the form is being used to accumulate data we'll display in the first form. If we displayed the second form normally (which you can certainly do, by the way), you would not know when to display the data in the first form. One restriction on the system is that the Delphi form does not understand C++, so you can't simply use the form to call back into the first (C++) form.

In order to show the form, we add a handler for the button (the one with the caption Show Delphi Form) to show the form in a modal state. Here is the code to add to the form button handler:

```
\void __fastcall TForm1::Button1Click(TObject *Sender)
{
    if (DelphiForm->ShowModal())
    {
        Label2->Caption = DelphiForm->Edit1->Text;
    }

}
```

You might be asking how the form knows about the DelphiForm form that it will be using. The answer is that it doesn't, and we need to take care of that now, before we try to compile or link the application.

Adding A Delphi Form To Your Application

In order to compile and link the Delphi form into your application, you need to tell the CBuilder project manager that the form exists in the first place. You do this by selecting the Project|Add To Project menu item and then navigating to the position of the Delphi form on your system. Move to the Type combo box at the bottom of the open dialog and select *.pas from the list. This will allow you to select Delphi forms. Find the DelphiForm form and select it to add.

Once you've added the form to your project, the next step is to tell the CBuilder form about it. There is nothing special or abnormal about this process. Bring up the CBuilder form code in the editor. Select File|Include Unit Hdr from the main menu in the CBuilder IDE. From the dialog displayed, select the DelphiForm entry and click on the OK button. This will automatically generate a C++ compatible header file for the DelphiForm unit and include that header into your CBuilder form. If you're interested in how the unit classes map to C++, take a look at the DelphiForm.hpp generated file that appears in the editor window. It's interesting to look at, if nothing else.

Once you've linked the DelphiForm object to the form object in CBuilder, you can use it as though it were a normal C++ builder object. The header file contains translations for all methods, properties, and types found in the Delphi form. You can use it as though it were a C++ form and, in fact, would never know the difference if you hadn't added it in the first place.

VCL objects being VCL objects, you can use the same methods for Delphi versions of the objects that you did in Delphi. Therefore, there is really no difference between using a Delphi form and using a CBuilder form.

Notice that when you build and link the form, the Delphi form is compiled exactly as the normal CBuilder forms, thanks to the complete, industrial-strength Object Pascal compiler that comes with the CBuilder system. In our next example, we'll use that compiler to exploit yet another way to reuse Delphi components—using Delphi functions in a CBuilder program.

Using Delphi Functions In CBuilder Applications

If you can use a form in an application, the reasoning goes, why can't you use a Delphi unit without a form attached to it? Wouldn't it be nice to have the functionality of all the Delphi code out there when you're writing new C++ code? Fortunately, you can.

Let's take a good example of what I'm talking about. When I started to write this book, I thought that a wonderful example of what you could accomplish with CBuilder would be to draw text rotated at an angle. This is pretty neat to look at and even easier to code. In short, it's the perfect example. Looking into the deepest depths of the back of my hard drive, I found some code that did exactly that, rotated the text about an angle on the screen. I have no idea what I was using it for, only that it was there and it worked. This is my idea of a source-code repository. Ignoring that for the moment, I unearthed the rotation code only to discover that it was, of course, for Delphi. Later on in the book when we work on components, you will see my translation of this code into C++. For now, it makes a great example of reusing Delphi code in CBuilder.

The code itself is in the form of a Delphi unit. This is a self-contained module that contains both the interface for the function the function itself. Unlike C++, which has separate header files for definitions and source files for implementations, Object Pascal uses a single unit for both. This makes life easier for maintenance, but doesn't mesh well with C++. Or does it? Let's see.

Create a new form in CBuilder. Add a label, an edit field, and a button component to the form as shown in Figure 11.3. The area in the center of the form canvas will be used for displaying the rotated text. One note about this form: In order for it to work properly, you'll need to set the font to be a TrueType font. If you select the font property and click on the ... button, you will see a list of fonts displayed in the lefthand list box of the dialog. This dialog lists all kinds of fonts which can be used in the system. What we want is one of the fonts listed with a pair of interlocked T's (TT) before it in the display. These are scaleable, TrueType fonts, which can be rotated. Normal, bitmap fonts cannot be rotated and will not work for this example.

Once you have the form set up, the next step is to create the Delphi unit to add to the project. You can either type in the unit code or pull it in from the accompanying

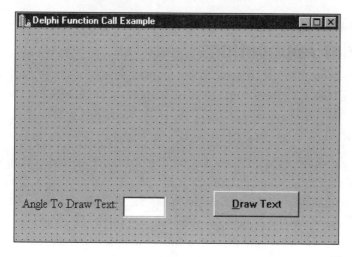

Figure 11.3
The text rotation example form.

CD-ROM, whatever makes you happier. If you prefer to type it in, create a new text file using the IDE editor and add the following code to the file:

```
unit Rotate;

interface

Uses
  Graphics, WinTypes, WinProcs;

procedure AngleTextOut(C : TCanvas; Angle, X, Y : Integer; Str : String);

implementation

procedure AngleTextOut(C : TCanvas; Angle, X, Y : Integer; Str : String);
var
  LogRec        : TLOGFONT;
  OldFontHandle,
  NewFontHandle : HFONT;

begin
  GetObject(C.Font.Handle, SizeOf( LogRec ), Addr( LogRec ));
  LogRec.lfEscapement := Angle * 10;
  NewFontHandle := CreateFontIndirect( LogRec );
  OldFontHandle := SelectObject(C.Handle, NewFontHandle);
```

```
   C.TextOut(X, Y, Str);
   NewFontHandle := SelectObject(C.Handle, OldFontHandle);
   DeleteObject( NewFontHandle );
end;
```

Save this unit as rotate.pas. This unit of code will implement the complete work needed to rotate some text on the canvas of the form. It will draw the text for the string by creating a new font temporarily, selecting that font into the device context for the form, drawing the text, and then getting rid of the old font. It's not a complex routine, but it serves its purpose.

In order to use the new form, you need to include the new unit in your form unit. Open the code for the form (Form1.cpp) and select the File|Include Unit Hdr command from the main menu. Select the Rotate unit and click on OK. This will automatically generate a new header file for the rotate.pas unit code as a C++ style header. If you look in the project directory at this point, you'll find a file called rotate.hpp, which contains the C++ translation of the definitions and functions found in the rotate.pas source file. This is what the file looks like:

```
//------------------------------------------------------------
// Rotate.hpp - bcbdcc32 generated hdr (DO NOT EDIT) rev: 0
// From: Rotate.pas
//------------------------------------------------------------
#ifndef RotateHPP
#define RotateHPP
//------------------------------------------------------------
#include <Windows.hpp>
#include <Graphics.hpp>
#include <System.hpp>
namespace Rotate
{
//-- type declarations ---------------------------------------
//-- var, const, procedure -----------------------------------
extern void __fastcall AngleTextOut(Graphics::TCanvas* C, int Angle,
  int X, int Y,  System::AnsiString Str);

}                 /* namespace Rotate */
#if !defined(NO_IMPLICIT_NAMESPACE_USE)
using namespace Rotate;
#endif
//-- end unit ------------------------------------------------
#endif       // Rotate
```

You should not modify this header file as the comment at the top of the file indicates. If you do, CBuilder will overwrite it when the rotate.pas file is next compiled and the changes may not mesh with what is in the actual source code for the Rotate unit. If you change this file, at best you may cause the program not to compile or at worst to bomb at runtime.

Notice that CBuilder automatically generates a complete namespace implementation around the functions and definitions in the unit and then adds a using clause to the header file. As we discussed earlier in the book, this is not the preferred way to work with namespaces, but does make it possible for you to call directly the function in your own code without having to worry about what namespace it is in. More importantly, though, this makes it possible to include numerous units without worrying about which unit a given function or object is in.

> **Note:** If the unit included happened to have a Pascal object in it, you would find that the generated header file contained a complete C++ class translation of that object. CBuilder is nearly completely compatible with all types used in Object Pascal for this express purpose.

The last parameter of the function is the last thing of interest in this conversion. In the Pascal unit, the **Str** parameter is of type String. This type is Pascal's implementation of the generic String type. In CBuilder, however, there is no direct **String** class that maps to this type. Instead, the parameter is treated as an AnsiString, which is the equivalent of the Delphi String type.

To call the function, among other things we need some text and an angle. The string we'll use is simply a hard-coded literal in the program. On the other hand, we'll allow the user to enter the angle into the edit field for the program. To complete the example, we need only add a new handler for the "Draw Text" button on the form. Add that handler, and then add the following code to the new handler:

```
void __fastcall TForm1::Button1Click(TObject *Sender)
{
    Canvas->Brush->Color = Color;
                AngleTextOut(Canvas, atoi(Edit1->Text.c_str()), Width/2,
                    Height/2, "Angled Text");
}
```

The background of the text is set to the same color as the background of the form in order to make it not stick out like a sore thumb on the screen. Once we've done this, we position the text so that it will start in the center of the form by dividing the Height and Width parameters by two as the starting point for the form. The user inputs the angle into the edit box. The angle represents the position from 0 degrees (normal text display from left to right) in a downward arc through 360 degrees. Once you've typed in all of the code, go ahead and compile and link the application in CBuilder. This will automatically compile the Pascal unit, compile the C++ form unit, and then link all of the things together. Notice that the Pascal compiler is automatically invoked for the module with a .pas extension.

When you're finished building the application, try running it. Enter a few different angles and click on the Draw Text button. When you finish, you'll see the result displayed that looks something like the figure shown in Figure 11.4. This completes the text rotation example and shows you just how little is involved in using Pascal functions in your C++ applications.

Although this example was not terribly complex, it does show you what you need to know about using Pascal units in CBuilder. As long as the unit will compile in Delphi, it will probably compile in CBuilder. For Delphi 3.0 applications, you may not use any of the new VCL components in a form to be used in CBuilder. Likewise, you cannot use any function in Delphi 3.0 that did not appear in Delphi 2.0.

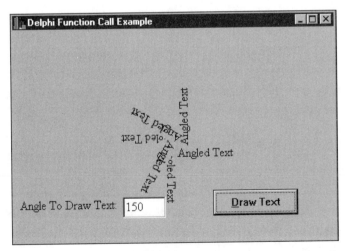

Figure 11.4
The text rotation form in action.

CBuilder is Delphi 2.0-compatible and mostly 3.0-compatible, although there are definitely differences between the two.

In general, when I was working at generating forms and units in Delphi 3.0 to work with CBuilder, I found that nearly all things translated perfectly. Using any of the new components (such as the **TCoolBar** component) in Delphi 3.0 resulted in not being able to use the form in CBuilder. The next release of CBuilder is intended to be completely compatible with Delphi 3.0, so you shouldn't have a lot longer to wait. By the end of 1997, Borland has promised to sync up the two products so that future releases of both products will provide the same functionality and will work together.

> **Note:** You might wonder whether, if CBuilder can use Delphi 3.0 forms, Delphi 3.0 can use CBuilder forms. The answer, surprisingly, is no. Delphi 3.0 does not ship with a complete C++ compiler in the same way that CBuilder includes a Pascal compiler. This makes it impossible to use CBuilder forms in Delphi 3.0.

What Did We Learn In This Chapter?

Hopefully, you have learned quite a bit in this chapter. The primary thing that you should take out of the chapter is that CBuilder does Delphi. You can reuse Delphi forms, Delphi units, and Delphi components directly in CBuilder. Here are the highlights of the chapter: CBuilder will automatically work with Delphi forms and units. Just add them to the project and you can use them as though they were C++ forms or units. CBuilder can directly import Delphi components as long as they are distributed in either object (.obj) or source (.pas) formats. Once a Delphi component is installed into the CBuilder component palette, you use it exactly the way you use any other component in the system. CBuilder can directly use Object Pascal units containing either objects, functions, or procedures. Any of these will be converted into their equivalent C++ prototypes and you will not even know that they were written in Pascal rather than C++. CBuilder forms cannot be used in Delphi 3.0 yet. Future releases of both products will become closer and closer together and may allow for completely interchangeable systems. As a note, it is much easier to convert Pascal to C++ than it is to go the other way. This is the primary reason that you cannot yet use C++ units and forms in Delphi applications. Nearly all Delphi applications could simply be converted into CBuilder applications by generating a new CBuilder project and then importing all of the units and data modules from the Delphi project into the CBuilder module.

That completes our discussion of Delphi. In our next segment, you will learn about using the CBuilder system with yet another "foreign" programming environment, this time the MFC system in Visual C++.

Using CBuilder In MFC

HIGH PERFORMANCE

- **Using The VCL In MFC**

- **Wrapper Functions And CBuilder**

- **What's A DEF File?**

- **Importing With Import Libraries**

- **Communicating With MFC**

- **Databases And MFC**

Using CBuilder In MFC

If you work in a corporate environment and are reading this book, chances are good that one of two situations is causing you to consider using CBuilder. The first situation is that your company already develops in Delphi and you're considering switching to CBuilder because the majority of your staff programs in C++ rather than Pascal. If so, this chapter might not be of terrific interest to you. The second situation causing you to consider CBuilder is that your company already uses Visual C++ and the MFC (which is the most prevalent C++ development tool in the Windows market). This chapter is just the place for you to get started.

It's a shame that most companies that use C++ also use the MFC to implement their front-end GUI development, because the MFC is really the dinosaur of Windows development tools. It requires that you work strictly within the environment it sets, with few chances to develop things your way. As a programmer who works extensively with Visual C++ and the MFC (hey, it pays the bills), I know exactly how frustrating it is when the user says, "That's almost a perfect dialog, but could you make the text appear in green?"

By this point in the book, you should really understand the differences between the VCL approach and the MFC approach. VCL is a set of components that allows you to build an application from the ground up, while the MFC is a class framework that lets you develop applications within the frame provided by the generated code from AppWizard. The biggest difference, of course, is that MFC determines how you'll present your application to the user (MDI-, SDI-, or dialog-based), while the VCL allows you to mix and match the pieces you want to construct the look that best fits your application.

With apologies to the many programmers devoted to MFC, I prefer the open approach of the VCL to the closed approach of the MFC. Your mileage may vary, of course.

If you do work in an MFC shop, perhaps after working through the book to this point you're wishing you didn't. Perhaps, you think, there must be a way to get all of this good stuff in your MFC application, but you can't see how. After all, MFC is MFC and VCL is VCL and never the twain shall meet.

I'm here to tell you that there is actually no good reason why you can't get the benefit of VCL forms in your MFC applications. It's a little harder to make the two development environments talk, but if you're willing to stretch yourself a little and work in two systems concurrently, you'll find that your Visual C++ programs can benefit from the VCL and the form-based approach.

Do you think that I'm crazy? Perhaps you think that I spent a little too much time out in the sun. Nope, it's really possible to mix in the VCL-based forms and the MFC-based system at the same time. In this chapter we explore this process, from developing the forms in CBuilder to linking them into your MFC application. We'll leave no stone unturned and no bug left unsquished (or something like that).

Using The VCL In An MFC Application

If you think about the problem for a moment, you'll realize that it's simply not possible to link VCL-based code into an MFC application. After all, the VCL uses its own object format, its own startup code, and a huge library of components that would certainly clash with the MFC. On the other hand, CBuilder is quite capable of creating a Dynamic Link Library (DLL), which can be used by any other system. After all, a DLL is a DLL is a DLL, and any system that knows how to work with DLL's will work with one written in any language. This is the approach we'll take in building a CBuilder form for use in an MFC-based Visual C++ application.

The CBuilder To MFC Example

In this example, we'll go through the steps one at a time to load a CBuilder form into an MFC application. I'll tell you the tricks and traps along the way to making the thing work, as well as some of the things you can do to make your life a little easier.

The first step to loading a CBuilder form into an MFC application is to create a CBuilder DLL containing the form to be loaded, not a particularly difficult task. Just create a new application in CBuilder by selecting File|New and select DLL as the type of application you want to create. CBuilder will automatically generate a complete skeleton DLL, including a main entry point function and a makefile. If you're accustomed to working with other systems, you probably know how nice it is to have this generated automatically for you.

Once you've created the DLL, the next step is to create a form that you can use in the DLL. There is nothing magical about this. You don't need to worry about initialization routines, linked libraries, or anything of that sort because the forms have all of the internals built into them to create themselves. Just create a new form using the FileINew command and select Form from the dialog box.

Figure 12.1 shows the form we'll use for this application. As you can see, there is nothing special about it. I'll assume at this point that you know enough about the CBuilder system to create whatever kind of form you need for your application. In this example, we're looking primarily at the stuff behind the scenes rather than worrying about what the GUI display will look like.

Once the form is defined, you'll need a way to create the form from within the MFC application. This brings us to the second step of the process: creating a wrapper function to access the form from the MFC application.

Creating A Wrapper Function

One of the problems in working in multiple development environments is worrying about the problem of C++ name mangling in the compiler. As it turns out, Microsoft's

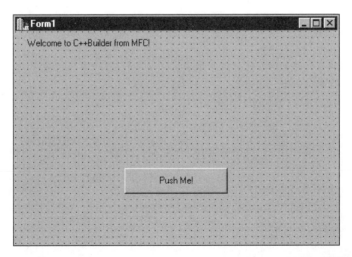

Figure 12.1
The CBuilder form for the MFC application.

Visual C++ and Borland's C++Builder compilers do not, of course, turn out the same names for the same functions when they are mangled, which makes it very difficult to link the two together. Fortunately, the C++ language provides a way around this problem in the form of removing the mangling from functions and objects defined in the system.

If you place the strange-looking statement **extern "C"** around a block of code in your program, the compiler will not mangle this block. It might appear, looking at the syntax of the statement, that this block would preclude you from using C++ code in the block, but it doesn't. You can do anything you like in a block defined with the **extern "C"** syntax without turning it into a mess.

Consider, for example, the following block of code:

```
void CreateAForm(long nWhichForm);
```

If you run this code through the compiler (Microsoft's Visual C++), you'll probably end up with a symbol in the output object file with a name something like "_CreateAForm@4". This represents a function that takes a long variable, I think. It also contains an underscore (_) at the front of the function. I have no idea why the compiler chooses to do this; it's probably for historical reasons.

If you're like me, you don't really care why the compiler does anything it does. All you want is for it to turn out working code that you can link into your application. The problem, therefore, is to make the two compilers turn out code that matches. This is the purpose of the **extern "C"** statement. Going back to our line of previous code, if you now write the following:

```
extern "C"
{
void CreateAForm(long nWhichForm);
}
```

The compiler will look at the previous code and turn out a symbol for it that reads more like this: "CreateAForm". There is no mangling of the argument list to create a function name, nor is there an underscore generated for the function header. Both of the compilers know how to deal with this syntax, so it's the perfect way to communicate between them.

Before you ask, there is simply no way that you can directly "talk" to a CBuilder VCL object from a Microsoft Visual C++ application. Visual C++ would choke and die on the syntax used in VCL object definitions with all of the extensions used (__property, __fastcall, etc.) and would never be able to link them together. As a result, you need to use an intermediary function to do the job.

In our first example, we'll only concern ourselves with putting the data up onto the screen and not with having anything returned to the calling program at this point. Consider this to be a splash screen or something of that sort. For this reason, we'll create a wrapper function that shows the form and then returns control to the calling MFC application.

Here is the code to add for the wrapper function in your DLL program. Add this code to the project1.cpp source file, which you can get at by selecting View|Program Source or by simply turning to the editor, which should already have this file loaded:

```
extern "C" void WINAPI __declspec(dllexport) ShowForm(void)
{
    Form1 = new TForm1((TComponent *)NULL);
    Form1->Show();
}
```

The first thing to notice about the previous code is the declaration of the interface for the function. **The extern "C"** segment we've already talked about. The **void**, of course, simply says that this function doesn't return anything. The WINAPI segment says that this is a normal Windows function.

The **__declspec(dllexport)** segment of the declaration, on the other hand, is an important addition that you should place in all of your functions that you want to call from an external program. This statement says that this function is to be automatically exported from the DLL and available to any calling program. If you do not define your function as exportable, no calling program will see it, and you will not be able to call it from your MFC program.

Building A DEF File

You might remember that when we were talking about DLLs in CBuilder, we talked about the implib program, which is used to create import libraries from DLLs. When these import libraries are linked into the program, the functions in the DLL act as though they are simply part of the program itself. Unlike dynamic loading, which requires that you load the DLL, find the function in the DLL, and call the function by indirection (as you saw in an earlier chapter), static loading is different. When you statically load a DLL via an import library, Windows will do the job of finding the DLL, loading it into memory, and translating your calls to the function into the indirect function calls. Import libraries are less flexible than static libraries. Once you've linked to an import library, you're stuck with the single implementation of the function and cannot change your mind at runtime. On the other hand, they're just as nice for patching. You can simply ship a newer version of the DLL to the user, and if none of the function definitions have changed, the user will simply load it as before.

Given this wonderful description of the import library, you would think that our job was mostly over. We would simply use the implib program to generate a complete import library for our DLL, load the import library into the Visual C++ MFC application, and call the function. You would, of course, be wrong. It's against the law, it seems, for compiler vendors to make anything this easy for a programmer. Instead you need to follow a straightforward, but definitely strange, procedure to make your DLL work with MFC.

You cannot simply use the implib program on the DLL because the library generated by the implib program is not compatible with Visual C++. Although a DLL is a DLL, a library is a collection of object files. In order for the code to be compatible, the object file format would have to be compatible. The object file format for CBuilder is quite different from that of Microsoft's Visual C++, so the import library will not load correctly. What we need to do is to create an import library in Visual C++ that is compatible with that system.

"No problem," I hear you saying, "just fire up the Visual C++ implib program and be done with it." Sorry, it isn't that easy. Microsoft, for reasons of its own, does not ship an implib.exe with its development tools anymore (they used to). They do provide a method for creating an import library, but it requires a little more work. Let's look at the steps you need to take to accomplish this task.

First you'll need a module definition file (DEF file) for the import library building. This file, which old-time Windows programmers will immediately recognize, is a definition of the DLL that includes a list of the exported functions. Rather than make you learn the arcane syntax of the DEF file, I'm going to give you a skeleton DEF file that you can simply clone into whatever format you need. Here is the skeleton file, along with a description of what you need to change

```
; project1.def : Declares the module parameters for the DLL.

LIBRARY      $$ProjectName$$
CODE                SHARED EXECUTE READ
DATA                READ WRITE
DESCRIPTION  '$$Description$$'

EXPORTS
    ; Explicit exports can go here
    $$FunctionName$$          @$$FunctionNumber$$
```

where you should replace **$$ProjectName$$** with the name of your project. The project is generally the same as the name you saved the project under in CBuilder.

$$Description$$ is a human readable description of the project that tells a reader why you created this DLL and what it's used for.

$$FunctionName$$ is the name of the function you want to export. There is one entry here for each function you want to define as exportable in the DLL.

$$FunctionNumber$$ is a simple ordinal number from 1 to the number of functions in the DLL. This number is used to speed the loading of the functions from the DLL at runtime.

For our program, we need to know the list of exportable functions in the DLL. Normally, of course, you know this list because you wrote the DLL in the first place, but sometimes you may be working with a third-party DLL that doesn't identify the exported functions. In other cases, you'll want to see what other functions a DLL has exported other than the ones they tell you about in the documentation (this is a common problem). To do this, you'll use another program shipped with the Visual C++ system: dumpbin.

To list all of the exported functions in a DLL, use the following syntax for the dumpbin program

```
dumpbin /EXPORTS filename.dll
```

where, of course, **filename.dll** is the name of the DLL for which you want to obtain a list of exported functions. Running the dumpbin program on the project1.dll file that we created in CBuilder results in the following printout:

```
dumpbin /EXPORTS project1.dll
Microsoft (R) COFF Binary File Dumper Version 4.20.6164
Copyright (C) Microsoft Corp 1992-1996. All rights reserved.


Dump of file project1.dll

File Type: DLL

        Section contains the following Exports for
          D:\matt\CBDLL\Project1.dll

                  0 characteristics
                  0 time date stamp Wed Dec 31 19:00:00 1969
               0.00 version
                  1 ordinal base
                  3 number of functions
                  3 number of names

          ordinal hint    name

                  1    0   ShowForm   (0000119C)
                  2    1   _DebugHook   (000313FC)
                  3    2   _ExceptionClass   (000347E0)

    Summary

        9000 .data
        1000 .edata
        2000 .idata
        4000 .reloc
        5000 .rsrc
       2F000 .text
        1000 .tls
```

There are a number of interesting things shown in this printout, but few that you really need to worry about. The most important is the block shown in highlighted print, which shows the exported functions as well as the numbers you need to put into the DEF file. We don't really care about the **_DebugHook** or **_ExceptionClass** exports; they're used internally by the CBuilder system. Instead, we're interested in the **ShowForm** function that we created in the DLL. Using the previous information, we can now define the DEF file for our DLL:

```
; project1.def : Declares the module parameters for the DLL.

LIBRARY      "PROJECT1"
CODE            SHARED EXECUTE READ
DATA            READ WRITE
DESCRIPTION  'Test DLL for using BCB from MFC'

EXPORTS
    ; Explicit exports can go here
    ShowForm    @1
```

Building The Import Library

We began this discussion about working with import libraries, so you may be wondering why we had to build this silly DEF file to begin with. The answer is simple: to create an import library that Visual C++ can use, we need a DEF file that contains the information about the DLL.

This might be confusing, unless you understand what, exactly, an import library really is. An import library is simply a strange sort of library that contains "stubs" for the functions in a DLL, along with some code that tells Windows to load the functions directly from the DLL rather than use anything in the library itself. Given this information, it makes sense in a strange sort of way that you can generate an import library for a DLL without needing the DLL in any way for the process. Well, at least it makes sense to Microsoft, and they created the things. What else do you need to know?

To build an import library for the DLL given a DEF file, you use the lib program that ships with Visual C++. Unlike tlib, which ships with the CBuilder system, lib is a more complicated program. The tlib program, you might remember, simply creates an archive of object files that can then be linked into an application. The lib program, on the other hand, does much more than this. Using the lib program, move to the directory that contains the DEF file for the DLL and use the following command to generate an import library for the DLL:

```
lib /DEF:project1.dll
Microsoft (R) 32-Bit Library Manager Version 4.20.6164
Copyright (C) Microsoft Corp 1992-1996. All rights reserved.

LIB : warning LNK4068: /MACHINE not specified; defaulting to IX86
project1.dll : warning LNK4017: MZP statement not supported for the
target platform; ignored
   Creating library project1.lib and object project1.exp
```

You can safely ignore the warning from the program that the MZP statement is not supported for the target platform. The message is there because we didn't define a **MACHINE** value for the library. The lib program defaults to the Intel architecture if you don't tell it otherwise, but because CBuilder currently runs only on Windows machines, this is not a problem.

When the lib program has finished running (which should take only a second or two), you should look in the directory for a file with extension .LIB and the same name as the DEF file. This is the import library that you can use for this DLL.

> **Note:** One of the problems with creating an import library indirectly is that if you make a mistake in the DEF file, the library will not link properly. If you get strange results from the linker, look at the entries in the DEF file to make sure that your typing is correct.

At this point, you have a complete DLL with a complete import library that you can use in your Visual C++ program. The next step, therefore, is to create the MFC application and call the function. Let's do that next.

The MFC Application

I'm assuming that you already know how to create a new application in Visual C++ using the AppWizard. If you don't, please consult the documentation for that product. This is a book on CBuilder, not Visual C++.

Generate a new application using AppWizard, name it MFCToBCB, and make it a Single Document Interface (SDI) application. Leave all other defaults alone for this example; we won't need them for this application.

If you're using Visual C++ 4.x, select Project|Insert Files Into Project and navigate to the import library that we created in the previous steps. Add the library to the project and click on the OK button. Visual C++ will now link in the import library for the DLL when the project is built. This example will not work with earlier versions of Visual C++, because you cannot link a 32-bit library and DLL with a 16-bit application.

The next step is to call the function. First, add a new menu item to your project main menu. Then give the new main menu the name Special and the menu item

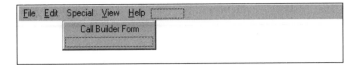

Figure 12.2
The menu structure for the MFCtoBCB application.

beneath it the caption "Call Builder Form". The complete menu structure is shown in Figure 12.2.

Once you've defined the new menu item, add a new handler for it to the **CMainFrame** class via the ClassWizard. Give the new method the name **OnBuilderForm**. This method will be used by the application to display the CBuilder form.

Open the **CMainFrame** class for editing in the editor of the IDE of Visual C++. Add the following code to the top of the mainfrm.cpp source file. This code represents the prototype for our function that the compiler will need to generate code to call the new DLL function:

```
extern "C"
{
void __declspec(dllexport) ShowForm(void);
}
```

Note that in the source file we also need to wrap an **extern** "C" statement around the function prototype. If you don't do this, the function will not link into the library, and you'll have an undefined link error at the end of the link process.

The other interesting thing is the __**declspec(dllexport)** modifier used in the function prototype shown previously. This modifier, when used in a DLL, indicates that the DLL function is to be exported. When used in an application program, however, it's automatically converted into a statement meaning that this function is to be imported from a DLL. Pretty nice little macro there.

Calling The Function To Display The Form

The last step in the process is actually to call the function. Move to the new method that we added to the **CMainFrame** class (**OnBuilderForm**), and add the following code to the new method:

```
void CMainFrame::OnBuilderForm()
{
                ShowForm();
}
```

That's really all you need to do to call the method and display the form on the screen. In this case, the compiler will compile all of the code, the linker will link into the import library for the DLL, and the entire application will be bound together.

At runtime, Windows will automatically load the DLL for the CBuilder form when the application is started. When you call the **ShowForm** method of the DLL, the import library stub will indirectly call the function in the DLL, and the form will be displayed for the user to see.

Don't believe me? Go ahead and build the Visual C++ application. Make sure that the DLL for the CBuilder form is in the same directory as the executable for the Visual C++ application and start the program up. Choose the Call Builder Form menu item and watch the form display itself on the screen. Congratulations. You've just successfully merged a CBuilder form with an MFC application.

Example 2: Communicating Between Visual C++ And The CBuilder Form

In the first example in this chapter, we explored the basics of linking a CBuilder form to an MFC application. While this is certainly important, there is more to working with the MFC than simply displaying a form that lets the user look at things. In this second example of the chapter, we explore how you can communicate between the MFC and CBuilder forms. We'll construct a simple address book-style form that allows the user to enter an address for a person. The MFC application will construct an object that is then passed to the address book form and used to retrieve the information from the form back into the MFC application.

To build this application, you'll need to once again create a DLL in CBuilder as your application type. Once you've done that, add a new form to the project and add the controls until it looks like the one shown in Figure 12.3. When you're ready, we'll move on to the next step, adding the data back into an MFC application.

The first thing we need to do in this application is to add a function wrapper to the DLL that will allow us to create the form. Let's look at the code first, and then talk about it a little.

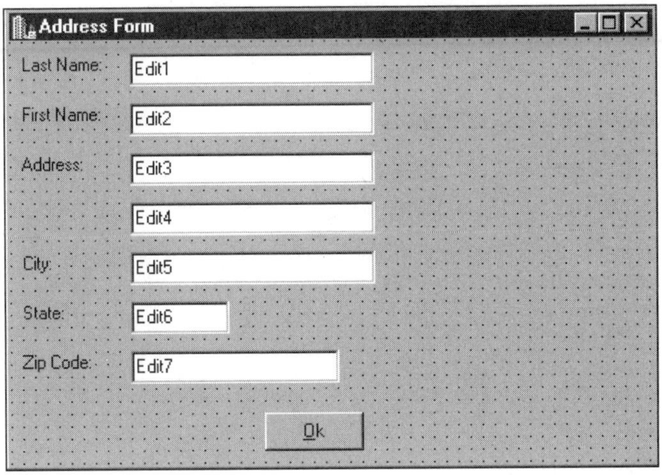

Figure 12.3
The address form for the CBuilder to MFC DLL.

```
extern "C"
{
void WINAPI __declspec(dllexport) CreateAddressForm(TAddress *pObject)
{
   // First create the form
   TForm1 *pForm = new TForm1(NULL);
   // Get the data from the user
   pForm->ShowModal();
   // Put the data back into the structure
   pObject->SetLastName( pForm->Edit1->Text.c_str());
   pObject->SetFirstName( pForm->Edit2->Text.c_str());
   pObject->SetAddress1( pForm->Edit3->Text.c_str());
   pObject->SetAddress2( pForm->Edit4->Text.c_str());
   pObject->SetCity( pForm->Edit5->Text.c_str());
   pObject->SetState( pForm->Edit6->Text.c_str());
   pObject->SetZipCode( pForm->Edit7->Text.c_str());
}
}; // End extern "C"
```

The first obvious fact here is that once again we're creating a wrapper function with an **extern "C"** declaration so that we can call it from MFC. The first odd thing you'll notice is that, unlike the last time, in this case the function takes a parameter that represents the object that will be created in the MFC application to store the data that the user enters into this form. Let's take a quick look at this object, which you should enter into a new file called "Address.h". This file will also be used in our MFC application to communicate.

```
#ifndef _ADDRESS_H_
#define _ADDRESS_H_

class TAddress
{
char strLastName[ 80 ];
char strFirstName[ 80 ];
char strAddress1[80];
char strAddress2[80];
char strCity[40];
char strState[4];
char strZipCode[10];

public:
    TAddress(void)
    {
    }
    ~TAddress(void)
    {
    }
    const char *GetLastName(void)
    {
        return strLastName;
    }
    const char *GetFirstName(void)
    {
        return strFirstName;
    }
    const char *GetAddress1(void)
    {
        return strAddress1;
    }
    const char *GetAddress2(void)
    {
        return strAddress2;
    }
    const char *GetCity(void)
    {
        return strCity;
    }
    const char *GetState(void)
    {
```

```
        return strState;
    }
    const char *GetZipCode(void)
    {
        return strZipCode;
    }
    void SetLastName( const char *strLast )
    {
        strncpy( strLastName, strLast, 80 );
    }
    void SetFirstName( const char *strFirst )
    {
        strncpy( strFirstName, strFirst, 80 );
    }
    void SetAddress1( const char *strAdd1 )
    {
        strncpy(strAddress1, strAdd1,80);
    }
    void SetAddress2( const char *strAdd2 )
    {
        strncpy(strAddress2, strAdd2,80);
    }
    void SetCity( const char *strC )
    {
        strncpy(strCity, strCity,40);
    }
    void SetState( const char *strSt )
    {
        strncpy(strState, strSt,4);
    }
    void SetZipCode( const char *strZip )
    {
        strncpy(strZipCode, strZip, 10);
    }
};

#endif
```

As you can see, this is just a simple object that contains address information contained inside of a C++ object. By using a standard C++ object, we make it easy to connect the DLL to the MFC application. The code in the wrapper function assigns the pieces of the address object by calling the member function, and we needn't worry about the alignment or definition of the object. We trust the object to store the information in whatever way it needs to in order for it to work with Visual C++ and the MFC.

One last note: You'll need to include the Address.h header file in the project.cpp source file so that the definition of the **TAddress** class is available to the compiler. You'll see that the forward function declaration of the wrapper function is at the bottom of the header file. This is for the use of the Visual C++ application.

The Visual C++ Application

Once we have the CBuilder side of the equation completed, the next step is to create a Visual C++ application to use that wrapper function in the DLL. Create a simple application using AppWizard, name it MfcBcbTest, and make it an SDI-type application.

Add a new handler for the File|New menu item to the CMainFrame class. Give this new handler the name OnFileNew, as the ClassWizard suggests. Add the following code into the OnFileNew method of the CMainFrame class:

```
void CMainFrame::OnFileNew()
{
        TAddress *pAddress = new TAddress;
        CreateAddressForm(pAddress);
        MessageBox(pAddress->GetLastName(), "Last Name", MB_OK );
}
```

As you can see in this code, we create a new instance of the **TAddress** class (for which you need to include the header file in the mainfrm.cpp source file). This object will be the interface between the MFC application and the CBuilder DLL. Once the object is created, we pass the pointer to the object to the wrapper function, which was prototyped in the Address.h header file. The function is called, which will display the address form as a modal dialog box. Once the user clicks on the OK button, the form will close and the object is returned to the MFC application. To verify that the data was sent correctly, we display the last name stored in the object in a message box after the function returns.

That's all there is to it. You now know what is involved in passing data back and forth between the CBuilder form and the MFC application—not much.

The Last Test: Working With Databases

You no doubt want your MFC application to take advantage of the vastly superior database handling functionality offered by the VCL database objects. In this final example of working between the MFC and VCL, we examine how to transform the previous address book example into a database-based address book search engine.

Figure 12.4 shows the new form that we need to add to the DLL in order to make the project work. One note: You won't need to modify the Visual C++ application that we developed in the previous example to work with this new DLL because the interface is the same.

You would think, if you work in Visual C++ a lot, that you would need to do some sort of initialization to make the database stuff work from the VCL. You would, rather fortuitously, be wrong. The VCL uses static libraries that require no initialization, and the VCL database components understand when it's necessary to open, close, and initialize the database engine. In short, all of this happens behind the scenes and requires no work on your part.

In this example, we'll allow the user to browse for entries in a database. They can type in certain fields (along with allowing them to enter asterisks or question marks to match multiple entries) and then select the desired address entry from the list presented to them.

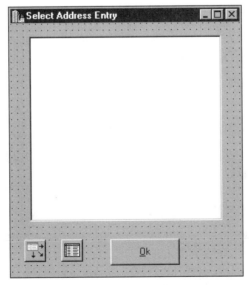

Figure 12.4
The database selection form.

You'll need to make one simple modification to the Unit1 form, which is the form displaying the address information. This form will now contain one additional button that will be used to search for the specified data. In order to make all this work, add a new button to the form with the caption "Search". Add a new event handler for the Search button click event and add the following code to the Search button event handler:

```
void __fastcall TForm1::Button2Click(TObject *Sender)
{
    AnsiString strSearch = "";
    AnsiString s = Edit1->Text;

    // Check each piece
    if ( Edit1->Text.Length() )
    {
        strSearch += "LASTNAME = '";
        strSearch += Edit1->Text;
        strSearch += "'";
    }

    if ( Edit2->Text.Length() )
    {
        if ( strSearch.Length() != 0 )
            strSearch += " AND ";
        strSearch += "FIRSTNAME = '";
        strSearch += Edit2->Text;
        strSearch += "'";
    }

    if ( Edit3->Text.Length() )
    {
        if ( strSearch.Length() != 0 )
            strSearch += " AND ";
        strSearch += "ADDRESS_1 = '";
        strSearch += Edit3->Text;
        strSearch += "'";
    }
    if ( Edit4->Text.Length() )
    {
        if ( strSearch.Length() !  0 )
            strSearch += " AND ";
        strSearch += "ADDRESS_2 = '";
        strSearch += Edit4->Text;
```

```
        strSearch += "'";
   }
   if ( Edit5->Text.Length() )
   {
        if ( strSearch.Length() != 0 )
           strSearch += " AND ";
        strSearch += "CITY = '";
        strSearch += Edit5->Text;
        strSearch += "'";
   }
   if ( Edit6->Text.Length() )
   {
        if ( strSearch.Length() != 0 )
           strSearch += " AND ";
        strSearch += "STATE = '";
        strSearch += Edit6->Text;
        strSearch += "'";
   }
   if ( Edit7->Text.Length() )
   {
        if ( strSearch.Length() != 0 )
           strSearch += " AND ";
        strSearch += "ZIP_CODE = '";
        strSearch += Edit7->Text;
        strSearch += "'";
   }

   TForm2 *pForm = new TForm2(NULL);
   pForm->SetSearchString(strSearch);
   pForm->ShowModal();
   // Copy the pieces from the database
   Edit1->Text = pForm->Table1->FieldValues["LASTNAME"];
   Edit2->Text = pForm->Table1->FieldValues["FIRSTNAME"];
   Edit3->Text = pForm->Table1->FieldValues["ADDRESS_1"];
   Edit4->Text = pForm->Table1->FieldValues["ADDRESS_2"];
   Edit5->Text = pForm->Table1->FieldValues["CITY"];
   Edit6->Text = pForm->Table1->FieldValues["STATE"];
   Edit7->Text = pForm->Table1->FieldValues["ZIP_CODE"];

   delete pForm;
}
```

This code is long, but it isn't really very complex. What we're doing here is checking each field in the form to see whether the user entered anything into it. If they did, we build it into a search string to pass to the database as a filter string. Basically, what we need to do is to create a string of the form

```
FIELD='Value' AND FIELD='Value'
```

where **FIELD** is one or more of the fields in the database and **'Value'** is the user-entered string representing the data they want to see in this field. In short, we're creating a Query By Example (QBE) form that can add this functionality to a Visual C++ application. Although you can write QBE things in Visual C++, it really isn't a great deal of fun. It involves either building runtime SQL and then extracting the fields you want, or writing horrible parameterized queries. In CBuilder, we could create the whole thing in a few simple lines of code by writing a general-purpose function that matches the field names to the edit fields.

Once we create the search string, it's time to do the database filter and display the matching records for the user. This is where the second form (Form2) comes into play. This form contains a list box that will be used to display all of the matching entries from which we want the user to select. Let's create that form now.

Creating The Record Selection Form

The record selection form contains two elements: a list box and an OK button. The list box must contain the records from which the user can select. The OK button is used to close the list box form and indicate to the calling form that we have successfully selected a record from the database.

The first thing that we need to do in this form is to handle the loading of the list box. It isn't directly possible to do this on a **FormCreate** event because we don't know at that point what the selection filter string will look like. Instead, we need to add a method that the other form (Form1) can use to set the filter string. Let's look at that code now:

```
void TForm2::SetSearchString(AnsiString strSearch)
{
    Table1->Filter = strSearch;
    Table1->Filtered = true;

    // Fill the list box with items
    Table1->First();
```

```
    while ( !Table1->Eof )
    {
        AnsiString s = Table1->FieldValues["LASTNAME"];
        s += ",";
        s += Table1->FieldValues["FIRSTNAME"];
        ListBox1->Items->Add( s );
        Table1->Next();
    }
}
```

This code simply applies the filter string that we created in the Form1 Search button click function, loops through the resulting strings in the database, and loads them into the list box. The strings displayed are of the form LASTNAME, FIRSTNAME in this case, although you could certainly display more information if you like. A better way to implement this might have been to display a grid with all of the data in it, but this example will suffice. Note that it's not necessary to clear the list box before loading the data because we'll always be creating this form for a given selection and then destroying it afterwards.

The final piece of the equation is that the user's selection needs to be processed when the user selects something in the list box and clicks on the OK button. What we really want to do at this point is simply position the database "pointer" (really called a cursor for you database sticklers) at the position of the selected record. The table is still "visible" to the calling form at this point (it's a published object of the form), so that form can simply read the information the form needs when the user completes the form.

Here is the code for the OK button to add to the click event hander:

```
void __fastcall TForm2::Button1Click(TObject *Sender)
{
    if ( ListBox1->ItemIndex == -1 )
        return;

    // Move to the table we need
    Table1->First();
    for ( int i=0; i<ListBox1->ItemIndex; ++i )
        Table1->Next();
    Close();
}
```

This code is pretty simple and straightforward. First, we check to be sure that the user actually selected something. If they didn't, we return out of the function. If they did select something, we position the database pointer to the correct position by moving through the records one at a time until we encounter the correct record. At that point we close the form using the **Close** method of the **TForm** class.

Once the form is closed, the **ShowModal** function will return in the first form. Please note that rather than using the **Close** method, it would have been just as easy to set the **ModalResult** property of the form to something other than 0, and the form would have closed and returned that result to the calling application form.

Once we've returned to the calling form, we grab each piece of the database form and set it into the edit fields. This allows the user to modify the data before closing the form and returning that data to the calling Visual C++ program. The final thing that the Form1 routine needs to do is to delete the **Form2** object because Form1 was the one that allocated it in the first place. Failure to delete this form would result in a memory leak (actually also a resource leak) because the form would never get cleaned up when the program ended. This will eventually crash the operating system, so we clean up after ourselves.

A few important things to notice in this little application. First, the initialization of the database is done inside of the database components. This is an important idea that you should carry on to your own application components. If you expect something to be set up and it isn't, you should set it up yourself. Don't expect the end user to set some global variables or call global functions for you. Failure to do this in a component-based system leads to problems later on. Components mean that everything should be encapsulated within the components, not left as an exercise for the application designer.

The other important thing to notice in this application is that you can easily create forms not only in the wrapper functions of your DLL, but also within any of the forms. Remember, though, that the memory you're consuming belongs to the application that is calling you, so be careful to free up any memory that you choose to allocate. The object passed into the DLL wrapper function (the **TAddress** object) is not allocated by the DLL functions, it's not your responsibility to handle them.

The final thing to notice in the application is something that you can only see at runtime. If an error occurs in the application, the CBuilder exception handling functionality will automatically catch it, even though there is no application to deal with the issue. This can be quite important to you, the application programmer. You can still use the **try .. catch** blocks in your code and still expect that unhandled exceptions will be dealt with by the underlying VCL. If an exception is thrown in a DLL, you can usually expect that the code will pick up at the end of the current method. This applies, of course, to non-fatal exceptions, which will terminate the DLL function. Try to catch as many exceptions as you possibly can in your own code so as to leave as little as possible to get through and stop the application from running properly.

That finishes the database DLL example. There are no changes needed to either the wrapper function of the DLL or to the calling MFC application from the last example. These changes are all encapsulated inside one of the forms of the DLL, so nothing needs to know about it. In fact, you need not even generate a new DLL import library for your DLL. Pretty amazing stuff, isn't it?

What Did We Learn In This Chapter?

This chapter covered quite a lot of ground. If you're a Visual C++ programmer, you saw enough to allow you to use VCL components in your Visual C++ programs, if only indirectly. If you're a corporate programmer trying to convince your company to use CBuilder, you should now have enough ammunition to show the company that there is at least a middle ground in the war between VC and CB. Here are some of the other highlights of this chapter:

- We saw how to create a **wrapper** function to encapsulate form creation in a CBuilder application and then embed that **wrapper** function in a DLL to be called from Visual C++.

- We learned how to use the dumpbin utility in Visual C++ to view all of the exported functions in a DLL created in CBuilder.

- We learned how to use the **lib** command to create import libraries from DLLs defined in CBuilder. By the way, this method will work with any DLL, not just those created in CBuilder. You Visual C++ programmers may have even learned something about your own system.

- We saw how to create a module definition file (DEF file), which could be used to create the previous import library in Visual C++.

- We saw how Visual C++ and CBuilder programs could talk to each other through intermediary objects.

- We saw how CBuilder database functionality could be dropped into a Visual C++ program through the use of CBuilder forms in a DLL.

- Although it wasn't directly mentioned here, you can directly use any functionality you want in a Visual C++ program from CBuilder by creating units in CBuilder that are called via **wrapper** functions. These units need not contain any visual code, but can simply use VCL components such as the database segments directly.

If you want to try something interesting, try creating components directly on a Visual C++ dialog to see if it can be done. Create a **wrapper** function that allows you to instantiate the component and pass in a dialog and position on which to instantiate it. You may need to use NULL as the parent of the component to make it all work.

That concludes our Visual C++ interface chapter. I hope that all of you MFC programmers see what you're missing in the ease of development in the VCL. I also hope you see that this is not an all or nothing proposition. You can use the VCL in your Visual C++ applications, if only indirectly.

Working With Threads

CHAPTER

13

- **What's A Thread?**

- **Why Use Threads?**

- **Creating A Thread**

- **Synchronicity Too?**

- **Searching For Threads**

Working With Threads

When I say the word thread, what do you think? Little white pieces of cotton on your business suit? The stuff sold on spools that is used for sewing? In the computer world, however, threads mean something quite different.

Threads in the computer world are independent processes that are running within your application. Your program already consists of threads, although you probably never think about it. When you display a form on the screen, it is running in a thread. All forms in an application usually run in the same thread, which is known as a single-threaded application. When you use more than one thread in an application, your program is multithreaded. So there. You know everything there is to know about threads. Well, not quite. There are a few questions yet unanswered: What are they really? Why do you want to use them? How do you use them? All of these questions will be answered in this chapter on threads and their uses in CBuilder applications.

A *thread* is simply an executing body of code whose processing time is controlled by the operating system rather than the program. While you might have multiple functions running in your program at the same time, the function processing is controlled by your application logic. A thread's execution is controlled by the time allotted to the thread by the operating system. Threads all run concurrently within an application and all run in the same global address space as the application. This means that a thread can "talk" to anything in the application it knows about. Global variables are accessible to a thread, as are global objects. A thread is like a mini-program running within your own program.

Why use threads? In the bad old days of MS-DOS programming, we created TSRs, which stood for Terminate and Stay Resident. A TSR was a background program that ran while the operating system was doing other things. A TSR was a good way to trap keystrokes, update the printer, update the clock display on the screen, or for whatever else you needed. They were fairly limited beasts and generally had to be written in assembler to be fast and small enough to be useful.

When Windows programming began, programs ran in a normal fashion. The Windows scheduler could tell a program to stop and start another one, but unless the other program acknowledged the request, it would keep running. Windows 95 and Windows NT are preemptive operating systems and can actually take control of the system and stop a running program. Other programs are then started at the discretion of the operating system. Threads are kind of like non-preemptive systems within a program. You can pause or resume a thread, but stopping one is at the whim of the thread itself. The operating system, of course, can kill a thread (as stopping a thread permanently is known) any time it wants. Your program, even though it created the thread, can only request that the thread stop.

In this chapter we begin to explore the programming of threads: why you would use them, what you can use them for, and how you communicate with them. We will look at thread examples from simple form displays to complex thread communications. By the time you finish this chapter, you should have a fuller understanding of not only how to use threads in your applications, but also when to use them.

Why Use Threads?

If you have worked in Windows for any length of time, you are probably accustomed to background processes, things you do in the idle time when your program is not processing user input or performing some action on the user's behalf. CBuilder has support built into it for idle processing, but using threads is the preferred method for doing such background work. A thread has numerous advantages over the idle processing system. In the first place, you need not worry about the length of time it takes to perform an action. Secondly, if you have several things to do in the background, you would have to perform your own time-slicing to do the job. You would need to do the first task, stop the processing, do the second task, and so forth. The thread system already has all of this time-slicing and process management built in.

A second reason to use thread processing is that it will not interfere with the normal message handling of your application. If you have written idle loops in standard Windows applications (non-framework-based), you often find that you have the equivalent of a message-handling loop embedded in your code. Usually, background processing loops look something like this:

```
while ( !done )
{
    // Do some processing

    // Process any waiting messages for the system to avoid stopping the
    // whole system
    while ( GetMessage(&msg) )
        DispatchMessage(&msg);
}
```

The purpose of the previous listing is to make sure that the loop of processing doesn't stop the user from doing anything else. Once you go down this road, you need to start worrying about re-entrancy of your code, having your code called from multiple places, and keeping track of where you are in the process. Using threads, you just worry about what you want to do and let the system do the rest.

A Simple Thread Example

For our first example, let's start with the inner workings of working with threads. We will create a simple form that uses a thread to update some text on the screen. The form will allow you to pause, resume, or stop the thread. In the meantime, the thread will be working away displaying numbers on the screen. We will explore how to create threads and how to add a thread object to your program.

Figure 13.1 shows the form we will be using to display the simple thread example. As you will notice, it consists of one label and three buttons.

Adding A New Thread

How you add a thread is the first issue that you need to be aware of in a thread-based application. You might have seen a class called **TThread** in the CBuilder documentation. This class is used to instantiate a thread in the system. Unfortunately, it is not quite as simple as just creating a new thread object by using the new operator.

Threads contain the method that implements all of the processing for the thread. This **Execute** method will be called when the thread is started, and is intended to continue running for the life of the thread. When the **Execute** method returns the thread exits or dies. In order to implement thread behavior, therefore, you will need to override the **Execute** method to do what you want. This overriding implies that

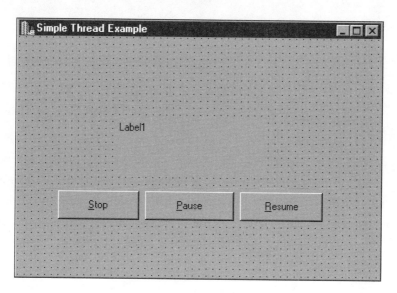

Figure 13.1
A simple thread example form.

you need to derive your own class from **TThread** to do the job, and this is exactly the case. You will derive a class from **TThread** and implement the **Execute** method for that derived class.

CBuilder makes it extremely easy to derive new classes from the **TThread** class by allowing you to create a new thread object. To do this, select the File|New menu item and select the Thread Object entry in the first panel of the New Items tab dialog. Selecting this object will bring up a secondary dialog, which will prompt you for a new name for your thread class. In our case, give the new thread class the name **TCheckThread**, because it will be checking the value of an entry and displaying it. When you click on the OK button, the **TCheckThread** class is generated in the Unit2.cpp source file (as well as the Unit2.h header file). Here is the implementation of the class as it is generated by the CBuilder wizard:

```
//-------------------------------------------------------------
#include <vcl\vcl.h>
#pragma hdrstop

#include "Unit2.h"
//-------------------------------------------------------------
//    Important: Methods and properties of objects in VCL can only be
```

```
//    used in a method called using Synchronize, for example:
//
//        Synchronize(UpdateCaption);
//
//    where UpdateCaption could look like:
//
//        void __fastcall TCheckThread::UpdateCaption()
//        {
//          Form1->Caption = "Updated in a thread";
//        }
//---------------------------------------------------------------
__fastcall TCheckThread::TCheckThread(bool CreateSuspended)
    : TThread(CreateSuspended)
{
}
//---------------------------------------------------------------
void __fastcall TCheckThread::Execute()
{
    //---- Place thread code here ----
}
//---------------------------------------------------------------
```

As you can see, the thread class generated by the wizard is quite complete. It doesn't do anything, but it is ready to be used. To modify this code, all you need to do is implement the **Execute** method.

In our first example, we want to explore the various methods of the thread class. For this reason, our **Execute** method is extremely simple, just counting up to 10,000 over and over. It illustrates the speed of the thread code, the interchange between the thread and the outside world, and the way in which you implement thread code. With all of that in mind, here is the code for the **Execute** method of the thread:

```
void __fastcall TCheckThread::Execute()
{
   while ( !Terminated )
   {
      Synchronize(UpdateLabel);
   }
   MessageBox(NULL, "All Done!", "Info", MB_OK);
}
```

In addition to the **Execute** method, we also need to update two other methods. First, the constructor for the class. Here is the initialization code we need to add to the constructor:

```
__fastcall TCheckThread::TCheckThread(bool CreateSuspended)
    : TThread(CreateSuspended)
{
    pLabel = NULL;
    nCount = 0;
}
```

This code will simply use the member variables to initialize the label object we will be using to show the progress and the count variable that maintains the current position in the 0 to10,000 range that we are incrementing. In addition to the constructor, we need a method to assign the label:

```
void __fastcall TCheckThread::AssignLabel(TLabel *pL)
{
    pLabel = pL;
}
```

The **Synchronize** method provides a way for you to avoid all of the multithread problems that exist while trying to update the same object from different threads in the application. Whenever you are working with a VCL object on a form in the main thread (the application), you should use a **Synchronize** method to make sure that this is the only thread that executes during this time. If you don't do this, you may find that multiple threads are trying to update the same object in different places, causing at best strange results and at worst program crashes.

The **Synchronize** method takes a single argument, which is a TTheadMethod type. This is simply a pointer to a thread member function that takes no arguments and returns no value. This method should be as fast as possible to make the process of thread interaction as painless as possible. Only the method will be executing while the method referenced in the **Synchronize** method is being called.

All of this code leads up to the **UpdateLabel** method, which is doing all of the work in the thread class. This method is quite trivial, as the following code listing shows:

```
void __fastcall TCheckThread::UpdateLabel(void)
{
    if ( pLabel )
        pLabel->Caption = nCount;
    if ( nCount < 10000 )
        nCount ++;
    else
```

```
        nCount = 0;
}
```

Once we have all of the code for the thread class implemented, the next task is to modify the form to create the thread and work with it. Let's turn our attention to that problem next.

Working With Threads In Forms

In order to work with a thread, first you need to create it. This task is relegated to the form containing the thread and is accomplished by simply allocating a new thread object using the new operator. In the case of our program, we will simply create the thread when the form is created. Add a new handler for the **Create** event to the form and add the following code to the **FormCreate** event handler:

```
void __fastcall TForm1::FormCreate(TObject *Sender)
{
    pThread = new TCheckThread(FALSE);
    pThread->AssignLabel( Label1 );
}
```

When you create a thread, you can start it in suspended mode or not in suspended mode. The argument to the thread constructor represents a boolean value indicating which form it should start in. Suspended mode is like putting the thread to sleep until the application wants it to start up. If you start a thread in suspended mode, it is your responsibility to start the thread by calling the **Resume** method of the thread.

Why would you want to start a thread in suspended mode? For two reasons. The first is that due to a problem in the Windows scheduler, it is possible for a thread to start before the constructor of the derived thread class completes. This will cause the **Execute** method to be called before the constructor has finished running. If this is a problem, you should start the thread in suspended mode in your own derived constructor and then call the **Resume** method as the last thing in the constructor. A simple example of such code might read:

```
TMyThread::TMyThread( bool bSuspend )
    : TThread( true ) // for suspend mode
{
    // Do some initialization
```

```
    // Start the thread if they wanted to
    if ( bSuspend == false )
        Resume();
}
```

You will need to decide whether or not to implement this in your own code. It is pretty simple code and doesn't hurt anything, so you might always want to implement your thread classes in this manner.

In our code, we create the thread in a non-suspended mode, indicating that the thread should start running as soon as it can. We can do this because we don't need any specific conditions to run the thread.

Once the thread is started, the user has three choices for stopping it. The first is to terminate the thread via the Stop button. To stop the thread, you need to tell the thread **Execute** method to stop. Looking at the **Execute** method, we see that the method ends when the **Terminate** flag is set to true. In order to make the **Terminate** flag true, you call the **Terminate** method of the class. Add the following handler for the Stop button in the class to do this:

```
void __fastcall TForm1::Button1Click(TObject *Sender)
{
    pThread->Terminate();
}
```

The second way to pause and resume the processing of a thread can be seen in action by adding a handler first for the Pause button on the form and adding the following code to the Pause button event handler in the form class:

```
void __fastcall TForm1::Button2Click(TObject *Sender)
{
    pThread->Suspend();
}
```

The third way to stop a thread is with the **Suspend** method of the class. It will temporarily stop the thread from running, but will not kill it. The **Execute** method is not called during a pause event. There is one strange note about Suspending a thread via this method. The Suspend call is not the expected on/off toggle. Calling the **Suspend** method multiple times results in a counter being incremented for each call. In order to restart a thread that has been called some number of times with the

Suspend method, you must call the **Resume** method an equal number of times. The process looks something like this:

Suspend : Count = 1
Suspend : Count = 2
Suspend : Count = 3
Resume : Count = 2 Thread not restarted
Resume : Count = 1 Thread not restarted
Resume : Count = 0 Thread is now restarted.

Why would you ever want to nest **Suspend** calls like this? There are numerous reasons, but the biggest is that you can be calling a derived class of a Thread in a derived class of a Form. If you had differing conditions in the different layers of inheritance in which you didn't want the thread to run, you would call Suspend at those different layers. In order to restart the thread, all of the different layers would need to agree that the conditions were right.

The final case, of course, is the Resume button. Clicking this button will cause the suspend condition to be decremented. If you click on the Suspend button followed by the Resume button, you will see the display first stop and then start updating on the form. Add a handler for the Resume button click event and add the following code to the handler:

```
void __fastcall TForm1::Button3Click(TObject *Sender)
{
    pThread->Resume();
}
```

That's all that you really need to know about working with forms and threads. CBuilder makes it particularly easy to deal with threads so that you hardly need to know what is going on behind the scenes. The important points to remember from this example are that the thread must be started, an exit condition must be specified for the thread, and the thread must be stopped. Throw in the condition that you need to remember to call the **Synchronize** method before interacting with any VCL controls on a form from a thread, and you know almost everything there is to know about thread-based programming.

Just to show you that it doesn't get much harder than this, consider the following slightly more complex example of working with threads.

The ThreadSearch Application Example

In our second example of working with threads, we are going to create a thread-based searching program. It will allow the user to select a given string to search in a given directory. We will also allow the user to specify a file mask (such as all source files *.cpp) to search in that directory. The form will then kick off a search thread that will locate all of the files in the given directory that contain the search string and load those file names into a list box on the main form.

While the thread is running, the user may want to view each of the files, and this is fairly accommodated. We will allow the user to double-click on the list box entry and bring up a form displaying the file in its entirety (provided it fits in memory). We don't necessarily know whether the search is finished, so we can't just process the entries as they are added. Using threads, however, the program simply looks at the user events as they happen and lets the thread worry about loading the list box. There is no need to worry about checking for user events during the search process because the thread is running on its own. We just write simple code.

This project uses two separate forms. The main one contains the edit fields to specify the search criteria for the search and the list box to contain the search results. The secondary form contains only a **TMemo** object, which will be used to display the file selected by the user. Figure 13.2 shows the main form for the application, while Figure 13.3 shows the secondary file display form.

Building The Main Form

The main form of the application is built with three labels, three edit fields, one button, and one list box. The edit fields are used only for gathering information; we will do no validation of input into these fields. If the user enters invalid data into the file mask or the directory fields, he just won't find anything. If you were building this form for a production environment, of course, you would add a browsing button to allow the user to select the directory and probably would allow the user to select a file mask from a predefined set of masks. That isn't the point of the example, so we won't worry about it here.

The first thing that needs to be dealt with in the form is the handling of the Do Search button, which will be used to kick off the search process and start a thread of

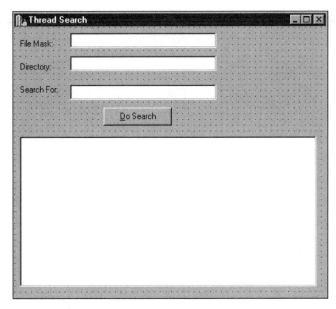

Figure 13.2
The ThreadSearch main form.

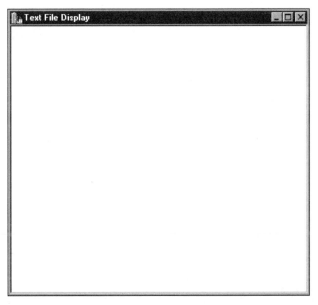

Figure 13.3
The File display form for the ThreadSearch application.

the proper type for the process. Add a new event handler to the form for the Do Search button click event and add the following code to that new event handler:

```
void __fastcall TForm1::Button1Click(TObject *Sender)
{
   pThread = new TSearchThread(Edit2->Text, Edit3->Text, Edit1->Text,
      FALSE);
   SetOkToSearch( false );
}
```

All we are doing is starting a new thread object and passing it the data that the user entered into the three edit fields of the form. We'll eventually tackle creating the thread class, but for now just assume it's going to work. The **SetOkToSearch** method is used to indicate whether a search is in progress, and it will be used to enable or disable the search button. Here is the implementation of this function, which you can add directly to the header file for the class:

```
void SetOkToSearch(bool bSearchOk)
   {
       Button1->Enabled = bSearchOk;
   }
```

Why are we making this into a function? Because by doing so we protect the implementation of the button-enabling. If we choose to do other things in this function, such as updating a status bar, displaying a message to the user, or even logging the event to an external file, the underlying classes need not know anything about the process. All the calling functions know is that this function stops a search from taking place or allows a new search to begin.

That out of the way, the next problem lies in the display of the text file when the user selects one from the list box by double-clicking on it. Add a new handler for the **DblClick** event for the **ListBox1** object and add the following code to the event handler for the form:

```
void __fastcall TForm1::ListBox1DblClick(TObject *Sender)
{
   // Get the text file at that location
   int nIdx = ListBox1->ItemIndex;
   if ( nIdx != -1 )
   {
      AnsiString strFile = ListBox1->Items->Strings[nIdx];
```

```
    // Create a new file viewer
    pFileViewer = new TForm3(this);
    pFileViewer->Memo1->Lines->LoadFromFile( strFile );
    pFileViewer->Show();
  }
}
```

In this method we get the name that the user selected from the list box. The list box will contain the full pathname of the files found, so this function can simply assume that the file name is valid (we'll make sure of that later) and just use it to display the file. The display itself is all taken care of directly from the VCL **TMemo** object, which already knows how to load itself directly from a file. By using the **LoadFromFile** method, we load the entire selected file directly into the memory of the **TMemo** object of the third form. Note that there is no code at all for TForm3 that you will need to implement. All of the work is already done for you. Isn't it wonderful to not write code once in a while?

That takes care of nearly all of the visual aspects of the form loading, searching, and displaying of text for the files found matching the search criteria. The only piece remaining, therefore, is the actual searching. This will all take place within our new thread object, which might be a good idea to create right now.

Creating The SearchThread Object

You create the thread for this example exactly the same way you did for the previous example. Use the CBuilder thread object creation system to create a new thread class and give this class the name **TSearchThread**. CBuilder will generate a source file (Unit2.cpp in this example) with the class defined in it.

The first modification that needs to be made is to the constructor for the class. Besides setting up the thread to run, we need to initialize all of the member variables for the class. In keeping with the policy I stated a bit earlier about not running the thread until you finish the initialization, we will add that tidbit to the code as well. Here is the complete constructor for the class:

```
__fastcall TSearchThread::TSearchThread(AnsiString strDir, AnsiString
    strMask, AnsiString strText, bool CreateSuspended)
   : TThread(false)
{
   FstrDirectory = strDir;
```

```
    if ( FstrDirectory[FstrDirectory.Length()-1] != '\\' )
        FstrDirectory += '\\';
    FstrFileMask  = strMask;
    FstrSearchText = strText;
    if ( !CreateSuspended )
        Resume();
}
```

With these changes, you will need to make several modifications to the header file for the thread class to contain the new member variables and methods for the **TSearchThread** class. Here are the changes to the Unit2.h header file for the **TSearchThread** class:

```
class TSearchThread : public TThread
{
private:
protected:
    void __fastcall Execute();
private:
    AnsiString FstrDirectory;
    AnsiString FstrFileMask;
    AnsiString FstrSearchText;
    AnsiString FstrCurFileName;

    int DoFind( AnsiString strSearchText, AnsiString& text );
public:
    __fastcall TSearchThread(AnsiString strDir, AnsiString strMask,
        AnsiString strText, bool CreateSuspended);
    void __fastcall AddToListBox(void);
};
```

The directory, file mask, and search text member variables are used for the searching process to determine which files will be looked through and what text will be looked for. The current file name member variable (FstrCurFileName) is used because the method to "talk" to the VCL object on the form, the list box, cannot take any parameters. Finally, we add a private member function, **DoFind**, to do the actual searching through the file to see whether it contains the desired text string.

Once we have the thread initialized and running (via the **Resume** call at the end of the constructor), the **Execute** method comes into play. In our previous example, the **Execute** method continued to run forever because there was no useful purpose to it. In this example, on the other hand, our purpose is quite explicit: To search through a finite number of files to find all of those files that contain a specified text string. For this reason, we won't simply loop forever but only until we have run out of text files to process. Here is the code for the **Execute** method for the **TSearchThread** class:

```
void __fastcall TSearchThread::Execute()
{
    // Loop through all files that match the file mask given us.
    // Use the Win32 API functions to do this.

    WIN32_FIND_DATA FindFileData;
    AnsiString strSearchFiles = FstrDirectory + FstrFileMask;
    HANDLE hFirstFileHandle = FindFirstFile( strSearchFiles.c_str(),
        &FindFileData );

    while ( hFirstFileHandle && !Terminated )
    {
                // Try to open the file for input
                FILE *fp = fopen(FindFileData.cFileName, "r" );
        FstrCurFileName = FstrDirectory + FindFileData.cFileName;
                if (fp == NULL)
                {
                        if ( FindNextFile( hFirstFileHandle,
                            &FindFileData ) == FALSE )
                                break;
                        continue;
                }

                // Search this file one line at a time.
                char szBuffer[ 256 ];

                while ( !feof(fp) )
                {
                        if ( fgets(szBuffer, 255, fp) == NULL )
                                break;
                        AnsiString s = szBuffer;

                if ( DoFind( FstrSearchText, s ) )
        {
          Synchronize(AddToListBox);
            break;
                        }
                }
}
```

```
                    // Close the file and move to the next file in the list.
                    fclose(fp);

                    if ( FindNextFile( hFirstFileHandle, &FindFileData ) ==
                        FALSE )
                                    break;
        }
        Form1->SearchComplete();
}
```

This code follows a simple and straightforward process. First, the file mask and directory are used to create a file list to search by using the **FindFirstFile** and **FindNextFile** API functions that we looked at previously in the Windows API chapter of the book.

Each file is opened (if possible, if not it is skipped), and the lines of text read in from the file one at a time. If the text string is found in a line, the file is then closed, the file name added to the form list box, and the search loop exited. Once the file is processed in one way or another, the file is closed and the next file is selected by the API function. As this is happening, the user is free to select any of the file names stored in the list box and view them using the file viewer form we developed earlier in the chapter.

Once all of the files are searched or the thread terminated, the **SearchComplete** method of the form is called. This method, shown in the following listing, simply terminates the thread if it has not already been killed or finished and then re-enables the Do Search button on the form. This prepares the form for a second, third, and so forth, search of the data:

```
 void __fastcall TForm1::SearchComplete(void)
{
    pThread->Terminate();
    SetOkToSearch( true );
}
```

The code for the search function is pretty easy. I've left in some extras, such as telling you how many instances of the text string were found, in case you get terribly ambitious and want to add relevancy to the search entry in the list box. If you make millions of dollars on this crummy piece of code, please drop me a postcard from Bermuda, okay?

```
// Method to do brute force searching of text in an input string.
int TSearchThread::DoFind( AnsiString strSearchText, AnsiString& text )
{
   int i=0;
   int nCount = 0;

   while ( i < text.Length() )
   {
      if ( !strncmp(text.c_str()+i, strSearchText.c_str(),
         strSearchText.Length()) )
      {
         i += strSearchText.Length();
         nCount ++;
      }
      else
      {
         i++;
      }
   }
   return nCount;
}
```

The final piece of the puzzle lies in the **AddToListBox** function. This function, which we set up to be synchronized with the form in the constructor for the class, is responsible for putting the currently selected file into the list box on the main search form. We needn't worry about whether anyone else is playing with the list box at the time we do our job, because this function is synchronized. The following is the code for the **AddToListBox** function:

```
void __fastcall TSearchThread::AddToListBox(void)
{
   if ( FstrCurFileName.Length() )
      Form1->ListBox1->Items->Add( FstrCurFileName );
}
```

This code simply checks to see whether there is anything in the current file name (just as a sanity check), and then adds the string to the list box by appending it to the end of the list. The user can then select the file they want to see by double-clicking on that entry in the list at any time during the run of the application.

Figure 13.4 shows a typical search of my hard-drive to find all of the source files (*.cpp) that contain the word "Text." The result is shown in the list box, and one of

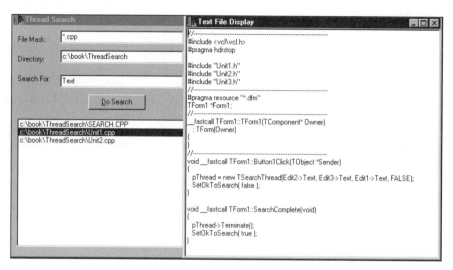

Figure 13.4
The search form in action.

those files is shown in the file viewer form at the same time. This search is complete, and the search button is re-enabled for another search.

Designing With Threads

Deciding when to use threads in an application is the most difficult part about working with threads. There are no hard and fast rules for when to use them, but certain kinds of applications do lend themselves to thread-based approaches.

The first clue that your application should use a thread is background processing. Checking a serial or parallel port, watching for file activity, or writing to a status log in the idle time of your application are events that will work well as threads. If the activities are separate entities, such as an idle loop, you can often simply "wrap" a thread around the code that implements the idle loop.

Another likely scenario for a thread is when you have multiple things you need to do at the same time that run discretely, such as starting code for your application or initializing code that must take place before the user can start an event. In general, your approach is to start the GUI interface (form) for the user to view while the background thread initializes the system for using that form. Loading project information for a system while the form displays, and parsing class data in a browser system (such as the one in Visual C++), are good examples of this.

The final case for thread-based applications occurs when you want to have the user start a process and then monitor that process while allowing the user to continue with other things. Suppose, for example, that the user was able to communicate with a host machine to retrieve a set of records from a host database. The user might define the search criteria for the set and then tell the application to view them. In the search process, much like in our search example, you could then allow the user to view detail records even as the records are being retrieved from the host. This would permit the user to do his or her job while the program is still in the process of doing its job.

The advantages to using threads are many. You can have each discrete set of code do the job it is intended to perform without worrying about any other part of the code. Your GUI code can simply assume that it has the data it needs when it needs it (a just-in-time solution to data retrieval) rather than worrying about the load process. Threads are a good way to separate the application-specific data retrieval code from the GUI code intended to display and manipulate that data. In this respect, threads lend themselves well to an object-oriented approach.

When are threads a bad idea? In many applications, adding threads to the system makes it overly complicated and slows it down. Threads add overhead to the system and make Windows itself run a little slower. The more threads in your system, the more overhead is involved in simply keeping track of each one and ensuring that each thread has time to run.

Before using a thread, ask yourself several questions.

1. Does this code interact with other code in the system? If it is tightly coupled to other pieces of code in the application, this code is a poor candidate for a thread.

2. Does this code need access to data that belongs outside of it? If the answer is yes, this code might be a poor candidate. Threads need to have total control over the data they are working with. While it would be okay to have a thread that loaded some records into a grid on the display, it would be a bad idea to have a thread that searched the records that a user was entering on the display. Your mileage may vary, of course.

3. Am I using threads just to say I'm using threads? Some programmers are anxious to use new technology even though it may not be the best solution to the problem at hand.

That really sums up threads in CBuilder applications. When used correctly, threads can speed up an application and help to make it more readable and easier to understand. CBuilder has some very nice debugging features specifically designed for working with threads (check the online help), which makes it a joy instead of a job to develop with them in your own applications.

What Did We Learn In This Chapter?

In this chapter we explored the concept of multithread programming. This technique, when properly used, can make your programs faster, more responsive, and much easier to use. We looked at how to add threads to your application and how to optimize them. Here are the highlights of this chapter:

- Threads are implemented by using the New Thread Object command in the CBuilder File|New Menu item.

- Threads run until they are either terminated via the Terminate command or paused via the **Suspend** method. Suspended threads can be restarted via the **Resume** method call.

- Threads implement all of their functionality in the **Execute** method, which generally runs forever or until a specific goal has been accomplished.

- If you want to work with a VCL object in a form not belonging to the thread, you should use the **Synchronize** method of the thread to call that method.

- To make sure that a thread doesn't start before the constructor code is finished, call the thread constructor with the **suspend** flag set to true and then call the **Resume** method as the last thing done in the constructor.

Once you get used to working with threads, you will find that you use them rarely in your own applications. Most of the time they are overkill. Use them for background processing, continuous updating or checking, or for concurrent processes that all need to be accomplished before a task can be completed.

That concludes our discussion of threads. In our next chapter, we get back into the meat of the CBuilder programming environment and take up the subject of creating your own components.

Creating Your Own Components

CHAPTER

14

- Component Development Process

- Designing A Component

- Properties, Methods, And Events

- Component Wizard

- Testing Components By Hand

- Installation

Creating Your Own Components

Components are the most exciting part of the CBuilder environment. They allow you to implement drag-and-drop programming, on-the-fly property manipulation, and true object-oriented design. Components are at the core of the CBuilder system and provide much of the flexibility of the IDE itself. Without components, there would be no CBuilder, and the world would be a much sadder place. In this chapter we explore creating your own components, from designing them to debugging them. We will look at installation issues, design time versus runtime issues, and much, much more.

In order to work with components, it is important to understand what a component really is. *Components* are simply encapsulations of data and methods. In short, they are objects. In the CBuilder system, a component is a specific object derived from TComponent. Components may (although they are not required to) have properties and methods. *Properties* are simply accessors for the data in the component. *Methods* are simply exposed functionality from the component. Components operate in one of two modes, design-time and runtime. In design-time mode, components are being displayed on a form in the CBuilder form editor. Design-time components cannot have their methods called, cannot interact directly with the end-user, and need not implement their full functionality. Usually, though not always, design-time components paint themselves in a default fashion for the properties assigned to them. A component in design-time is not required to look the same as it does at runtime, and many, such as forms, do not.

Runtime is the other component mode. At runtime, the component is operating in a real running application. It must render (draw) itself properly, handle method calls, and work effectively with other components. Although all components are

401

visible in some form at design time (how else could you select them?), they need not be visible at runtime. Database components, such as **TTable**, **TQuery**, and **TDataSet**, are not visible at runtime, but perform important functions nonetheless.

In this chapter we will explore several important facets of creating components to work with CBuilder. They won't be world-class components, and they aren't likely to end up in your commercial applications. They will teach you the basics of writing components for the system and the problems associated with them. In addition, we will cover the design and documentation of components, as well as the issues of property publishing, registration, and debugging. In short, this is a primer on component development, not an encyclopedia. There are other good books on component development and design (mostly written for Delphi, but the principles are the same), so please consult one of those if this is something you want to do professionally.

The Process Of Component Development

Creating components requires a specific process. This process is not specific to any kind of component, nor is it necessary only in the case of commercial component development; and the degree to which you implement each step may vary depending on the reusability required for the component and the importance of protecting the system from component failure. Here's an overview of the process; later, we'll explore each step in more detail:

1. Define the problem you are trying to solve.

2. Define a specific solution to the problem you are trying to solve.

3. Generalize the specific solution.

4. Design a component to implement the general solution.

5. Make the component design as flexible as possible for the end user.

6. Implement the component solution.

7. Debug the component.

8. Test the component.

9. Document the component interface for the end user (the programmer who will be using the component in the real world).

10. Miscellaneous work (help files, icons, palette page determinations).

11. Install the component.

12. Using what you have learned, start over at Step 1.

As you can see, the component development process is a never-ending solution in search of a problem. Seriously, the day you complete work on a component, the chances are quite good that you will start working on it all over again, as you can see Step 12 is trying to indicate. Fred Brooks, in his landmark software development book, *The Mythical Man-Month*, says that you should always write one version of a project to throw away because you will do that anyway. This truism is certainly appropriate in the component development world. The simple act of designing, developing, debugging (the three D's), and then using a component, will usually lead you in directions you never imagined when you started the component work in the first place. If you simply plan to rewrite the thing (saving a lot of work from the first time) once you are finished, you will probably be a lot happier in the end. Components and applications not rewritten following the first release usually end up so badly patched that the original code is unrecognizable even to the original author. Trust me. I've been there too many times to ever think that I can get it right the first time.

The Component Process In Detail

Let's look at each one of the steps that make up the process in a little more detail. If you are impatient with reading all this holier than thou stuff about how to design your components, you are free to skip forward to all of the code following this section, but I don't recommend it. People who think they know everything there is to know about a subject generally go in one of two paths: they realize they know very little about it or they become unemployed (and often unemployable). Learn from others' mistakes and you will go far in the industry.

Define The Problem You Are Trying To Solve

I couldn't count the number of times I have run across code that contained bugs. The bugs ranged from pure stupidity on the part of the coder (gee, you mean that 1 divided by 0 causes a problem?) to the extremely sublime mistake caused by some esoterica in the Windows (or even the MS-DOS) operating system. But most bugs occur because the programmer isn't sure what he or she is doing.

Writing components is like writing any other sort of code, only more so. If you make a mistake defining the interface of a method in one of your C++ classes in an application, that problem is serious but localized to the application in which it appears. If you later discover that you really needed more, or different, parameters to the method, it is just a matter of changing the interface in the method and then updating the application. If your class is part of a library, however, you will find that the change ripples across several applications in your company's system. When you get down to the component level, on the other hand, your one little change could affect hundreds of applications written at dozens of companies (assuming you sold your component to others). It's the little things that drive us all crazy.

When you sit down to write a component, write a problem statement that defines the problem you are trying to solve. Problem statements can be simple, as in "Solves the need to display JPEG images," or more complex, as in "Solves the problem of communicating between multiple components on a form to notify each of a change in the other." If you can't summarize the component's purpose in a single statement, you probably don't understand the problem well enough to offer a useful solution. At the initial stage of development, your problem statement is likely to cover only the current application you are handling. For example, your program might need a piece that allows the user to click on an embedded bit of text to jump to another form or another piece of text. Maybe you have some help instructions that require you to jump to other help instructions. The problem statement is to create a component that allows you to jump from one piece of help text to another using a mouse click.

You will be amazed at how much progress you'll make by simply writing a problem statement. It establishes what you are doing. When your boss asks what you've been working on for the last week, you can simply hand over the problem statement. When you look back at the component and see all its capabilities, you can return to the problem statement and see if it really does what you said it would. Problem statements often isolate an application's problems. Given a problem statement, you can often find an existing component that solves the problem without you writing any code of your own. All this from one little sentence written on a piece of paper.

Define A Specific Solution To The Problem

Once you have a problem statement, you can define a solution to the problem. At this point in the development effort, we don't need to worry about any other problems this component might solve, just that it solves this one. If the problem statement were to jump between help text entries, for example, you might define a solution that allows the user to go from point A to point B when point C is clicked.

Implementing a specific solution is quite often all that is needed for a problem. You may never go to the next step (generalization), but you will have at least considered the problem and offered a documented solution. Once you have the specific solution, you can offer it up for criticism by your coworkers. You might find that you have solved the problem, or you might find that your solution fails to take into account certain other conditions. Perhaps your solution was to check the word under the cursor and jump to another help file based on that word. Your coworkers could point out that jumping from the word "intent" in a document about programming HTML pages to a document about legal issues probably wasn't what the user wanted at all. Offering the specific solution can also drive you back to the drawing board and make you redefine the problem.

Generalize The Specific Solution

Once you have a specific solution to a specific problem, take a few minutes, hours, days, or whatever it takes, to step back and look at the problem and the solution. By examining the problem more generally instead of focusing only on the specific issue you are trying to solve, you may find a whole class of problems that can be solved. Some of the most brilliant ideas in the computer industry have come about from generalizing a solution to a specific problem.

Rather than trying to explain the generalization process, which is mostly a matter of individual work, let's look at a simple example of the process.

Fred Jones has a problem in his CBuilder application. He needs to restrict the input for a given field only to numeric entries. The entries can be of any length, but they must be positive and must contain only numbers and the decimal point. No exponentiation is allowed, no hexadecimal entry, and so forth. The user is only allowed to enter the digits zero through nine (0 through 9) and the decimal point (.). Immediately, Fred leaps into action, hacking together some code from the brilliant book he picked up just the other day (this book, of course) and comes up with a function in his form that does exactly what he wants. Fred is happy, the user is happy, the program works perfectly, and the world is a better place.

Unfortunately, Fred is working on the enhanced version of the program and discovers that there are three more forms that need the same sort of validation. Fred thinks he needs another programmer to do the job. Nah. Fred thinks about the fact that his career at this company isn't going anywhere and he really ought to learn how to write components if he wants a better job at the next company. With this in mind, Fred decides to implement his new knowledge of the validation of the numeric entry as a component. Components, after all, are a good thing, and Fred wants to minimize the amount of code he needs to cut and paste between forms. Cut and paste errors, in Fred's estimation, account for at least half of all of the bugs in his programs. If he avoids the problem by localizing the code into a component, he will avoid half the bugs.

Once the decision has been made to create a new component, Fred works at it diligently. Pretty soon he has a complete component that will check for numbers only on the input and reject anything else. For about two weeks, Fred is happy. Then, marketing decides that the Social Security input field needs to be validated for numbers and dashes, the date field needs numbers and slashes, and the special registration number field needs both letters and numbers. Fred is despondent.

What went wrong? Fred solved the specific case of needing a component to filter out data that was not valid for a given field. In his case, however, Fred never took the next step of generalizing the solution. Had he considered the problem for a little while, he would have realized that allowing the user to define a filter set of characters would have been much easier. You might ask why Fred didn't use the **Masked Edit** component that ships with CBuilder. The answer is that this component doesn't provide the very flexibility he sought. A mask is fixed in appearance, so that if I wanted to enter 1.234 or 123.4 or 12.45, I would not be able to write a simple mask that solves the problem. A filtered edit component, which accepted entries of 0,1,2,3,4,5,6,7,8,9, would have done the job. When the other component requirements came about, Fred would merely have had to change the filter string to add the new components.

One word of caution about generalization: It can be taken too far. If you try to solve all of the world's problems in a single component, you will find that you have created a component that no one will use because it doesn't solve their problem easily enough. Stick to a single problem and generalize the solution for other problems with the same underlying issue.

Design A Component To Implement The General Solution

Once you know what it is that you are going to do, the next step is probably the most crucial step in the component development process: designing the component to solve the defined problem. If you have designed the component properly and laid out the steps it will follow, writing the component is usually a pretty simple matter. As one of my ex-bosses used to say, "SMOP: Simple Matter Of Programming."

Design is one of the hardest jobs there is to teach. Schools don't do it; they generally hand you a completed design and tell you to implement it. Companies don't do it; they will generally hire an experienced designer to write the program specifications for a project. Design is one of those things you learn the hard way by doing it wrong a few times.

When you are designing a component, you need to get three major things right before you can start writing the thing: the component's properties, methods, and events. Unfortunately, this is a function of how many components you have designed in the past and how well you understand the component you are working with. It's a matter of practice, practice, practice. In addition to properties, the methods for a component need to be well thought out. Methods must be available to do the job users want (or properties must be available; in CBuilder the line is often blurred) or they will quickly lose interest in your component. Finally, you must define any events that you want handled in the component. Events are the hardest part of the process, and you often need to go back and study them after the fact. Many events are commonly added to components in future releases; few properties or methods are added. This is a function of how the component is used by the programmer.

Make The Component Design As Flexible As Possible

This step is really just the same as the progression from a specific design to a general one. Once you have defined the properties, methods, and events that will solve the problem you have defined in the specific case, try to generalize the component a bit to allow more flexibility. Add hooks before, during, and after each critical section. Look through the design for properties that have dependencies built into the system.

For example, if you were building a date component, you would, of course, have properties for the month, day, and year. This would be a specific solution to the problem. You would also likely have a method to return the date as a string so that the user can view it. This display method has a dependency that might not be immediately obvious. You need the data and the format to display a string. The format is not specified in our specific solution, so we should add it to the general solution. The format would be made up of the actual display type (MMDDYY, DDMMYY, MMDDYYYY, or whatever) along with the separator for the components of the date—usually a / or a -).

You often learn the flexibility issue in the heat of development. It is really okay to go back and add new properties and methods while defining a component. It is also not at all unusual for a single component to lead to others. If you realize that one component could easily be split into three separate ones that do the job better, by all means do so.

Implement The Component Solution

Once you have the component's design in mind (or on paper), it's time to get to the fun stuff—implementing the design in code. CBuilder provides some help in doing this, but most of the work will be on your own. First, you need to create the skeleton component, adding in the properties, methods, and events called for by the component's design.

After the component has its properties and methods, it is time to flesh out the implementation by using those properties and methods to build a working model. If you find during the implementation of the component that there are missing methods or properties, don't simply add them in. Drop back a step to the component design (either the specific or general solutions) and look at the problem again with the new properties or methods in mind. This might not lead anywhere, but it just might lead you to discover a few other missing ingredients as well.

Component development, like most RAD styles, is an iterative process. It is hard to get things right the first time, and it is impossible to do a good job if you are not willing to change the design when a better idea comes up. The real art to developing components, in fact, is knowing when to stop redesigning the system and when to put things off for another release.

We aren't going to talk a lot about the component development process here, other than to focus on the pieces you might otherwise overlook during the development phase of the process. Most of this chapter is code development, not verbiage.

Debugging The Component

As soon as the component development is finished, the next step is to debug it. In this chapter we will explore how to debug components initially and then how to work with them after they are installed.

Debugging is most certainly an art, and maybe even a black art. If you learn some tricks to debugging, you will go far in the programming world. Make the CBuilder debugger your friend instead of your enemy, and you'll find quite a few powerful tools.

One last comment before we move on. Debugging is not testing. Debugging is making the component work the way it says it should work. If I say that the component will draw a line from one corner of the component window to the other, it should do that. Debugging is making sure that it does do that. Testing is a whole other subject.

Test The Component

As I just said, debugging is not testing. So what is testing? It's verifying that not only does the component do what it is supposed to, but also that it doesn't do what it is not supposed to. While debugging verifies that valid input leads to valid results, testing often validates that invalid input also leads to valid results (or at least valid processing).

When you create a component you should test it extensively. This means considerably more than simply validating that the numbers you enter result in correct display. It means that if I indicate that a field should be between 1 and 10, that entering 11, 0, or −32768 will not cause problems. It means that if one property relies on another, the component doesn't crash when the second field is omitted. It means checking boundary conditions for properties and methods.

Boundary conditions are the extreme limits on input. If your number is supposed to be a positive integer, then the boundary conditions would be 0, −1, 32767 and −32768. You should also select one valid input in the middle, such as 1234, to test that everything is working correctly. Unless you are using some strange algorithm that has problems in the middle of the range, testing these five entries would be more useful than sitting at your keyboard for 12 hours testing every number you can think of.

In order to be truly useful, testing should include a regression component. This means that as I implement version 2.0 of a component product, this new component will pass all of the old tests for version 1.x along with any new tests that I come up with for the new functionality of version 2.0.

Fair warning: Most programmers are lousy testers. If you really want your component tested well, have other people help you, what is called Beta testing.

Document The Component Interface

If you have created the component well, the job of documenting it should be easy. You can simply list the published methods and properties for the component and explain what each one does. Your documentation should include any assumptions made in the component, as well as any dependencies between properties or methods.

Put simply, if you do not document your component, no one will use it. People simply don't have the time to look through source code for examples of how to do things. They don't have time to guess at valid entries in your properties. Borland has made the component usage in CBuilder as simple as it could without sacrificing flexibility and power in the components themselves. It is up to you to make your component as user-friendly as possible.

Don't inundate the user with documentation. Make your documentation clear and concise without being cryptic. If you are developing a date component, for example, you can take for granted that people will know what the **Month** property represents, can't you? Not really. If the month component runs from 1 through 12, that is quite different than if it runs from 0 through 11. The documentation must tell the user this, although it can be as simple as:

Month: The month number of the date, 0-based from 0 through 11.

This tells me everything I need to know. The **Day** component, on the other hand, is not as straightforward. Is it the day of the month or the day of the week? Naming your properties more explicitly makes this easier. Give the property the name DayOfMonth and no one will mistake it for the weekday. They still won't know if it is 0-based or 1-based, however. Be consistent and people will understand. The greatest compliment to the component writer is when the programmer stops looking at the documentation because the components all work the same way.

Think about your use of the components built into CBuilder. Once you understand how a property works in one component, don't you generally take it for granted that the property will work the same way in others? Of course you do. That's why the documentation is so important.

Miscellaneous Work

In this section of the development process, you need to address some other issues: Where will the component live in the component palette? What icon will represent it in the palette? What kind of a help file is offered and how do you tie it to the component?

Installing The Component

Although the installation of a component is taken care of by the development system IDE, there are issues here for you as well. There are two ways to test a component in CBuilder, as we will see in this chapter. In general, you will test your component initially without installing it (because that takes quite a while for many tests). In this chapter, I'll show you how to test a component without installing it. After the installation is complete, however, you will need to retest your component (regression testing, remember?). Components do not necessarily behave exactly the same way when installed versus when they are tested internally. You need to verify that the component works properly in both places.

*It might not appear that there is any way to install a component without the source for that component or without an object file for that component. This is not strictly true. Nor is it true that you can only install a single component at a time in CBuilder's VCL library. If you go outside of the IDE and build a library file for your components, you can add multiple components at the same time, as well as components that require multiple files. This trick comes with a price, however. You need to add a new unit to your component with the same name as the library that contains the Register functions for all of the components in the library. To see how this works, check the comps.lib library on the accompanying disk with this chapter's code. You will find a unit called comps.cpp that contains a **namespace** with the **Register** function defined for that library.*

Using What You Learned To Start Over At Step 1

Excellent components are never really finished: In the future you will update them, fix them, and add features to them; so, after creating a component, you should take time to look back and see what you have learned. Quite often you will find that the process of developing the component tells you something about the way you should have done it. Remember, develop one to throw away; you are going to anyway.

Now you know everything there is to know about component development, right? Well, maybe. Let's get you started on that road by writing some real components right here. We will start simply and then move our way up, as usual.

The AngleText Component

First, we'll develop a simple component to display text. In this case, however, we will be displaying text in whatever font the user wants (with certain restrictions, as we will see) rotated at whatever angle the user wants. This kind of a component is used for the display of an axis label on a graph, as the sidebar on a Web-style page, or in any kind of a form where you need the text displayed other than horizontally.

For this first component, we'll work through the process from start to finish to give you a firm background on how things are done in the CBuilder environment. After this first component, I will skip over the details of how to do the common portions of component development and will simply refer you back to this section if you need more help. The process of writing components is similar regardless of the component you are writing, as you will see.

The first step to developing a component, as we talked about earlier in the chapter, is to define what the component is to do and how it is to work. This is the problem statement for the component. Why are we creating this component? In the case of the **AngleText** component, the problem we are trying to solve is to display a vertical text string to show the y-axis label for a graph. In order to solve this problem, we need to rotate the text at a 90-degree angle from the horizontal. This is the specific problem statement we are solving.

The specific solution to the problem is to rotate the text at an angle when it is drawn. This isn't hard to do (we actually did this a bit earlier in the book when we looked at using Delphi units in our code), and involves manipulating the font object assigned to the canvas. In our case, we want to have the component have its own **Canvas** property so that we can work with it rather than the form on which it lives.

Normally, the next step of the process is to generalize the problem and the solution. In this case, there really is no generalized solution to the problem other than the one that solves the specific problem we are trying to solve. Instead of focusing on the general solution, therefore, we will focus on properties the component needs to do the job we have assigned to it.

Like the problem phase, the design phase has only the general solution, rather than both a general and a specific solution. Our solution involves two basic design decisions. First, we need to decide what properties the component will have. This first decision affects the second problem, which is the VCL class from which the component will be derived.

Selecting The Properties

Components have two types of properties. The first type are the properties inherited from the base component class that are exposed by the new component. These properties represent basic functionality that is based in the VCL for the component class that you get for free by deriving from the proper base type. In the case of the **AngleText** component, we would like to get certain properties for free in order to use them in our implementation. The second set of properties are new properties that we define specifically for our component. These properties are unique to the component we are implementing and do not require a choice in the base class.

When you create a component, you will derive it from a base class in the VCL. This base class selection affects the properties available to you when you write the component. All components must be at least derived from **Tcomponent**, the base class for all components in the VCL that implements almost no functionality for you. Alternatively, you could select a base component class that does a lot of the work for you. The choice of this class will affect how much work you have to do and how much work is done for you. Generally, you look for the highest level class that still fits the criteria of the component you are trying to write. You would not, for example, select a combo box to derive your component from if you were writing a new button class. You might, though, select the **TButton** class to derive from.

What this is all getting at is that, to determine the properties for a class, you need to determine the base class of the component. But in order to determine the base class for the component, you need to know what properties the component needs. This only seems like an infinite recursion; it really isn't that bad. Deciding which component class to derive from is usually a lot easier than it seems. If you want to derive a visual component that needs to paint itself, you need one of the **TCustomxxx** component class. If you are working with a component that implements the basics of a button, but with some twist (like repeating the click event on some predetermined interval, perhaps), you would derive from **TCustomButton**.

In the case of the **TAngleText** class, we need the basic control functionality to work. Basic control functionality includes the properties for Text, Canvas, Font, Color, and so forth. Therefore, the base class of the **TAngleText** class will be the **TCustomControl** class. This is the basic class that implements control properties and will give us the basic properties we need.

Let's move back to determining what component properties we need to implement for the **TAngleText** component. First and foremost, we need the Text to display at an angle. The **Text** property is a base property belonging to the **TCustomControl** class, so there is no work to do here. All we need to do is to expose this property (we will look at how to do this momentarily), and it will work as advertised. The next obvious property to define is the angle at which to display the text. This will be called the **Angle** property.

Once the two easy properties are out of the way, let's look at what other properties we need to define for the component. All VCL components automatically have the properties for position and parent. These properties are the **Left**, **Top**, **Height**, **Width**, and **Parent** properties. None of these properties needs to be implemented by you, the component developer.

The first thing that you need to think about is how you draw a text string at an angle. To do this, you need three things. First, you need the string to draw. This is the **Text** property of the component. Secondly, you need the angle at which to draw the component. This is the **Angle** property we already defined. Finally, you need a position at which to draw the text. This is the base point of the text string. We could simply define this point automatically, but this isn't really a good idea. Some users will want the string to appear centered vertically, others will want the string to appear butted up against the top of the component region, while still others might want it jammed down at the bottom of the component. Rather than making this decision for the user, we will simply allow the end user (the programmer using our component) to define the point. A point is hard to edit, so we will implement two separate properties, the X position of the base point and the Y position of the point.

Following the base point, the next issue involves the actual drawing of the component. In order to modify the component display, we need the font for the display. We could simply always use the parent font, but this would be an unnecessary restriction on the user. For this reason, we will expose the **Font** property of the **TCustomControl** class to the end user. Similarly, we need to allow the user to change the background color of the component so that it can blend in to the form it is displayed on (if so desired). For this, we expose the **Color** property. At this point we have six properties defined for the component. Three of them are implemented by the base class **TCustomControl** (**Font**, **Text**, and **Color**), and three need to be implemented by our component (**Angle**, **XPos**, **YPos**). Now let's get started on the actual coding.

Implementing A New Component

CBuilder isn't a great help in creating components. The Component Wizard can be used to generate a very simple skeleton for the component but can't be used past that point. We are going to do something about that a little later in the book, but for now, it will do you some good to actually create a component from scratch and learn what all the little pieces do.

The CBuilder Component Wizard is used to create a new component skeleton in CBuilder. You might think that this sort of a tool would be in the Tools menu, but it isn't. Select Component|New from the main CBuilder menu and you will see the Component Wizard screen, which is shown in Figure 14.1. This simple screen allows you to define the component name, the base class of the component, and the palette page you want to display the component on. These are the only options you have in the wizard. There are no entries for the properties you want to add to the component, any methods you might want to add, or any events to process. These are all things that you need to do on your own, but don't panic. We'll go through the process step-by-step in this chapter.

For this example, enter TAngleText for the component name. Select the **TCustomControl** component as the base class and leave the Samples page for the Palette Entry. Click on the OK button, and the component will be generated and added to your project. This is useful because we can then test the component within the project before actually installing it in the system. It is much easier to test and debug a component within a project than it is to do so after it is installed.

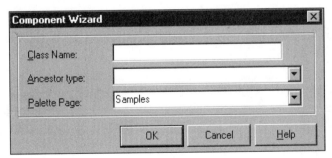

Figure 14.1
The Component Wizard in CBuilder.

Adding Predefined Properties

Adding properties to the component is the first step toward implementing the component. There are two ways to add a property, each corresponding to the two different kinds of properties. First, you can add a property of your own, as we will do for the **Angle**, **XPos**, and **YPos** properties. When you define a property on your own, you are responsible for specifying its type, as well as the read and write access to it. The second kind of property, predefined, is much easier to work with. Let's add the easier, predefined properties first.

Within your component header file, you will find an entry called **__published**. All entries within this section will be displayed in the Object Inspector of the CBuilder IDE when the component is selected on a form in Edit view. If you add a component outside of this region, the property is still available to the programmer at runtime (assuming it is in the public section of the header file, of course), but will not be displayed at design time. Properties outside of the **__published** section are known as runtime-only properties.

To add a predefined property to the component, which is implemented by the base class, you just add the property to the component with the keyword **__property**. Other than the fact that it exists, you really don't need to know a great deal about this keyword at this point. For a predefined property, you generally just add the keyword **__published**, followed by the name of the property you want to expose for this component class. In this example, add the three component properties we have talked about by modifying the header file section as follows:

```
__published:
__property Text;
   __property Font;
   __property Color;
```

In this case, we are not modifying any pieces of the property, but you are permitted to change anything about a predefined property except its type. The other modifications can include the **read** function, **write** function, and default. We will look at these shortly.

Adding New Properties

Once we have added the predefined properties for the component, the next step is to add the component-specific properties. Let's first handle the header file changes needed for these properties, then worry about the implementation.

Add the following lines to the **__published** section of the header file for the **TAngleText** component class:

```
__published:
    __property double Angle={read=FAngle, write=FAngle, default=0};
    __property int    XPos={read=FXPos, write=SetXPos};
    __property int    YPos={read=FYPos, write=SetYPos};
```

In each case, the property definitions define a new property that will be available at design time for this component class. The **Angle** property is defined as a double. The basic format of the **__property** statement is as follows:

```
__property <type> <PropertyName>={ [read=<ReadFunctionOrProp>]
    [,write=<WriteFunctionOrProp>][,default=<value>};
```

where:

- <type> is the valid C++ type for this property. Usually, property types are one of the basic C++ types such as short, long, int, etc.

- <PropertyName> is the name of this property that you want to appear in the Object Inspector.

- <ReadFunctionOrProp> is either a function to use to read the value or a property value itself. We will talk about this one shortly.

- <WriteFunctionOrProp> is the same as the **Read** function but applies to changes to the property value.

- <value> is a default value for this component that should appear in the Object Inspector. Note that the default values are NOT set in the actual property in the component, only in the Inspector at design-time.

So what, exactly, is this **Read** and **Write** function stuff? At this point we reach the most critical difference between a property and a member variable. Although properties appear to be simple member variables in your code using the component, they are actually anything but. Member variables simply permit the user to assign values to the component property and modify them. You can stop them from directly assigning values by using accessor functions, but this also makes the code ugly. If my component property is an array of integers, for example, why do I need to write code like this:

```
myComponent->SetArrayElement(3,12);
```

when I would prefer to write:

```
myComponent->Array[3] = 12;
```

The first entry (3) is the index of the element to set, or is it the value? You can't really tell without consulting the documentation. It only gets worse if you want to implement a two-dimensional array:

```
myComponent->Set2DArrayElement(1,2,12);
```

Again, which is the row? Which is the column? Which is the value to set? Imagine, instead, if you simply write:

```
myComponent->[1][2] = 12;
```

Doesn't this seem a whole lot less error-prone? Of course it does. With **Read** and **Write** functions, this kind of thing is easy. Also, if you don't want the user to be able to modify the component property, you can just omit the **Write** function on the property and the user won't be able to change the value. Isn't this is a lot nicer than worrying about accessor functions using **Get** and **Set**? As a note: you can, in fact, leave off the **Read** function and allow the user to set the value using a **Write** function. I'm not sure what validity there is to implementing a write-only property, but the power is there if you need it.

> **Note:** The default value can be specified using the **default=** clause in the property statement. This does not set the value of your property variable to that value. It only places the value into the Object Inspector when the component is first created. If you want to initialize the value using the default statement, you must also set the value of the property value in the constructor for the class.

I hope you can see why you would use **Read** and **Write** functions in your component, but the next question is how to use them. If you don't want to worry about what the user sets the value of a property to (as we wouldn't in the case of the **Angle**), then you simply assign the variable itself to the **Read** and **Write** function. In the case of the **Angle** property, this is exactly what is happening. In the case where you actually want to filter out some input, you assign a member function to the function. Let's first add the property member variables to the class so that you can see what is going on. Add the following lines to the private section of the header file:

```
private:
    double FAngle;
    int    FXPos;
    int    FYPos;
```

These member variables are the normal, garden-variety, C++ variables that you are probably accustomed to in working with C++ classes. They are not directly accessible by the end-user (programmer). It is conventional to use the F prefix when working with member variables that implement properties in your components. This is a hangover from the Delphi origins of the components, but is a good convention to have, nonetheless.

These variables are the ones that you will use in your code. The properties, on the other hand, are used directly by the end-programmer. How do the two meet? In the case of direct properties, such as **Angle**, **Read**, and **Write** functions, specify that when the user changes the value of the property by writing a line of code such as:

```
pAngleText->Angle = 90.0;
```

This code will automatically update the value of the FAngle member variable to 90.0. This is accomplished internally within the component base class implementation and the CBuilder C++ compiler. On the other hand, when the programmer enters a line of code like this one:

```
pAngleText->XPos = 100;
```

something quite different occurs. In this case, the component property is set and the **Write** function for the component is called. If you will recall, the **XPos** property used a function called **SetXPos** to set the data. When the user tries to write to the value of the property called **XPos**, the value is converted into a function call. You will need to add two lines of code to the header file as prototypes for these function calls. Add the following two lines to the protected section of the header file:

```
virtual void __fastcall SetXPos(int XPos );
virtual void __fastcall SetYPos(int YPos );
```

When you write a **Set** function (or **Write** function), your function needs to take a single parameter. There are exceptions to this, such as when you are implementing an array property, but we will look at these cases later in the chapter.

Note the use of the __**fastcall** modifier for the function. All property **Read** and **Write** functions must use the __**fastcall** modifier. If you don't, strange things will happen at best, and the environment will throw a nasty exception at worst. Remember the __**fastcall**.

Implementing these functions is pretty easy. All you need to do is decide what data you will allow to pass through to the member variable and what data you are not. It is entirely up to you. Although you cannot return an error from a **Read** or **Write** method, you can throw an exception if the data is invalid. Unless the data would cause a serious program error, I don't recommend doing this in your components.

Here is the implementation of the previous two methods:

```
void __fastcall TAngleText::SetXPos(int XPos )
{
   if ( XPos < 0 || XPos > Width )
      return;
   FXPos = XPos;
}

void __fastcall TAngleText::SetYPos(int YPos )
{
   if ( YPos < 0 || YPos > Height )
      return;
   FYPos = YPos;
}
```

As you can see in the previous code, the function simply verifies that the point you want to set lies within the component boundaries. This really is just common sense. If the value is valid, the member variable is assigned the new value. If the value is not valid, the method simply returns. What happens to the member variable in this case? Nothing. You have effectively protected the actual property from receiving invalid data in your component, which is a whole lot nicer than **Sets** and **Gets**.

The next piece is to initialize the variables in the class. As with all C++ classes, it is important that you initialize all variables before you use them. In the case of components, this initialization should match the default statement in the property definition if there is one. Add the following code to the constructor for the class:

```
__fastcall TAngleText::TAngleText(TComponent* Owner)
    : TCustomControl(Owner)
{
    FXPos = -1;
    FYPos = -1;
    Angle = 0;
}
```

Note that we do not initialize, set, or get the **Text**, **Font**, or **Color** properties. These properties belong to a lower-level component and are initialized there. You could initialize them in your own constructor, and this value would override the base class settings.

At this point, we have a fully functional but totally useless component. This component will allow itself to be created, have properties assigned, and initialize itself. It will not, however, draw itself as rotated text on the screen. Let's take care of that little detail next.

Painting The Control

The most important part of any component is generally the visual aspects of the control. In the case of a component, which is only visually oriented, this is even more important. In the case of a component derived from **TCustomControl**, the handler method called to draw the control is called **Paint**. The **Paint** method takes no parameters, as you are expected to use the **Canvas** property of the component class to do the actual drawing. This also allows your component to paint itself to the printer, if necessary.

There is no simple way other than by brute force to add a new component method. This is an area that needs some work in CBuilder, and will almost certainly improve in future versions. For now, though, here is what you need to do.

First, determine which method in the component you need to override. This can be done by examining the methods listed in the online help for the component class you are working with. Select the one you want and copy the text for the prototype of the method to the clipboard, move to the header file for the class, and add the following line to the header file in the protected section. Most overridden methods will fall in the protected section of the component header file:

```
virtual void __fastcall Paint(void);
```

Note the use of the virtual keyword. Only virtual methods can be overridden by derived classes. Fortunately for you, most handlers in the CBuilder VCL classes are implemented as virtual methods.

Once you have the prototype defined in the header file, it is time to add the functionality for the method to the source file for the class. Add the following method to the end of the source file for the **TAngleText** component:

```
void __fastcall TAngleText::Paint(void)
{
  // Set text display angle
  LOGFONT LogRec;
  GetObject(Font->Handle,sizeof(LogRec),&LogRec);

  // Note: Angle in tenths of degree
  LogRec.lfEscapement = Angle * 10.0;

  // See if position is defaulted
  if ( FXPos == -1 )
     FXPos = Width / 2;
  if ( FYPos == -1 )
     FYPos = Height / 2;
  Canvas->Font->Handle = CreateFontIndirect(&LogRec);
  Canvas->Brush->Color = Color;
  Canvas->TextOut( FXPos,FYPos, Text );
}
```

This code is straightforward, really, in that it just sets the properties of the Canvas for the font and the color and then draws the text at the user-specified location. The modification of the font is done by changing the lfEscapement portion of the structure, which defines the angle (in tenths of a degree) at which this font should be created. The rest of the code is simple Windows magic.

That completes the implementation phase of the component development for the **TAngbleText** component. The next stage is to test the component to make sure that it is working properly before we try to install it.

Testing The Component

Once we have written the component, the next logical step is to test it. Testing an installed component is easy; just drag it and drop it onto a form and then set the component properties for which you want to view changes. This also works well for testing the methods of the component. The problem with testing this way is the turnaround time. If you need to make a change, you need to change the component, compile it, and then reinstall it, which takes a lot of time for each test. It would be easier, therefore, if we could just test the component before we install it. Thanks to some things we learned earlier in the book, we can do just that.

As you learned way back in the chapter on using the VCL, components can be created dynamically at runtime by the programmer. We can take advantage of this fact to test the visual aspects of the component, where most problems will occur. Another round of testing is necessary for the installed component because the Object Inspector interface needs to be verified.

To test this component, we are going to use the form shown in Figure 14.2. As you can see, this form consists of just a paintbox control and two buttons. The buttons will be used to increment (>) and decrement (<) the angle of the **AngleText** control we are going to create on the form.

Add a **Create** event handler to the form and add the following code to it. This will simply create a new instance of the component in the space occupied by the paintbox. This works because the paintbox has no window of its own, so we can treat it as a placeholder for the component we want to create there:

```
void __fastcall TForm1::FormCreate(TObject *Sender)
{
    pAngleText = new TAngleText(this);
    pAngleText->Parent = this;
    pAngleText->Top = PaintBox1->Top;
    pAngleText->Left = PaintBox1->Left;
    pAngleText->Width = PaintBox1->Width;
    pAngleText->Height = PaintBox1->Height;
    pAngleText->Angle = 0;
```

```
    pAngleText->Font = Font;
    pAngleText->Color = Color;
    pAngleText->Text = "Test String";
}
```

As you can see, we set the **position** and **angle** properties as well as the **Text**, **Color**, and **Font** properties. Before we go on, though, there is one little piece that I forgot to tell you earlier that applies now. The **Font** property of the Form must be selected and set to a TrueType font (a font with interlocked T's) because these are the only fonts that can be rotated.

Once all of the pieces are set up, the text will appear in the paintbox area when the form is run. In order to change the angle, add two handlers for the increment button and the decrement button. The increment button (caption >) should have the following code attached to it:

```
void __fastcall TForm1::IncrementClick(TObject *Sender)
{
                // Increment by 10 degrees
    pAngleText->Angle += 10.0;

}
```

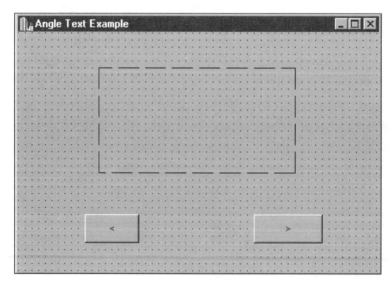

Figure 14.2
The **AngleText** component test form.

As you can see, because the **Angle** property is treated as a member variable, we can even use the += operator to modify it. The remainder of the method is pretty tame; it just adds 10 degrees to the current Angle value. Likewise, the Decrement button (caption <) should have a method called **DecrementClick** attached to it like this:

```
void __fastcall TForm1::DecrementAngle(TObject *Sender)
{
                // Decrement by 10 degrees
   pAngleText->Angle -= 10.0;
}
```

The final piece of the test is to add an instance of the **TAngleText** class to the form header file. Add the TAngleText header file to the form header file by moving to the header file (right-click and select Open Source/Header file from the speed menu) and then selecting File|Include Unit Hdr. Select the TAngleText unit from the list, and then add a line to the private section of the form header file:

```
private:    // User declarations
   TAngleText *pAngleText;
```

Compile and run the application. You should see the **AngleText** component displayed in the center of the form like the one shown in Figure 14.3.

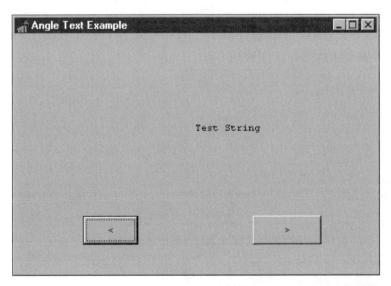

Figure 14.3
The **AngleText** component at runtime.

Now, the testing can begin. Click on the increment button. Notice that…nothing happens. Why? Well, this is our first bug. If you track through the problem, you will find that the component **Angle** property does change (you can look at it in the debugger), but that the control doesn't change the display of the text. Why? A good way to find the problem is to minimize the form window and then restore it to normal size. The angle text is suddenly angled. The problem, therefore, is that the component is not being repainted properly. Actually, the real problem is that the component is not being repainted at all.

There are two solutions to this problem. First, we could make the user force a repaint of the component when the angle is changed. This would involve code like this all over the user code:

```
pAngleText->Angle += 10.0;
pAngleText->Repaint();
```

Code like this is annoying to users. Why should they need to worry about when the component is displayed? That's the component writer's problem, not the component user. The visual aspects of the component are completely within the component.

To fix this problem, we need to know when the angle changes, and when it does, to repaint the control. The **Write** method of the component property is called when the user tries to change the property. We can modify the component to redisplay itself when the component angle property is changed. Modify the header file for the **TAngleText** component as follows:

```
class TAngleText : public TCustomControl
{
private:
   double FAngle;
   int    FXPos;
   int    FYPos;
protected:
   virtual void __fastcall Paint(void);
   virtual void __fastcall SetXPos(int XPos );
   virtual void __fastcall SetYPos(int YPos );
   virtual void __fastcall SetAngle(double Angle);
public:
   __fastcall TAngleText(TComponent* Owner);
__published:
   __property double Angle={read=FAngle, write=SetAngle};
```

```
    __property int    XPos={read=FXPos, write=SetXPos};
    __property int    YPos={read=FYPos, write=SetYPos};
    __property Text;
    __property Font;
    __property Color;
};
```

Now, add the following code to the source file for the component:

```
void __fastcall TAngleText::SetAngle(double Angle)
{
    if ( Angle != FAngle )
    {
        FAngle = Angle;
        Repaint();
    }
}
```

This code does a little more than I said. It first checks to see if the angle that the user specifies is the same as the angle that the component is already using. This just stops unnecessary redrawing of the component when the component is not really changed, and it's just a nice thing to do for the end programmer who might not know whether or not the angle is changing, but doesn't like the flicker of the component continually redrawing.

When you add that code to the component and rerun the application, the component will work properly as shown in Figure 14.4. This concludes the first portion of the component test, testing the visual aspects of the control.

Installing And Testing The Component

You install a component the same way that you install any other sort of component. Select the Component|Install menu item and click on the Add button. In the small dialog that appears, select the Browse button and navigate to the component source file that is in the directory of your current project. Select it and click on the OK button to close the window. Keep clicking on OK until you have closed the Component Installation window. At this point, CBuilder will compile and build the VCL library for use with the system. When it has finished (assuming there are no compile errors), the Component Palette will be rebuilt and the new component will be displayed on the palette page that you specified in the **Register** function. If you

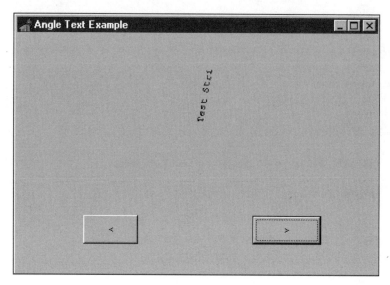

Figure 14.4
The **AngleText** component working properly at runtime.

look back at the component source code, you will see that CBuilder automatically generated a **Register** function for the component:

```
namespace Angletext
{
    void __fastcall Register()
    {
        TComponentClass classes[1] = {__classid(TAngleText)};
        RegisterComponents("Samples", classes, 0);
    }
}
```

In this case the new component will be installed on the page called Samples (which will be created if necessary). If you successfully compiled and installed the component, you can now test it in the environment. Create a new form and drop an instance of the component onto it. Change the text and see whether the component text redisplays. Change the angle and verify that the component displays at the new angle. When you are completely satisfied with the component, the testing is over.

The Icon

The last issue that I need to take up with you concerning simple components (and all components, in fact) is that of the icon displayed for the component. This icon is normally the same as the base class from which the component is derived. In the case of the **TCustomControl** class, the icon is quite simple and not very useful. Here is how you can change the icon for a component.

First, you need to create a new icon for the component. You can do this in a variety of ways, but the easiest is to use the Resource Workshop that ships with Borland C++ or the Resource Editor that ships with Visual C++. Create a resource file that contains the icon and give it the name <component.rc> (where component is the same as the name of the file containing the component). Build the new resource file into a compiled form and rename it to a DCR file. CBuilder will now automatically place that icon into the palette page with the component. The most important issue is that the resource identifier of the bitmap in the resource file must match the name of the component. If, for example, you have a component named **TNewControl**, the resource ID must be **TNEWCONTROL** (bitmap identifiers are case-insensitive, but it is conventional to put them in uppercase).

Shipping Components

Once you have a complete component implemented and installed, the next step is to determine what you need to do in order to ship it or use it in another application. The first stage is to copy needed files into the directory that CBuilder expects to have present when it uses the component.

When you install the component, you need to copy the OBJ file and the header (.h) file into the lib directory for the CBuilder tree. When you do this, the compiler and linker can find the files it needs to make the system work.

When you want to ship your component, on the other hand, you will want to ship the OBJ object file for the component as well as the header file (.h), and optionally the project resource file (DPR) that can go with the component.

That concludes the first example of component design and development. In this section we learned how to create a new component, we saw how to add new properties to a component, and how to publish those properties so that they could be seen in the Object Inspector of the CBuilder system. In our next example, we will explore some more aspects of component design and development as we look at a more complex example, the **FilterEdit** Component.

The FilterEdit Component

Way back when, in Chapter 4, we discussed how you could filter out unwanted characters from user input by capturing the edit keys as they were pressed by the user and not allowing any that were undesired to make it to the edit control itself. At that time, we explored the problem of trapping the individual keystrokes for each different field on a form and how this could cause the code to get very large. It's time to fix that particular problem by creating a single component to filter out characters.

Although this example is quite useful as a standalone component that you can certainly reuse in your own application, it is also an important example of one of the benefits of using the VCL over using ActiveX components. In the VCL, it is quite easy to create new components from your own base components and make the child component classes specialized for special needs. In this example, as an illustration of this power, first we will create a base class that filters out any kind of input and then derive a base class from that class that filters out specific kinds of input.

The Problem Statement

As with all good component designs, this one begins with a statement of the problem we are trying to solve. In this case, the problem is that we need to be able to filter out some forms of user input, specifically anything that isn't a number. We would like to have a single component that can be used on all forms that accept only numeric entries. This is the specific problem.

The specific problem is easily generalized to a component that accepts only specific input to a component that can either accept or reject specific input. Suppose, for example, that you want to put out a functional demo, but not so fully functional that the user wouldn't pay you for it. One solution would be to allow the user to enter anything she wants in the program, as long as it doesn't contain the letter N. Another possibility is a telephone entry program that accepts letter combinations for the numbers. A-B-C would be accepted for the number 1, for example. In this example, the letters not on the telephone, Q and Z, would not be accepted for valid input because they aren't on the telephone dial. I hope that you can see that the idea of filtering input can be as much about filtering what should be there as for what shouldn't. In this way, we can create a generalized component that only allows certain input or one that only disallows certain input.

The Specific Solution

In this particular example we are going to implement not only the specific solution, but also the general solution, which will serve as the base class for the specific numeric-entry only solution.

To begin with, we need to define class properties for the specific solution of a numeric-only entry control. As it turns out, there aren't any. All we want is for the control to behave exactly the same way that a normal edit control behaves without allowing the user to enter anything that isn't a number.

The general solution, however, is a different story. Let's tackle that one first.

The General Solution

In the case of a general solution for requiring or prohibiting data from being entered into the edit control, we need two bits of information from the user, and these two bits of information will become the properties of the control. The first property will be the data that is to be allowed (or not allowed) to be entered into the control. For our purposes, a string that holds all of the characters will be sufficient. This will also give you some experience in working with non-basic property types. The second property will be a flag indicating whether the characters in the string are to be the only characters allowed in the entry (flag=true) or whether the control should screen out the characters entered in the string (flag=false). We will call the property of characters **Allowed** (for the allowed characters) and the flag property **Include** (as to whether the characters should be included or not).

Implementing The Base Component

In order to implement the base component, create a new component in CBuilder. Give this new component the name **TFilterEdit**, and set the **TCustomEdit** class as the ancestor type for the component. This will give us all the functionality of the edit component and allow us to filter out the data we don't want without having to duplicate all of the functionality of the underlying Windows edit control.

Once you have the basic component generated by the Component Wizard tool in CBuilder, it is time to add the properties we need to the component. Add the following lines to the header file for the component:

```
#include <vcl\System.hpp>
//————————————————————————————
class TFilterEdit : public TCustomEdit
{
private:
    System::AnsiString FFilterString;
    bool                FbInc;
protected:
                virtual void __fastcall KeyPress(char &Key);
public:
                __fastcall TFilterEdit(TComponent* Owner);
__published:
    __property System::AnsiString Allowed = {read=FFilterString,
write=FFilterString};
    __property bool Include = {read =FbInc, write=FbInc, default=true };
};
```

In this case, we are adding a few internal member variables to hold the actual property values and overriding the **KeyPress** member function of the **TCustomEdit** class to do our filtering of data from the user.

The properties added are the **Allowed** string, which is an AnsiString type, and the **Include** flag, which is a boolean value. Note that the AnsiString type is contained within the System namespace, so we need to qualify the type fully by using the System:: scope identifier to tell the compiler where to find the AnsiString type. In addition, we need to include the System.hpp header file from the system include area (CBuilder\include\vcl) to get the definition of this class. CBuilder's Object Inspector and other tools understand the AnsiString type and will allow the user to edit these strings using the standard string editor in the system.

Once we have the properties defined and set up in the header file, it's actually time to implement the component code. The first change occurs in the constructor for the class, which needs to implement the default value for the **Include** flag as we set it in the previous property declaration:

```
__fastcall TFilterEdit::TFilterEdit(TComponent* Owner)
                : TCustomEdit(Owner)
```

```
{
   FbInc = true;
}
```

The only other code needed for this component is the **KeyPress** method, which will check the user input character against the Allowed list and either permit or prohibit the entry, based on the setting of the **Allowed** and **Include** properties. Here is the code for the **KeyPress** method:

```
void __fastcall TFilterEdit::KeyPress(char &Key)
{
   // Look for the keystroke
   for ( int i=0; i<FFilterString.Length(); ++i )
      if ( Key == FFilterString[i]  )
         if ( FbInc )
            return;
         else
         {
            Key = 0;
            return;
         }

   // Didn't find it. If this is inclusive,
   // this is bad
   if ( FbInc )
      Key = 0;
}
```

Again, no magic here. The method loops through the available characters in the string looking for the one the user typed. If it finds one and the **Include** flag is true, this character is fine and the function returns to allow the edit component to do its job. If the character is not found, the loop drops out of the loop. At this point, the **Include** flag is checked again. If the flag is set, this indicates that the character is not valid, because it would have had to have been in the list. If this happens, the keystroke is eliminated by setting it to 0, which indicates to the control not to process the key.

Narrowing The Field: The TNumericEdit Class

Once you have the **TFilterEdit** component written, the next step is to create a class based on that class called **TNumericEdit**. This class is even simpler than the **TFilterEdit** because it only accepts numeric entries. To do this, you will first need to

compile and then install the **TFilterEdit** component by doing the usual
Component|Install. Test the component by entering a string for the Allowed value
and the Include value and make sure it is working properly. If so, install it and move
on to the next step.

When you install a new component in the CBuilder system, you will then have the
full use of that component for all purposes. These purposes include deriving another
class from that component and using it as well. If you have worked in other systems
that only permit the ability to derive classes from the base classes in the system, this
is certainly a welcome change. Remember that once you install a component, it
becomes a part of the base CBuilder system. There is no difference between a component you write and one that was written by the Borland VCL team. This power to extend
the CBuilder system fully makes it ideal for working in a corporate environment.

Once you have the **TFilterEdit** component installed, use the Component Wizard
to derive a new component called **TNumericEdit**. This component should have an
ancestor class of **TFilterEdit** (which will now appear in the combo box).

The only thing you will need to do in the code for the **TNumericEdit** class is to
modify the constructor for the class to initialize the **Include** and **Allowed** properties
to allow the user to include only numeric characters. Here are the changes to the
constructor for the **TNumericEdit** class:

```
__fastcall TNumericEdit::TNumericEdit(TComponent* Owner)
    : TFilterEdit(Owner)
{
    Allowed = "1234567890";
    Include = true;
}
```

Unfortunately, that's not all there is to it. There's a problem. To see it, add some test
code to your project to build a new component of this type on the fly. Here is the
code you could try:

```
void __fastcall TForm1::FormCreate(TObject *Sender)
{
    pEdit = new TNumericEdit(this);
    pEdit->Left = 10;
    pEdit->Top = 10;
    pEdit->Width = 100;
    pEdit->Height = 30;
```

```
pEdit->Parent= this;
pEdit->Allowed = "ABCDEFG";
pEdit->Include = false;
}
```

If you add the TNumericEdit header file to this form and define a member variable called pEdit of type TNumericEdit in the class, you will find that the previous code compiles just fine. What's the problem? The issue here is that your properties from the **TFilterEdit** component were inherited into the TNumericEdit and allow the user to override the settings you have established in your new component class. This is normal behavior in a C++ class, as the **__published** section is analogous to the public section of a class definition. This is obviously not the way we want things to work. Is there any way to fix this problem without rewriting all the code in the base component? Kind of. The problem with publishing properties in a base class is that those properties will always be available in a derived class of that type. In other words, we can't really stop the programmer from using the **Allowed** and **Include** properties in the derived class the way that things are done now.

How do you fix this problem? Basically, the only way that you can guarantee that a property will work properly is to create an abstract base class for both components and then make the property protected in this base class. For example, we could create a class **TBaseFilterComponent** that defined:

```
class TBaseFilterEdit : public TCustomEdit
{
private:
   System::AnsiString FFilterString;
   bool              FbInc;
protected:
               virtual void __fastcall KeyPress(char &Key);
   __property System::AnsiString Allowed = {read=FFilterString,
      write=FFilterString};
   __property bool Include = {read =FbInc, write=FbInc, default=true };
public:
               __fastcall TBaseFilterEdit(TComponent* Owner)
      : TCustomEdit( Owner )
   {
   }

__published:
};
```

Then the new **TFilterEdit** class would look like this:

```
class TFilterEdit : public TBaseFilterEdit
{
private:
protected:
public:
                __fastcall TFilterEdit(TComponent* Owner);
__published:
   __property Allowed;
   __property Include;
};
```

This class simply republishes the **Allowed** and **Include** properties so that the end-user will be able to see them in the Object Inspector and modify them. Likewise, the **TNumericEdit** class also derives from the **TBaseFilterEdit** class.

```
class TNumericEdit : public TBaseFilterEdit
{
private:
protected:
public:
   __fastcall TNumericEdit(TComponent* Owner);
__published:
};
```

Note that in this case we do not publish the **Allowed** and **Include** properties to the user, so a component of type TNmericEdit does not permit the use of these properties by the end user. Within the class, the **Include** and **Allowed** properties are available directly because they are protected members of the class. The member variables representing these properties in the base class (**FbInc** and **FFilterString**) are not available in either of the two derived component classes. The complete source for all three classes will be found—you guessed it—on the accompanying CD-ROM for this book.

We went through this exercise rather than simply presenting the base class first to illustrate two points. First, this is the reason that the VCL components are all based around abstract classes like **TCustomEdit** and **TCustomListBox**. By making all of the properties that implement these classes protected, the component writer doesn't need to worry about restrictions. The second reason is to illustrate that properties may be made more, but not less, available by republishing.

The final point to gather from this example is to understand that the component development process is iterative. You will often find that you need to go back to the design phase when you have already reached the implementation stage of the component development. Regardless of the number of iterations you need to go through to get there, it is important to get it right. Once your components are released into the public usage (or escape easily, as the case may be), you will be unable to change them easily without affecting existing code. You can usually add to an existing component, but not subtract from one.

With this in mind, let's move on to the last example of component design and development, in which we create a component from scratch that actually does something. Along the way, you will learn something else about properties—how to make properties that are arrays.

The LineGraph Component

Windows is, of course, a graphical user interface. As a result, programs written for the Windows operating system are graphical in nature. One of the most common uses for graphics is to graph data for the user to view. CBuilder provides an ActiveX component that does graphics, but it suffers from two major drawbacks. First, it is an ActiveX component, which means that you need to ship it separately from your application, install it on the user's machine, and register it with the operating system. Secondly, the **VCFormulaOne** component is massive overkill for many applications. When all you want to do is graph some lines on the screen, you don't need giant 3D effects, symbols at every point, labeled axes, and so forth. What you really need is a simple graphing component.

We're going to develop such a simple graphing component.

The Problem Statement

The purpose of this component is to allow the user to draw comparative graphs for data sets supplied for the user. This component should allow scaling of data to fit user-defined data limits, colors for different lines, and the number of tick marks to display. The purpose of the component is to allow the user to compare data, so the component needs to support multiple line display and should retain persistent information when moved or resized.

In short, we are developing a graphing tool that allows the user to display multiple line graphs on the surface of the component. This component could be combined with the **TAngleText** component to display a graph with axis labels, or placed onto a tab of a dialog to display stock market data.

The Specific Solution

In order to solve the problem, we need to be able to draw the graph data on the surface of the component. The user will supply this information, and we will render it by plotting the data based on user-defined axis information. A rough cut at the solution would be to accept two line point arrays and plot them on the canvas of the component. This would be sufficient to satisfy our requirements, but would not be a general-purpose component. Instead, we need a more basic graphing tool.

Determining The Properties For The Component

Once you have defined the problem the component is to solve, the next step, as always, is to determine the component properties to be useful to the user. For the **LineGraph** component, this is no exception.

The most obvious property for the component is the points. Actually, we need multiple sets of points, so we will also need another property, the number of lines to plot. Finally, we need to plot the lines in different colors, so we need a property to hold the colors of the lines. There are quite a few other properties, but let's look at them all at once before we go on.

The component we are going to create will be called the **LineGraph** component. Use the Component Wizard in CBuilder to generate a new component with that name and give it an ancestor class of **TCustomControl**. The custom control class is used because we don't need anything other than basic windows functionality, but we do need a canvas on which to draw our graph. The **TCustomControl** class is the basic windowing component in the VCL system.

Adding The Properties To The Component

The **LineGraph** component has quite a few properties attached to it. Let's take a look at the changes to the header file for the component and then talk about what each property will do and how it is implemented.

```
public:
    __property Graphics::TColor LineColors[int nIndex]=
        {read=GetLineColor, write=SetLineColor };
    __property double XPoint[int nLine][int Index] = {read=GetXPoint,
        write=SetXPoint};
    __property double YPoint[int nLine][int Index] = {read=GetYPoint,
        write=SetYPoint};

__published:
    __property int NumberXTicks = { read=FNumXTicks, write=FNumXTicks,
        default=5 };
    __property int NumberYTicks = { read=FNumYTicks, write=FNumYTicks,
        default=5 };
    __property double XStart = { read=FXStart, write=FXStart};
    __property double YStart = { read=FYStart, write=FYStart};
    __property double XIncrement = { read=FXInc, write=FXInc};
    __property double YIncrement = { read=FYInc, write=FYInc};
    __property int NumberOfPoints = { read=FNumPoints,
        write=SetNumberOfPoints, default=0 };
    __property bool XGrid = { read=FXGrid, write=FXGrid, default=true };
    __property bool YGrid = { read=FYGrid, write=FYGrid, default=true };
    __property int NumXDecimals = { read=FXNumDecimals,
        write=FXNumDecimals, default=2 };
    __property int NumYDecimals = { read=FYNumDecimals,
        write=FYNumDecimals, default=2 };
    __property int NumberOfLines = { read=FNumberOfLines,
        write=SetNumberOfLines, default=0 };
```

You probably noticed right away that the list is quite long. The **LineGraph** component has a lot of functionality and, as a result, has quite a few component properties as well. The next thing that you might notice is that not all of the component properties are published. Several of the properties are simply listed as public values. Why would we do something like that?

Look at the properties that are not published and notice what they have in common. They are all listed with a strange syntax. Each of these properties is listed as an array property. In CBuilder, properties can look like arrays regardless of whether the underlying property is actually implemented as an array or not. Actually, as you will see a little later, the component properties in this case are not implemented as true arrays at all. This is real encapsulation at its best. Here we have something that looks like an array, works like an array, and is treated as an array by the user, but isn't implemented as an array.

Let's tackle those array properties first. There are three such properties, corresponding to the X points on the graph, the Y points on the graph, and the colors for the lines on the graph. The X and Y points are two-dimensional arrays in the component because you treat the lines as arrays of points. The two properties, therefore, are simply arrays of lines containing arrays of points. The colors are a one-dimensional array because only a single color is assigned to each line in the graph.

How would you use these properties in your own code? By treating the points as arrays. Basically, you would have code in your application that looks something like this:

```
pLineGraph->XPoints[0][0] = 10.0;
pLineGraph->YPoints[0][0] = 10.0;
```

The previous lines of code define a single point on the graph at location 10,10, the first point of the first line. To set the color, you would simply set the line corresponding to the index you want. To set the color of the first line to red, for example, you would write a line of code which read:

```
pLineGraph->LineColors[0] = clRed;
```

> **Note:** In CBuilder, indices for array properties do not need to be integers like they have to be in C or C++. You can also use strings, objects, or anything else you would like. This is the basis for the **FieldValues** property in the **TDataSet** component class.

The remainder of the properties are also related to the graph, as you might guess. The **NumberXTicks** and **NumberYTicks** properties refer to the number of "ticks" (lines) to use in dividing the axes of the graph. The XStart and YStart values represent the starting point on the X and Y axes. Likewise, the increment values represent the values to use for each tick mark starting at the start position on each axis.

When you are defining the X and Y points for the graph, you need two bits of information. The **NumberOfPoints** property stores the total number of points to plot for the lines, and the **NumberOfLines** property represents the number of lines we are going to plot. In other words, the line graph will be a two-dimensional grid of NumberOfLines lines, each containing NumberOfPoints points. If you don't want to restrict the user to a fixed number of points for all lines, it would be easy enough to allow the user to set these values individually, as you will see as we begin to implement the actual code for the component.

Most of the other properties are really self explanatory. The one that bears looking at is the **X/YGrid** property. If this property is set to true, the graph will be drawn with a grid (horizontal and/or vertical lines) across it. If these properties are false (either or both), the lines will not be drawn. It can be a lot easier to look at a graph with the grid lines on, so the default for these values is **true**.

Implementing The Control

Once we have the properties defined for the control, the next stage of development is to begin the implementation phase. Let's start out by defining the member variables we'll need to implement all these properties.

In the case of the points and color properties, we need some sort of array to hold the data. This is evident by the property definition. What is not obvious is how big an array we'll need to use to hold the data. How do you know how big the user will want the array sizes to be? Obviously you don't know at design time what the largest array size could be. One user might only want 10 points, another might want 1,000 or so. To be a useful component, you need to avoid building limits into the design and implementation unless those limits are absolutely necessary. Fortunately, earlier in the book we learned about the Standard Template Library, the library that supplies data structures that allow, among other things, arrays with no fixed size and can grow at runtime. We will use the STL vector class to hold the point data for the component.

Let's take a look at the header file changes needed for the property member variables that we will be adding to the code:

```
typedef std::vector<double> DblArray;

class LineGraph : public TCustomControl
{
private:
    int FNumberOfLines;
            int FNumXTicks;
            int FNumYTicks;
    double FXStart;
    double FYStart;
    double FXInc;
    double FYInc;
    int    FNumPoints;
    std::vector<DblArray> FXPoints;
```

```
std::vector<DblArray> FYPoints;
std::vector<Graphics::TColor> FLineColors;
bool    FXGrid;
bool    FYGrid;
int     FXNumDecimals;
int     FYNumDecimals;
```

The typedef at the top of the header file is used to make it easier to work with the vector class for multiple index arrays. Otherwise, we have to worry about writing things like this:

```
vector < vector<double> > FXPoints;
```

This leads to problems when you have multiple > signs in a row. Rather than deal with the problem, we will typedef the vector type into a new type, called DblArray, which is simply a flexible array of double values.

Once we have all of the member variables defined, it is time to initialize them all in a useable fashion. This is done, of course, in the constructor for the class. Let's take a look at that code now:

```
__fastcall LineGraph::LineGraph(TComponent* Owner)
              : TCustomControl(Owner)
{
              // Component properties must be initialized
              FNumXTicks = 5;
              FNumYTicks = 5;

    FXStart    = 0.0;
    FYStart    = 0.0;
    FXInc      = 10.0;
    FYInc      = 10.0;

    FNumPoints = 0;
    NumberOfPoints = 0;
    FNumberOfLines = 0;

    // Default to showing grid lines
    FXGrid = true;
    FYGrid = true;

    FXNumDecimals = 2;
    FYNumDecimals = 2;
}
```

As you can see, we set up reasonable defaults for all values in the member variables. What about the arrays of points and colors? These cannot be initialized in the constructor because we don't know how big to make them. When will we know this information? When the user sets the number of lines and the number of points. If you look back at the property definitions for the **NumberOfLines** and **NumberOfPoints** properties, you will find that they both use the variable itself for reading, but have a function used for the writing of the data. These functions are necessary because there are side effects when the values are changed. This is the power of working with properties. Although the user is unaware (or at least uncaring) of the fact that changing the number of lines allocates some memory in the background, it is going on nonetheless. Here are the two functions for the property change:

```
void __fastcall LineGraph::SetNumberOfLines( int nLines )
{
    // Set number of x and y points
    FXPoints.reserve( nLines );
    FYPoints.reserve( nLines );
    // Set number of colors
    FLineColors.reserve( nLines );
    // Initialize all line colors to black
    for ( int i=0; i<nLines; ++i )
        FLineColors[ i ] = clBlack;

    // Save number of lines
    FNumberOfLines = nLines;
}

void __fastcall LineGraph::SetNumberOfPoints( int nPoints )
{
    // Set number of x and y points for each line
    for ( int i=0; i<FNumberOfLines; ++i )
    {
        FXPoints[i].reserve( nPoints );
        FYPoints[i].reserve( nPoints );

        // Initialize all points to 0.0 for
        // safety
        for ( int nPt=0; nPt<nPoints; ++nPt )
        {
            FXPoints[i][nPt] = 0.0;
            FYPoints[i][nPt] = 0.0;
        }
    }
}
```

```
    // Save the number of points
    FNumPoints = nPoints;
}
```

Okay, so we now have the properties assigned and initialized. We have the arrays allocated and waiting for data. What's next? First, we need to be able to put data into the various properties. These methods are simple, because the vectors have already been allocated and initialized in the previous methods. Here are the methods that set the data into the arrays:

```
double __fastcall LineGraph::GetXPoint( int nLine, int nIndex )
{
    return FXPoints[ nLine][ nIndex ];
}


void __fastcall LineGraph::SetXPoint( int nLine, int nIndex,
    double dPoint )
{
    if ( nLine >= FXPoints.size() )
        FXPoints.insert( FXPoints.end(), DblArray() );

    FXPoints[ nLine ].insert(FXPoints[nLine].end(),dPoint);

}


double __fastcall LineGraph::GetYPoint( int nLine, int nIndex )
{
    return FYPoints[ nLine ][ nIndex ];
}


void __fastcall LineGraph::SetYPoint( int nLine, int nIndex,
    double dPoint )
{
    if ( nLine >= FYPoints.size() )
        FYPoints.insert( FYPoints.end(), DblArray() );

    FYPoints[ nLine ].insert(FYPoints[nLine].end(),dPoint);
}


void __fastcall LineGraph::SetLineColor( int nIndex, Graphics::TColor
    clrNewColor )
{
    FLineColors[ nIndex ] = clrNewColor;
}
```

```
Graphics::TColor __fastcall LineGraph::GetLineColor( int nIndex )
{
return FLineColors[ nIndex ];
}
```

It is quite simple to understand how this code is written, but the interesting part is how it's used. When you have an array property (one defined as property[index]), your **get** functions need to accept one parameter for each index of the array. If your array is one-dimensional, as is the line color property, then your **get** function will take a single argument, the index of the entry to return. If your array is two-dimensional, the **get** function takes two parameters, and so forth.

Similarly, the **set** functions for array properties take multiple parameters. The **set** function will take one parameter for each array index plus one more parameter for the value to set at those indices. To use these array properties, you work with them as if they were arrays:

```
pLineGraph->XPoints[nLine][nPt] = x;
```

The previous line of code is translated into a call to:

```
pLineGraph->SetXPoint(nLine, nPt, x);
```

Now you can understand why it is so important to have the ability to use the functions to read and write property values. On top of the ability to use whatever data structure you feel is most useful in your underlying code, you have the ability to screen out or fix any data coming in. If the line or point index is out of range, for example, you could elect simply to ignore the problem, throw an exception, or move the line or point into range.

The drawing code is almost the last major piece of the component. Although straightforward, the drawing code is daunting because of its size, and you might consider breaking it up into separate pieces in your own component. We implement the drawing code in its own procedure, called DoPaint, rather than simply handling paint, for a very good reason. By handling the procedure using an arbitrary Canvas object, the code can be used to paint not only on the screen but also to a printer, fax, or other device.

```
void __fastcall LineGraph::DoPaint(TCanvas *pCanvas)
{
    int nYStart = Top + 20;
```

```
int nXStart = 50;
int RightMargin = 40;

// Draw the axes for the graph
pCanvas->MoveTo( nXStart, nYStart);
pCanvas->LineTo( nXStart, Height-30 );
pCanvas->LineTo( Width-RightMargin, Height-30);

// Draw the tick marks. First the horizontal

if (FNumXTicks > 0)
{
    // Determine spacing.
        int nSpaceTicks = (Width-nXStart-RightMargin) / FNumXTicks;
    double xVal = FXStart;

        for ( int i=0; i<=FNumXTicks; ++i )
        {
            pCanvas->MoveTo( nXStart+(i*nSpaceTicks),Height-30);
            pCanvas->LineTo( nXStart+(i*nSpaceTicks),Height-25);

        // Label the tick mark
        char szBuffer[ 20 ];
        sprintf(szBuffer, "%5.*lf",FXNumDecimals,xVal);

        // Get the width of the string.
        int nWidth = pCanvas->TextWidth( szBuffer );

        // And put in the right place.
        pCanvas->Brush->Color = Color;
        pCanvas->TextOut(nXStart+(i*nSpaceTicks)-nWidth/2, Height-20,
          szBuffer );

        // Increment value
        xVal += FXInc;

        // If grid desired, show it
        if ( FXGrid )
        {
            pCanvas->MoveTo( nXStart+(i*nSpaceTicks), nYStart );
            pCanvas->LineTo( nXStart+(i*nSpaceTicks), Height-30 );
        }

        }
}
```

```
// Now the vertical
if (FNumYTicks > 0)
{
    double yVal = FYStart;

    // Determine spacing.
            int nSpaceTicks = (Height-30-nYStart) / FNumYTicks;

            for ( int i=0; i<=FNumYTicks; ++i )
            {
        int nYPos = Height-30-(i*nSpaceTicks);
                    pCanvas->MoveTo( nXStart-5, nYPos );
                    pCanvas->LineTo( nXStart, nYPos );

        // Label the tick mark
        char szBuffer[ 20 ];
        sprintf(szBuffer, "%5.*lf",FYNumDecimals,yVal);

        // Get the width of the string.
        int nWidth = pCanvas->TextWidth( szBuffer );
        int nHeight = pCanvas->TextHeight( szBuffer );

        // And put in the right place.
        pCanvas->Brush->Color = Color;
        pCanvas->TextOut(nXStart-nWidth-7, nYPos-nHeight/2,
          szBuffer );

        // Increment value
        yVal += FXInc;

        // If grid desired, show it
        if ( FYGrid )
        {
            pCanvas->MoveTo( nXStart, nYPos );
            pCanvas->LineTo( Width-RightMargin, nYPos );
        }
            }
}

// Draw the lines connecting the points
if ( FNumPoints > 0 )
{
    for ( int nLine = 0; nLine < FXPoints.size(); ++nLine )
    {
                // Set the colors for this line
            pCanvas->Pen->Color = FLineColors[ nLine ];
```

```
                    // Convert to screen units
                int nXPos = XPointToScreen(FXPoints[nLine][0]);
        int nYPos = YPointToScreen(FYPoints[nLine][0]);
                    for ( int i=1; i<NumberOfPoints; ++i )
                {
                  pCanvas->MoveTo(nXPos, nYPos);
                    nXPos = XPointToScreen(FXPoints[nLine][i]);
                    nYPos = YPointToScreen(FYPoints[nLine][i]);
                  pCanvas->LineTo(nXPos, nYPos);
                }
        }

                    // Reset the colors
        pCanvas->Pen->Color = clBlack;

    }
}
```

Given this function, therefore, we can implement two other functions to display or print the graph without modifying the display:

```
void __fastcall LineGraph::Paint(void)
{
   DoPaint(Canvas);
}

void __fastcall LineGraph::Print(void)
{
   TPrinter *printer;
   printer = new TPrinter();
   printer->BeginDoc();
   DoPaint(printer->Canvas);
   printer->EndDoc();
   delete printer;
}
```

There is no particular reason to create a new **TPrinter** object, by the way. You could just as easily use the **Printer()** function in the place of the **printer** object in the previous **Print** method.

Finally, two utility functions in the code actually translate the data point to the screen point. Here they are, in all their glory:

```
int __fastcall LineGraph::XPointToScreen(double pt)
{
    int RightMargin = 40;
    int nXStart = 50;

    // Calculate width of screen
    int nSpaceTicks = (Width-nXStart-RightMargin) / FNumXTicks;
    int nNumPixels = nSpaceTicks * FNumXTicks;

    // Calculate the width of the data
    double dWidth = (FNumXTicks * FXInc) - FXStart;

    // Figure out the percentage of the screen
    // occupied by this point
    double dPercent = (pt-FXStart) / dWidth;

    // Now, convert that to a pixel
    int nX = dPercent * nNumPixels;

    // Good! Now position it from the start
    nX = nXStart + nX;

    return nX;
}

int __fastcall LineGraph::YPointToScreen(double pt)
{
    int nYStart = Top + 20;

    // Calculate width of screen
    int nSpaceTicks = (Height-30-nYStart) / FNumYTicks;
    int nNumPixels = nSpaceTicks * FNumYTicks;

    // Calculate the height of the data
    double dHeight = (FNumYTicks * FYInc) - FYStart;

    // Figure out the percentage of the screen
    // occupied by this point
    double dPercent = (pt-FYStart) / dHeight;

    // Now, convert that to a pixel
    int nY = dPercent * nNumPixels;

    // Good! Now position it from the start
    nY = (Height-30) - nY;
```

```
    return nY;
}
```

That completes the graph control, except for the testing. You will find a complete test program for the graph component on the accompanying CD-ROM for this book. It shows you first how to create the control dynamically, then how to load it with data. When you run this program, you will see the display shown in Figure 14.5.

Understanding the complete component described in the LineGraph section may take some study. This component is a non-trivial implementation, but you'll find it can really be useful in your own projects. Don't hesitate to take some time and go back through the code to understand how things work.

What Did We Learn In This Chapter?

This chapter has been a brief, but filling, introduction to the wonderful world of component development, stressing the need to make components flexible and reusable.

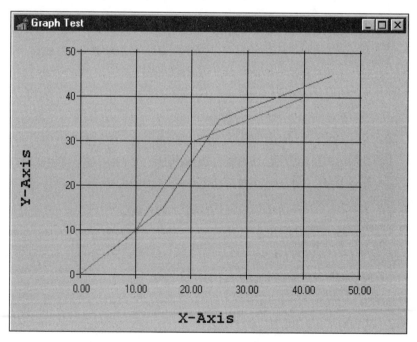

Figure 14.5
The **LineGraph** component in action.

Components are the building blocks of the CBuilder system, and allow you to extend the systems to solve your own specific problems. By writing components, you promote the reuse and sharing of code within your company or area, and you'll gain some recognition for developing quality code. Components are a reflection of your programming skills; treat them that way. If you intend to write them professionally for resale to other programmers, I suggest that you pick up a book specifically on component development.

Here are the highlights of this chapter:

- The component development process starts with the definition of the problem you are trying to solve and ends with testing and documenting the component. In between, you define the specific problem more thoroughly and then generalize that problem into a component solution.

- You can bundle components into a library to register with CBuilder.

- Components can be created from existing code to encapsulate a given technique, as shown in the **AngleText** component, which encapsulates our rotated text code.

- Component properties may be simple, such as integers or doubles, or complex, such as arrays (even multidimensional) or strings.

- Selecting the proper base class for a component will make the job of writing the component easier.

That's really about all there is to say in this chapter. Although we barely scratched the surface of component development, I hope you have learned enough to strike out on your own and learn more about the subject. Components are the most exciting part of CBuilder, and writing your own components can be a rich and fulfilling experience.

HIGH PERFORMANCE

Frequently Asked Questions

CHAPTER

15

HIGH PERFORMANCE

- **Look Here First For Answers**

- **Working With The STL**

- **Where To Find Answers**

- **Working With Expectations**

Frequently Asked Questions

The questions in this section have appeared on the Borland newsgroups, CompuServe forums, and in email messages I have received from other users of the CBuilder system. Each question is followed by a brief answer in order to include the maximum number of questions. If you don't understand enough about a problem or solution after reading the questions and answers, consult the relevant portions of the book.

This section is broken down into nine basic sections:

1. General Topics
2. General Programming Questions
3. Standard Template Library
4. Visual Component Library
5. Help Files and Problems
6. Database Questions
7. Exception Handling
8. Miscellaneous
9. Building Components

General Topics
What Is C++Builder?

C++Builder is the proper name for Borland's new RAD (Rapid Application Development) tool. In this book we shorten the name to CBuilder. It is basically Delphi using C++ as the development language. CBuilder permits rapid development of form-based applications using a simple drag-and-drop editing style. All CBuilder components are property-based, so defining a new entity on an input or display form is as simple as dropping the component onto the form and setting some properties to define its behavior.

CBuilder also features two-way tools. Changes made in the form editor are reflected immediately in the code. Changes made in the code are likewise reflected in the form display.

Why Should I Use CBuilder?

If you are a C++ developer creating applications for the desktop (which is most of us), you should seriously consider using CBuilder instead of the environment you are using. CBuilder features an industry-standard C++ compiler complete with templates, exception handling, namespaces, the Standard Template Library, and other important C++ features.

The environment provides a maximum productivity gain over older environments like Visual C++ or Borland C++. In addition, CBuilder can use MFC or OWL code written for legacy applications. Finally, because CBuilder can use Delphi components, it comes with an existing code base of thousands of modules that require no coding or manipulation.

Can CBuilder Work With MFC?

Yes, but: You must have the version of MFC shipped with Borland C++ 5.02 or later. You must use the Borland-supplied makefile to build the MFC, as well. You can use CBuilder forms in MFC applications directly, as well. See later topics in the FAQ.

The question, however, is really whether you want to use MFC with CBuilder. MFC is an older framework that is huge, poorly written, and generally a pain in the neck. Before you whine at me for being a CBuilder snob, remember that I'm a professional MFC programmer who has worked with it since it came out (with Microsoft C 7.0). Believe it or not. I do know what I am talking about.

Can C++Builder Work With OWL?

Yes, OWL can be compiled with CBuilder. You must rebuild the libraries using the CBuilder compiler because CBuilder has changed the object file format in order to support the exception handling built into the new system.

Is Borland Getting Rid Of OWL?

Borland's position on OWL is that it is not getting rid of it, but that its future will be driven by the market. All things considered, it will probably keep OWL for the foreseeable future due to the number of industrial applications that use it.

What Is VCL?

VCL stands for Visual Component Library. The VCL is a library of prebuilt components that encapsulate most of the common Windows objects. VCL objects can be either visual or non-visual. Most importantly, the VCL is a library, not a framework. Individual VCL components can be used independently of the system as a whole. This behavior makes it possible for the VCL forms to be used in DLLs and supported by other compiler environments, such as a CBuilder form in Visual C++ applications.

Where Can I Get More Information

There are numerous sources of information about CBuilder. The best one is the Borland Web Site (**http://www.borland.com**), which has the most up-to-date information on the product and any bug fixes. Borland does maintain a bug knowledgebase at this site and has numerous technical information papers available there.

In addition, any site that supports Delphi will, in general, work with CBuilder.

How Do I Do A "Make" While In Brief Emulation Mode?

The Ctrl+F9 keyboard combination will do a **make** in Brief mode.

How Do I Change The Default Project?

The Object Repository window controls the default application type when you select File|New Application. To select the current application type for defining (the default project), bring up the Object Repository window by selecting File|New. Move to the Projects tab of the repository dialog (intuitively labeled New Items) and select the type of application you want to generate as default. This will be the type generated when you select File|New Application.

My Error Window Disappeared. How Do I Get It Back?

Try resizing the Edit window to be larger. Sometimes this will fix the problem. Or right-click on the Edit and select Message View.

My Console App Doesn't Use VCL. How Do I Remove It From The Link?

Choose View|Project Makefile from the main menu. Locate the line beginning with 'ALLLIB'. Delete VCL.LIB from the makefile. Change CP32MT.LIB to CW32MT.LIB. Your ALLLIB line should now look like this:

```
ALLLIB = $(LIBFILES) import32.lib cw32mt.lib
```

How Do I Use Third-Party DLLs With CBuilder?

Use the IMPLIB.EXE that comes with builder to build an import library for your third-party DLL. Then simply link it in as normal.

How Do I Build A Static Library With CBuilder?

You can't. CBuilder can only create executables and DLLs. The command line versions of the compiler and the LIB tool must be used to create static libraries.

Where's The Dialog Wizard?

The Dialog Wizard only ships with the Professional and above levels of CBuilder and is found in the Examples directory. You have to compile it and install it to use it.

Why Doesn't Turning Off Debug Information Reduce The Size Of The EXE File?

Debug information is stored in the TDS file that has the same name as your project. It is stored externally to your executable so it adds no space to the executable. For this reason, turning off debug mode does not reduce the actual EXE file.

What Are All The Files Created By CBuilder? Which Can I Delete?

Aside from your source files (*.CPP, *.H, *.DFM), CBuilder creates several files in your source directory. Some of these, such as the *.MAK and *.RES files are needed to build your application. Others can be deleted after the executable is built. The following file types can be safely deleted: *.OBJ, *.TDS, *.IL?. The OBJ files are object files bound into the executable. The TDS file is the debugging symbols file. The IL? files are the incremental linker files. In addition, any file of the form *.~?? is a backup file and can be deleted if you like. Backup files are created when you make changes in the Editor.

Where Are The Samples On The Samples Tab?

You will find them in the \cbuilder\examples\controls directory. You need to compile them and install them in order to use them (unlike the beta of the software).

Where Are The Internet Controls?

Internet controls are only in the Professional and above editions of the product. They will then be found on the Internet component palette tab.

> **Note:** Borland recently has made the Internet controls available on its Web site. Check **www.borland.com** for details.

How Do I Make Several Components On A Form Have The Same Property Value?

The easiest way is to select all of the properties using the SHIFT key. Hold down the Shift key and select each component you want to change. Then, simply select the Object Inspector and modify the property you want to change. All selected objects will share this change.

General Programming Questions
What Is A "Compiler Error #1" And How Do I Get Rid Of It?

Compiler Error #1 is caused by a variety of things. Generally, you can fix the problem by simply shutting down CBuilder and then restarting it and reloading your project via File|Reopen. If this doesn't work, you may need to find out what problem is actually occurring. Go out to a DOS command box, run the make program on the makefile in your project directory, note the error that is reported, and fix it.

What Is An AnsiString And How Do I Convert It To A Char *?

AnsiStrings are Delphi-compatible strings used throughout the CBuilder system. If you have a choice, you should use AnsiStrings rather than the STL string or character arrays. Their many, nice, overloaded methods make them easier to use than **char ***'s or strings.

For example, rather than using error-prone methods such as **strcat** or **strcpy**, you can use overloaded methods of AnsiString such as += or =, as in the following example:

```
// If you used to do this:
char szBuffer[20];
strcpy ( szBuffer, "This is a good test");
strcat ( szBuffer, " and so is this!");
// You can now do this:
AnsiString strBuffer;
strBuffer = "This is a good test";
strBuffer += " and so is this!";
```

In the previous example, you will find that the text copied into szBuffer will actually overflow the buffer and cause a hard-to-find error. In the second case, using AnsiStrings, there is no such problem.

As to the second part of the question, you use the **c_str** method of the AnsiString class to convert it to a **char ***. For example:

```
void func(char *strBuffer);  // Prototype for some function
AnsiString s = "This is a good test";
func(s.c_str());
```

How Do I Add Items To A Set?

The overloaded << operator is used to add data into a set such as the **Font Style** property. To add the bold attribute to a font style object, you would use the following:

```
pMyFont->Style << fsBold;
```

What Does The Error "Member Function Must Be Called..." Mean?

This error will happen quite frequently to Pascal programmers moving to CBuilder or to C++ programmers who forget parentheses. Basically, this error means that you have a class **Foo** that has a method called **Bar**. You typed:

```
Foo f;
f.Bar;
```

when what you really meant to do was:

```
Foo f;
f.Bar();
```

In Pascal, you can call a function or method not requiring arguments without including the parentheses. In C++, the parens are always required for function calls. This is how the compiler knows that you are trying to call a function and not pass the address of a member function to something. For example:

```
void func(int x)
func( f.Bar() );
```

is quite different than:

```
func( f.Bar );
```

The first example will pass the result from the **Bar** method call to the function. The second example will pass the address of the member function **Bar** to the **func** function as an argument. This will result in a compiler error.

What Does The "Structure Required" Error Mean?

The structure required error means that you are trying to call something using the dot (.) syntax instead of the arrow (->) syntax. When you are using a pointer to a structure or object, use the arrow syntax. When you have a real object or reference to an object, use the dot syntax. For example:

```
Foo *pFoo;

pFoo->Bar(); // Okay.
pFoo.Bar();  // Error: -> required (This generates the error above).

Foo foo;
foo->Bar();  // Error: . required
foo.Bar();   // Okay.
```

How Do I Fix The "Linker Error: Failed To Create Map File" Error?

Again, this is an error that appears to have multiple causes. A lack of disk space will cause it, as will a corrupted set of incremental link files. To fix it, close CBuilder and delete all .IL? files (*.IL?) in the project directory of your project that is having the problem. Sometimes you can get by simply doing a Build All.

How Do I Add Resources To A Project?

Choose the Add To Project item and add the RC or RES file that contains the resources you want to work with in your project. CBuilder automatically knows to run the resource compiler and the RC file and to link in the RES file for the resources. You can also use the USERC or USERES macros in your project file:

```
USERES("myresources.res");
USERC("myresources.rc");
```

Can I Dynamically Link The VCL Library?

No. At this point, the VCL library can only be statically linked into programs. Borland has said that future releases of CBuilder will allow VCL to be linked in dynamically.

How Do I Step Into The VCL Source When Debugging?

You need to link with the debug version of the VCL. There are three steps involved in using the VCL source. First, you need to have debugging info turned on in order to use it. Select Options|Environment from the main menu and click on the Library tab. Click on the Build with debug info button. Next, you need to link with the debugging version of the VCL. On this same tab, click on the Link with debug VCL checkbox. Finally, you need to tell the debugger where to find the source code for the VCL when stepping into it. Click on the Preferences tab of the property sheet and enter the source code path in the Path for Source field at the bottom of the page. Separate each path with a semicolon (;).

Why Is Debugging So Slow? How Can I Speed It Up?

Here are several ways to speed up debugging. Probably the biggest is to add RAM to your system. No serious work should be attempted with less than 32MB of RAM. Remove all unneeded variables from the watch windows. The fewer things the system has to keep track of, the faster it will be. Close the object inspector window while debugging. This window is updated as you step, so this will speed things up a bit.

The Compiler Is Buggy! My Variables Have The Wrong Values

Probably not. Try the following code in CBuilder:

```
int func()
  {
    int x = 2;
              int y = 3;

    MessageBox(NULL, "Got to here!", "Info", MB_OK );
  }
```

Call **func** in your application and step into it in the debugger. Examine the values of x and y in the watch window or object inspector. You will notice that they are likely to have the value 0. Is this a bug? No. The compiler realized that you were never using the values x and y in your function and optimized them out of existence. The debugger knows that they exist (because they are in the source code) but also knows they have no value. As a result, they are 0. If you do not use the variables, they will have no value in the debugger. If you really want to keep them, try the following:

```
int func(void)
{
   int x = 2;
             int y = 3;

   AnsiString strTemp = "X = " + AnsiString(x) + " Y = " +
      AnsiString(y);
                MessageBox(NULL, strTemp.c_str(), "Info", MB_OK );
}
```

You should see the proper values in the message box.

How Do I Access The Printer Or Clipboard Properly In CBuilder?

In CBuilder there are predefined objects for the printer and clipboard. It is best to use them in place of creating your own objects. For the Printer, the object is called Printer and is called as a function. For example:

```
// To start a new page on the printer
         Printer()->BeginPage();
```

Likewise, the clipboard is used as a function, **Clipboard**().

How Do I Set Byte Alignment In CBuilder?

Unfortunately, CBuilder ignores the alignment options in the compiler and substitutes it own. Therefore, you cannot use the -a1/2/3 flags to the compiler. In place of this, use the pragma pack as follows:

```
   // Set single byte alignment
#pragma pack(push,1)
struct StructureNeedingAlignment {
// Data for structure
};
```

```
// Turn off byte alignment
#pragma pack(pop)
```

How Do I Accept Dragged-And-Dropped Files In My Form?

In the usual manner <grin>. Actually, you just handle the WM_DROPFILES method. Example:

```
void TMainForm::WMDropFiles(TWMDropFiles& Msg)
{
  char szTemp[ 256 ];
  int  nNumberOfFiles = DragQueryFile(Msg.Drop,
    0xFFFFFFFF, szTemp, 256 );
  for ( int nFile = 0; nFile < nNumberOfFiles; ++nFile )
  {
    // Get the dropped file name
      DragQueryFile( Msg.Drop, nFile, szTemp, 256 );

// Do something with the file
            ProcessFileName( szTemp );

      }

// Complete the process
          DragFinish(Msg.Drop);
      }
```

How Do I Resize A Component To The Size Of The Form?

The easiest way to do this is simply to set the **Alignment** property of the component to alClient. This will automatically set the size of the component to the full client size of the form every time the form is resized (including the first time).

If you have some specific reason to resize the component at runtime (like you want to leave 1 pixel around the thing for some reason), you do it via the **Top**, **Left**, **Height**, and **Width** properties of the component. For example:

```
// Move the component Edit1 to be the size of the form with a two
         // pixel boundary around id
```

```
Edit1->Top = 2;
           Edit1->Left = 2;
           Edit1->Width = Width-4;
           Edit1->Height = Height-4;
```

How Do I Use The TRACE Macros In CBuilder?

To use the TRACE macro, you need to do two things. First, define the __TRACE symbol. Next, include the checks.h header file. Example:

```
#define __TRACE
           #include <checks.h>

  TRACE("I am here!\n");
```

> **Note:** The output from the TRACE macro is written to a file named OutDbg1.TXT, which will be loaded into the file editor. It is not automatically saved, so if you want to keep it, you will need to save the file in the editor. In addition, CBuilder will not prompt you to save this file when you close a project, so remember if you have one open.

How Do I Draw Just A Piece Of A Bitmap?

Use the **TImageList** class. The **TImageList** component has a method called **Draw** that accepts boundaries much like the **BitBlt** function of the Windows API.

How Do I Dynamically Create A Component At Runtime?

Easy. You use the new operator:

```
*pEdit = new TEdit(this);
           pEdit->Parent = this;
           pEdit->Left = 10;
           pEdit->Top = 10;
           pEdit->Height = 20;
           pEdit->Width = 200;
           pEdit->Visible = TRUE;
```

Remember to set the parent property of the component, or it will not display. In the previous example, the "this" is assumed to be a form, but it can be any windowed component.

How Do I Emulate Sprintf With Strings?

Use the **String** class. For example, to format a decimal number, you would use something like the following:

```
// Rather than sprintf(szBuffer, "%d", nNumber );
        String s = String(nNumber);

// This also allows you to create formatted strings with text
        String s1 = "Hello world, I am " + String(nNumber) +
          " years old!";
```

Standard Template Library
Why Do I Get A Whole Bunch Of Errors When I Use The Vector Class?

You are probably doing something like this:

```
#include <vector.h>

int func(void)
        {
            vector<int> array;
        }
```

and are getting a bunch of errors on the line vector<int>. To fix this, just use the namespace for the STL, which is called std. Here is the code that fixes the problem:

```
#include <vector.h>
        use namespace std;   // ADD THIS LINE

int func(void)
        {
            vector<int> array;
        }
```

Can I Use The STL In Components?

Absolutely. Just remember to add the correct header file (vector, list, etc.) and to fully qualify the STL component name with the std:: qualifier. Other than that, STL components work exactly the same way in components as they do in applications.

Visual Component Library (VCL)
How Do I Add Items Programmatically To A List Box Or Combo Box?

In simple terms, you use the **Add** method of the **Items** property. In other words, when you are working with the items of a list or combo box, you are directly working with the **Items** property. CBuilder has encapsulated all of the functionality of the pieces of list/combo boxes into separate pieces for the data and attached information of the boxes.

For example, to add an item to the end of a list box list, you would use the following piece of code:

```
ListBox1->Items->Add( "MyItem1" );
```

To modify a given item of a list box, you treat the **items** property as an array and write:

```
ListBox1->Items[nIdx] = "MyItem1";
```

Finally, you can remove items from the class by using the **Remove** method:

```
ListBox1->Remove(0);  // Remove the first element of the list box
```

How Do I Handle A Windows Message (WM_USER) In My Component Or Form?

Any Windows message not already handled by a CBuilder component can be added to it via the message map construct. To do this, define your message as a constant:

```
#define WM_MY_MESSAGE (WM_USER+1)
```

Next, in your header file for the component or form, add the following lines within the class definition:

```
BEGIN_MESSAGE_MAP
MESSAGE_HANDLER(WM_MY_MESSAGE, TMessage, OnMyMessage)
END_MESSAGE_MAP
```

Finally, define the **OnMyMessage** method in your class as a method of the class accepts a **TMessage** argument:

```
void __fastcall OnMyMessage( TMessage& msg );
```

In your code for the function, you can then implement whatever you want to do when the user-defined message is received. If you are using a message that is defined by Windows but not implemented by CBuilder, leave out the previous step in defining the message. All other steps are the same.

When Do I Need To Use __Fastcall?

You do not have to use **__fastcall** for your own methods. Only methods that are added to components need to use it. Methods in your derived components that override VCL methods need the **__fastcall** modifier.

All of this is caused by the fact that the VCL is written in Pascal. Because C++ and Pascal use different calling conventions, the **__fastcall** modifier was created so that the arguments would be interpreted properly.

Why Do I Get Weird Errors In Installing My Component?

The original question usually runs like this: Everything appears to work properly in the installation, but the component behaves oddly and generates access violations. How do I fix this?

Chances are the component is not compiled using word alignment. If you have changed the alignment via a C++ or Pascal compiler directive, the component will do strange things.

How Do I Add A Horizontal Scrollbar To A ListBox?

This is a common Windows programming problem. The addition of a horizontal scrollbar to a listbox is simple, but the scrollbar doesn't appear to work. The reason for this is that you must set the horizontal extent of the list box to tell it how far it can scroll. To do this, find the widest string in the list and set the horizontal scroll extent to this value:

```
List1->SendMessage( LB_SETHORIZONTALEXTENT, m_nMaxLength, 0);
```

where m_nMaxLength is an integer value representing the length of the longest string in pixels. You can find the length of a string by using the **GetTextExtent** method.

```
SIZE sz;
GetTextExtentPoint32( List1->Handle, szString, strlen(szString), &sz );
m_nMaxLength = sz.cx;
```

I Like MessageDlg From Delphi. Can I Use It In CBuilder?

Yes, you can use the **MessageDlg** function in CBuilder. The function has a rather odd syntax, but you just have to use a little ingenuity:

```
MessageDlg( "Status Message", mtError, TMsgDlgButtons() <<mbYes <<
    mbNo, 0);
```

How Do I Install A Delphi Component In CBuilder?

In order to install a Delphi component in CBuilder, you must have the original source code for the component. DCUs cannot be installed in CBuilder. To install the source, follow the usual procedure for component installations and select the PAS source file for the component. All the rest of the process is the same. CBuilder can easily compile both Pascal and C++ source code.

> **Note:** Not all components in Delphi will work in CBuilder. Generally, they will, but if the Pascal component uses a **Real** property, which is not supported in CBuilder, you will get a strange compile error (Real not supported) when trying to use the component in your application.

Why Can't I Define A Simple Instance Of My Component In My Program?

What you would like to do is something like:

```
TEdit myEdit;
myEdit.somfunc();
```

Unfortunately, you can't do this. Instead, you need to create an instance of the **TEdit** class on the heap using the operator **new**. Borland requires this because the VCL objects are in Pascal and are destroyed differently. To create an instance of a VCL object within your application use the following:

```
TEdit *pEdit = new TEdit(this);
pEdit->Parent = this;
```

How Do I Break Down An Input File Name Into Its Components?

The **ExtractFileExt** function will extract the extension from a file name and return it as a string.

```
string Ext = ExtractFileExt(FileName);
```

How Do I Get To The Individual Pieces Of An Image?

Use the Pixels property of the image.

How Do I Change Items In A List Box Without Deleting And Re-Adding Them?

The items in a list box are stored in the **Strings** property of the Items array. You can directly (sort of) modify these strings by using that array property. For example, to get the first string (0 indexed) of a list box and append the letter W to it, you would do the following:

```
string s = List1->Items->Strings[0];
        s += "W";
        List1->Items->Strings[0] = s;
```

How Do I Change The Text Color Of A Button?

You can change the text color (but not the background color) of a button by using the **Font->Color** property. For example, to change the color of a button text to red, you would use:

```
Button1->Font->Color =clRed;
```

How Do I Store Information Associated With List Box Items?

Use the **Items** property and set or get the **Objects** property of the **Items** property for the item you want to work with.

How Do I Draw Bitmaps On A TBitBtn At Runtime?

This is ugly. Like all bitmaps, a glyph button (TBitBtn) starts out life as a 1 by 1 pixel bitmap (like all Windows bitmaps). To make it the size you want it, set the **Width** and **Height** properties of the bitmap to the size you want. Once you have done that, you can use the **Canvas** property of the button to draw on it. One thing you need to remember is that the lower-left corner pixel of the bitmap is used as the transparent color of the bitmap.

By the way, this only applies if you create the **TBitBtn** object at runtime. If you are simply drawing on an existing bitmap button, you can skip the **Height** and **Width** stuff.

My MDI Child Window Won't Close! How Do I Close An MDI Window?

In the **FormClose** method of your MDI child form, you need to put the following line of code:

```
Action = caFree;
```

The default behavior for an MDI child is to minimize it when closing. Don't ask me why.

How Do I Put The Date And Time In A Status Bar In CBuilder?

Putting the date and time in a status bar is pretty easy. You can get the current date and time via the **Now**() function of the VCL, which returns you the current date and time as a **TDateTime** object.

To put that data into the status bar, you need to create panels for the status bar. You then use the **Items** property of the Panels to set the text via something like:

```
StatusBar->Panels->Items[nTimeIndex]->Text = strTime;
        StatusBar->Panels->Items[nDateIndex]->Text = strDate;
```

where nTimeIndex is the index of the panel you want to hold the time, and nDateIndex is the index of the panel you want to hold the date. strTime and strDate are the date and time strings, respectively. If you aren't comfortable using the **TDateTime** object, just include <time.h> and use the **localtime** function to retrieve the date/time in local format.

How Do I Change The Background Color Of A Form?

You would think that this would be a simple matter of setting the color property of the form to whatever color you want. Unfortunately, this doesn't seem to work (at least in Version 1.0). Fortunately, the solution isn't much harder. Simply add a Create handler for the form and set the color of the form in that handler:

```
Color = clRed;  // Sets background color to red.
```

How Do I Convert An Edit Field To A Floating Point Number?

That depends on what you are talking about. Assuming that what you want to do is to get the information stored in the edit control as a double, you need to convert the **Text** property of the edit field into a double as shown in the following code fragment:

```
double dValue = atof(Edit1->Text.c_str());
```

This code fragment will extract the result of the Edit field input into a **char** * buffer and end that result to atof, which will do the conversion from char * to double. You may need to include <math.h> for the definition of atof.

How Do I Load A Bitmap At Runtime?

That kind of depends on what you are trying to load it from. To load a bitmap from a file at runtime in your application, use the **LoadFromFile** method. Given a bitmap called Bitmap1 you would use:

```
Bitmap1->LoadFromFile("c:\\windows\\somebitmap.bmp");
```

> **Note:** You need two slashes to get a backslash in C++.

How Do I Disable A Single Member Of A Radio Group?

When you want to work with a member of a radio group, you usually refer to the **Items** property (**RadioGroup->Items**). For enabling and disabling of the control, you don't want to work with the strings of the group, but rather with the controls. It is not surprising, therefore, that to do what you want, you use the **Controls** property of the radio **Group** object. Here is a snippet of code that will disable the third element (0 based) of the radio group:

```
RadioGroup1->Controls[2]->Enabled = false;
```

Help Files And Problems
Why Do I Get An Empty Message Box When I Press F1?

You need the updated help files from the Borland Web Site. The URL for the updated help files is: http://www.borland.com/techpubs/bcppbuilde.

Why Is The TStringGrid Help Missing?

Actually, the TStringGrid is pretty much exactly the same as the TDrawGrid, so you can use it. If you are a perfectionist and must have the updated help files, check the previous URL and you will find the addenda to the Help files to contain this information.

Are There A Lot Of Links Missing In The Help Files?

Yes. Borland is aware of the problem and is working on a patch to the Help files for the missing links. Some of the missing links, however, are in the Microsoft Help files, which Borland simply licenses. Check the Borland Web site for updated information.

How Can I Add F1 Help For My Component?

If you have written a new component and want to have your help file come up when the F1 key is pressed in the IDE tab containing the component, you need to use the Borland OpenHelp system. The steps to installing a help file for your component are as follows:

1. Create a new help file for your component. Move the help file to where you would like it to reside permanently. Your help file must have a TOC (Table Of Contents) or CNT file with it.

2. Run the OpenHelp application. Click on the Add button below the list of currently available help files.

3. Select your help file from wherever the help file for your component is found. This should be the place you put it in Step 1.

4. Move the Help file to the selected list by selecting it in the available list and then clicking on the > button to move it to the selected list.

5. Click on Apply and then OK.

CBuilder Crashes When I Click On The Find Tab Of Help

In your Windows directory, locate the winhelp.ini initialization file. Edit it with any standard text editor and remove all references to any previous Borland products (like Delphi or C++) you might have had installed in your system and then removed. Next, delete any GID files in the CBuilder\help directory. This should fix the problem.

Database
Why Am I Getting A Record/Key Deleted Message In My Btrieve File?

This is usually caused by one of two things. First, you may be including NULL (0) bytes in your strings. Btrieve expects strings from the BDE to be filled with spaces. Secondly, you may require a non-unique field. When you initially add a record to the table, the indexed fields are checked for validity. Make sure the records have valid index data in them.

How Do I Put Today's Date In A Date Field Of My Dbedit?

Use the **Now**( ) function of the **TDateTime** class to put today's date in a field.

How Do I Set A Filter Which Contains A Special Character Like '/' ?

If your field name contains a special character like /, as in a field such as Last/First, you need to enclose the field name in square brackets [Last/First] in your filter statement. Example: Filter = "[Last/First] = 'Telles/Matt'"

How Do I Use Indices In A Database?

You need to use the TTable access to a database in order to take advantage of indices. Check the **TTable** class for the relevant properties to set.

How Do I Log On To My Access (Or Other) Database Without Having The User Enter The Data?

As you are probably aware, when connecting to "foreign" databases such as Access, CBuilder's BDE will require the user to enter a login name and password for the database. If you use a **TDatabase** component to connect to the Access database (rather than the default database), you can fix this. Set the **login** prompt property of the database object to false. Then set the **Params** property to the name and password you want to use:

```
USER NAME="ADMIN"
PASSWORD="ADMIN"
```

How Do I Know If My Database Record Is Modified?

Add an **OnDataChange** event to your form that contains the data source you are interested in. If you want to work with the data directly, add the handler to the data source. Otherwise, add it to the data-aware control you are working with.

How Do I Cancel A Record Edit In My Database?

Use the **Abort** method of the database object.

Exception Handling
How Do I Make Use Of The Try .. Catch Statements?

Basically, anything that might throw an exception needs to be surrounded by a **try** block if you want to do exception handling on it. The basic structure of the **try .. catch** block is as follows:

```
try {
    // Statements that might cause an exception
}
```

```
catch(Exception& ce)
{
    // Do something with exception
}
```

How Do I Make An Exception Handler A Form Member Function?

The application object in CBuilder processes most exceptions when they bubble up from the base classes such as forms. In order to make the exception handler correspond to your own form's exception handler, you just assign it in your form's **create** method:

```
__fastcall TForm1::FormCreate()
{
    Application->OnException = MyHandler;
}
```

Then, define a handler in your form like this:

```
void __fastcall TForm1::MyHandler( System::TObject* Sender,
  SysUtils::Exception *e)
{
    // Handle exception e here
}
```

Miscellaneous
What Are Other Sources Of Information About CBuilder?

The best sources of information are the newsgroups located at **forums.borland.com**. They contain up-to-date information about the various aspects of CBuilder programming (ActiveX, VCL, Databases, General). In addition, the Borland group on CompuServe is a good source of information (BCPPWIN). Finally, check out the CBuilder home page at **www.borland.com**.

How Do I Use CBuilder Forms In My MFC Application Using Visual C++?

Make a DLL in CBuilder containing the forms you want to use. For each one, create a wrapper function defined as extern "C" to call from MFC. Create an import library in MFC using the **dumpbin /exports** command to find the names of the functions and then create a DEF file containing those entries. You will then be able to use the lib /def: option to create a new import library to call the functions in your MFC application.

How Do I Access The Volume Name Of My CD Using CBuilder?

Check the **GetVolumeInformation** Windows API function. CBuilder can directly call API functions with no problem.

How Do I Use OLE Automation In CBuilder?

Basically, you use the **CreateOleObject** function to create an OLE automation object in your CBuilder application. Then, use the **OlePropertySet** and **OlePropertyGet** methods of the object returned to get and set the properties of the object.

Finally, to call a method of the object, use the **OleProcedure** method of the object to call the procedure in the object you need.

How Do I Do Idle Time Processing In CBuilder?

The best way to do this is by creating a thread to handle the idle time processing. If you really want to do it in an idle loop, you can use the **OnIdle** event handler of the application. Just set **Done** to true when you have finished whatever you are doing so that the **WaitMessage** method is called to update the system properly.

Building Components
How Do I Add A Class Property To My Component, Like TFont?

If you are using an existing property like **TFont**, you just define a property of that type. If, however, you are trying to create a new property that is a class and use it in your component, you need to make sure of a couple of things. First, the class you are using must be derived from **TPersistent** somewhere in its hierarchy (in other words, derived from some class derived from TPersistent). Next, you need to define the previous property class where you are going to use it.

Finally, just add a __**published** property to the component containing the property class you want as a "normal" variable. Use the variable itself for the **read** and **write** property methods.

The tricky part is that you must override the **Create** method of the component to create an instance of your class property. Otherwise the thing will crash when the Object Inspector tries to load it.

> **Note:** If you want the user to be able to edit the individual properties in the Object Inspector of the IDE, you need to publish the properties in the class that you are making into a property.

Why Do I Get A Stack Overflow When I Try To Look At A Property Of My Component In The Object Inspector?

Chances are that your set function for the property is assigning to the property name instead of the member variable. For example:

```
int Fx; // Property member variable
__property int X={read=X, write=SetX};
__fastcall void SetX(int x)
{
    X = x; // This should be Fx instead of X!
}
```

How Do I Create A Round Button?

Use the CreateEllipticRegion to create a round region and then use the **SetWindowRgn** API function with the handle of the button and the round region that you got from the **Create** function.

What Files Do I Need To Put Where When Creating A Component?

The OBJ file and the header file (.H or .HPP) should be copied to the CBuilder\Lib directory when creating a file. This will allow CBuilder to link and compile applications properly using that component in their forms.

How Do I Create A Component That Looks Like An Array?

You just create an indexed component. An indexed component looks like this:

```
__property double XPoint[int nLine][int Index] = {read=GetXPoint,
    write=SetXPoint};
```

This example shows a property called XPoint, which represents a two-dimensional array. The **GetXPoint** function would look like this:

```
virtual double __fastcall GetXPoint( int nLine, int nIndex );
```

while the SetXPoint function would look like this:

```
virtual void __fastcall SetXPoint( int nLine, int nIndex, double dPoint );
```

It is not necessary to implement the property as a true array. That is up to you.

How Can I Test My Component Without Adding It To The Palette?

You can test any component by simply creating an instance of it in the parent form and assigning the properties you want. For example, to create a new **edit** component on a form, you would use:

```
TEdit *pEdit;              // This goes in header file
pEdit = new pEdit(this);   // Create with owner of form
pEdit->Parent = this;      // IMPORTANT! Create with form as parent
pEdit->Left = 10;
pEdit->Width = 100;
pEdit->Top = 10;
pEdit->Height = 20;
```

The previous code will create an **edit** component starting at position 10,10 on the form and running 100 pixels to the right and 20 pixels down. The previous code can be used for any kind of component, as all components support these attributes.

Other Sources Of Information

CHAPTER
16

- Web Sites

- Mailing Lists

- Newsgroups

- Other Computer Sources

Other Sources Of Information

One of the most frustrating things about working with new technologies is the fact that there is so little reference material out there. If you are working in Visual Basic, Delphi, or Oracle, you will have little or no problem finding books, Web sites, journals, and other sources of information about problems you may encounter while working with the tools. With CBuilder being a nearly new technology, however, you will probably find that there is a dearth of good information available to you. While CBuilder Web sites, books, and magazines are growing by leaps and bounds, you may be having some problems tracking them down. In this chapter we will look at some of the available sources of information for CBuilder, focusing especially on areas of the Internet and computer networks that will have the most up-to-date answers to your questions.

Borland's Web Site

The first, and most obvious source of information for CBuilder tools, questions, and updates is the Borland Web site. The Borland site, **http://www.borland.com**, has a wealth of technical information about CBuilder. Here you will find white papers comparing CBuilder with other products and technical papers showing how to accomplish tasks and get around problems in the system. Borland maintains a bug-tracking database on its site for looking up and reporting bugs and a Frequently Asked Question (FAQ) section.

In addition to the Web site itself, Borland has a number of Usenet newsgroups available for CBuilder discussions. These are under the umbrella site of **forums.borland.com** for your newsreader. On this server you will find the following newsgroups devoted exclusively to CBuilder:

- **borland.public.cpp.jobs**: A newsgroup devoted to jobs for either Borland C++ or CBuilder.

- **borland.public.cbuilder.activex**: A newsgroup devoted to handling ActiveX questions associated with CBuilder. Here you will find descriptions of using, writing, and finding ActiveX controls.

- **borland.public.cbuilder.commandlinetools**: A newsgroup devoted to using the command line tools that ship with CBuilder. Here you will find information about using the command line versions of the compiler, linker, make tools, grep, and all of the other tools that make up the CBuilder command line system.

- **borland.public.cbuilder.database**: A newsgroup devoted to the database aspects of using the CBuilder system. You will find questions and answers about using CBuilder with various available databases (such as Oracle, dBase, or Access) as well as subjects like SQL statement tuning, index manipulation, and other interesting topics.

- **borland.public.cbuilder.ide**: A newsgroup devoted to the Integrated Development Environment of CBuilder. Questions here often include keyboard shortcuts, installing and using tools, working with Wizards, and other topics involved with using and extending the IDE.

- **borland.public.cbuilder.jobs**: A newsgroup devoted entirely to CBuilder jobs in the industry. Companies are free to post jobs here, and consultants who use the system often post notes concerning their availability. Past threads in this newsgroup have concerned themselves with rates for CBuilder consultants, how to hire a CBuilder programmer, and companies using the system.

- **borland.public.cbuider.language**: A newsgroup devoted to the CBuilder language, C++, and the Borland extensions to the language. This newsgroup handles not only standard C++ questions and how they are dealt with by the CBuilder compiler, but also the proprietary extensions Borland has added to the language.

- **borland.public.cbuilder.non-technical**: A newsgroup devoted to the non-technical aspects of CBuilder. Information is found here about installation problems, upgrade issues, new patches, new Web sites for the system, and other questions about the system that are not technically oriented.

- **borland.public.cbuilder.vcl**: A newsgroup devoted to the VCL system found within the CBuilder system. Questions in this newsgroup range from issues about using the VCL components that ship with the system to writing your own VCL components. This is the most active of the Borland newsgroups to date and will probably continue to be so in the future. If your question concerns programming with CBuilder and forms, you should probably check this newsgroup first for your answers.

- **borland.public.cbuilder.winapi**: A newsgroup devoted to working with the Windows API and CBuilder. You will find questions and answers here dealing with not only what API functions are available to do a job, but also what their impact is in CBuilder. In addition, you will learn how to extend existing VCL components using the Windows API and how to encapsulate API functions within your own components. This is also a well-frequented newsgroup.

The Borland newsgroups generally receive several hundred messages per day. If you have a newsreader that allows searching within messages, you will find it worth your while to first check the newsgroups to see whether the problem or issue you are encountering has been found and fixed by another user. Don't try to go it alone in this brave new world of programming.

CompuServe

Besides its own Web site, Borland also maintains a presence on the CompuServe forums as well. Although no longer officially maintained by Borland, the CompuServe groups often provide a wealth of information about using and extending the system. If you have not used CompuServe before, there are two different ways to access information in a forum. The first is the message boards, which are quite similar to Usenet newsgroups. The primary difference between the forums and the newsgroups is that the forums tend to have a higher signal-to-noise ratio, that is, the newsgroups tend to have a lot of information not related to the subjects at hand, such as advertisements for other products, spamming, and cross-posted information that doesn't tie to the newsgroup topic. Forums, on the other hand, tend to stay on the subject for which they were created without a lot of fluff.

In addition to message boards, the other source of information on CompuServe is the file library, which contain uploaded files for the CBuilder system. Files can be text containing Borland tech information or they can be user-uploaded files containing new VCL components and test applications. Demonstrations of commercial products and shareware can also be found in the file libraries on a try-before-you-buy system.

On CompuServe, you will find Borland sites at CIS:BCPPWIN, the official CBuilder forum, which contains libraries with information about all of the various aspects of CBuilder. You will find patches to the Help files, uploaded VCL components, messages on how to do things, and other useful information about CBuilder here.

Another useful forum is the CIS:DELPHI32 forum. This forum, although devoted to Borland's Delphi product, contains information that can be used with the CBuilder system as well. Delphi and CBuilder are extremely closely intertwined, so that you can often take Delphi code and either use it directly in your application or easily convert it into C++ code to use in CBuilder. In addition, usually Delphi components can simply be dropped directly into the CBuilder system and used from the Component Palette, as we have seen earlier in the book. Because of this, you can use the file libraries on this forum to search for components that do the job in your CBuilder applications as well. Although not all components will work with CBuilder (Delphi 3.0 components will not, for example), most will work and are well worth the time and effort to download.

Mailing Lists

Several mailing lists are available for the CBuilder programmer. One of these is maintained by Borland and can be found at the Borland Web Site (**http://www.borland.com**). It provides update information, patches, and other non-technical data about the product, and keeps you informed of what is going on in the CBuilder world.

In addition to the non-technical Borland mailing list, there is also a mailing list devoted to working with CBuilder. This moderated list is maintained by Ziff-Davis and can be reached by going to the ZD Web site (**http://www.cobb.com**) and adding yourself to the list via the Web pages found there. The Ziff-Davis mailing list is found at the Ziff-Davis Cobb group Web site at **http://www.cobb.com/cpb**. Here you will find, in addition to the mailing list, information from the *C++Builder Journal* magazine.

Web Sites

Here are quite a few Web sites that I have found useful over the course of programming in CBuilder and writing this book.

Alan Garny's Web site (**http://pc-heartbreak.physiol.ox.ac.uk/programming.html**) contains information and downloadable components for CBuilder. Here you will find a transparent bitmap component, as well as threaded timer and **OpenGL** components.

The next site you should consider on your Internet trek is the unofficial C++Builder Home Page. In spite of the name, this site is not maintained by Borland, but rather, is an individual home page. There are some nice components here and some pretty decent links to other sites. The unofficial C++Builder Home Page is found at the Internet location **http://www-rohan.sdsu.edu/home/mattison/bcb/**.

Another good source of information on CBuilder is found at the C++Builder Solutions page. This page, run by Kent Reisdorph (another CBuilder author and programmer) is sponsored by TurboPower, a vendor of Delphi and CBuilder components. This page, found at **http://www.turbopower.com/bcb**, contains many articles about CBuilder, several frequently asked questions with answers, and other ramblings about the system. Kent is an excellent source of information about CBuilder, a member of TeamB (Borland's volunteer support), and an all-around nice guy. You will often find him in the aforementioned Borland news forums answering questions.

Daniel Carey's home page, at **http://www.multipro.com/whawke/**, is an excellent source of CBuilder components, articles, FAQs, and news about CBuilder. Updated regularly, this Web site features a download section, what's new, and links to many other sites concerning CBuilder and Delphi. Daniel is a CBuilder programmer at heart and keeps his Web site updated with new components and articles. This is a good place to start if you want to get a sense of what is available on the Web for CBuilder programmers.

The Many Roads To CBuilder Web site, **http://www.iks.aqua.com/r2bcb/**, started out life as a page devoted to holding links to other sites about CBuilder. Since its inception, this site has grown to contain its own question-and-answer articles, as well as pointers to a number of good downloadable components. Before you start searching around the Web for a list of CBuilder sites, try this site. It probably already has it. I used this site as an excellent launching point for my Web meanderings.

Possibly the best single source of information on the Web outside of the Borland Web site itself is The Bits They Forgot, at **http://www.jpmg-group.mcmail.com/bcb.htm**. This site features really good articles for beginners (how-to articles on threads, databases, and forms) to advanced users (internals of the CBuilder system).

Also found on this site are downloadable components, frequently asked questions and answers, and links to other sites. If you are a beginner and are frustrated with the documentation that shipped with CBuilder, check this site for answers about your questions. The tutorials found here will not only answer your basic questions, but will teach you as much as many of the beginner books on the market. This site, in case you hadn't guessed, is highly recommended.

ZBuilder Software is a company devoted to writing components for CBuilder and its older brother Delphi. ZBuilder maintains a Web site on America Online at **http://www.members.aol.com/zbuilder/index.htm** that contains downloadable versions of components as well as shareware information. ZBuilder also offers custom programming in CBuilder for those projects that you just don't have the time to do yourself.

The Unofficial Home Page of CBuilder, at **http://www.nh.ultranet.com/~bsturk**, is another great source of information about CBuilder. Run by Brian Sturk, a frequent visitor to the Borland forums and an avid CBuilder programmer, this site features downloadable components, articles, and links to other sites. Updated frequently, this site is another invaluable resource when searching the Web. Brian is also heavily involved in IRC (check the next section for details).

Dr. Bobs' CBuilder Gate is a great place to go if you want to learn about (or just download) wizards and experts for CBuilder and Delphi. Dr. Bob is the expert on the Web about Wizards and Experts and has written quite a few for use with CBuilder and/or Delphi. In addition to the wizards, you can find press releases, components, book reviews, and other Delphi and CBuilder related information at this Web site. This should be considered essential for anyone doing serious development in CBuilder. Dr. Bob's CBuilder gate can be found at **http:/www.members.aol.com/CppBuilder/index.htm**.

By the time this book finally arrives on the scene, there will probably be considerably more sites devoted to CBuilder. Check one of the previous sites for links to these sites or find them with one of the many Web search engines. In addition to the CBuilder-only sites listed previously, you can generally find good information at any site related to Delphi. One of the best is the Delphi Super Page, which has information and components for Delphi 1.0, 2.0, and 3.0. The Delphi 2.0 components will work with CBuilder quite well, and most of the others can be adapted to work with CBuilder. The Super Page has a small section on CBuilder components, which is likely to grow as time goes by. The Delphi Super Page can be found at **http://sunsite.icm.edu.pl/delphi/**.

The final Web site that I have to mention (because otherwise my editor will kill me) is the Coriolis Group Web site at **http://www.coriolis.com**. This site has many books, articles, and downloads for books on CBuilder and Delphi and is a good starting point for exploring the wide world of CBuilder programming.

Other Sources

In addition to computer networks, the Internet, and Web Sites, there are other ways to get information about CBuilder. Several books (including this one, of course) and magazines are already on the stands waiting for you, and more will be coming out as the world waits to learn more about this system. In addition, there is an IRC channel for CBuilder discussions found at #cbuilder. If you are not already on IRC, give it a shot and see what you are missing.

You probably won't need all the help that is available to you for CBuilder. The system itself is easy enough to use, and most things you want to do are already thought of and implemented in the VCL. On those occasions when the VCL is not quite enough, however, it is nice to know that you can gather both code and components for use in your applications. Remember, CBuilder is all about code reuse. If you need something that is not immediately available, check around on the nets before you decide to write it yourself. It might be that someone else has already done the job for you.

Applications And Wizards

CHAPTER 17

HIGH PERFORMANCE

- **Creating A Wizard**

- **The Internals Of The IDE**

- **Wizards And Databases**

- **Generating A New Component**

Applications And Wizards

In Chapter 14, we learned to extend the CBuilder development system by using the VCL to develop new components, but there is another way to extend the system. CBuilder offers an extensive API (Application Programming Interface) that allows you to extend the system itself through the creation of new programming wizards.

What is a wizard? Basically, it's a quick and easy way to create something in an IDE. Wizards can do the job of automating difficult or time-intensive tasks, make it easier to clone an existing structure or application, and do many other jobs that make a programmer's life easier. The purpose of a wizard is to make a job quicker and easier. What could be better than making it easier to construct a component in the CBuilder environment?

As you saw in Chapter 14, the component development process is not terribly difficult, but it is involved. CBuilder offers a Component Wizard, which will generate the skeleton for a new component, but that skeleton is extremely limited in what it can accomplish. It would be better, in my humble opinion, to have a wizard that not only allowed you to specify the base class for a component, but also allowed you to pre-select properties and methods to override and add new properties and components. We will develop just such a wizard (albeit not the perfect solution, of course).

In this chapter we develop a complete application to parse and display the component classes found in a standard CBuilder include file. This application will display for the user the classes found in the include file. When one of these classes is selected, the methods and properties of the component class will be displayed as well.

The second phase of our development process is to turn our application into a database front-end that will take selected classes from the display and load the data into database tables.

In the third and final phase of the development effort, we will create a full-blown wizard to use the database tables we created in phase two to generate new component classes. Along the way, you will learn more about the structure of C++ classes in CBuilder, how to add utility units, and more about how to generate CBuilder applications.

Creating The Class Parser Application

The purpose of the Class Parser application is to be able to parse and display class information about C++ component classes based on information stored in the header files for those classes. This is not a full-blown class browser (although, with a fair amount of work you could make it into one) or a perfect parser (it can be fooled without a lot of trouble if you want to), but it does the job the majority of the time. If you have the time and energy, I am quite sure you could make this application into a full-blown class browser and parser, but I am not that energetic.

Figure 17.1 shows the main form for the application. This form contains list boxes, which will list the available classes, and the methods and properties for those classes. It is worth noting at this point that the parser itself does not differentiate between an event and a property, as they are really the same thing within the CBuilder system. If you want to know which is which, you can generally rely on the fact that events begin with the string "On" and properties do not.

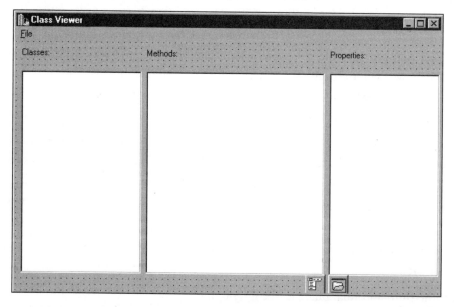

Figure 17.1
The ClassViewer application form.

To create the application, we will need quite a bit of supporting code to do the parsing and create the lists. If this is your first exposure to working with heavy-duty C++ coding in CBuilder (and probably not your last), you'll be getting a good introduction to the idea of writing real C++ code (instead of working strictly with the GUI elements of the system). Remember, CBuilder contains a complete and powerful C++ compiler. Use that compiler to its best advantage.

The Utility Unit

The utility unit is the first piece of the system that we will implement. This unit will contain utility functionality that is going to be used throughout the system. In general, it is best to separate the GUI code (that code that implements and supports the visual aspects of the application) from the true utility code (reusable classes and functions) in your projects. We will do this in our example by factoring out the non-visual code and moving it to a utility file.

Create a new unit in CBuilder by selecting File|New Unit. This unit will be called Utility, so save it under that name. When you have finished creating the new files, add the following code (or copy it from the CD-ROM) to the file. The listing is quite long, so you might want to just copy it from the disk. We will look at the individual functions as we go along.

```
#include "Utility.h"
//-------------------------------------------------------------------
#include <stdio.h>
#include <string.h>
#include <stdlib.h>
#include <ctype.h>

int GetWordQuoted ( char *string, char *word, char *brkChar )
{
    // Find the start of the string

    int nEndPos = 0;
    for ( int i=0; i<(int)strlen(string); ++i )
        if ( !isspace(string[i]) && (string[i] != ',' && string[i] != '|') )
        {
            nEndPos = i;
            break;
        }
```

```
// Find the end of the word

char term_char = 0;
if ( string[nEndPos] == '"' && string[nEndPos-1] != '\\' ) {
    term_char = '"';
    nEndPos++;
}

int nWordPos = 0;
for ( int j=nEndPos; j<(int)strlen(string); ++j ) {
    if ( term_char ) {
        if ( string[j] == term_char ) {
            word[j-nEndPos] = 0;
            j++;
            nWordPos = j;
            break;
        }
    }
    else
        if ( isspace(string[j]) || string[j] == ',' || string[j] == '|' )
        {
            nWordPos = j;
            break;
        }
    word[j-nEndPos] = string[j];
                nWordPos = j;
}

word[nWordPos-nEndPos] = 0;
if ( brkChar )
    *brkChar = string[nWordPos];
if ( string[nWordPos] == ',' || string[nWordPos] == '|' )
    nWordPos++;

return nWordPos;
}
```

The **GetWordQuoted** function will return a single "word" in a line, a word being any set of characters, optionally enclosed in quotation marks (hence the Quoted part of the name), that begins and ends with a valid terminating character. This function is quite nice for parsing out the individual words of a block to allow you to look at them one at a time, and we will use it to look for classes, properties, and methods in the code we parse in the include files.

```
int IsEndOfLine( char ch )
{
   if ( ch == ';' )
      return 1;
   if ( ch == '{' )
      return 1;
   if ( ch == '}' )
      return 1;
   return 0;
}
```

The **isEndOfLine** method is a C++ parser method that verifies whether a given character can end a line in a C++ statement. Statements in C++ are anything that end with a semicolon, open, or close brace. As a result, this method checks for those three characters and indicates if they were found.

```
BOOL CheckClass( char *strLine, char *strClassName )
{
   char szWord[ 256 ];

   int nPos = GetWordQuoted ( strLine, szWord, NULL );
   if ( !strcmp(szWord, "typedef") || !strcmp(szWord, "extern") )
      return false;

   if ( !strcmp(szWord, "class") && strLine[strlen(strLine)-1] != ';')
   {
      nPos += GetWordQuoted ( strLine+nPos, szWord, NULL );
      // Skip declspecs
      if ( !strncmp(szWord, "__declspec", 10) )
                        GetWordQuoted ( strLine+nPos, szWord, NULL );

      strcpy( strClassName, szWord );
      return true;

   }

   return false;
}
```

The **CheckClass** function looks to see if the current statement is a class definition. To be a class definition, the function extracts the first word of the statement using the **GetWordQuoted** function. This word is then checked to see if it is a class statement. This function ignores forward class definitions, only returning true in the case of a true class declaration.

```
int SkipToEndOfComment(FILE *fp)
{
   int c = 0;
   int last_c = 0;

   do {
      c = fgetc(fp);
      if ( c == '/' && last_c == '*' )
         break;
      if ( c == EOF )
         break;
      last_c = c;
   } while ( !feof(fp) );
   // Get whatever follows the comment.
   if ( !feof(fp) )
      c = fgetc(fp);
   return c;
}
```

The **SkipToEndOfComment** method reads through the file looking for the end to a matching comment. It will not process nested comments. The method returns the character immediately following the comment block.

```
BOOL PreScanClasses(char *strFileName, TListBox *pListBox)
{
   FILE *fp = fopen(strFileName, "r");
   if ( fp == NULL )
   {
      return false;
   }

   char szBuffer[ 1024 ];
   char szClassName[ 256 ];
   int  brace_cnt = 0;

   while ( !feof(fp) )
   {
      int c = 0;
      int  pos = 0;

      // Clear the line buffer
      memset ( szBuffer, 0, 1024 );

      int last_c = 0;
```

```
    do {
      c = fgetc(fp);
                    if ( c == '{' )
          brace_cnt ++;
                    if ( c == '}' )
          brace_cnt ++;
      if ( c == '#' && pos == 0 )
                      break;
                    if ( c == '/' && last_c == '/' )
          break;
                    if ( c == EOF )
                      break;
      if ( c == '*' && last_c == '/' )
      {
                      last_c = 0;
                      pos --; // Skip backwards over start of comment
          c = SkipToEndOfComment(fp);
                      }

                    // See if we should add this character

      if ( c != '\n' )
        if ( pos || !isspace(c) )
                    szBuffer[pos++] = c;

      last_c = c;
    } while ( !IsEndOfLine(c) );

    if ( ( (c == '#' && pos == 0) || (c == '/' && last_c == '/') )
    {
                    while ( c != '\n' && !feof(fp) )
                      c = fgetc(fp);
    }
    else
      if ( brace_cnt )
                  {
          if ( CheckClass(szBuffer, szClassName ) )
            pListBox->Items->Add( szClassName );
                  }
  }
  fclose(fp);
}
```

The **PreScanClasses** function is used to extract the class names from a file for display in the initial Class list box. It looks through the C++ include file for valid C++ statements and runs them through the **CheckClass** function to see if they fit.

```
BOOL ProcessLine( BOOL bDisplay, char *strLine, char *szClassName,
   TListBox *pPropList, TListBox *pMethodList )
{
   char szWord[ 256 ];

   int nPos = GetWordQuoted ( strLine, szWord, NULL );
   if ( !strcmp(szWord, "typedef") || !strcmp(szWord, "extern") )
      return bDisplay;

   if ( !strcmp(szWord, "class") && strLine[strlen(strLine)-1] != ';')
                 {
      nPos += GetWordQuoted ( strLine+nPos, szWord, NULL );
      // Skip declspecs
      if ( !strncmp(szWord, "__declspec", 10) )
                  nPos += GetWordQuoted ( strLine+nPos, szWord, NULL );

      if ( !strcmp(szWord, szClassName) )
         return true;
      else
         return false;
   }


   // Don't bother going any further if we didn't find the
   // class yet.
   if ( bDisplay == false )
      return false;

   // Look for properties
   if ( !strcmp(szWord, "__property") )
   {
      char szType[ 256 ];
      char szPropName[ 256 ];
      nPos += GetWordQuoted ( strLine+nPos, szType, NULL );
      nPos += GetWordQuoted ( strLine+nPos, szPropName, NULL );
      if ( !strcmp(szPropName, "*") || !strcmp(szPropName, "&") )
      {
         strcat( szType, szPropName );
               nPos += GetWordQuoted ( strLine+nPos, szPropName, NULL );
      }

      // Inherited properties that are published just have a name
      if ( strlen(szPropName) && strcmp(szPropName, ";") &&
         strcmp(szPropName, "=") )
                  pPropList->Items->Add(szPropName);
      else
```

```
                   pPropList->Items->Add(szType);
      }
      else
         if ( strstr(strLine, "__fastcall") )
         {
            pMethodList->Items->Add(strLine);
         }

         // Once we find it once, we will always
         // find it until it is over!
         return true;
}
```

The **ProcessLine** method is a utility function used by the next function (**GetMethodsAndProperties**) to extract any methods or properties found in a given C++ statement.

```
void GetMethodsAndProperties(char *fileName, char *className, TListBox
  *pPropList, TListBox *pMethodList )
{
   FILE *fp = fopen(fileName, "r");
   if ( fp == NULL )
   {
      return;
   }

   char szBuffer[ 1024 ];
   int  brace_cnt = 0;
   BOOL bFoundIt = FALSE;
   while ( !feof(fp) )
   {
      char c = 0;
      int  pos = 0;

      // Clear the line buffer
      memset ( szBuffer, 0, 1024 );

      char last_c = 0;

      do {
         c = fgetc(fp);
                     if ( c == '{' )
            brace_cnt ++;
                     if ( c == '}' )
            brace_cnt ++;
```

```
            if ( c == '#' && pos == 0 )
                    break;
                if ( c == '/' && last_c == '/' )
        break;
                if ( c == EOF )
                    break;
        if ( c == '*' && last_c == '/' )
        {
                    last_c = 0;
                    pos --; // Skip backwards over start of comment
            c = SkipToEndOfComment(fp);
                }
        if ( c != '\n' )
            if ( pos || !isspace(c) )
                    szBuffer[pos++] = c;

                if ( !strcmp(szBuffer, "public:") ||
                    !strcmp(szBuffer, "private:") ||
                    !strcmp(szBuffer, "protected:") )
                {
                    pos = 0;
            szBuffer[pos] = 0;
                }


        last_c = c;
    } while ( !IsEndOfLine(c) );

    if ( (c == '#' && pos == 0) || (c == '/' && last_c == '/') )
    {
                    while ( c != '\n' && !feof(fp) )
                        c = fgetc(fp);
    }
    else
        bFoundIt = ProcessLine( bFoundIt, szBuffer, className,
            pPropList, pMethodList );
    }
    fclose(fp);
}
```

The final function listed, the **GetMethodsAndProperties** function, is used to load the second and third list boxes on our form. These methods will be responsible for parsing the lines and placing the data into the processing area for the other utility functions to work with.

Once we have the utility functions out of the way, it is time to code up the form itself to use all of these wonderful functions. The first thing to do is to add a new handler for the File|Open menu item. Add an event handler for this menu selection and add the following code to the menu handler:

```
void __fastcall TForm1::Open1Click(TObject *Sender)
{
    ListBox1->Clear();
    if ( OpenDialog1->Execute() )
    {
        FstrFileName = OpenDialog1->FileName;
                      PreScanClasses(FstrFileName.c_str(), ListBox1);
    }
}
```

This method will display the Open File dialog and allow the user to select a header file from which to parse. If they successfully select one, the first list box (class names) is loaded by calling the **PreScanClasses** function that we added to the utility unit of the project.

The other menu item is File|Exit, which will simply exit our application and terminate the process. Add a new menu handler for the File|Exit menu item and add the following code to the menu handler:

```
void __fastcall TForm1::Exit1Click(TObject *Sender)
{
    Application->Terminate();
}
```

The final step in the form development process is to handle the selection of a class in the first list box. When this happens, we want to update the other two list boxes with the methods and properties of the selected class. Add a handler for the first list box click method and add the following code to that new handler:

```
void __fastcall TForm1::ListBox1Click(TObject *Sender)
{
    AnsiString s;
    // Get the selected item in the list
    for ( int i=0; i<ListBox1->Items->Count; ++i )
        if ( ListBox1->Selected[i] )
        {
            s = ListBox1->Items->Strings[i];
        }
```

```
// Load the other list boxes.
ListBox2->Clear();
ListBox3->Clear();
            GetMethodsAndProperties(FstrFileName.c_str(), s.c_str(),
                ListBox3, ListBox2 );

// If there was something selected, go ahead
// and allow import of that data into the
// database
if ( ListBox1->ItemIndex > -1 )
{
    Button1->Enabled = true;
}
}
```

As you can see from the previous code, the majority of the work is done by our utility functions, which can parse the include file, load the list boxes, and make sure that everything is displayed correctly for the user. At this point, you have a complete Class Parser application, which can be used to display the information for all classes in a selected include file. Figure 17.2 shows the program in action showing several classes in the CBuilder include tree (found in the VCL directory of the include tree).

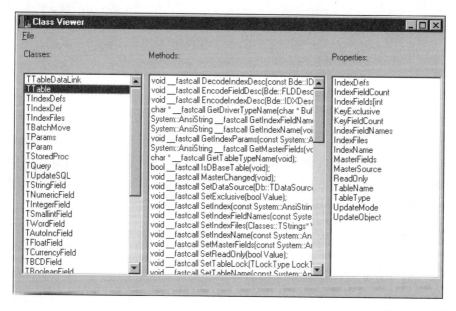

Figure 17.2
The ClassViewer in action.

Phase II: Adding To The Database

Once we have the data loaded from the include files about the classes found there, it would be best to store that information so it wouldn't have to be loaded each time the user wants to work with it. That would slow things down and make the program inefficient. We need to store the information (class list, methods, and properties) persistently so that we can use it in another project. In other words, we need a database.

It isn't difficult to add the pieces we need to store the information in a database upon load. All we need to do is add a couple of tables and a button to start the import process into the database. The updated version of the ClassViewer form is found in Figure 17.3.

In this version of the form, we are going to add a function that will persistently store the data for the class into the database tables. The first thing we need, of course, is a couple of tables to use to store that data. In this case we will use the Database Creation program that we learned about earlier in the book to create the tables (after all, isn't that the ultimate purpose of code reuse?).

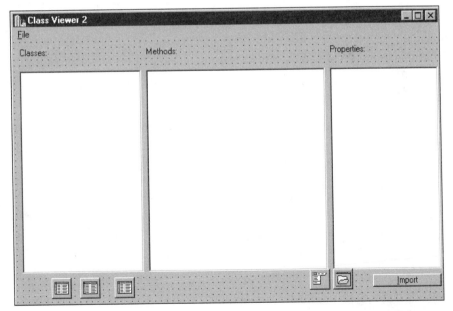

Figure 17.3
The Updated ClassViewer form.

For this application, we need three different tables: ClassNames, Methods, and Properties. The ClassNames table, representing the class names loaded from the include files, obviously needs to have the class name and a unique identifier stored in it. Because class names are only unique within a namespace, we will store this unique identifier for use as a link between this table and other tables. Table 17.1 shows the fields we will be using in the first table for the classes.

Once we have the fields defined, you can use the CreateDB program to add all of the fields to the table. Create the table with the name Names.DBF. This will be a dBase file that we will then use in the rest of our application.

The Methods Table

Once we have defined the main table for the application, the next step is to build the supporting tables. The first will hold the method information for the class. In our case, we only need the actual method signature for the method. We don't need to parse out the individual pieces of the method (such as the return type and arguments). In fact, we don't actually need the name of the method at all. Why? All we are going to do is allow the user to generate the methods into a class header and source file for the new component being generated. For this reason, there is no need to split out the method names, return types, or parameters. In fact, this would be a bad idea, as it would be impossible to determine overloaded methods in a list. For this reason, all we need to store is the class for which these methods exist (so that we can find them) and the method signature for the method.

Table 17.2 shows the layout of the method information table. The class identifier is simply the same ID that we put into the class names table. The method name identifier is the complete string that holds the method signature. When the user selects a method to write into the new component, we just write out the complete method name.

Use the CreateDB program to create a new table with the name Methods.DBF. This will be the dBase file we will use to store the method information for the components

Table 17.1 The ClassNames table.

Field	Type	Length
ClassName	CharacterString	80
ClassId	CharacterString	10

Table 17.2   The Methods table.

Field	Type	Length
Class Id	Character String	10
Method	Character String	255

that we parse in the include files. When each component is placed into the Class table, we will hold onto the class identifier string that is written with it. This same class identifier string will then be used for the Method table as well, so that we can easily cross-reference the two tables and join together the information we need.

The Properties Table

Our third table will store the properties. You might think that this would be more difficult than storing the methods. After all, you would think, the Properties table would need the property name, the property type, the **read** and **write** functions for the property, and so forth. Fortunately, it is not that difficult, and we won't need nearly all of that information.

Table 17.3 shows all of the fields that we will need for the Properties table in this application. Surprised?

Why is it possible for us to define the entire properties field in a single database field definition? Where are the types? Where are the read and write functions? How is it all going to work? Relax, it isn't really that difficult.

When you define a property for a component, you might remember, you need to define the property name, the type of that property, and a way for the user to set and get the information for that property. A typical property definition might look something like this in your code:

```
__property int AProperty={read = FAProperty, write =SetAProperty,
   default=32 };
```

Table 17.3   The properties table definition.

Field	Type	Length
ClassID	Character String	10
PropertyName	Character String	80

It is true that you need most of this information to define a new property in your component. In fact, as an absolute minimum, you need the property name, the type of the property, and a member variable in which to store the property (with no **read** or **write** functions). This is true for all new properties added to a component.

For properties that are simply exposed from a base class of the component, however, it is not necessary to override any of the previous information. A so-called hoisted property requires only that you name the property that you are exposing from the base class in the published section. Given a property definition in a base class, for example, like this:

```
protected:
    __property System::AnsiString Text={read =Text, write=SetText};
```

If you wanted to use the **Text** property in a component class derived from this one, you would not need all of the information stored in that property. You would need to hoist that property into the derived component class. This is done by writing a line or two of code that looks like this:

```
__published:
    __property Text;
```

Remember, the compiler already knows the type of the property from the base class. You aren't allowed to change the type of the property, as this would hopelessly confuse the user. You would have two different properties with different types allowed for them appearing in the Object Inspector. Which one would be which? Are they order-dependent? And if you could use both, how would you know which one was being referred to in code?

The answer to all of this is to disallow the use of multiple properties of the same name. When you hoist a property to a higher-level component (derived class) you maintain most, if not all, information about the property. While it is acceptable to change the **read** and **write** functions for a property in a derived class, and to change the default value, we will not handle these somewhat strange cases in our component generator wizard. If you get ambitious later on, feel free to add this capability on your own.

So we now have the three tables we need to store the information. The next question is how to get the data into those tables. To store that data persistently, we need to modify the code that we have written in the ClassViewer application. Although it might be possible to use the data-aware controls to accomplish this task, it is much easier to simply use the **TTable** object to store the data we want into the databases from the listboxes in the form. Let's do that now.

Saving The Data

The modifications we need to make to our form for the ClassViewer application to support persistence are pretty straightforward. First, we add a new button with the caption Import to the bottom-right corner of the form. This button will be used by the user to import the current selection into the database. In addition to this button, we need to add three **TTable** objects to the form. These tables will represent the three tables that we created in the last step of the procedure: Class, Properties, and Methods tables.

For the Class Table, set the database name to ".\". This indicates to CBuilder that the table is to reside in the same directory as the application. Because this is a relative path, this program will run properly in any directory that we install it into. If we put in a hard-coded path (such as c:\Program Files\ClassView\), we would now have to install the system in that directory to have it work properly. Alternatively, we could set the database name at program startup, but this is an easier approach overall. By simply making sure that all of the component pieces are installed in the same place, we reduce the program overhead. You might wonder why we didn't simply assign a BDE alias to the application and use that, but that is more complicated and, as a result, more error-prone. You would need to define the BDE alias on your target machine, make sure that everything was set up correctly, and so forth. Aliases are wonderful for networked applications or remote-database systems, but overkill for simple tools like this one.

Once you have the database name set in the component, set the Table name to Names.DBF. This is the table we created a bit earlier. Set the Name of the component to be **NameTable**. I don't always set the **Name** property of my components unless there is a real chance of confusing two of them. In this case, we will have three **TTable** objects on our form with no way to differentiate them. The **Name** property works well as a user-interpretable difference, so we will set the names of each of the tables to represent the different tables with which we are working.

After you have defined the Names table, do the same for the Methods table and the Properties table. The Methods table gets the same database path (.\) and a table name of Methods.DBF. The Properties table gets the database path and a table name of Props.DBF. In each case, set the **Active** flag of the database table object to true so that we can directly use the tables in our own code.

Adding The Data To The Tables

Once you have all of the tables defined for the form, it is time to write the code that will put the user's data into the tables. To do this, we will need to add a handler for the Import button Click event. This handler will only be called when the user has made a selection. For this reason, first we need to modify the selection handler for the list box full of class names. Modify that function as follows:

```
void __fastcall TForm1::ListBox1Click(TObject *Sender)
{
   AnsiString s;
   // Get the selected item in the list
   for ( int i=0; i<ListBox1->Items->Count; ++i )
      if ( ListBox1->Selected[i] )
      {
         s = ListBox1->Items->Strings[i];
      }

   // Load the other list boxes.
   ListBox2->Clear();
   ListBox3->Clear();
                GetMethodsAndProperties(FstrFileName.c_str(), s.c_str(),
                   ListBox3, ListBox2 );

   // If there was something selected, go ahead
   // and allow import of that data into the
   // database
   if ( ListBox1->ItemIndex > -1 )
   {
      Button1->Enabled = true;
   }
}
```

Once you have added this code, the Import button will be enabled only when a selection is made from the list box. To be sure, set the **Enabled** property of the Import button to be false initially, or the button would be enabled when the application starts up. This is not what we want to have happen, so we initialize it to disabled.

When the user clicks on the Import button we need to add the data. Add a handler for the Import button Click event to the form to accomplish this.

```
void __fastcall TForm1::Button1Click(TObject *Sender)
{
   // First, add the selected item in the
   // list box
   if ( ListBox1->ItemIndex != -1 )
   {
      AnsiString strClass = ListBox1->Items->Strings[ ListBox1->
         ItemIndex ];

      // Add it to the database
      int nRecordNo = NameTable->RecordCount;
      NameTable->Append();
      NameTable->FieldValues["ClassName"] = strClass.c_str();
      NameTable->FieldValues["ClassID"] = AnsiString(nRecordNo+1);
      try
      {
         NameTable->Post();
      }
      catch ( Exception& te )
      {
         MessageBox(NULL, te.Message.c_str(), "Error", MB_OK);
      }

      // Now, handle the properties
      for ( int nProp=0; nProp<ListBox3->Items->Count; ++nProp )
      {
         PropertyTable->Append();
         PropertyTable->FieldValues["ClassID"] = AnsiString(nRecordNo+1);
         PropertyTable->FieldValues["PropertyNa"] = ListBox3->
            Items->Strings[nProp];
         PropertyTable->Post();
      }

      // Finally, handle the methods
      for ( int nMethod=0; nMethod<ListBox2->Items->Count; ++nMethod )
      {
         MethodTable->Append();
         MethodTable->FieldValues["ClassID"] = AnsiString(nRecordNo+1);
         MethodTable->FieldValues["Method"] = ListBox2->
            Items->Strings[nMethod];
         MethodTable->Post();
      }


   }

}
```

This code will do several things. First, the class name selected in the first list box (Classes) will be added to the Names table. The unique identifier will be set to the number of records in the table, so we don't need to generate any sort of unique ID or worry about duplicate identifiers by using some algorithm to generate the identifiers. Instead, we just allow the database to take care of the issue by creating an "auto-incrementing" field by using the record number of the record we are adding. Name table identifiers, therefore, will start at 0 and run to the number of records in the database.

After the master record is added to the Names table, we then repeat the process for each of the properties and methods in the other two list boxes. There is no need to check selections for these list boxes because all of the entries in the list box represent either a property or a method in the class we have selected. Note the use of the **FieldValues** property of the table to assign the property value. This property is of type Variant. A Variant item is one that can hold any number of different field types. In this case, a Variant can hold strings, numbers, and booleans. The field type within the database determines whether a given data type can be converted successfully into the type stored in the database. For character string types, the AnsiString can be used for easy setting of the data.

Note the names of the fields in the table. Although we have the name PropertyName to the property name field in the props.dbf table, dBase supports only ten characters for the name of the actual field, so we need to truncate the field name to the tenth character, resulting in the name PropertyNa in the **FieldValues** property call. If you try to send the whole property name, the BDE engine will choke on it and complain that the field wasn't found. You need to take a little care in this situation. Use the Database Field Browser application we developed earlier in the book to examine the actual field names (or, of course, you can just bring up the Database Desktop application that ships with CBuilder).

Trying It Out

Once you have the application compiled, linked, and running, the next step is to test the whole thing out. On some systems, you will get a strange error (Database Structure Corrupted) if you try to run this application within the CBuilder environment. If this happens, just close down CBuilder and run the program from Windows Explorer or the command-line prompt. I have not determined why this error occurs, but that it only happens within the IDE.

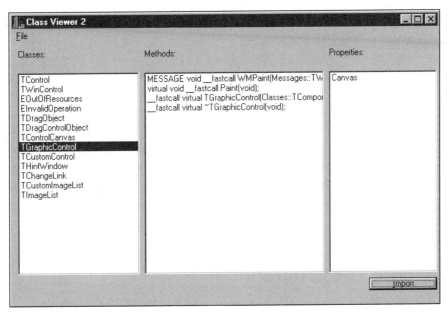

Figure 17.4
The ClassViewer program in action.

Figure 17.4 shows the application with a selected item and the methods and properties assigned to that item class. Once you have the application loaded and running, import a few of the classes into the database so that we will be able to use them in the next section of the chapter.

We're Off To Build The Wizard

It would be really nice at this point to build the database of classes, methods, and properties that we have assembled into a bigger, better Component Wizard. It would be really nice for two reasons. First of all, it would help me fill this chapter with something, and my editors would be grateful. Secondly, it would give you the starting point for your own wizards and your own Component Wizard++. Our component wizard, unlike the one shipped with CBuilder, will permit you not only to select a base class, but also to add other information. The component wizard we will build will allow you to promote (or hoist, in CBuilder parlance) properties from the base class. It will let you override methods in the base class. In addition, it will allow you to define new methods and properties and add them to the class. In short, it is a Component Wizard++, the next generation of Component Wizard.

Before you get too excited about it, let me tell you a few things about the program. It is a work in progress. The program itself is not particularly error-tolerant, nor does it handle all cases. It has several known bugs. They are not the end of the world, but you will need to be aware of them. In spite of this, I am sure it will teach you something about writing wizards.

In order to create a wizard, you first need to have the functionality in place to do the wizardry. The best way to approach a wizard is first to implement its functionality in an application. Then the code for the application can be moved into the wizard framework (which I will present a little later), and the whole thing built into a wizard application. The last step to working with wizards is the installation step. We will look at that piece when we have built the wizard code.

Building The Program

As a program, the wizard code consists of a tabbed dialog implementation. This dialog is shown in Figures 17.5 through 17.7. These are the three pages that make up the dialog and represent everything we need to know about the form for the app.

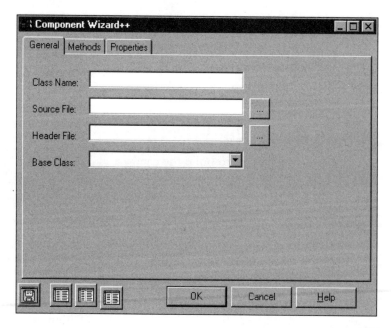

Figure 17.5
Page one of the ComponentWizard form.

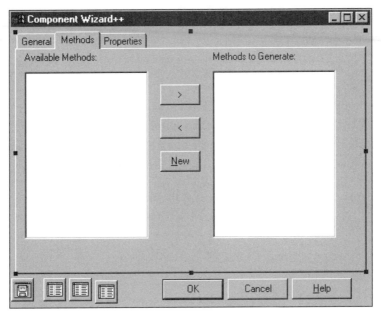

Figure 17.6
Page two of the ComponentWizard form.

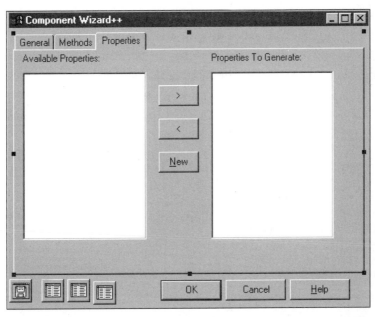

Figure 17.7
Page three of the ComponentWizard form.

To create the form, use the File|New menu item to create a new Tabbed Dialog form in the Forms section. Add three pages to the tabbed dialog that look like the previous ones. Once you have done this, you are ready for the coding task.

First, we'll do a couple of things on the first page (naturally). We need to load that base class combo box with the list of classes found in the table we built using the previous ClassViewer program. This is accomplished in the **Create** event handler for the form. Add a new handler for the **Create** method, called **FormCreate**, and add the following code to the handler for the form:

```
void __fastcall TPagesDlg::FormCreate(TObject *Sender)
{
    // Load the combo box
    Table1->First();
    while ( !Table1->Eof )
    {
        ComboBox1->Items->Add(
            Table1->FieldValues["CLASSNAME"]
        );
        Table1->Next();
    }
}
```

This code will load the combo box with the class names found in the table. The user will select one and use that data to select the methods and properties already existing in the table for that class to promote properties and methods into their own class. To accomplish this, we need to deal with the user making a selection from the combo box. Add a new handler for this case and add the following code to that event handler:

```
void __fastcall TPagesDlg::ComboBox1Change(TObject *Sender)
{
    // Get the class name for this id
    Table1->Filter = "CLASSNAME = '" + ComboBox1->Text + "'";
    Table1->Filtered = true;

    // Move to that record
    Table1->Last();

    // And get the id
    AnsiString strClassId = Table1->FieldValues["ClassID"];
    Table1->Filtered = false;
```

```
// Load the properties
Table2->Filter = "CLASSID = '" + strClassId + "'";
Table2->Filtered = true;
Table2->First();
ListBox1->Clear();

while ( !Table2->Eof )
{
    ListBox1->Items->Add( Table2->FieldValues["Method"] );
    Table2->Next();
}

// Load the methods
Table3->Filter = "CLASSID = '" + strClassId + "'";
Table3->Filtered = true;
Table3->First();
ListBox3->Clear();

while ( !Table3->Eof )
{
    ListBox3->Items->Add( Table3->FieldValues["PropertyNa"] );
    Table3->Next();
}
}
```

Here we simply filter the database for the specific class name that was given to us, and we will be permitted to load the proper methods and properties from the tables into the list boxes on the other pages. Once the user makes a selection from the combo box, the list boxes are loaded and the user is ready to go. That basically completes page one of the tabbed dialog except for the OK and Cancel buttons, which we'll skip for now and come back to later.

The next batch of items for us to handle are the buttons to move items to and from the selected list from the list of existing items. These buttons will be used to promote properties and override methods in the base class into our class. For page two, add two handlers for the > and < buttons (buttons 3 and 4 of the form):

```
void __fastcall TPagesDlg::Button3Click(TObject *Sender)
{
    // Is anything selected in the first list?
    if ( ListBox1->ItemIndex != -1 )
    {
        ListBox2->Items->Add( ListBox1->Items->Strings[ListBox1->ItemIndex] );
    }
);
```

```
      ListBox1->Items->Delete( ListBox1->ItemIndex );
   }
}
//-------------------------------------------------------------------
void __fastcall TPagesDlg::Button4Click(TObject *Sender)
{
   // Is anything selected in the second list?
   if ( ListBox2->ItemIndex != -1 )
   {
      ListBox1->Items->Add( ListBox2->Items->Strings[ListBox2->
         ItemIndex] );
      ListBox2->Items->Delete( ListBox2->ItemIndex );
   }

}
```

Likewise on the third page we have the same issues. We need to move items from the first list box to the second list box and vice versa. Moving an item to the right-hand list box will add it to the class when the class is generated, while moving it from the right-hand to the left-hand list box will make it not added to the list. Here are the appropriate event handler methods and their code:

```
void __fastcall TPagesDlg::Button6Click(TObject *Sender)
{
   // Is anything selected in the first list?
   if ( ListBox3->ItemIndex != -1 )
   {
      ListBox4->Items->Add( ListBox3->Items->Strings[ListBox3->
         ItemIndex] );
      ListBox3->Items->Delete( ListBox3->ItemIndex );
   }
}
//-------------------------------------------------------------------
void __fastcall TPagesDlg::Button7Click(TObject *Sender)
{
   // Is anything selected in the second list?
   if ( ListBox4->ItemIndex != -1 )
   {
      ListBox3->Items->Add( ListBox4->Items->Strings[ListBox4->
         ItemIndex] );
      ListBox4->Items->Delete( ListBox4->ItemIndex );
   }
}
```

The two buttons remaining on the form interface are the New buttons on the method and properties pages of the tabbed dialog form. These buttons are used to create new methods and/or properties that are defined only in this layer of the class. These properties are the ones that add value to the component, and in order to implement them, we need two more forms for gathering the data from the user.

The New Method Form

The first form we need to implement for the project is the form to add new methods to the component. This form will allow the user to specify the method name, the return type of the method, and the argument types and names. All of this information will be combined into a standard C++ style method declaration and added to the list of methods to be generated for the class. This permits us to use the same code in all places to deal with the methods. Figure 17.8 shows the form we will be implementing for the new method form.

The only code that we need to add to this form is in the creation process. We need to set the column headers for the grid and make the column widths the right size. Add a handler for the **Create** event called **FormCreate** and add the following code to the new handler for the form:

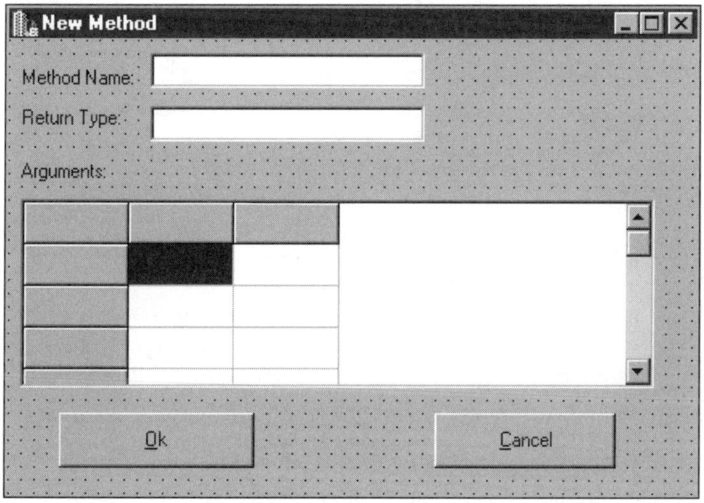

Figure 17.8
The New Method form.

```
void __fastcall TForm2::FormCreate(TObject *Sender)
{
    StringGrid1->Cells[1][0] = "Field Type";
    StringGrid1->Cells[2][0] = "Argument Name";
    StringGrid1->ColWidths[0] = 10;
    StringGrid1->ColWidths[1] = 100;
    StringGrid1->ColWidths[2] = StringGrid1->Width-140;
}
```

There is nothing terribly complex here. We are simply setting the column headers and widths so that the form looks right when it is entered by the user. The only other thing that might not be obvious on this form is that you should modify the **Options** property of the **StringGrid** object so that the **goEditing** and **goTabs** selection flags are set to true. The **goEditing** flag allows the user to edit the data directly in the grid (so that the user can enter the types and names), while the goTabs selections allows use of the Tab key within the grid in order to move the cells of the grid around.

Once we have the form defined and initialized, the next step is to display it in response to the user clicking on the New button in the Methods page of the tabbed dialog. We do this in the event handler, of course, after adding a reference to the new form by using the File|Include Unit Hdr command. Here is the relevant code to add to the event handler for the Methods page:

```
void __fastcall TPagesDlg::Button5Click(TObject *Sender)
{
    if ( Form2->ShowModal() )
    {
        // Build method string.
        AnsiString s = Form2->MethodReturn->Text;
        s += " ";
        s += Form2->MethodName->Text;
        s += "( ";

        // Do the arguments
        boolean bFlag = false;

        for ( int i=1; i<Form2->StringGrid1->RowCount; ++i )
        {
            AnsiString strArg = "";

            // There has to be something in the type column
            if ( Form2->StringGrid1->Cells[1][i].Length() )
```

```
        {
            if ( bFlag )
                s += ", ";
            strArg += Form2->StringGrid1->Cells[1][i];
            strArg += " ";
            strArg += Form2->StringGrid1->Cells[2][i];
            s += strArg;
            bFlag = true;
        }
    }
    s += ");";

    // Add to the list
    ListBox2->Items->Add( s );
    }
}
```

At this point, the Methods page is more or less complete. We will need to get data out of it, of course, but not before we put more data into it. Let's move on to the Properties page to see what lies in wait for us there.

The Properties Page

As you might guess from the previous code, we will need to implement another form to handle the new property input. Unlike the method code, this form requires no coding at all. Figure 17.9 shows the New Property form in all of its glory.

Once we have the New Property form in place and have added to the project, we can use it in the event handler for the New button on the Properties page of the tabbed dialog. Add a new handler for this button and add the following code to the handler:

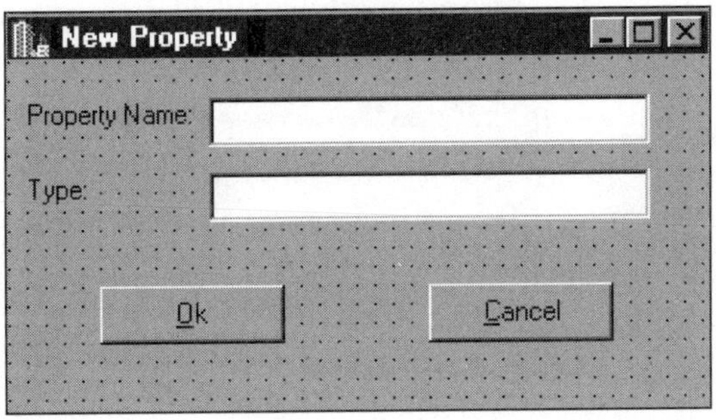

Figure 17.9
The New Property form.

```
void __fastcall TPagesDlg::Button8Click(TObject *Sender)
{
    if ( Form1->ShowModal() )
    {
        AnsiString s = Form1->PropertyType->Text;
        s += " ";
        s += Form1->PropertyName->Text;
        ListBox4->Items->Add( s );
    }
}
```

This code displays the form as a modal dialog box. The form gathers the information and waits for the user to click on the OK button. Once the OK button is clicked, the form then builds a valid property string of the form:

```
<prop-type> <prop-name>
```

Each property that we need to add to the component, in other words, will have the type in front of it. This contrasts with hoisted component properties, which are usually simply listed by their name. This difference will allow us to generate the properties and the member variables associated with them properly in the generation phase of the component creation.

We have already handled the case of the moving of properties to and from the list boxes, so we are now finished with the development of the Properties page. At this point it is time to move on to the good stuff: generating the actual component definition.

Generating The Component Source Code

When the user clicks on the OK button of the tabbed dialog form, the application is expected to go ahead and generate the code for the new component. Obviously, there is a little bit of validation that needs to be done by the program (verifying that we have source and header file names, for example), but in general, the program takes your word for what you have entered. If you create properties that have invalid names, for example, the application will let it go. This is a necessary evil for an application written in this scope. You are certainly welcome to enhance the application and make it more robust. Let me know if you do so; I would love to see the result.

Add a handler for the OK button to the tabbed dialog in CBuilder. Add the following code to the OK button:

Add a handler for the OK button to the tabbed dialog in CBuilder. Add the following code to the OK button:

```
void __fastcall TPagesDlg::OKBtnClick(TObject *Sender)
{
   // Check that they gave us enough info
   if ( ClassName >Text.Length() == 0 )
   {
      MessageBox(NULL, "The class name is required!", "Error", MB_OK );
      return;
   }
   if ( SourceFile->Text.Length() == 0 )
   {
      MessageBox(NULL, "The source file name is required!", "Error",
         MB_OK );
      return;
   }
   if ( HeaderFile->Text.Length() == 0 )
   {
      MessageBox(NULL, "The header file name is required!", "Error",
         MB_OK );
      return;
   }

   // Create the output header file
   FILE *fp = fopen(HeaderFile->Text.c_str(), "w");
   if ( fp == NULL )
   {
      MessageBox(NULL, "Unable to open header file", "Error", MB_OK );
      return;
   }
   GenerateHeaderFile(fp);
   fclose(fp);
   FILE *sfp = fopen(SourceFile->Text.c_str(), "w");
   if ( sfp == NULL )
   {
      MessageBox(NULL, "Unable to open source file", "Error", MB_OK );
      return;
   }
   GenerateSourceFile(sfp);
   fclose(sfp);
}
```

There are a couple of things worth noting in this code. First of all, you can see how we can abort the process of generating the code by displaying an error (optional) and then returning from this routine. Secondly, you should see that it is perfectly okay to use the old fashioned **stdio** functions, such as **fopen** and **fprintf**. They work extremely well in CBuilder. While you certainly could use streams, this application makes extensive use of formatted output, a weakness of streams.

The function itself simply verifies that the required fields of the form (the class name, base class, source, and header files) are entered. Once this is done, the program tries to open the header and source file for output. This is an iffy decision. In this case, I have chosen to overwrite the complete source and header file when the generation is done, but a better choice might have been to append to an existing file. There are more problems with this choice than are immediately apparent, however, especially in the case of a header file. You need to worry about multiple inclusions of the header file, including the base class header files, and so forth. To avoid these problems, I opted for the simpler solution of always re-creating the files. This isn't that major an issue, but I wanted to point it out as a pitfall of the development process. Just another example of the need to think outside the immediate world of your program.

This function makes use of several utility functions at different levels. First, let's tackle the header file generation. The header file for the component class will contain only the definitions for the class, no code. Here is the **GenerateHeaderFile** function to add to your class. Don't forget to add the prototype for the function to the header class definition of your own class.

```
void TPagesDlg::GenerateHeaderFile(FILE *fp)
{
    fprintf(fp,"//-----------------------------------------------------
    -----------------\n");
    fprintf(fp,"#ifndef %sH\n", ClassName->Text.c_str() );
    fprintf(fp,"#define %sH\n", ClassName->Text.c_str() );
    fprintf(fp,"//-----------------------------------------------------
    -----------------\n");
    fprintf(fp,"#include <vcl\SysUtils.hpp>\n");
    fprintf(fp,"#include <vcl\Controls.hpp>\n");
    fprintf(fp,"#include <vcl\Classes.hpp>\n");
    fprintf(fp,"#include <vcl\Forms.hpp>\n");
    fprintf(fp,"//-----------------------------------------------------
    -----------------\n");
    fprintf(fp,"class %s : public %s\n",
        ClassName->Text.c_str(),
```

```
        ComboBox1->Text.c_str() );
    fprintf(fp,"{\n");
    fprintf(fp,"private:\n");
    GenerateMemberVariables(fp);
    fprintf(fp,"protected:\n");
    fprintf(fp,"public:\n");
    for ( int i=0; i<ListBox2->Items->Count; ++i )
    {
        fprintf(fp, "    %s\n",
            ListBox2->Items->Strings[i].c_str() );
    }
    fprintf(fp,"__published:\n");
    GenerateProperties(fp);
    fprintf(fp,"};\n");
    fprintf(fp,"//---------------------------------------------------------
        -----------------\n");
    fprintf(fp,"#endif\n");
}
```

This function isn't very impressive. It actually was written by taking an existing simple component, copying the lines into the function for the header file of that component, and then changing the specific class names to general class names. To generate the header file, we need certain basics. The header file will always have an ifdef/endif pair that prevent the header file from being included multiple times. Once this is done, the base class header files are included for the VCL. Next, the class itself is defined. This consists of the class statement, open brace, and the public, private, and protected sections. We reach our first minor problem—generating the member variables—within the private section. Each property defined in the class solely at this class level will require a member variable to which to assign the data.

To generate member variables, you need two bits of information: the type of variable to define and the name of the variable. In this generator, we are going to make the reasonable assumption that the variable type is the same as the property type it represents. Most of the time the two will be the same. This generator does not support indexed properties (another limitation, I am afraid), so we need not worry about the other cases, which make up most of the differences.

Once we have the type of the variable, the next step is to come up with a name. Fortunately, convention helps us out here. The CBuilder convention for member variable names for properties is to put a capital F in front of the property name, and this is exactly what we are going to do in our components. If you can't rely on conventions, what can you rely on?

One problem is that we do not want to generate member variables for all properties, only non-hoisted properties. In fact, if we did generate variables for hoisted properties, they would become local to our class and be of no help at all. How do we get around this problem? The answer lies in the way that we generated the new properties. Remember that we included both the type and the name of the property for new properties. Hoisted properties only have a name. We can check, therefore, for properties that contain a space in the name (representing the space between the type and the name) as an indicator. This is exactly what we will do. Here is the code for the **GenerateMemberVariables** function, which you will need to add:

```
void TPagesDlg::GenerateMemberVariables(FILE *fp)
{
  // Look for any properties that have a space in
  // them. These must have a member variable given
  // to them.
  for ( int i=0; i<ListBox4->Items->Count; ++i )
  {
    AnsiString s = ListBox4->Items->Strings[i];
    if ( strchr( s.c_str(), ' ') )
    {
        char szProp[ 256 ];
        char szType[ 256 ];

        // So we can find the end of the string.
        s += " ";

        int nPos = GetWordQuoted( s.c_str(), szType, NULL);
        GetWordQuoted( s.c_str()+nPos, szProp, NULL);

        // Generate a member variable of this type
        fprintf(fp, "    %s F%s;\n",
            szType,
            szProp );

    }
  }
}
```

For the properties themselves, we call the **GenerateProperties** method. This method also needs to make some decisions based on whether or not the property is hoisted. If it is, it simply generates a property prototype:

```
__property Fred;
```

If, on the other hand, the property is a new one for this class, we need a full property declaration:

```
__property int Fred={read=FFred, write=FFred};
```

Here is the complete code for the **GenerateProperties** method:

```
void TPagesDlg::GenerateProperties(FILE *fp)
{
  // Look for any properties that have a space in
  // them.
  for ( int i=0; i<ListBox4->Items->Count; ++i )
  {
    AnsiString s = ListBox4->Items->Strings[i];
    if ( strchr( s.c_str(), ' ') )
    {
        char szString[ 256 ];
        char szProp[ 256 ];
        char szType[ 256 ];
        strcpy ( szString, s.c_str() );

        // So we can find the end of the string.
        strcat ( szString, " " );

        int nPos = GetWordQuoted( szString, szType, NULL);
        GetWordQuoted( szString+nPos, szProp, NULL);

        fprintf(fp, "    __property %s %s={read=F%s, write=F%s};\n",
            szType,
            szProp,
            szProp,
            szProp );

    }
    else
        fprintf(fp, "    __property %s;\n", s.c_str());
  }
}
```

The methods are already generated in the header file via the **GenerateHeader** method. The methods are already in their correct format in the list box we select them into (or generate them into), so we just get each selected/generated entry and write it out to the header file for the application.

Once we have generated the header file, it is time to generate the source file. The **GenerateSourceFile** method is used to create the source file and generate all of the verbiage necessary to create the source methods. Here is the **GenerateSourceFile** method for the class:

```
void TPagesDlg::GenerateSourceFile(FILE *fp)
{
    fprintf(fp,"//-------------------------------------------------------
                  -----------------\n");
    fprintf(fp,"#include <vcl\\vcl.h>\n");
    fprintf(fp,"#pragma hdrstop\n\n");
    fprintf(fp,"#include \"%s\"\n", HeaderFile->Text.c_str());
    fprintf(fp,"//-------------------------------------------------------
                  -----------------\n");
    fprintf(fp,"static inline %s *ValidCtrCheck()\n",
        ClassName->Text.c_str());
    fprintf(fp,"{\n");
    fprintf(fp,"    return new %s(NULL);\n",
        ClassName->Text.c_str());
    fprintf(fp,"}\n");
    fprintf(fp, "//-------------------------------------------------------
                  -----------------\n");
    fprintf(fp, "__fastcall %s::%s(TComponent* Owner)\n",
        ClassName->Text.c_str(),
        ClassName->Text.c_str());
    fprintf(fp,"    : %s(Owner)\n",
        ComboBox1->Text.c_str());
    fprintf(fp,"{\n");
    fprintf(fp,"}\n");
    GenerateMethodsSource(fp);
}
```

This method is pretty simple. It generates the include files listing at the top of the source file, including the header file for the class itself. It generates a **ValidCtrlCheck** method called by the VCL to create a valid instance of this component for use in the form editor. Once that is out of the way, the method generates the basic constructor needed by the VCL to call the base class constructor. All of this code, as you might guess, comes from a basic component that has been generalized and dropped into our code.

The last piece of the puzzle is generating the individual methods for the class. This is done by the **GenerateMethodsSource** method. Create this new method and add the following code to the method:

```
void TPagesDlg::GenerateMethodsSource(FILE *fp)
{
   for ( int i=0; i<ListBox2->Items->Count; ++i )
   {
     AnsiString s = ListBox2->Items->Strings[i];
     char szString[ 256 ];
     char szType[ 256 ];
     strcpy ( szString, s.c_str() );
     int nPos = GetWordQuoted( szString, szType, NULL);

     // Get rid of trailing ;
     szString[strlen(szString)-1] = 0;

     fprintf(fp, "%s %s::%s\n",
         szType,
         ClassName->Text.c_str(),
         szString+nPos );
     fprintf(fp, "{\n}\n");
   }
}
```

At this point, we have completed the component generator application. The point of this exercise, though, was to create a true wizard for CBuilder. Let's do that now.

Creating A Wizard

A wizard, or expert, is an add-in to the CBuilder system that aids the user in performing common or complicated tasks. For component generation, CBuilder offers the Component Wizard, an add-in accessible through the Component|New menu item. Other wizards in the system include the Dialog Form Wizard, the Dialog Wizard (available only in the Professional edition or higher), and the basic form wizard found in the Object Repository. Nicely exposing the API (application programmer interface) for the wizard structure, Borland has enabled you to drop in your own add-ins for CBuilder.

There are quite a few wizards available in the CBuilder shareware market. Probably the most interesting one is actually freeware. Written by Daniel Carey, a CBuilder programmer on the Internet, it offers the ability to generate simple CBuilder wizard skeletons. Basically, it's a Wizard wizard that lets you create your own wizard application. I have used this wizard on several occasions to generate the skeletons for my own code, and you can certainly use it for yours. You will find the wizard in both source and binary (DLL) form on the accompanying CD-ROM in the Extras directory.

A wizard is simply a DLL that is hooked into the CBuilder system. You need to conform to certain rules for the wizard, such as providing a set of fixed interface functions. Much like the **Register** function needed for components, the wizard interface functions allow the CBuilder system to load and execute the functionality found in the wizard without having to know a lot about it.

When you create a new DLL in the CBuilder system, you have done most of the basic work needed to generate a wizard application. By using the Wizard wizard, we can create a basic skeleton for the Component Wizard++ and take a look at it. If you don't want to install this wizard or just would prefer not to deal with it, I'll do the work for you and we can look at the code together.

```
#include <vcl\sharemem.hpp>
#include <vcl\vcl.h>
#include <vcl\exptintf.hpp>
#pragma hdrstop
USERES("CompWiz.res");
USELIB("Bcbmm.lib");
//------------------------------------------------------------------
TExpertState tx;
//------------------------------------------------------------------
int WINAPI DllEntryPoint(HINSTANCE hinst, unsigned long reason, void*)
{
                return 1;
}
```

This is simply the entry point for all DLLs. A DLL is required to have this function and to export it so that Windows knows how to load the DLL into memory. Any global initialization or allocation/deallocation will be done here. This function is called at various points during the lifetime of a DLL, most notably the loading and unloading of the DLL.

```
//------------------------------------------------------------------
class __declspec(delphiclass) CompWiz;

class CompWiz : public TIExpert
{
public:
                System::AnsiString __stdcall GetName(void);
//Short, descriptive name
                System::AnsiString __stdcall GetAuthor(void){};
```

```
//not needed for this expert
            System::AnsiString __stdcall GetComment(void){};
//not needed for this expert
            System::AnsiString __stdcall GetPage(void){};
//not needed for this expert
            HICON __stdcall GetGlyph(void){};
//not needed for this expert
            TExpertStyle __stdcall GetStyle(void);
//Expert style, Form,Project,Standard,Add-in
            TExpertState __stdcall GetState(void){};
//not needed for this expert
            System::AnsiString __stdcall GetIDString(void);
//Unique, internal identifier
            System::AnsiString __stdcall GetMenuText(void){};
//note needed for this expert
            void __stdcall Execute(void){};
//not needed for this expert

            void __fastcall OnClick( TIMenuItemIntf* Sender);//
called when user clicks menu option

            void __fastcall AddMenuItem(void);

            __fastcall CompWiz(void){};
            __fastcall virtual ~CompWiz(void){};
};
```

This class definition is our expert itself. Notice that the class is derived from a VCL class called **TIExpert**. This class, which is not documented in the online help for the CBuilder VCL system, forms the basis for all experts in the CBuilder system. Notice the comments on the right-hand side of the class methods. The expert generated these comments to help you know what methods are and are not used in this kind of an expert. The expert we are building is an add-in expert, which means that it appears in the Tools menu and can do pretty much anything. Other kinds of experts include Form experts (generate different individual kinds of forms), Project experts (create entire projects), and Standard experts (do normal repetitive tasks).

```
//-------------------------------------------------------------------
void
HandleException(void)
{

}
```

This method is used to handle local exceptions within the DLL so that they do not bubble up to the main level application (in this case, CBuilder).

```
//------------------------------------------------------------------
void
__stdcall RunExpert( TIMenuItemIntf* )
{
}
```

The **RunExpert** method is the main entry point in any expert. It is responsible for doing all of the work in the expert. When we begin to add the code for the wizard, we will primarily be adding to this method.

```
//------------------------------------------------------------------
System::AnsiString
__stdcall CompWiz::GetName(void)
{
    try
    {
                    return "CompWiz";
    }
    catch(...)
    {
                    HandleException();
    }
    return "";
}
```

The **GetName** method returns the short, simple name for the wizard. We want our wizard to generate components, so the short name for it will be CompWiz, a name that is returned to the CBuilder IDE for use in displays and message boxes.

```
//------------------------------------------------------------------
TExpertStyle
__stdcall CompWiz::GetStyle(void)
{
                try
    {
                    return esAddIn;
    }
    catch(...)
    {
                    HandleException();
```

```
    }
    return esAddIn;
}
```

The **GetStyle** method is called by CBuilder to determine the kind of wizard it is dealing with. In our case, we are an add-in expert, so we return the constant esAddIn. The different available types are: esStandard, esForm, esProject, and esAddIn. These constants are defined in the EXPTINTF.HPP header file found in the include\vcl directory in the CBuilder install tree.

```
//-------------------------------------------------------------------
System::AnsiString
__stdcall CompWiz::GetIDString(void)
{
    try
    {
                    return "CWZ100";
    }
    catch(...)
    {
                    HandleException();
    }
    return "";
}
```

The GetIDString is intended to return a unique identifying string. In this case I chose the nice and simple CWZ100 (for Component WiZard 1.00). Choose anything you want as long as it is unique among the wizards you write.

```
void
__fastcall CompWiz::OnClick( TIMenuItemIntf* Sender)
{
    try
    {
        RunExpert( 0L );
    }
    catch(...)
    {
    }
}
```

The **OnClick** event handler is called by the system when the menu item in the IDE associated with this expert tool (we will get to this step in a few moments) is clicked by the system. We will add our own handler for the menu item to the actual IDE menu item in the registration function for this expert. When the menu item is called, the **RunExpert** method is called, which, as I mentioned earlier, is where everything of any importance happens in the system.

```
//------------------------------------------------------------------
void
__fastcall DoneExpert(void)
{
}
```

The **DoneExpert** method is called when the expert is completed. If you have any cleanup work to do in your wizard code, you should put it into this method.

```
//------------------------------------------------------------------
void
__fastcall CompWiz::AddMenuItem(void)
{
    int index;
    TIMainMenuIntf *mmi;
    TIMenuItemIntf *miparent;
    TIMenuItemIntf *michild;
    TIMenuFlags mf;

    try
    {
            mf << mfVisible << mfEnabled;

        mmi = ToolServices->GetMainMenu();
        michild = mmi->FindMenuItem( "ToolsGalleryItem");

        index = michild->GetIndex();
        index++;
        miparent = michild->GetParent();

        miparent->InsertItem( index, "ComponentWizard++",
                "CompWiz",
                "", 0, 0, 0, mf, OnClick );
            michild->Release();
            miparent->Release();
        mmi->Release();
    }
    catch(...)
    {
```

```
        }
}
```

The **AddMenuItem** method is called to add a new menu item to the IDE main menu. In this case, we are adding the menu item with the caption "ComponentWizard++" to the menu that contains the item ToolsGalleryItem, which is found on the Tools menu. The identifier for this menu item is simply incremented to add the new menu to the end of the menu. The new item is inserted into the parent menu (Tools) for this menu item and the **OnClick** method is assigned as the callback for this menu item. This is the connection between the expert code and the IDE code.

```
//---------------------------------------------------------------------
extern "C" __declspec(dllexport)
bool
__stdcall INITEXPERT0016(      Toolintf::TIToolServices* ToolServices,
                               TExpertRegisterProc RegisterProc,
                               TExpertTerminateProc &Terminate)
{
            // make sure we're the first and only instance
            int Result = Exptintf::ToolServices == NULL;
            if (!Result) return false;

            Exptintf::ToolServices = ToolServices;
             if (ToolServices != NULL)
                    Application->Handle = ToolServices->
                        GetParentHandle();
             else
                    return false;

            Terminate = DoneExpert;

            // register the experts
            CompWiz *ew = new CompWiz;
            (*RegisterProc)(ew);

            ew->AddMenuItem();

            return true;
}
```

This is our registration function, which is called by the CBuilder IDE when the DLL is first loaded. The DLL is loaded when it is registered with CBuilder (we will talk about this later), and the system starts. At that point, each wizard in the system is interrogated and loaded by the registration function. This function first checks to see if we have already been registered. If not, a new instance of the **CompWiz** class is created and the menu item for this expert added to the Tools menu.

> **Note:** *Throughout this chapter the terms wizard and expert are used interchangeably, just as Borland does throughout its documentation. You just sort of get used to it.*

Adding Functionality To The Wizard

Having a wizard skeleton is all well and good, but it doesn't get the job done. What we need is all of the functionality from our previous application added to the wizard. How can we accomplish that?

As it turns out, all of that functionality is already there. After all, we already have the form defined to accept all of the data we need, right? And we have all of the code written to generate the component class based on that data. Therefore, we have already done all the work. All we need to do is to add the form and units that we created in our previous application to our DLL, show the form when the expert is called, and the rest is done for us. This was the whole purpose of first making the form into an application. We could work out the bugs, test the system, and make sure that everything was working correctly before we integrate the whole thing into the CBuilder system as a full-blown expert. Always take things one step at a time in the development world, and you will do just fine.

Copy the files for the forms and units from the application project (ignoring the project file, make file, and intermediate compile files) into the new expert directory. Once you have done this, make the following modifications to the expert code. The biggest change, of course, is in the **RunExpert** method because it is responsible for doing all of the work in the expert. Here is the new **RunExpert** method for our wizard code:

```
void
__stdcall RunExpert( TIMenuItemIntf* )
{
   TPagesDlg *frm;

            try
      {
```

```
                    frm = new TPagesDlg(Application);
    Form1 = new TForm1(frm);
    Form2 = new TForm2(frm);

            if( frm->ShowModal() )
            {
                    TCreateModuleFlags mf;

                    mf << cmAddToProject << cmNewUnit <<
                      cmMarkModified;

                    ToolServices->CreateCppModule( frm->
                      SourceFile->Text,"",
                    "","", 0L, 0L, 0L, mf );
            }
            frm->Free();

        }
        catch(...)
        {
            HandleException();
        }
}
```

There are a couple of important things to notice here, the first being the use of the **try .. catch** block around the code to make sure that an error will not percolate to the IDE and crash the user's system. The next thing to notice is that we create instances of all of the forms in the system here in the **RunExpert** function. Because the DLL has no main application object, there is no auto-creation, and if there is no auto-creation, you must create the forms before you use them. Failure to create the forms will cause the VCL to raise an exception and the expert will crash. Once all the forms are created, we go ahead and display the first form modally. This displays the usual tabbed dialog on the screen and allows the user to enter data for the new component just as he did when he was working with the application version of the code.

Following the form display and processing, you will notice another block of code that calls the **CreateCppModule** method of the **ToolServices** object. This important call adds the new module to the current project, just the way that CBuilder does in its own Component Wizard. To be compatible, we need to do this as well. Finally, the form is deleted by calling the **Free** method of the base form.

Side Trip: The ToolServices Object

One of the more important objects for use in creating wizards is the **ToolServices** object, which contains methods for working with the IDE itself. Table 17.4 lists the available methods in the **TIToolServices** class, which is the actual class type of the object.

As you'll probably notice in the table, the methods available in the **ToolServices** object give you full control over the IDE. With these methods available to you, you can add any functionality you would like to the system from within your wizards. If you are accustomed to writing add-ins for other systems, I think you will find CBuilder is quite a nice system. It extends the same functionality available to the system itself to your wizard and handles internal errors in wizards with the same grace it handles its own problems. It is quite hard to crash CBuilder through a wizard (although I have no doubt someone out there will manage it).

Now back to our regularly scheduled code.

Problems, Problems, Problems

One of the first things you will notice when you install the wizard and run it within the environment is that it doesn't work. Surprise? Not really. After all, we told the forms to use the databases local to the directory of the application. In the case of a DLL, the local directory is the current CBuilder directory, not the current DLL directory. Change the database directory for the tables to point to the place where you are installing the DLLs and databases.

One immediate note. If you are installing the DLL in the same directory you are creating it, you will quickly find that you cannot build the DLL in the environment. The reason for this is pretty simple. CBuilder is loading the DLL into the memory of the operating system, and the operating system isn't going to let you overwrite that file while it has it loaded; and you get a strange sharing violation if you try. Always install your DLL from another directory on the system (perhaps CBuilder\bin) rather than the directory in which you are testing it. Of course, to test the changes to the DLL you need to close down the IDE and restart it. This is more an operating system problem than a CBuilder one. Once loaded, the DLL stays loaded until the IDE is shut down. For this reason you can't just copy over it (you get the same sharing violation error).

Table 17.4   The **TIToolSerives** class methods.

CloseProject	Closes the current project.
OpenProject	Opens a new project specified by caller.
SaveProject	Saves the current project.
CloseFile	Closes the current file in the editor.
OpenFile	Opens a specified file into the editor.
SaveFile	Saves the current file in the editor.
ReloadFile	Reloads the current file in the editor from disk.
CreateModule	Creates a new module in the current project.
CreateModuleEx	Same as CreateModule, but with more options.
GetParentHandle	Returns the window handle of the parent of the caller.
GetProjectName	Returns the current project name
GetUnitCount	Returns the current number of units in the current project.
GetUnitName	Returns the name of a specified unit (by index number) in the current project.
EnumProjectUnits	Loops through each of the units in the project, calling a user-defined handler for each one.
GetFormCount	Returns the number of forms in the current project.
GetFormName	Returns the name of a specified form (by index number) in the current project.
IsFileOpen	Indicates whether or not the specified file is loaded in the editor.
GetNewModuleName	Returns the name of the next module name using the standard formula for the project (i.e., Unit1, Unit2).
GetModuleCount	Returns the number of modules in the current project.
GetModuleName	Returns the name of a given module (specified by index number) in the current project.
GetComponentCount	Returns the number of components defined in the current system.
GetComponentName	Returns the name of a given component (specified by index number) in the current system.
GetMainMenu	Returns a handle to the main menu of the IDE system.
CreateCppModule	Creates a new CPP file in the project and optionally adds it to the project.
RaiseException	Allows the programmer to raise an application exception in the system.

Installing The Wizard

Looking back over the last piece, I realize that I haven't told you how to install a wizard in the first place. Reminds me of a MASH episode I watched a few years back. The doctors were trying to disarm a bomb. One (Hawkeye Pierce, I think) was doing the surgery on the bomb while the other (Henry Blake) was reading the instructions. The whole conversation went something like this: "Okay, now cut the blue wire." Snip. Pause. "After cutting the red wire." Oops.

Well anyway, let's go through the installation process. In order to install a wizard so that CBuilder sees it, first shut down the CBuilder system. Next, bring up the regedit program by launching a command-prompt window and typing regedit at the prompt. Press Return and the program will start up. When you bring up the regedit program you are confronted with a list of registry keys. Double-click on the **HKEY_CURRENT_USER** key and then the Software key within it. You should see an entry for Borland. Double-click on that to reveal the CBuilder key, and within that key, the 1.0 key. Finally, you will reach a level showing a large number of entries. If there is an entry for Experts, add a new string value to it. The name of the string value isn't important (it is for your use), but the value of the string must be the complete path to the wizard DLL file you have created. Figure 17.10 shows the display you should see for a wizard in the CBuilder system.

The Expert Install Program

This is all pretty horrible and annoying. I really don't understand why Borland chose to not give you a simple "Install Wizard" menu command. There is no reason, however, why you need to suffer this way. CBuilder is all about convenience, so let's create a simple application that will let you install wizards at your convenience. Figure 17.11 shows the form we will be using for this purpose.

To implement this application, we need to add two pieces of code to the system. First, we need the handler for the "..." button, which will display the Open dialog to allow the user to select a DLL or other file to install. Here is the handler for that code.

```
void __fastcall TForm1::Button1Click(TObject *Sender)
{
    if ( OpenDialog1->Execute() )
    {
        Edit2->Text = OpenDialog1->FileName;
    }
}
```

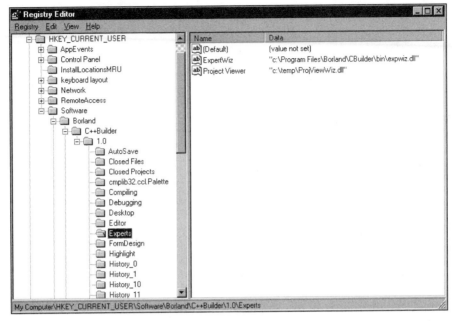

Figure 17.10
Regedit showing CBuilder Wizard entries.

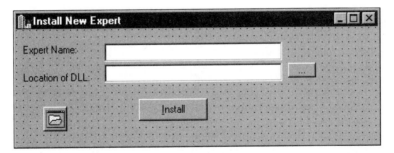

Figure 17.11
The ExpertInstall form.

The next issue is to add the registry key in response to the user clicking on the Install button on the form. Add the following code to the handler for this event.

```
void __fastcall TForm1::Button2Click(TObject *Sender)
{
    TRegistry *pReg = new TRegistry;
    AnsiString Key = "Software\\Borland\\C++Builder\\1.0\\Experts";
```

```
try {
  pReg->OpenKey(Key, true);
    pReg->WriteString(Edit1->Text, Edit2->Text);
}

catch(Exception& e)
{
    MessageBox(NULL, "Unable to install!", "Error", MB_OK );
    delete pReg;
    return;
}
delete pReg;
MessageBox(NULL, "Expert Installed", "Success", MB_OK );
Application->Terminate();
}
```

That's all you need to do. Once the code compiles and links, all you need to do is run the application. You can even install it as a Tool on the Tools menu if you like.

That pretty much sums up the wizard work in this chapter. Writing a wizard isn't much different from writing an application in CBuilder, so by now you should know everything you need to know.

What Did We Learn In This Chapter?

In this chapter we learned quite a bit about writing wizards that can extend the CBuilder system. You saw just how easy it is to create your own wizards, test them in a standalone application, and install them. Specifically, here are the things you should take away with you from this chapter:

- Wizards can be used to extend the basic functionality of the CBuilder system.

- Wizards fall in one of four types: AddIn, Form, Project, or Standard.

- To create a wizard, first create the forms in a standalone application and test them. Then you can use the code in a wizard.

- New modules, units, or even forms can be added to a project via wizards.

- The **ToolServices** class is available for working with Wizards to provide the wizard with the full functionality of the IDE.

- Installing a wizard involves writing new keys to the system registry.

- The **TRegistry** object can be used to work with the system registry in a CBuilder VCL application.

That concludes the application programming development section of the book. I really hope you have learned a bit about working with CBuilder and extending the system. You probably have already noticed just how easy it is to create extensive, complex applications using the VCL. One of the biggest challenges I faced in writing this book, in fact, was coming up with hard-core problems that were not easily handled. CBuilder is an extremely powerful system that makes application development a breeze. I only hope that you enjoy working with the system as much as I have.

Extensions To C++ For CBuilder

CHAPTER

18

- Extensions To C++

- New Keywords

- What Does It All Mean?

- Summary

Extensions To C++ For CBuilder

Traditionalist C++ programmers knock CBuilder because Borland has implemented its compiler with non-portable extensions to the language. All things considered, this is a pretty silly argument. After all, if you want to write simple C++ code, CBuilder can certainly handle it. You don't have to work with the extensions if you don't want to. CBuilder is quite capable of working with ANSI standard C++ and can create fully capable C++ Windows applications without using the VCL. You could do this if you wanted to, but why?

The argument against using the VCL usually runs to portability. You won't be able to move your code from the CBuilder environment. Oddly enough, no one makes this argument against Visual Basic or Delphi, but C++ purists insist on portability, which is pretty dumb, really. You aren't going to use CBuilder to develop cross-platform applications; you are going to use it to create the best Windows applications in the shortest time period possible.

Extensions

In this chapter we will explore the extensions that make the CBuilder language unique, when to use the extensions, and when not to use them. There are only a few times that you are actually required to use one of the extensions to the C++ language, and we will examine those cases. C++ is a complex language to begin with, and you don't want to use more than you need to in your own applications.

Let's look at each of the Borland extensions used in CBuilder.

_asm And __asm

The **asm** keywords can be used interchangeably. Each of these (including the un-listed **asm** keyword) will simply allow you to place assembly language instructions into your application source code without linking in assembler modules. The __**asm** keyword has been around for some time in the Borland compilers, and works well for embedded assembler. You will generally only use this kind of code for extreme speed or to interact directly with system registers and ports. If you don't already know how to write assembler code, practicing in CBuilder is not the place to start.

__automated

The __**automated** keyword is used for OLE automation properties in your components. Any property declared as __**automated** is, by default, public in your class. The difference is that automated properties require that you use member functions for access. You may not simply use member variables for interacting with automated properties. In addition, you must use the __**fastcall** modifier for these member functions. You may not use the index, stored, default, or nodefault modifiers for automated properties.

_cdecl And cdecl

These keywords define a method or function to use the C-style protocol, which means that the function is linked in using a case-sensitive process with a leading underscore (_) prepended to the function name. The use of **cdecl** variants also affects the way CBuilder passes arguments on the stack to change. The last parameter is pushed onto the stack first, and the caller of the function is required to clean up the stack. When using the modifier in your own programs, it is unnecessary to do anything extra to work with **cdecl** functions or variables. The compiler will do all of the work for you.

__classid

The __**classid** function is used to return a pointer to a vtable (C++ virtual table) for a class in the VCL library. The __**classid** is used internally by the CBuilder system to work with VCL objects and methods that require a **this** pointer indicating the object on which they operate. Although the __**classid** is a major part of the internal runtime type identification system built into CBuilder, this statement should not be used in application programs. Borland reserves the right to change the behavior of this functionality, and applications that rely on certain inner workings of the compiler will be broken by future releases. As a general note, this statement is the basis for the interaction between the C++ objects in CBuilder and the underlying Pascal-based VCL.

__closure

The __closure keyword is used in event handler function declarations. Closures are a special form of the function pointer used in most callback functions found in Windows frameworks. Unlike normal function pointers, a closure maintains not only the address of the function to be called (a four-byte pointer) but also a pointer to the object for which the event is being called (the **this** pointer). The use of the __closure statement is somewhat limiting in the system, as it allows for only a limited number of objects of the same class. Fortunately, this number is quite large because it represents a pointer to memory. Don't worry too much in the near term about running out of object pointers in your applications.

Closure is an important concept in CBuilder that you need to understand if you are going to write your own event handlers in the system. The basic format of a closure is that of a member function in the system:

```
class MyClass
{
    void ACallbackFunction( int x, double y, char *z);
}
// To set up a closure, you first define it
void (__closure *CallbackEvent)(int, double, char *);
// Now, you can assign it to an object of the correct class
MyClass *obj = new MyClass;
CallbackEvent = obj->ACallbackFunction;
```

This is what really goes on when you are working with event handlers: You are assigning and modifying pointers to member functions. Although working with member functions is a confusing topic at best in C++, CBuilder uses the idea to its best potential with the concept of the __closure statement.

__declspec

The __declspec modifier is a true oddball in the CBuilder system, with two completely discrete uses. The first is as a modifier for imported or exported functions in a CBuilder DLL. This statement takes the place of the older __export modifier present in older compilers. This statement had several problems, the most basic of which was that it had to appear in a specific position in the code. For example, you could not write:

```
__export void funct(void);
```

if you wanted to export a function called **funct** that took no parameters. Instead, it was required that you write:

```
void __export func(void);
```

This is an annoying limitation. There are rarely any conditions in C++ where it matters what order you place things in. The only comparable condition that I can think of is the **const** modifier, which is legal in different positions, but means different things depending on its position. The __**declspec** modifier is different. Use it as follows:

```
void __declspec(dllexport) funct(void);
__declspec(dllexport)void funct(void);
```

Both of these statements are legal and correct. They both export a function called **funct** in the DLL from CBuilder. It is quite common to use this statement in your application programs and dynamic link libraries, so you had better become accustomed to seeing it in code.

__except

The __**except** statement is the same as the **except** statement. It is used in C++ exception handling to specify the actions that should be taken when a given error is raised within a **try** block. The primary difference between the **try .. catch** and the __**try** .. __**except** statements is that **try .. catch** is used in C++ applications, while __**try** .. __**except** statements are used in structured C applications. The general form of the __**except** statement is this:

```
__try
{
// some statements that might raise an exception
}
```

```
__except(someexpression)
{
}
```

If you write code only in C++ applications for CBuilder, you will never use the __except or __try statements. These statements will, however, be used in legacy C code, which is included in CBuilder projects. By using the structured exception handling, you are working within the Win32 operating system support for exception handling, and you will be compatible with the CBuilder exception handling mechanism built into the VCL.

__export And _export

You use the __export statement to export classes, functions, and data within your CBuilder DLL for use in other applications. There are several forms of the modifier to be used in your application.

```
class __export MyClass
{
}
```

This form of the statement specifies that the entire class **MyClass** is to be exported for use in other applications. By including the proper header file for the class and linking to an import library for your DLL, other application developers can simply use the **MyClass** class as though it were part of their own applications.

```
void __export Function(void)
{
}
```

This form of the statement allows a single C++ (or C) function to be exported from the given DLL module. Note that you can elect to export any or all of the functions in a DLL individually without giving the user access to internal functions if you don't want to. One warning about exporting functions from a DLL in this way. You are exporting the function by name rather than by ordinal number, and the ordinal number entry is much more efficient to use and quicker to load. So this isn't really the way to go if your concern is the speed of loading functions from the DLL. The difference is milliseconds, but for high-performance applications it can be noticeable, especially so if the function is called many times in a short period of time from the DLL.

```
int __export nDataValue;
```

This final form of the **__export** statement is used to export actual data values from within a DLL to an application. Although you normally wouldn't do something like this in your own applications, in some cases you might want to export error flags or status information variables.

Why would you want to use the **__export** statement? Basically, if you don't like to mess around with module definition files (DEF files) and EXPORT statements in the definition file that define the DLL entries you want available to other applications in the system.

__fastcall And _fastcall

One of the most important extensions in the CBuilder system is the **__fastcall** statement, which makes it possible to use Pascal-based VCL objects within your C++ applications. Using the **__fastcall** modifier instructs the compiler to generate code that passes parameters to the functions in the system registers, which is the way that Pascal expects the functions to be passed.

The rules for using **__fastcall** are very simple. If you are exporting a method from your class that is to be used by the Object Inspector or other place, you must use the **__fastcall** modifier in your function declaration. If you are overriding a VCL method that is defined using the **__fastcall** modifier, you also must use the modifier in your own method. Because **__fastcall** is not inherited, it must be defined for each level of class that implements an override for a given method.

For example, if you are overriding the **Paint** method of a component in a class derived from a VCL object, you must declare it as follows:

```
virtual void __fastcall Paint(void);
```

This is necessary because **Paint** is really implemented down at the Pascal level by the VCL object. If, on the other hand, you want to implement a brand new function in your class that calls a low-level VCL object, you are not required to use the **__fastcall** modifier for your new method.

Suppose, for example, you wanted a new method that toggled the Hide/Show state of the form without knowing the current state. The method, called **Toggle**, could be declared as this:

```
virtual void Toggle(void);
```

No __fastcall modifier is needed because this function does not exist within the VCL. The fact that it probably is implemented using VCL methods is not important. Here is one possible implementation, showing the use of the underlying VCL component methods:

```
void TMyComponent::Toggle(void)
{
   if ( Visible )
      Hide();
   else
      Show();
}
```

It is important to remember to include the __fastcall modifier when you override methods. At best, the function simply won't work because your version of it is not called. At worst, the program will throw an exception and crash.

__finally

The __finally is used along with the __try statement to implement exception handling using structured exceptions. Because the __try and __finally statements are only used in C files and functions, it is not necessary to worry about them in CBuilder because it has no direct knowledge of C functions (aside from the extern C statement), and therefore, will not use this statement within the IDE.

To use external C functions and the structured exception handling provided by CBuilder and the C++ language, you must use the command line version of the tools and link the object files produced by the compiler into the IDE project.

_import And __import

The purpose of the **import** statements in CBuilder is to specify that a class, function, or piece of data is to be imported from an external source. You can import specific classes from an external DLL or library as well as C-style functions. By using one of the import statement forms, data elements defined in an external DLL can be treated as though they were part of the program in which they were running.

To use the import statements, use the _import or __import statement as a modifier for the type of element you are importing. There are three different types of this statement, one for each of the types that can be imported in this manner:

```
class _import MyClass
{
}
```

This statement will define a class that is imported. CBuilder will generate all of the necessary code to load the class from the linked DLL (assuming it is found), so you can then simply define instances of that class within your CBuilder application.

```
int __import MyFunction(int arg1);
```

This statement defines an externally defined function, found in a library or DLL, that accepts a single argument of type integer and returns an integer. Note that the __import modifier goes after the return type for externally defined functions.

```
int _import MyData;
```

This final form of the import statement defines an externally defined integer value that will be resolved at link time by the compiler and linker. The import statement modifier for a data element will always go between the data type and the variable name. Other modifiers can also be applied within this space (volatile, for example).

__int8, __int16, __int32, And __int64

These entries allow you to specify the size of an integer in the system for your variables. The number following the __int indicates the number of bits the variable will occupy in memory. For example, the __int16 variable type will define a variable that occupies 16 bits in memory (a standard Windows integer).

As an example, consider defining a constant equal to the value 8. You might want to have this value take up less space in the system by defining it as only 8 bits in memory. To do this you would write:

```
int8 iVal = 0;
```

_pascal And __pascal

The **__pascal** keyword specifies the way in which data is passed to functions and methods in the CBuilder system. The Pascal-calling convention has two notable differences from standard C-style calling functions. First of all, Pascal functions are case-insensitive because they are all stored in uppercase. This allows the compiler to link the modules easily into the system. In C++, Pascal-style functions are still mangled, but the function name is translated into uppercase.

The second difference in the Pascal-calling convention is the order in which arguments are pushed onto the stack. Although this is not a concern unless you are writing assembler code to call the functions, it is important that you note when a function is in Pascal format. Failure to use properly the Pascal format will cause program exceptions at runtime. Always use the **__pascal** modifier when calling VCL methods.

__property

Certainly one of the most important of the new modifiers is the **__property** modifier statement. The property statement indicates to the compiler that this is a property of a VCL-style object. Properties will allow specialized **read** and **write** access to the data within an object. When you specify the **__property** modifier, you are telling the compiler that direct access to this property is not always the case, as for example, in the following property:

```
private:
int FMyInt;
public:
void __fastcall SetInt(int iNewInt);
__published:
__property int MyIntProperty={read=FMyInt, write=SetInt};
```

In this case, we are indicating that the user has the right to read the property. When they do this they will receive the value of the internal member variable **FMyInt**. When, however, they try to write to the property, the compiler will silently call the **SetInt** method of the object. Here's some code to make it a little more straightforward to understand:

```
TMyObject *pObject = new TMyObject(NULL); // Create an instance
pObject->MyIntProperty = 164; // Calls SetInt
int nInt = pObject->MyIntProperty; // Gets value of FMyInt variable
```

Remember that using the **property** statement automatically causes some overhead code to be created when the property is accessed. Given the enormous gains of the property functionality, this code is fairly minimal, so you shouldn't worry about it. The __**property** statement is used quite commonly in CBuilder applications and components.

__published

The **published** keyword is used to tell the compiler that you want this object to have properties that appear in the Object Inspector within the IDE. Only objects derived from **TObject** may contain a __**published** section. The __**published** statement is not like properties that apply to single lines. Instead, it can be considered to be an access-specified statement (like **private**, **protected**, or **public**) that specifies the object properties which follow are public entries that will also appear in the Inspector. Using the __**published** statement also means that the Information for the object in which the __**published** statement is used will contain Delphi-style runtime time identification (RTTI) data, which can be used to query the object for available properties and methods.

__rtti

Similar to the __**published** statement, the __**rtti** statement forces the compiler to generate runtime-type identification for a class or structure. Unless you tell it otherwise, by default the compiler will generate RTTI information. From the command line, you may use the **-RT-** flag to tell the compiler not to generate RTTI information for the program and its data as a whole. If you do this and wish to have certain classes or structures within the program use RTTI, you can use the __**rtti** modifier to force the compiler to do so. To do this, use the following syntax:

```
struct __rtti MyStructure {};
```

This will force the structure **MyStructure** to be generated with runtime type identification data. Once it is generated, you can then query that information at runtime using the **typeinfo** and **typeid** classes in your application.

__thread

The **__thread** modifier is used to declare global variables unique to each thread. For example, if you want to have a single global variable as a flag to indicate whether or not a given file has been loaded, you might use a boolean global variable. This variable, though, might be different for different threads. Each thread might need to load its own version of the file. Perhaps the files are output logs. You would not necessarily want each thread to write to the same output log. In this case, you would want the output log flag to be unique to the thread it is running in. To do this you use the **__thread** modifier on the variable.

The syntax of the **__thread** modifier is as follows:

```
int __thread bFileOpen = FALSE;
```

There are a few caveats about using the **__thread** modifier, the most important of which is that the statement may not occur in a line containing a runtime initializer. This means that statements such as this:

```
int __thread nNumTimes = GetNumberOfTimes();
```

don't work because the function call can only be evaluated at runtime. This limitation also applies to objects, because they require a constructor call to be created, which can only happen at runtime. Only simple data types can be used with the **__thread** modifier. The other important caveat is that you may not use the **__thread** modifier on functions or pointers because these are simply memory addresses that cannot be moved for each thread.

__try

Like the **__except** statement, the **__try** statement is a version of exception handling only used in C programs. When you are working with C++ programs like CBuilder, use the **try** statement instead. For more details on **__try**, see the previous **__except** statement.

Conclusion

That concludes this chapter and this book. I hope that you have learned a bit about this amazingly simple system called CBuilder that is so easy to use and work with.

With the possible exception of the entries found in this chapter, CBuilder is straightforward and follows established standards. Delphi programmers will have no problem moving to CBuilder, of course, and neither will programmers inexperienced with Borland products.

I hope I have adequately demonstrated the simplicity of using the objects and environment. I tried to make the chapters complete enough to show you things that aren't immediately obvious, and I can tell you that it was hard to make the easy look complex and hard to use. I hope that by now you are over any fear you might have had of the system and that you are well on your way to creating brilliant new applications for the computers of today and tomorrow. Good luck and happy programming.

Index

D

E

F

M

N

Name property, 57
Namespaces, 346
  and scope, 165
  closing one and opening another, 176
  code for two classes defined in single
    source file, 175
  simple program, 165
  wrappers, 164
Not symbol
  and drag and drop lists, 103
Notebooks, 129. *See also* Controls/Tab.
NumberOfPoints method, 41

O

Object Pascal, 6
Object Repository, 24, 457, 531
Object-oriented code
  important points about, 185
Object-oriented design
  good example of, 126
Objects
  Application, 44, 281
  OpenDialog, 57
  PageControl, 131
  Sender, 104
  Source, 104
  TColor, 121
  TDBNavigator, 229
  TFont, 120
  ToolServices, 540
  TTable, 213
  VCL TForm, 24
ODBC Administrator, 245, 246
ODBC-compliant databases
  and C++Builder, 211

ODBC database
  using with C++Builder, 245
ODBC files
  and BDE, 269
OK button
  code, 525
OleCtrl class, 197
OnBuilderForm
  code to call, 363
OnClick
  code to add, 238
  code to add to handler, 290
  code to allow the user to open the first
    database file, 242
  complete code for the filter button to
    add to the event handler, 240
OnCreate
  code to add to, 289
OnDragDrop
  code to add to the handler for the list
    boxes, 103
  code to modify method, 107
OnDragOver
  code, 103
OnExit
  code to add to new handler, 98
OnFileNew
  code to add into CMainFrame class, 368
OnFormCreate
  code to add to event, 16
OnlyOnce application, 280
OnMouseDown
  code for new handler, 19
  code to modify method to store
    something, 26
OnMouseMove
  code to handle drawing, 22

T

W

X

Z